The Unavoidable Issue

U.S. Immigration Policy in the 1980s

Edited by
DEMETRIOS G. PAPADEMETRIOU
and
MARK J. MILLER

A Publication of the
Institute for the Study of Human Issues
Philadelphia

Manufactured in the United States of America

1 2 3 4 5 6 7 8   90 89 88 87 86 85 84 83

Library of Congress Cataloging in Publication Data

Main entry under title:
The unavoidable issue.

   Bibliography: p.
   Includes index.
   1. United States—Emigration and immigration—
Addresses, essays, lectures.   I. Papademetriou,
Demetrios G.   II. Miller, Mark J.
JV6483.U52   1983   325.73   82-15650
ISBN 0-89727-047-9

For information, write:

Director of Publications
ISHI
3401 Science Center
Philadelphia, Pennsylvania 19104
U.S.A.

The Unavoidable Issue

"Good laws lead to the making of better ones;
bad ones bring about worse."

—*Jean Jacques Rousseau*

To Sigrid and Jane

Preface

This volume arises from a deep concern over the future of the immigration and refugee policy of the United States. A succession of federal task forces and commissions have studied U.S. immigration law and concluded that reform is badly needed, but meaningful reform has proven to be an elusive goal.

One barrier to reform is the enormous complexity of the immigration issue itself. Immigration, whether regulated or clandestine, affects the fundamental fabric of society. Hence, its effects are myriad and difficult to ascertain with precision. Furthermore, many of the determinants of immigration lie outside the ambit of U.S. sovereignty and consequently are less malleable to U.S. policy. Recognition of the complexity of the immigration issue has stymied reform since uncertainty over the consequences of policy changes favors maintenance of the status quo. Perhaps nowhere more than in the realm of immigration policy has an old adage rung true: Better the devil you know than the devil you don't.

The complexity of the immigration issue need not preclude reform. Considerable advances have been made in our understanding of discrete areas of the immigration issue. The plan behind this book was to invite experts on the various components of U.S. immigration policy to contribute chapters that would make "state of the art" reviews of learning in the respective areas and, if desired, draw out the implication of that learning for public policy. The goals of the book, then, are twofold: to acquaint the reader with the principal controversies in the debate over immigration and to provide the reader with comprehensive understanding of the immigration issue within the space limitations of a single volume. It is hoped that the reader will emerge with a sense of urgency about the need for immigration policy reform and with a sense of the course that reform should take.

The editors would like to thank Betty Crapivinsky-Jutkowitz of

PREFACE

ISHI Publications for her early endorsement of this project and for her steady encouragement in the face of delays that would have strained the goodwill of less understanding publishers. This volume developed out of a 1980 American Political Science Association convention panel on the Political Economy of International Migration, chaired by the editors.

DEMETRIOS G. PAPADEMETRIOU
MARK J. MILLER

Contributors

Vernon M. Briggs, Jr., is Professor of Labor Economics and Human Resource Studies at the New York State School of Labor and Industrial Relations at Cornell University. Among the books he has either authored or co-authored are *The Chicano Worker, Chicanos and Rural Poverty, The Negro and Apprenticeship, Employment, Income and Welfare in the Rural South,* and *Labor Economics: Wages, Employment, and the Trade Unionism.* Since 1977, Professor Briggs has been a member of the National Council on Employment Policy.

Walter A. Fogel is Professor of Industrial Relations and Associate Director of the Institute of Industrial Relations at the University of California, Los Angeles. He has written widely on immigration and minority labor market experiences, including the volume, *Mexican Illegal Alien Workers in the United States.* Professor Fogel was a staff member of President Carter's Interagency Task Force on Immigration Policy.

Leon Gordenker is Professor of Politics and faculty associate at the Center of International Studies at Princeton University. He has written widely on the subject of international organization and has been conducting a study of the international handling of refugee problems.

Elizabeth Hull taught for three years at the State University of New York in Oswego, and is presently Assistant Professor of Political Science at Rutgers University. Professor Hull, whose research focuses on the constitutional rights of noncitizens, has written a number of articles on this theme for law reviews and policy journals. She is currently at work on a book about the rights of aliens in the United States.

Ellen Percy Kraly is a Visiting Assistant Professor of Sociology at Hamilton College. Her current research interests include emigration from the U.S., international migration statistics, immigration policies and ethnic relations, and the use of demographic methods in the analysis of international migration and ethnicity. Dr. Kraly has served as a consultant to the United Nations Statistical Office, the National Academy of Sciences, and the Interagency Task Force on Immigration.

Elizabeth Midgley has observed the making of U.S. immigration policy as a State Department analyst, as research assistant to Walter Lippmann, and as a television news producer for the Public Broadcast Laboratory and CBS News. She has been a trustee of the German Marshall Fund of the United States since its establishment in 1970 and is presently Vice-Chairman of the Board of Trustees.

Mark J. Miller is Associate Professor of Political Science at the University of Delaware. He has served as a consultant to the Interagency Task Force on Immigration and to the U.S. Department of Labor on foreign labor questions.

Demetrios G. Papademetriou is Executive Editor of the *International Migration Review*. He has taught at the University of Maryland, Duke University, and at the New School for Social Research, where he is a member of the Graduate Faculty. Dr. Papademetriou has chaired and participated on a large number of national and international panels on migration and has conducted and directed funded field research on the topic both in Europe and the United States. His latest book is *Emigration and Return in the Mediterranean Littoral*.

Sidney Weintraub is Dean Rusk Professor at the Lyndon B. Johnson School of Public Affairs of the University of Texas at Austin. He was a Senior Fellow at the Brookings Institution, and served for 25 years as a career diplomat, including assignments as Deputy Assistant Secretary of State for Economic Affairs and Assistant Administrator of the Agency for International Development.

Contents

U.S. Immigration Policy: International Context, Theoretical Parameters, and Research Priorities

Demetrios G. Papademetriou and *Mark J. Miller*

International migration has been an enduring component of the global economic, social, and political milieu. Although such migration has usually been considered an unmitigated benefit to both the sending and the receiving societies, its exponential and almost uncontrolled growth during the past twenty-five years has prompted a fundamental reassessment of the process. The initial results of this reassessment have had a sobering effect on all the principals in the migration chain and have gradually led them to the realization that migration has failed to resolve and in fact may have exacerbated the very condition it was believed to ameliorate.

Over the past quarter of a century, many advanced industrial societies have found themselves at a point in their development where the confluence of a variety of forces precipitated a chronic condition of selected labor shortages. The structural nature of these shortages was the result of a combination of such social, demographic, economic, and political factors as:

- the deteriorating demographic structure of many advanced capitalist societies that exhibit low birthrates, a consequent aging of their

The first author would like to thank the staff of the Center for Migration Studies, and especially its Director, Lydio F. Tomasi, for their dedication and commitment to the study of international migration. Without their cooperation and support, this book would not have been possible. Without Dr. Tomasi's constant encouragement and thoughtful comments, this chapter would have been far less rigorous and comprehensive. Only the authors, however, are responsible for errors of omission or commission.

1

population, and a significant contraction of their active work forces;
- the compounding effect of measures that contract work forces even further, such as earlier retirement, longer vacations, shorter work weeks, and psychological inducements to work-age youths to postpone entering the job market in favor of additional education;
- the concomitant proliferation of highly technical and white-collar occupations, which require a continuous evolution in the skills and education of personnel—itself a product of advanced development;
- the restructuring and increasing dichotomization of labor markets into primary and secondary sectors with their own distinct manpower and skill requirements;
- the continuing and increasing vitality of the secondary sector through the confluence of such factors as variable demand patterns for industrial products, continuously important but marginally profitable industries, a bullish market for private and public services that are archetypically labor-intensive, a persistent demand for temporary and seasonal work, and a proliferation of jobs that native workers are increasingly reluctant to take because of low wages, poor working conditions, and undesirable social status;
- the coupling of the human losses from World War II with the demands for vast manpower resources during the subsequent economic boom and the only moderately successful rationalizations of labor forces and incomplete capital-intensive expansion of some economic sectors in advanced industrial societies.

The optimistic and, as it currently appears to many observers, shortsighted response to such usually relative (although at times absolute) labor scarcities was either the instituting of bilateral agreements with many of the labor-surplus countries in the periphery for a controlled importation of labor (the European model and the U.S. *bracero* program), or the formulation and implementation of immigration policies that, although restrictive in their legal requirements, tolerated and thus encouraged the inflow of a largely spontaneous, clandestine, and thus exploitable immigrant force (the dominant U.S. model). Both processes gradually evolved into a condition in which the labor importers became increasingly dependent on a constant supply of foreign labor while, concomitantly and imperceptibly, the labor supply was becoming more and more independent of the actual labor needs of the host economies. In other words, what had always been assumed to be the biggest asset of the foreign labor "recruitment" course—its ability to act as a flexible cushion that could be called upon as a temporary expedient with which to overcome un-usual labor demand pressure (what the Germans call the *Konjunktur-puffer* function)—became increasingly less reflective of the actual situation. In fact, as the migration flows became more mature and (selected) labor demand pressure persisted, the temporary and revo-cable nature of the arrangement began to recede and, in the resulting policy void, was replaced by the de facto (though unintended) expan-sion of opportunities for longer-term stays, family reunifications, some modest occupational mobility, and all but the formal establish-ment of an immigration flow.

These universally unanticipated consequences gradually resulted in the conclusion that the "importation" of foreign labor not only failed to solve the structural problems of the intermittently labor-scarce industrial societies, but may actually have contributed toward maintaining and institutionalizing these scarcities. In fact, it now ap-pears that, except for the obvious economic benefit accruing to the worker and the significant contribution of the worker to the short-term profitability of certain industrial sectors—to which the worker is now indispensable—the importation of labor has otherwise given rise to severe longer-term economic, political, and social problems. The latter two have been only inadequately and slowly understood by most labor-receiving countries.

Although the initial coincidence of interests between labor-scarce and labor-surplus societies gave rise to a buoyant, almost reckless, enthusiasm for both organized and spontaneous migration flows, these same actors are beginning to view migration as a process whose short-term economic benefits are seriously undermined both by the negative sociopolitical consequences and, increasingly, by unforeseen longer-term economic liabilities. Under these circumstances, outside of the profitability of private capital, the major structural contribution of the process may have been the progressive disappearance of na-tional boundaries for labor and its transformation into a structural component of the international political economy.

Many critics of the international political and economic system view international migration as a process structurally central to both sending societies and receiving societies. The flow of labor is seen as neither temporary nor limited to a specific region. Rather, it is viewed as one of the most important "defining features of the contemporary world economy."[1] The departure point of this perspective is its treat-ment of development and underdevelopment as parts of the same single integral totality, a world capitalist economy that simultaneously

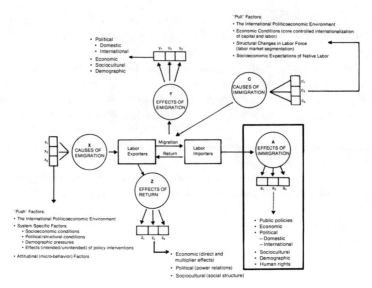

Figure 1.1   A Detailed Causal Model of Migration

This model offers a detailed and comprehensive view of the causes and conse-
quences of international migration for both sending and receiving countries. The
model follows the Partial Least Squares (PLS) technique developed by Herman O.
Wold and his associates. See Karl G. Jöreskog and Herman O. Wold, "The ML and
PLS Techniques for Modeling with Latent Variables: Comparative Aspects" (Paper
delivered at the Conference on Systems Under Indirect Observation [Causality/
Structure/Prediction], Centre de Rencontres, Cartigny, University of Geneva,
Geneva, Switzerland, October 1979); R. Noonan and Herman O. Wold, "NIPALS
Path Modeling with Latent Variables: Analyzing School Survey Data Using Non-
linear Iterative Partial Least Squares," *Scandinavian Journal of Educational Research*
21 (1977): 33–61; and Herman O. Wold, "Soft Modeling: The Basic Design, and
Some Extensions," in *Systems Under Indirect Observations: Causality-Structure-
Prediction*, ed. Karl G. Jöreskog and Herman Wold (Amsterdam: North Holland,
1981).

   PLS is a latent variable causal modeling approach that occupies a midpoint
between data-oriented, narrowly inductive analytical strategies and more sophisticated hard modeling. The softness and paucity of the migration data make PLS an
appropriate research tool for studying international migration. The arrow scheme
involves *manifest* (directly observed) variables, which are depicted as squares, and
latent (indirectly observed) variables, shown as circles. Analytical complexity is reduced by treating *blocks of observables* as the *structural units* of the model. Each block is
assumed to have a *block structure* according to which the manifest variables are
treated as linear indicators of a latent variable; the latter is estimated as a *weighted*
aggregate of the indicators. The arrows of the scheme characterize the model's
structural relations.

Source: Demetrios G. Papademetriou and Gerald W. Hopple, "Causal Modelling in International Migration Research: A Methodological Prolegomenon," *Quality and Quantity*, forthcoming, Figure 5.

depends on and recreates conditions for international economic inequality.[2] In this scenario, although migration can still be viewed as partly the result of decisions by individuals and/or households, the range of options available to them is shaped by such structural factors as the place of each state into the global political economy.

This perspective is principally useful in highlighting the structural components of international labor migration, in terms of the internal division of labor (and its consequent social class relations) and the international political and economic hierarchy of national systems that often have limited room for independent action with respect to the production and distribution of commodities and the emigration of their citizens.[3] Although the appeal of this often procrustean theoretical bed varies with one's acceptance of the basic components of the arguments made by "world system" and *dependencia* advocates, one cannot deny the need for a more comprehensive ("holistic") perspective in the study of the place of international migration in international politics and economics, and particularly of the manner in which it interacts with the global system's structures, patterns, and processes. As Figure 1.1 indicates, however, one cannot obtain a thorough understanding of the causes and consequences of international migration by looking only at the structural components of international migration. To gain such an understanding, one must also appreciate the explanatory power of such competing frameworks as those emphasizing important intrasystemic forces (labor market, demographic, social, and domestic political) or the myriad of individual motives that influence the actual profile of specific migration flows.

U.S. Immigration Policy: An Overview

Comprehensive analyses of the place of international migration in the social, economic, political, and demographic milieu of both sending societies and receiving societies are rare and usually either fail to identify the broad political/economic parameters of international migration or lose sight of the multitude of individual/group motives for emigration and the precise impact of specific migration flows on the economy and society of sending and receiving societies. By necessity, then, we embark on this task in this volume with considerable apprehension. The goal of the endeavor will be to identify and understand the broad interplay of the complex forces that have traditionally shaped the multiple population, social, economic, and political (internal and external) dimensions of U.S. immigration policy and to offer some insights, guidelines, and alternatives to the future course of action in this area. The ultimate objective will be to identify the policy instruments necessary for a goal-oriented labor market, population, and foreign policy of which immigration should be an integral component—a policy sensitive to the demographic, social, economic, and domestic and international political priorities of the United States.

The challenges to be met are substantial. The literature on immigration suffers from paucity and frequent unreliability of data; published works are frequently superficial and weak both in their designs and in their methodologies; and, because of the topic's high degree of emotive and political salience, many works are obvious products of polemicists or apologists for particular points of view and seek to promote single-interest political or economic philosophies.

If there is one aspect of U.S. immigration policy that is marked by substantial consensus, it is the need to rethink immigration policies and to make them an integral component of a national population, labor market, and foreign policy. Yet, as the U.S. policy apparatus gropes toward that goal, the confusion generated by masses of contradictory "evidence" about every possible impact of legal and illegal immigrants on the American society and economy is heightened. Simultaneously, a confrontational public spirit is evolving, resulting in an "us" versus "them" debate and in hyperactive involvement by contending interest groups. Such hyperactivity further polarizes the attitudes of opinion makers and the mass public and deprives policymakers of some of the options they may have wished to consider; it also contributes toward increasing popular uncertainties and working class and minority insecurities.

If the historical experience of the United States and other advanced industrial democracies with immigration is relevant to the future, myths and rumors about immigrants may be expected to challenge the legitimacy of virtually any government action in this matter and interfere both with the improvement of the conditions under which illegal immigrants exist and with the consequent amelioration of some of the negative societal consequences attendant to the problem. In fact, the appearance of elite ambivalence and confusion encourages negative race and ethnic stereotyping, supplants the real population and labor market issues, and may compel the government to respond to the former (rather than the two latter) challenges.

It is in the context of de facto clandestine immigration that use of the one ready source of useful experience—the grappling of European advanced industrial societies with the consequences of an "organized" temporary foreign worker program—can be quite instructive. We have looked at the European experience in Chapter 10. At stake is who should be allowed to articulate and implement decisions that have an impact on the whole society: private citizens, special-interest groups, or government (the latter presumably aware of the full spectrum of pertinent issues). The case of Europe affords one the unique opportunity to evaluate alternative policies in terms of their aims and their performance. Similarly, it affords one the luxury of immediate longitudinal observations about the private/public, long/short, and latent/manifest costs and benefits of labor migrations. The experiences of France, West Germany, and Switzerland (i.e., their similarities and differences both among themselves and between them and the United States) can help the United States choose which policies are best suited to its own population goals (themselves the subject of another equally acrimonious debate) and its social, economic, and political requirements.

In the final analysis, the ability to make informed observations about the impact foreign workers have on the European advanced industrial democracies can better enable the United States to identify and comprehend the behavior and impact of total immigration on domestic population growth and on the socioeconomic and political realms of American society, while providing a barometer on what appears to be a most seriously contemplated policy option in many U.S. policy circles today: the instituting of some form of a temporary foreign worker program.

A Brief History of U.S. Immigration Policy

The immigration policy of the United States has usually reflected a particular period's preoccupation with its immediate past rather than its present or future. Its dimensions, at least until recently, have been influenced by a host of often inadequately understood and contradictory forces in such areas as the demographic composition of the population, economics, and foreign and domestic politics. The resulting responses have usually denied U.S. policymakers the opportunity to articulate and implement immigration policies that best complement long-term goals in the increasingly interdependent foreign and domestic political and economic spheres.

In fact, U.S. immigration policies, although viewed as domestic matters with only an incidental relationship to diplomacy, have always had a global impact and, as such, have often been a vital component of U.S. foreign policy.[4] Accordingly, and in spite of the infrequency with which U.S. immigration policy has had deliberate foreign policy implications, the manifest (intended) and latent (unintended) international consequences of U.S. immigration policies have always been significant. Even during the so-called laissez-faire period prior to 1882, a host of legislation that seemed to be unrelated to immigration[5] had a significant impact on and helped shape the composition of the U.S. population and subsequently the direction of U.S. society.

The history of U.S. immigration policy can be best understood within the parameters of capital and labor relations, with an almost uninterrupted series of victories by the former, which were often (but not always) to the detriment of the latter.[6] In fact, even during the restrictionist policies of the last sixty years, capital has always been clearly at the controls either by being successful in instituting "temporary" foreign labor programs (in 1917–1922 and 1942–1964) or through the de facto "open" immigration policies of recent years, where vast numbers of illegal foreign workers have been allowed to enter the country and perform critical economic functions with only a small risk of detection and apprehension and little fear of punishment (other than voluntary deportation).

Organized labor in the United States traditionally has been suspicious of, if not outrightly opposed to, immigration. Throughout the nineteenth century, capital prevailed on both the executive and legislative branches and won legislation that responded to often contrived labor shortages. In some cases (such as the transportation industry in the confusing days following the Civil War), capital actually secured legislation that included incentives and indirect public subsidies for labor procurement. As Vernon Briggs points out in Chapter 4, for instance, the 1864 Contract Labor Act passed Congress in spite of strenuous efforts by such nascent worker organizations as the National Labor Union (NLU) to block it. Although repealed four years later, this act set the tone both for a pattern of business practice of hiring foreign workers regardless of their legal status and for a pattern of impotence by successive labor organizations in checking this practice. In fact, labor was most successful in obtaining restrictive and/or exclusionary legislation only when variables other than labor market conditions intervened, most notably those of race and ethnicity. Thus, buoyed by the openly anti-Chinese California state constitution of 1874, no less than six federal Chinese Exclusion Acts were passed between 1882 and 1904, the last one not repealed until 1943; in 1907 the gentlemen's agreement reached with Japan prohibited Japanese immigration; and in 1917, immigrants originating in the "Asia Pacific Triangle"[7] were excluded from entering the United States.

Similarly, labor was most successful in checking the influx of southern and eastern Europeans only after it formed alliances with those who questioned the moral, physical, and political fitness of these groups. As a result of such alliances, literacy requirements and a head tax were imposed on prospective immigrants over sixteen years old in 1917, and numerical quotas were imposed in subsequent legislation. By that time, the climate of antiimmigrant sentiment was running so high that organized labor was able to control the immigration "main door" with relatively modest expenditures of political capital. In fact, beginning with 1917, the antiimmigrant coalition was firmly in control. In 1921, quotas became fixed at 3 percent of the total representation of each ethnic group in the U.S. 1910 census—except those from the western hemisphere. When this formula still allowed in too many "undesirable" and "unassimilable" southern and eastern Europeans, and armed with "scientific" evidence by psychologist Henry Herbert Goddard, who in 1924 "found" 80 percent of incoming Russians, Hungarians, Italians, and Jewish immigrants "feebleminded," Congress passed the 1924 National Origins Act. This act placed a ceiling of 150,000 annual admissions, reduced the quota to 2 percent, and rolled back the effective census date to 1890, thus controlling for the ethnic makeup of new immigrants even further.[8] Western hemisphere immigrants, of course, were again exempted from numerical controls.

In spite of these de jure limits to immigration, capital remained successful in maintaining a "back door" to meet its "need" for labor of little social consciousness, no political power, and an essentially temporary and revocable nature. This labor, whether recruited through a temporary worker program or allowed to enter outside the law, enabled capital to remain profitable in marginal enterprises by postponing the expensive restructuring of the labor market. In the words of Aristide Zolberg, this "main gate"/"back door" system "emerged from a specifically American configuration and has structured our immigration policy from approximately 1880 to the present."[9] Within this framework, labor and immigration policies, particularly in the Southwest, have consistently resulted in "conscientious human efforts . . . to keep wages low, to keep incomes depressed, and to keep unionism to a minimum by using waves of legal immigrants [from China, Japan, Mexico, and from Europe as well], *braceros* [from Mexico], border commuters [from Mexico], and now illegal aliens [mainly from Mexico and the Caribbean, but by no means exclusively so]."[10]

By the early 1920s, both "main gate" (i.e., legal and intended) and "back door" avenues for immigration had been restricted—the former with the requirements outlined above, the latter with the termination of what some students of U.S. immigration have termed "the first *bracero* program"[11] (see Chapter 4, below). This program was the result of the first significant exception to the immigration law, when Congress, under pressure from southwestern agricultural interests, authorized a temporary worker program and exempted recruits both from literacy requirements and from the head tax required of each immigrant. With the termination of that program and the uncertain economic times of the 1920s and 1930s, the illegal and explicitly "temporary" labor immigration to the United States became less significant for a time, while the pressure for voluntary and involuntary returns increased exponentially.

Substantial pressure for "back door" immigration was renewed during World War II (1942), when the United States was again experiencing severe labor shortages. In response to these shortages, a temporary worker program was instituted which after its official reconfirmation by Public Law (P.L.) 78 (1951)—during the height of U.S. involvement in the Korean War—would last until 1964. This law was the result of another bizarre alliance of American special interests, such as agribusiness, organized labor, and the Mexican government, while most opposition came from the Mexican-American community in the Southwest.[12] During the later stages of the *bracero* program, this odd alliance became even more intriguing. By the time the program was discontinued in 1964, the climate of special-interest opinion had shifted considerably: U.S. agriculture had come to resent the increasingly interventionist policies of the Department of Labor with regard to wages and working conditions and was willing to have the program terminated; an increasing outcry about the conditions of life and employment of the *braceros* from many quarters had created an anti-*bracero* program alliance between the Mexican government and the liberal voices in the United States; finally, an increasingly vocal and politically important coalition of the Mexican-American and black communities was now actively opposing the program. This shifting of opinion occurred, characteristically, in the midst of increasing official and unofficial confusion over the precise impact of the *braceros* on local and regional labor markets, over the relationship between the *bracero* program and illegal immigration, and over the program's effect on the social and economic well-being of the region's most disadvantaged and politically powerless groups—the minorities, youth, and women.

Meanwhile, beginning with the early 1950s, the "main gate" was also moving toward reform. Although Senate Report 1515 (1950) reviewed immigration policy and recommended a few legislative changes, one could feel the undercurrent of change in the mood of both the executive branch and the multitude of public and private-interest groups involved in the review process. In spite of evolving attitudes about immigration, Congress symbolically maintained the official status quo (restrictionist) policies by enacting the McCarran-Walter Immigration and Nationality Act in 1952 over President Harry Truman's veto. The act's failure to respond to the changing climate of opinion with regard to immigration led to a plethora of subsequent amendments as well as the simultaneous liberalization of "back door" opportunities.[13] By the end of the decade the substance of the 1952 legislation had changed beyond recognition. It was only a matter of time, then, before President John F. Kennedy's commitment to immigration reform and President Lyndon B. Johnson's emphasis on the "Great Society" would result in the first major revision of U.S. immigration policy in nearly half a century.[14]

The resulting 1965 Immigration and Nationality Act (INA) (P.L. 89-236) placed an immigration ceiling of 290,000, split between the western (120,000) and eastern hemispheres (170,000). This legislation has been frequently hailed for having abolished national-origin and anti-Oriental discrimination and, in conjunction with the civil rights legislation of the 1960s, for tearing down the institutional racism of previous U.S. immigration legislation. Zolberg calls the act a "political triumph and a historical vindication."[15] Two other eminent immigration authors celebrate the act because it made immigration "oblivious to such factors as color, religion, and language."[16] Yet the 1965 Immigration and Nationality Act continued to maintain the dual identity of U.S. immigration policy by treating the two hemispheres differently, by discriminating against colonies, by favoring the rich (through special provisions for investors) and the highly skilled, by failing to provide adequately for refugee flows, and by avoiding the issue of "back door" immigration. With regard to numbers, visas to *western hemisphere* immigrants were granted on a first-come, first-served basis; relatives of U.S. citizens and residents had equal preference with workers—regardless of the order of relationship or skill level involved; and in order to protect the labor market from undue competition, a labor certification was required of all non-first order relatives. This requirement charged the secretary of labor with certifying that there was a shortage of "able, qualified, willing, and available" workers in a particular skill category and that the prospective immigrant would not affect "prevailing wages and working conditions" adversely.

Table 1.1 *The Seven-Category Preference System*

Preference Category	Visa Applicants Eligible	Percentage of Annual Worldwide Ceiling	Total Visas Available
First	Unmarried sons and daughters of U.S. citizens	20	54,000
Second	Spouses and unmarried sons and daughters of lawful resident aliens	20 (26)[a]	54,000 (70,200), plus any unused first-preference visas
Third	Members of the professions and scientists and artists of exceptional ability, and their spouses and children	10	27,000
Fourth	Married sons and daughters of U.S. citizens, and their spouses and children	10	27,000, plus any unused first-and second-preference visas

Fifth	24	Brothers and sisters of U.S. citizens, and their spouses and children	64,800, plus any unused first-, second-, and fourth-preference visas
Sixth	10	Skilled and unskilled workers in occupations for which a shortage of employable and willing persons exists in the U.S.	27,000
Seventh[a]	6	Refugees	16,200
Non-preference[b]	—	Remaining unused allocations	—

Source: Adapted from U.S. Commission on Civil Rights, *The Tarnished Golden Door: Civil Rights Issues in Immigration* (September 1980), p. 150, Chart A1; and Select Commission on Immigration and Refugee Policy, *U.S. Immigration Policy and the National Interest, Final Report*, March 1, 1981 (Washington, D.C.: Government Printing Office, 1981), p. 89. Modified by the authors to reflect amendments to the Immigration and Nationality Act through 1981.

[a]This preference was removed by the Refugee Act of 1980, P.L. 96-212. Its share is added to the second preference. The current worldwide immigration ceiling (exclusive of refugees) is 270,000, with the 20,000-visas-per-country and 600-per-dependency (former colonies) limit uniformly applied.

[b]Other applicants, vying for any positions left after the first six preferences are exhausted.

Eastern hemisphere immigrants, however, were subject to a seven-preference category system, with each country awarded a certain proportion (but no more than 20,000) of the total number of visas (see Table 1.1). Furthermore, eastern hemisphere immigrants entering under the third and sixth preference were prohibited from exhausting any unused visas from the other categories and were required to obtain labor certification.[17]

The preference system, although in basic philosophical accord with a race/color/language neutrality, is flawed by a series of pronounced intended and unintended inequities. For instance, there is a strong bias in the third and sixth preference categories in favor of those who can contribute immediately to the American economy but whose immigration may represent significant losses for the sending countries—a practice which has generated increasing attention in proposals for some sort of a compensatory scheme for the countries of workers' origin.[18] Furthermore, there is a strong preference for skilled over unskilled workers (sixth preference). There may be, consequently and indirectly, a dampening of U.S. incentive to develop and train its own manpower. And finally, there are a host of probably unintended loopholes that have been fully exploited by immigration lawyers. Among those, one must note the opportunity to travel to the United States to have one's child born there and thus gain the right to immigration without a labor certification requirement as the parent of a U.S. citizen (almost one-third of total western hemisphere immigration since 1965 took that route); or to bring one's retired parents to the United States (exempt from labor certification), who then can bring along their children under the second preference—a process significantly reducing the total waiting time for citizenship. Although the former loophole was closed in a 1978 amendment to the INA, the important variable is one's ability to afford these avenues.[19]

Some of the other unintended consequences of the 1965 act reflect the naiveté of the architects of P.L. 89-236. The refugee category has been inadequate—an issue not addressed satisfactorily until the 1980 Refugee Act. The labor certification program has a Catch-22 effect, in that one has to be offered a job in order to be eligible to apply for certification, a provision that "encourages" illegal entry and/or unauthorized employment. The unequal treatment for the two hemispheres was continued (eliminated in P.L. 94-571 [1978] by extending to the western hemisphere the same preference system as for the eastern hemisphere and eliminating the exemption from labor certification for the first and second preferences; the separate numerical ceilings for the two hemispheres were also abolished in 1978, in favor of a worldwide ceiling of 270,000). The failure to anticipate more accurately the pressure for immigration from such countries as Mexico and the Caribbean, whose nationals often have to wait for more than three years to reunite with their families in the United States (see Table 1.2), undermined one of the most important improvements of the 1965 act. And many of these provisions spurred additional illegal immigration.[20]

Parallel to these "main gate" reforms, the 1965 act reaffirmed the continuation of a system of small-scale "back door" immigrant waves by empowering the attorney general to authorize the entry of several categories of temporary workers as an exemption to the rule prohibiting nonimmigrant labor (provision 101a [H] ii of the 1952 Immigration and Nationality Act, dubbed the "H-2" program). Although this discretionary power rests with the attorney general, it is the Department of Labor which actually certifies that "indigenous labor is unavailable and that recourse to temporary alien labor will not be detrimental to local wage scales or working conditions" and recommends to the Immigration and Naturalization Service that it issue temporary work permits.[21] Under this program, one finds not only farm workers, sheepherders, and woodcutters, but also large contingents of foreign entertainers, athletes, and musicians who get permits valid for eleven months, renewable up to three times.

Although this program is intended to respond to genuine labor shortages, several problems hamper its operation. For instance, when is a shortage real and when is it contrived? What is the potential for confusion of the practice of having two separate agencies responsible for the program? How can one reconcile the fact that by tying a worker to a single employer who has arbitrary powers over him during his tenure as an H-2 worker, one creates an extremely one-sided power relationship potentially leading to what critics of the program call an indentured-servant condition. And finally, how can one reconcile the fact that issuance of permits often reflects a specific industry's governmental contacts rather than success in demonstrating need?[22]

Assessing the Impact of Immigration on the United States

In addition to the factors identified earlier in this chapter, elucidation of the impact of legal and illegal immigrants on the American society is hampered by the twin problems of voluminous information on *illegal* migration with equivocal and contradictory results, and a relative paucity of reliable and current research on *legal* immigrants, the

Table 1.2 *Countries with Greatest Number of Active Immigrant Visa Applicants (by Preference), January 1, 1980*

Country	First Preference	Second Preference	Third Preference	Fourth Preference	Fifth Preference	Sixth Preference	Non-Preference	Total
Mexico	2,412	59,207	19	11,059	26,904	1,556	173,681	274,838
Philippines	912	32,914	32,266	14,830	165,776	3,138	1,111	250,947
China	431	10,538	633	9,692	81,093	3,469	5,681	111,537
Korea	19	4,008	198	144	67,953	1,174	835	74,331
Dominican Republic	217	16,491	—	186	4,677	67	13,419	35,057
India	7	2,480	4,798	69	21,109	684	2,553	31,700
Vietnam	32	6,232	11	74	13,980	63	245	20,637
Colombia	38	3,856	9	149	4,895	343	9,834	19,124
Cuba	427	1,904	—	2,243	11,751	1	838	17,164
Jamaica	249	5,594	6	577	3,892	346	6,436	17,100
Italy	63	917	30	970	11,044	330	522	13,876
Canada	252	532	496	741	3,151	876	6,097	12,145
Other countries	1,266	31,414	2,484	4,884	91,531	18,562	59,457	209,598
Total	6,325	176,087	40,950	45,618	507,756	30,609	280,709	1,088,054

Total applications, by preference, as of January 1, 1979, were:

	First Preference	Second Preference	Third Preference	Fourth Preference	Fifth Preference	Sixth Preference	Non-Preference	Total
	5,909	145,881	51,397	33,487	285,783	28,217	363,691	914,365

Source: Department of State, Visa Office, unpublished data. Adapted from Select Commission on Immigration and Refugee Policy, *U.S. Immigration Policy and the National Interest*, Final Report, March 1, 1981 (Washington, D.C.: Government Printing Office, 1981), Table 9.

result of anticipatory choices by those who serve the policy community. Consequently, the usual problems of jealously guarded discipli-
nary parochialism are compounded by both too much information
and too little reliable information. We will attempt to bridge these
interdisciplinary gaps in an effort to offer a comprehensive overview
of the impact of immigration on the American society and economy.

THE ECONOMIC (LABOR MARKET) COMPONENT

The impact of international migration on the economies of the receivers is the most analytically complex dimension of the migration
phenomenon and has generated considerable intellectual acrimony.
This acrimony spans the spectrum of the issues. For instance, foreigners are held responsible for both dampening and fueling inflation by
reducing and increasing aggregate demand; for depressing wages or
at least moderating wage increases; for improving the economic condition of some members of the indigenous work force, but also for
contributing to the deterioration of working conditions and of the
economic condition of the receivers' disadvantaged native strata; for
being crucial to the economic health of advanced industrial societies,
but also for creating a persistent structural economic dependence on
continuous flows of migrants through the creation of "immigrant"
occupations within certain economic sectors, particularly in the secondary labor market; for displacing indigenous workers and for
filling a genuine labor market shortage; and finally, for dampening
the industry's enthusiasm for capital investment, mechanization,
labor force rationalization, and restructuring jobs and for having no
discernible impact in these areas.[23]

Of course, elements of truth appear in both dichotomies. For
instance, short-term migrants usually come alone and often go
through extraordinary personal deprivations in order to meet their
savings goals. As a result, aggregate demand is affected little by their
presence here. However, as allegedly and even self-intended temporary flows mature into longer-term and permanent stocks, family
reunification occurs and consumption patterns begin to approach
those of natives. In the absence of preparation for the resulting increased consumption, demand-pull inflation in affected markets is
likely. A similar situation obtains with the impact of immigration on
the economic position of indigenous workers. At entry, both clandestine and legal immigrants are likely to compete with native disadvantaged workers for entry-level positions. The abundance of labor

supplies for such jobs acts as a disincentive for these industries to raise wages significantly or to improve working conditions. In time, however, most legal immigrants advance to better jobs in which they are in competition with other native workers and older immigrant groups in the better-paying and more stable positions. In fact, Barry Chiswick has found that within eleven to sixteen years the earnings of immigrants surpass those of natives with similar sociodemographic characteristics.[24] The advancement of these groups has obviously occurred at the expense of the disadvantaged who—for reasons ranging from inadequate human capital and failure to be sufficiently mobile to take advantage of new opportunities, to deep-rooted ethnic and racial biases—have remained in the pool of workers from which entry-level jobs are filled. The full implications, and some rare hard evidence documenting these hypotheses, are discussed forcefully by Walter Fogel in Chapter 3 of this volume.

The degree of complexity, controversy, and richness of the competing hypotheses about the place of foreign workers on the labor markets of advanced industrial societies is best illustrated by a brief discussion of the "segmented" or "dual" labor market hypothesis. The controversy to which this hypothesis addresses itself is whether foreign labor, and particularly, "temporary" and clandestine foreign labor, displaces native labor or simply occupies a structural and needed place in the jobs hierarchy in industrial democracies. Segmentation sociologists and labor economists focus on the analysis of the internal structure of labor markets and the economic, social, and political forces that operate in such markets. This analysis has led to the discovery of the existence of two relatively nonporous segments with few established mobility channels between them.[25] Although few social scientists would deny the existence of this segmentation, its etiology and such issues as the degree of intersegment mobility and the choice of appropriate ameliorative policies are the subject of intense debate.

Liberal economists subscribe to the "human capital" approach and make two basic assumptions: (1) individuals can act as rational human beings and "purchase" enhanced skills as they would any other commodity and (2) that wages reflect an individual's marginal productivity, that is, his value to the employer. Education and technical training are seen as investment decisions involving time and money which give the investor a rate of return analogous to the slope of a regression line. Thus, income differences, as well as unemployment and poverty, are largely voluntary.[26] While the analytical focus of the human capital model is predictably the individual, the "structural" approach championed by Michael Piore gradates jobs according to such criteria as prestige, access to power, unionization, race, sex, and ethnicity.[27] The emphasis of the latter approach is on the inequalities in labor markets which result from the confluence of both supply- and demand-side reasons. In this view, mobility between the two sectors is negligible, not because of the worker's own lack of human capital but because of institutional restraints, most notably discrimination.[28]

But what of the characteristics of the two principal labor markets? Piore goes beyond the internal structure of these segments to look at the nature of the dominant working-class organization in different employment sectors. The upper tier of this dual market (primary market) is made up principally of "monopoly" and "oligopoly" firms, while the lower tier (secondary market) is composed of "competitive" firms. Firms in the former segment exercise significant control over their markets. They utilize high capital intensity to enhance productivity and are able to pass wage increases on to consumers through their control of the marketplace.[29] For firms in the lower segment, the economic environment is uncertain. Their markets tend to be local, or at best regional, and rely on labor-intensive processes of production. Since these firms are neither monopolistic nor oligopolistic, they cannot manipulate their markets and thus cannot pass on increases in their wage bill to consumers.

Furthermore, the social relationships of production which prevail in each segment are shaped by their respective internal structural determinants. Accordingly, the monopoly/oligopoly market emphasizes stability and tenure in social relationships and reinforces it with the bureaucratization of production processes and the creation of *internal markets*. Work is stratified into "finely graded job ladders," which provide for institutionalized promotion and advancement. The secondary market, on the other hand, is unstable, enforces "discipline" in a direct and arbitrary manner, does not generate an internal market, and offers no incentive for *either employer or worker* to stabilize employment.[30] It is precisely this market that suffers from a relative labor scarcity as the disadvantaged indigenous groups—as well as the second-generation external and internal immigrants—begin to reject secondary market jobs. Piore's explanation of this rejection focuses on the social component of secondary labor market jobs. He argues that jobs in the lower segment of the labor market carry negative social implications in addition to low wages, substandard working conditions, and irregular tenure. Thus, most indigenous workers find them unappealing. But with economic uncertainty and demand unpredictability on the rise, the secondary labor market is constantly expanding and thirsts for more labor. Gradually, an area's supply of marginal groups, such as women, teenagers, and students, becomes exhausted, and employers are confronted with limited alternatives involving intervention at either the fixed or the variable production-factor end. Because additional capitalization of the production process through investment in laborsaving machinery is not warranted by the nature and structure of the product-demand market, and because increasing wages and benefits in order to attract and retain workers involves both an undesirable qualitative change in the relationship between labor and management and a reduction in the latter's flexibility vis-à-vis the former, neither alternative is a viable option. Other alternatives, such as relocation to areas of abundant supplies of inexpensive labor, may be worth considering, but their viability is constrained by market considerations, expense of relocation, and the transferability of the operation.

The most feasible response, then, is the search for a steady and docile yet expendable and infinitely flexible labor supply. Foreign workers are ideal targets because they seem to satisfy most requirements of lower-segment employment in that they form an elastic labor supply, regardless of the mode of their "recruitment" and their legal status. They are more expendable than indigenous labor because of a system that formally and informally gives them few procedural rights to contest dismissals. Frequently they are interested only in temporary (i.e., flexible) commitments and will accept relatively modest wages and have modest expectations about working conditions. They are docile, not interested in organizing or afraid to, hardworking, usually honest, and quite exploitable. Finally—and here is Piore's innovative thinking at work—they usually retain their home social identity. By remaining rooted in the social structure of their point of origin, they view and treat work abroad in purely instrumental terms, in a social vacuum, without regard to the social component of their job. Foreign workers, then, at least initially, derive their social identity from another socioeconomic structure and view work abroad as a "temporary adjunct to their primary roles."[31] This convenient, one-dimensional (economic) identity is fully coincident with their employers' requirements.

This most intriguing scenario has some interesting implications, the most important of which is hinted at by the social context of the identity of foreign workers. As long as the social identities of migrants are anchored in their home community, they indeed are the conjunctural and convenient target workers needed by marginal and traditional industries. Once they begin to develop roots in the community of destination and become conscious of the social component of their jobs, a shift in their job aspirations will occur, and they are likely to begin to avoid the jobs for which they "came" even at the risk of unemployment. At this point, these "migrants" have become de facto permanent additions to the native labor force and, as such, begin to compete with natives for better secondary-segment jobs and eventually for jobs in the primary labor market. While this transition takes place, the need for low-skilled and flexible labor by marginal firms does not abate and additional numbers of foreign workers are engaged. In the process, entire categories of jobs become labeled "foreign-worker jobs," thus adding to their already negative social connotation; wages fail to keep up with rising living costs because of the dampening effect of an adequate labor supply; working conditions undergo only marginal improvement; and we finally observe the coexistence of high levels of unemployment among indigenous marginal groups with a constantly increasing demand for foreign workers.

Such multiple controversies regarding the impact of immigration on the economy and the labor market make unequivocal answers elusive. Yet the untangling of this seemingly endless web of competing hypotheses by evaluating both their internal logical consistency and empirical foundations must become a priority of the academic and research communities. A starting point for this assessment must be the fundamentally neutral observation that the growth of the economies of both Europe and the United States since the end of World War II has been premised, to varying degrees, on a steady supply of foreign labor. The obvious strategy, and the only one that can be expected to produce significant results, will distinguish between short- and long-term impacts; describe how micro-level decisions of both individual migrants and specific employers have helped shape this flow; assess the economic interests of both the intended protagonists (workers/employers) and of the unintended protagonists (consumers of public and private goods) in the immigration process; search for the *juste milieu* between private and societal goals; distinguish between the manifest and latent consequences of the process; and finally, outline the present and probable future distributional (sectoral and regional) impacts of legal and illegal immigration.

It is interesting that, in spite of diverse ideological views, most immigration scholars share a common emphasis toward reforming the U.S. labor market. The obvious implication of Piore's work is that in the present segmented labor market the interruption of the illegal inflow would actually result in severe labor shortages in such economic activities as restaurants and hotels, the garment industry, maintenance, and other low-skill/pay employment, and various agricultural jobs. Finally, the dualists' recommendations to restructure the labor market range from the stringent enforcement of anti-discrimination legislation, the retraining of redundant workers and workers with obsolete qualifications, and the stringent enforcement of minimum-wage legislation, to an increase in public service employment *specifically* for secondary labor market workers, the aggressive defense of worker rights, and the improvement of working conditions.

THE POPULATION COMPONENT

Another crucial question that must be addressed in a comprehensive analysis of U. S. immigration policy is the demographic profile of immigrants (legal and illegal) and their anticipated impact on and contribution to the growth (or, more accurately for many advanced industrial democracies, the stemming of the decline) of indigenous populations. Explicit issues of population size have been only marginally important factors in the shaping of post–World War II immigration programs in most advanced democratic societies. One of the few exceptions has been France. As Gary Freeman notes, however, even the French effort to ground immigration policy on a population policy fell victim to the economic planners' insistence on a labor market approach, in spite of significant support among French political elites for the population option.[32] Policy fluctuations notwithstanding, French immigration practice has exhibited an unofficial tolerance of a spontaneous, unregulated immigrant worker inflow and has periodically offered foreign workers ample opportunities to regularize their position post facto and become permanent residents and citizens, most recently during a "one-time only" amnesty program in 1981.

It is clear that labor import and illegal migrant flows which are allowed to develop in the midst of policy voids become de facto immigration and population policies. It thus becomes critical that the demographic characteristics, fertility behavior, and regional dispersion patterns of both legal and illegal immigrants in the United States be known. In Chapter 5 of this volume, Ellen Percy Kraly makes a plea for the articulation of national goals in the sociodemographic composition of U. S. population. Echoing Leon Bouvier,[33] she decries the absence of an overall population policy and the failure to have even a tentative optimum population goal. Any serious efforts in this direction, however, are likely to confront a host of data voids and inconsistencies. Along with the many problems encountered in obtaining reliable data on legal immigrants, the problem is further exacerbated by the paucity of reliable data on clandestine workers. An increasingly accepted interim source of such information utilizes the demographic portrait of legal immigrants as an indicator of the profile of illegal immigrants. The reasons used to justify recourse to this indirect method range from the fact that many legal immigrants often serve an "apprenticeship" as illegals in this country[34] to the empirically observed finding that the various population variables of net immigration can be extrapolated with some degree of confidence from obtainable data, particularly since profiles of immigrants closely resemble those of natives.[35] Furthermore, there is increasing evidence that immigrant households are often composed of both legal and undocumented members who have very similar demographic characteristics.[36]

The debate over the effects of immigration on population, however, should not be defined exclusively by demographic concerns. It must also include the more critical discussion of the appropriate population size for the United States. As Charles Keely and Ellen Percy Kraly have shown, the annual net *legal* immigration flow to the United States is around 270,000, from a gross inflow of about 400,000.[37] The annual gross *illegal* immigration flow may be as high as 750,000, but on the basis of very tentative research, some observers think that only about 100,000 of them settle here for longer terms.[38] Arguments advanced by special-interest groups (such as Zero Population Growth) seeking to restrict total immigration severely make little sense in that they are premised on faulty data.[39] Current fertility rates are at about 1.7 live births per woman, down from 2.11 births per woman, which is the absolute population replacement level, and down from 2.9 and 3.7 births per woman in the 1960s and 1950s respectively. Hence, with reduced immigration the level of stationary population and the consequent decline stage will be reached in a relatively short time. For instance, depending on the estimate of permanent illegal settlement, the total U. S. population by the year 2000 can range from 234 million with no net immigration to 286 million with the present net number of legal immigration plus 1 million net illegal population per year. The true number will obviously lie somewhere between these two extremes and be much closer to the lower, rather than the higher, figure.[40]

THE SOCIAL COMPONENT

The third aspect of U. S. immigration policy that requires serious reappraisal is the social one. As Philip Martin points out, it is in the "social arena that benefits and costs [of immigration] are most important for policy prescription, yet even qualitative assessments are not unambiguous."[41] Receiving societies do benefit from the migrants' contributions to the various social insurance programs, particularly since there is evidence that clandestine migrants expecially utilize social services infrequently.[42]

The experience of the Europeans with utilization of social services by foreign workers points to a series of unanticipated changes in usage patterns as migration flows mature. These changes are relevant to the United States both in the event that a temporary worker program should be instituted and in understanding the likely impacts of long-term clandestine workers on the social infrastructure of the receiving country. Especially relevant is the exponential growth in social and infrastructural services required by immigrant *families*, regardless of their legal status. Education is an excellent example, and Elizabeth Hull's incisive discussion of the *Doe* v. *Plyler* case in Chapter 8 of this volume develops the constitutional implications of Section 21 of the Texas Education Code masterfully. This Texas provision denies children of illegal aliens in Texas the right to free education because of the "outlaw status" of their parents. The Texas test case is being watched with interest in many quarters as localities try to grapple with overcrowded schools and deteriorating services which result from congestion in areas where legal and undocumented workers are concentrated.

In a recent study, Michael Greenwood argues persuasively that the cost of immigrant use of public goods (services) depends on whether such goods are produced under conditions of falling or rising average cost.[43] Since immigrants usually have a low (local) tax base (because of low rates of property ownership), they contribute *less than their share* of the cost of services they use; this leads to higher-than-average contributions on the part of the natives (principally in infrastructure areas). Furthermore, the "price" for such infrastructure will also rise (in nonpecuniary terms), because their quality deteriorates from overuse or, in the case of finite resources (such as police), because they are spread more thinly. These increasing costs must be juxtaposed, however, against the declining average cost of producing certain other public goods (services such as health, retirement, unemployment, national defense, and agricultural assistance). These are areas where the participation of migrants through tax and withhold-ings contributions makes a marked difference. Furthermore, one must also consider such other factors as the opportunities migrants afford some of the indigenous primary labor market-based popula-tion for social advancement (while also "pushing" secondary labor market workers downward) and the often nonquantifiable conse-quences of the formation of a permanent underclass of workers who are suspended at the social fringes of societies. As former INS com-missioner Leonel Castillo frequently observed, societies have allowed themselves to drift into a policy of "half-open door" without "plan-ning or conscious expression of national intent."[44]

Social marginality, when constantly reinforced by in-stitutionalized political and economic discrimination and widely dis-cretionary and often capricious administrative practices by immigration bureaucracies, becomes fertile ground for severe sys-temic alienation, which in turn portends severe sociopolitical conse-quences. At the heart of this problem is the receiving societies' political ambivalence toward migrants, and their failure to accept the reality that their previous relative cultural homogeneity (European case) or seemingly abating social/ethnic cleavages (U. S. case) is now challenged by new cultural/linguistic/ethnic entities. In this new and evolving environment, receiving societies will come under increasing internal/international pressure to accept the moral and political im-perative of granting their new de facto citizens the rights and privi-leges that correspond to their economic contributions.[45]

THE POLITICAL COMPONENT

The final dimension of a comprehensive U.S. immigration policy is intimately related to the social one, but it centers on the political realm. Although it has received only scant attention among the major concerns of the immigration field, it must be of genuine interest to any student of international migration because it constantly intrudes upon—indeed, undergirds—all other dimensions. There is little doubt that it is partly in response to internal and international polit-ical pressure that the U.S. government has undertaken the current reassessment of its immigration and refugee policies. The essays in this volume by Mark J. Miller and Demetrios G. Papademetriou (Chapter 6) and Leon Gordenker (Chapter 9) reflect these concerns. At stake here seems to be the ability of the United States and other immigrant-"receiving" states to exercise one of the most jealously guarded expressions of sovereignty—control of their borders—and to formulate and implement immigration policies that reflect their national interests. As Miller and Papademetriou point out in Chapter 6, the chimerical nature of this vision in an increasingly interdependent world is rapidly becoming obvious, especially in view of the vast and porous U.S. borders. Unlike the European advanced industrial societies, which at least for the first decade of their experience with labor migration programs were in more than nominal control of the situation and could adjust the inflow volume and its composition according to perceived needs, the United States seems to be reacting to conditions "imposed" upon it by the region, and by its own traditionally dominant (and exploitative) political and economic role in it.[46]

In spite of the serious policy implications of the immigration issue, one of the most remarkable facts is that, had it not been for the nexus of Indo-Chinese/Cuban/Haitian refugees, the topic might not have become a centerpiece in the U.S. political agenda. Prior to that point, the salience of the immigration reform debate was viewed as relevant primarily to the southwestern regions, although the issue has been recognized as a key one by the overwhelming majority of Americans in every poll on illegal workers for nearly forty years.[47] The folly of such self-deceptive thinking has been the subject of much literature.[48] Meanwhile, the debate has become all-encompassing and sometimes includes shrill warnings about the Hispanicization of the United States as well as more reasoned concerns about the obvious violation of the most basic human rights of those who are in the United States without valid immigration documents.

The range and depth of the immigration controversy seems to test the will and ingenuity of political elites who have often reacted with uncertainty on the place of immigration in the ideological spectrum and instinctively seek consensus by appointing commissions, task forces, and study groups. Center stage is occupied by a nagging identity crisis that expresses itself in a constant equivocation between "main gates" and "back doors" and by frequent scapegoatism, xenophobia, and negative stereotyping. Illegal immigrants are often viewed as "intolerable burdens," "racial and cultural contaminants," "freeloaders," "welfare cheats," and "mañana minded."[49] Fears of future separatist movements in the Southwest are increasingly prominent and are discussed more fully in Chapter 10 of this volume. Finally, increasingly polarized public perceptions reduce "the degrees of policy space within which the U.S. and the Mexican governments can maneuver [and thus reduce the prospects] for a gradualist, cooperative solution [while pressuring for] narrow punitive responses by the U.S. government."[50]

Elite ambivalence and competing special interests have created a political climate in which strange bedfellows and odd couples operate in the eternal morass typical of plural political settings. The following list, adapted partly from the work of David North,[51] identifies some of these bizarre and deadlocked alliances.[52] The *restrictionists* include, among others, many liberals, conservatives, taxpayer groups, population-control advocates, ethnic and racial bigots, environmentalists, conservationists, law-and-order people, organized labor, and the black leadership. *Anti restrictionists* can count among themselves agribusiness and secondary labor market employers of illegals, the State Department, the Mexican government, the church, the Hispanic leadership, the civil libertarians, the Left, and the immigration bar. However, each alliance can count in its midst members with special interests whose presence defies conventional political and ideological logic. For instance, liberals who place the well-being of minorities on the top of their political agenda would be found in the restrictionist camp. If the protection of the rights and liberties of all people within the borders of the United States is one's most immediate concern, however, a relatively more open immigration policy may be advocated.

Among all these groups, organized labor must be singled out for its failure to become a veto group on immigration policy even under successive pro-labor administrations. Continuing a one-hundred-year-old tradition, it has been consistently outmaneuvered by business interests—at least with regard to "back door" policies. Underlying this lack of policy impact may be labor's basic ambivalence about the place of both legal and illegal immigrants (but particularly the latter) in the syndicalist movement. Are the two groups in similar antithetical positions vis-à-vis capital? Are immigrants a threat to the security, advancement, organization, or even the embourgeoisement of native workers? Is immigrant exploitation, particularly by secondary labor market employers, detrimental to the union movement? The answers to these questions hold the key to whether organized labor in the United States will perceive illegal immigration in a clearer light. Illegals may indeed harm the well-being of some union members, although the dualists would deny that, because the secondary labor market is not really organized. Yet it is in the class interests of organized labor to accept the reality of the existence of a large foreign work force, and in recognition of the negative impact that the exploi-

tation of foreign workers has an overall working class solidarity, organized labor should demand and obtain equal economic and social
treatment for all workers, regardless of nationality, and try aggres-
sively to organize illegals in a common front vis-à-vis business.[53] The
point cannot be emphasized enough: Such a course of action is indeed
in the best interests of the working class. In fact, unions should actively demand a principal role in both formulating and implementing
new pragmatic immigration initiatives in recognition of their legitimate interests in this matter.

The Public Policy Significance of Immigration Research

As Philip Martin has observed in the European context, labor migration occurred because "economic circumstances provided migration
incentives while [the] complexity [of the process] and self-interest
obscured costs."[54] This observation also applies to the American
scene. Thus, the United States finds itself again at the crossroads.
Unconvinced by competing claims with regard to the impacts of illegal immigration on our labor market, class structure, population,
social services and infrastructure, and domestic, regional, and international political responsibilities, policymakers have apparently come
to the conclusion that the status quo is unacceptable. The empaneling
in 1979 of the Select Commission on Immigration and Refugee Policy
initially gave the appearance of a high-level executive and legislative
commitment to addressing the problem in all its facets and arriving at
a consensus about the future direction of immigration policy. The
commission's work and final report (discussed at length by Elizabeth
Midgley in Chapter 2 of this volume), however, failed to obtain the
necessary consensus and were quickly superseded by the Reagan administration's own recommendations.

It appears that conflicting claims by analysts, especially with regard to the undocumented component of immigration to the United
States, will again prevent the articulation of a coherent policy. The
problem with undocumented workers is that, because they are in the
United States clandestinely, they are extremely difficult to identify
and locate—and even more difficult to interview. Furthermore, as
Walter Fogel points out in Chapter 3, there are significant regional
variations in both the composition of such flows and the manner of
their impact on regions, local labor markets, and local communities.
Because of the complexity and unreliability of most such data, and the
small n, the knowledge base about these groups is extremely scarce

and assumptions about impacts on host communities are frequently inaccurate. As a result, the formulation, implementation, and enforcement of policies aimed at addressing the problem in a thorough and integrated manner are handicapped by the usually only suggestive, and not conclusive, nature of data and, perhaps even more so, by scholarship that often approaches advocacy and thus carries with it a significant ideological burden.

A frequent reaction to the seemingly insurmountable problem of paucity of reliable data is the conviction that since data cannot meet the requirements of stringent scientific rigor—particularly the tests of randomness and replication—all efforts at profiling undocumented foreign workers should be abandoned as an exercise in futility.[55] Others react by taking an equally fallacious and dangerous course. They have noted the few studies available on clandestine immigrants and have sought to generalize and apply their findings to the entire illegal immigrant universe. The reactions, of course, need not be such polar opposites.

Although randomness would be ideal, the alternative must never be the abandoning of research. Concomitantly, analysts and interpreters of such research must resist the urge to confuse detail with social structure and overgeneralize from research findings. For instance, those who would rely on the study by David North and Marion Houstoun[56] should bear in mind that the sample on which that study was based was one of *apprehended* illegal aliens in the custody of the immigration authorities. Furthermore, the focus was heavily on Mexicans (481 out of 793 interviews) and western hemisphere aliens (an additional 273 of 793 respondents). Only 75 respondents came from other destinations. Finally, 457 of those interviewed were in the custody of the states of Texas, Arizona, and California. The remaining 40 percent were interviewed in seven other eastern, midwestern, and northwestern locations. Such a distribution biases the sample toward the Southwest and Mexico, while research has indicated that Mexicans may comprise only about 50 percent of the total undocumented population and that the spatial distribution of that population is quite diffuse.

Some more recent studies have set more modest objectives. For instance, many of the recent studies by Wayne Cornelius and his associates have set for themselves attainable goals and have made important contributions to our understanding of many aspects of the migration process.[57] Cornelius's often innovative work, however, has frequently been misused to support claims his data simply do not support. This problem is common to research on Mexican illegal aliens.[58] The root of the problem is that these studies, however carefully designed and executed, have inherently low generalizability levels, because they give information about only some Mexican illegal aliens, in certain types of occupations, in one (or from one) particular region. They will not disclose much about the Mexican population in Illinois, for instance, let alone undocumented non-Mexican workers in the eastern regions. Extrapolating from such studies is always dangerous and fails to generate wide support for such findings among either the research community or the policy community.

The question one must ask is whether such basic accord should be an expected or necessary prerequisite for research in areas of such extreme policy and political salience. We would argue that it must not. In cases where generalizable quantitative evidence is extremely hard to obtain, one can opt for such alternatives as initiating and fostering a catalog of systematic case studies that allow one to move "iteratively"[59] from quantitative to case-study designs and back. What is needed here are innovative research strategies which build on case studies that shed light on specific migration flows while specifying (and thus making more accurate) extant theoretical models. The studies of Mexican workers in the Southwest are well on the way to establishing the parameters and the foundation of such knowledge. Some equally interesting research is also being conducted with non-Mexican groups, in other geographical settings, and in a variety of working contexts. For instance, Thomas Bailey and Marcia Freedman have recently completed the first phase of a study on the impacts of "new" immigrants (legal and illegal) on the New York City restaurant industry;[60] Roger Waldinger is currently involved in a study of illegal foreign worker participation in New York's garment industry;[61] Sheldon Maram has recently completed a similar study involving the Los Angeles labor market;[62] Eleanor Glaessel-Brown, and Richard Cuthbert and Joe Stevens, have been studying impacts of foreign workers in New England's light manufacturing industry and Oregon's Hood River valley apple orchards respectively.[63] These studies represent a novel and fruitful research strategy that identifies the impacts of immigrant groups on specific industries in a particular setting, and their usefulness cannot be emphasized enough.

A final type of study is represented by collecting and analyzing data obtained from social service agencies. One such large-scale study was recently completed by Maurice Van Arsdol and his associates.[64] In that study, the authors examined the social, labor force, and earning patterns of a sample of unapprehended, undocumented migrants in Los Angeles who had sought the assistance of the One-Stop Immigration Center in regularizing their status. The sample was drawn from the center's records for the period from 1972 to 1975. The more "unusual" findings of the study included a significantly stronger female component than other studies of illegal aliens, a lower labor-force participation rate (due to the larger overall household component of the sample), and confirmation of the existence of a kinship network that plays a crucial role in facilitating clandestine immigration. More recently, a similar study utilizing data from the Catholic Migration Offices of the New York metropolitan area is investigating the labor-market profile of unapprehended undocumented immigrants who seek the assistance of these agencies.[65]

The controversy about the impacts of clandestine workers on the U.S. economy and society, although by no means resolved, is already on the way to becoming more fruitfully and systematically studied. What has not been adequately studied and understood is temporary worker programs. In fact, outlines of variations on the foreign worker theme have appeared with regularity in professional journals and commissioned reports.[66] They range in magnitude, intended impact, and conceptual clarity from the expansion of the H-2 program and a revised *bracero* program, to a massive "guest worker" policy like that in Europe. Such proposals seem to respond to the wrong question. There can be no disagreement that illegal immigration has been a source of troubled bilateral relations, has diminished American international prestige, has led to a divisive domestic public-policy debate, and has "invited" the wholesale violation of immigration law.[67] As is discussed in Chapter 10 of this volume, the foreign-labor programs under consideration, in addition to specific internal logical and philosophical problems, also suffer from some basic generic deficiencies in that they address merely the symptoms and consequences, rather than the causes, of the problem. As we have already pointed out, the causes of illegal immigration are structural and labor-market related. Therefore, in order to relieve immigration pressure one must focus on reforming the labor market.[68]

Furthermore, an immigration policy per se may be ancillary to other more fundamental questions such as population and social policies. Only when the United States agrees on a clear ordering of these priorities can immigration reform become the right tool in the attainment of long-term societal goals. In addition, immigration policy must be sensitive to important internal and external political pressures. While many of the internal political forces have already been identified, the external (international) political pressures must also be taken seriously into account. The formulation and implementation of immigration policies that merely palliate or even ignore other societal problems invites failure and will likely lead to another round in the seemingly interminable immigration policy debate. The United States must focus on the articulation and execution of population, social, labor market, and foreign policies, and then adjust its immigration policy accordingly. A necessary first step in this direction is studying the impact of legal immigration on American society, a topic that has taken a back seat to the much more "relevant" topic of illegal immigration. Only after we understand how legal immigrants behave can we begin to make intelligent policies about immigration in general.

Implicit in this recommended course of action is the nagging question of whether the United States is indeed engaged in the right debate. Foreign-labor programs do not address the fundamental questions outlined above. Furthermore, they may well be capital's latest entry into the "back door" sweepstakes of the 1980s. Although they obviously serve employer interests, they have severe negative impacts on U.S. class structure, the ability to enforce laws, and ultimately the need to adjust immigration to a clearly understood national program. In a climate of "expert" opinion running strongly in favor of more stopgap measures, we take the minority viewpoint that if there is a demonstrable need for more workers in secondary labor market activities in the face of high unemployment, we must first address the problem of why certain jobs are abandoned by native workers. Importing more "workers" solves nothing; it only postpones, reinforces, and eventually exacerbates structural labor market problems and compounds them with institutionally sanctioned exploitative programs that in return hurt our own disadvantaged citizens. If we indeed need more workers, let us opt for an immigration policy of flexible quotas which can best respond to our social, political, and human rights commitments. Changing the intolerable status quo with ill-conceived plans about foreign-worker programs is ostrichlike behavior; not only does it fail to remove the threat, it simply institutionalizes what Vernon Briggs calls a subclass of "rightless" and "deprived" persons.[69]

Notes

1. Alejandro Portes, "Toward a Structural Analysis of Illegal (Undocumented) Immigration," *International Migration Review* 12 (Winter 1978): 482.

2. Alejandro Portes and John Walton, *Labor, Class, and the International System* (New York: Academic Press, 1981), pp. 21–65.

3. Francisco Alba, "Mexico's International Migration as a Manifestation of Its Development Pattern," *International Migration Review* 12 (Winter 1978): 502–513; J. Craig Jenkins, "The Demand for Immigrant Workers: Labor Scarcity or Social Control?" *International Migration Review* 12 (Winter 1978): 514–535; Demetrios G. Papademetriou, "Emigration and Return in the Mediterranean Littoral: Conceptual, Research, and Policy Agendas" (Paper delivered at the First European Conference on International Return Migration, Rome, Italy, November 1981); D. G. Papademetriou, *The Impact of International Migration on the Development of the Countries of Worker Origin: The Case of Greece,* forthcoming; D. G. Papademetriou, "Rethinking International Migration: A Review and Critique," *Comparative Political Studies,* forthcoming; Portes, "Toward a Structural Analysis"; I. Wallerstein, "The Rise and Future Demise of the World Capitalist System: Concepts for Comparative Analysis," in *The Capitalist World Economy: Essays by Immanuel Wallerstein* (New York: Cambridge University Press, 1979).

4. As Aristide Zolberg observes in "The Main Gate and the Back Door: The Politics of American Immigration Policy, 1950–1976" (Paper delivered at the Council on Foreign Relations, Washington, D.C., April 1978).

5. Such as the various *passenger acts,* which influenced the cost and pattern of ocean crossing; *land policies,* which controlled the incentive for immigration; *naturalization laws,* which controlled the composition of the U.S. body politic; and, perhaps less directly, policies with regard to *slaves and Indians* (see ibid.).

6. The reference is to the periods of genuine labor shortages during which the economic vitality of a nation as a whole hinges on the availability of adequate foreign labor supplies willing to immigrate and ease labor bottlenecks in advanced economies.

7. The exceptions were Russians, Persians, and Afghans.

8. A 1929 amendment to the 1924 act set the 1920 census results as the effective date for calculating quotas.

9. Zolberg, "The Main Gate and the Back Door," p. 10.

10. Ibid., p. 11.

11. See, e.g., Vernon M. Briggs, "Foreign Labor Programs as an Alternative to Illegal Immigration into the United States: A Dissenting View," Center for Philosophy and Public Policy, University of Maryland, College Park, Maryland, 1980.

12. Ibid.; Mark J. Miller and David J. Yeres, "A Massive Temporary Worker Programme for the U.S.: Solution or Mirage?" Working Paper for Migration for Employment Project, World Employment Programme, International Labor Organization, Geneva, Switz., November 1979; Aristide Zolberg, "International Migration Policies in a Changing World System," in *Human Migration: Patterns and Policies,* ed. William H. McNeill and Ruth S. Adams (Bloomington: Indiana University Press, 1978); Zolberg, "The Main Gate and the Back Door."

13. The McCarran-Walter Act continued the racial focus of the 1920s legislation. In this spirit, it maintained a quota system already heavily skewed

toward advanced European societies, while making only nominal concessions to the rest of the world. For instance, Greece was awarded a ceiling of 308 entries, while most Asian countries were given 100 positions. The anachronistic nature of the legislation was recognized and adjusted, however, by allowing almost two-thirds of all those admitted in the 1950s to come in as exceptions to the law and in recognition of American skill and population needs, as well as of U.S. responsibilities to Eastern European refugees. The 1952 act is equally instructive in what it did *not* include: neither a penalty provision for hiring illegal immigrants nor permanent legislation to permit temporary agricultural labor as a nonimmigrant category—if U.S. workers could not be found. Both provisions had been integral parts of Senate Report 1515, on which the act was largely based. See Zolberg, "The Main Gate and the Back Door"; Elliott Abrams and Franklin S. Abrams, "Immigration Policy: Who Gets in and Why?" *The Public Interest* 38 (1975) 3–29; Interagency Task Force on Immigration Policy, Departments of Justice, Labor, and State, *Staff Report,* August 1979.

14. Abrams and Abrams, "Immigration Policy"; Interagency Task Force, *Staff Report;* Miller and Yeres, "Massive Temporary Worker Programme"; David S. North and Allen Lebel, *Manpower and Immigration Policies in the United States* (Washington, D.C.: National Commission for Manpower Policy, 1978); Zolberg, "The Main Gate and the Back Door."

15. Zolberg, "The Main Gate and the Back Door," p. 49.

16. North and Lebel, *Manpower and Immigration Policies,* p. 11.

17. See Charles Keely, *U.S. Immigration: A Policy Analysis* (New York: Population Council, 1979); Miller and Yeres, "Massive Temporary Worker Programme"; Select Commission on Immigration and Refugee Policy, *U.S. Immigration Policy and the National Interest,* Final Report, March 1, 1981 (Washington, D.C.: Government Printing Office, 1981); and U.S. Commission on Civil Rights, *The Tarnished Golden Door: Civil Rights Issues in Immigration,* September 1980.

18. See W. Roger Böhning, "International Migration and the Western World: Past, Present, Future," *International Migration* 16 (1979): 1–23. The magnitude of this problem often escapes the attention of all but specialists in immigration matters. For instance, this brain drain is responsible for finding more Filipino medical doctors than black doctors in practice in the United States and for admitting more foreign medical doctors in certain years than the number graduating from U.S. medical schools. One should not need guidance in understanding the role of the American Medical Association (AMA) in this. The AMA would rather fill excess demand with foreign doctors than expand the number of graduates of American medical schools, a practice that may be difficult to reverse when the shortage ceases to be as pronounced. Furthermore, the practice is a significant bonus to the United States because it does not have to absorb the high costs for the upbringing and professional training of these welcome immigrants.

19. Abrams and Abrams, "Immigration Policy"; Interagency Task Force, *Staff Report.*

20. Abrams and Abrams, "Immigration Policy"; Zolberg, "The Main Gate and the Back Door."

21. Miller and Yeres, "Massive Temporary Worker Programme," p. 8.

22. Briggs, "Foreign Labor Programs"; Interagency Task Force, *Staff Report;* Miller and Yeres, "Massive Temporary Worker Programme."

23. Briggs, "Foreign Labor Programs"; Wayne A. Cornelius, "Building the Cactus Curtain: Mexican Immigration and U.S. Responses" (Paper prepared for the Latin American Program of the Woodrow Wilson International Center for Scholars, Washington, D.C., September 1979); Michael Greenwood, "The Economic Consequences of Immigration for the U.S.: A Survey of the Findings," in Interagency Task Force on Immigration Policy, Departments of Justice, Labor, and State, *Staff Report Companion Papers,* August 1979, pp. 1–108; George Johnson, "The Labor Market Effects of Immigration into the U.S.: A Summary of the Findings," in Interagency Task Force, *Staff Report Companion Papers,* pp. 109–162; Keely, *U.S. Immigration;* Ray Marshall, *Employment Implications of the International Migration of Workers* (Washington, D.C.: National Council on Employment Policy, 1976); Philip L. Martin, "Guestworker Programs: Lessons from Europe," Report prepared for the Joint Congressional Economic Committee, June 1979; North and Lebel, *Manpower and Immigration Policies;* Papademetriou, "Rethinking International Migration"; Demetrios G. Papademetriou, "U.S. Immigration Policy at the Crossroads," in *Foreign Policy as Public Policy,* ed. Don C. Piper and Ronald Tercheck (Washington, D.C.: American Enterprise Institute, 1982); Michael J. Piore, *Birds of Passage: Migrant Labor and Industrial Societies* (New York: Cambridge University Press, 1979).

24. Barry Chiswick, "An Analysis of the Economic Progress and Impact of Immigrants," Paper prepared for the Employment and Training Administration, U.S. Department of Labor, June 1980.

25. E. M. Beck, Patrick M. Horan, and Charles M. Tolbert II, "Stratification in a Dual Economy: A Sectoral Model of Earnings Determination," *American Sociological Review* 43 (October 1978): 704–720; Suzanne Berger and Michael J. Piore, *Dualism and Discontinuity in Industrial Societies* (New York: Cambridge University Press, 1980); Peter B. Doeringer and Michael J. Piore, "Unemployment and the 'Dual Labor Market,'" *The Public Interest* 38 (Winter 1975): 67–79; Bennett Harrison and Andrew Sum, "The Theory of 'Dual' or Segmented Labor Markets," *Journal of Development Economics* 5 (1979): 215–231; Piore, *Birds of Passage.*

26. For example, since unemployment reflects the absence of relevant skills that would make one desirable to prospective employers, poverty and unemployment form a mutually reinforcing vicious circle. Explanations of and prescriptions for relieving unemployment abound. The Keynesians would naturally focus on government initiatives; the "structuralists" would focus on the disruptive effects of technological displacement, shifting industrial production factors, and the effects of foreign competition on labor markets; finally, the "job search" theorists would focus on the searcher's limited information, uncertainty, and distorted expectations about the labor market.

27. Piore, *Birds of Passage*.

28. Beck, Horan, and Tolberg, "Stratification"; Berger and Piore, *Dualism and Discontinuity;* Doeringer and Piore, "Unemployment and the 'Dual Labor Market'"; Harrison and Sum, "Theory of 'Dual' or Segmented Labor Markets"; Piore, *Birds of Passage*.

29. Berger and Piore, *Dualism and Discontinuity;* Doeringer and Piore, "Unemployment and the 'Dual Labor Market'"; Piore, *Birds of Passage;* Alejandro Portes and Robert L. Bach, "Dual Labor Markets and Immigration: A Test of Competing Theories of Income Inequality," Occasional paper, Comparative Studies of Immigration and Ethnicity, Center for International Studies, Duke University, Durham, N.C., 1979; Michael L. Wachter, "Primary and Secondary Labor Markets: A Critique of the Dual Approach," *Brookings Papers on Economic Activity* 3 (1974): 637–680.

30. Berger and Piore, *Dualism and Discontinuity*; Doeringer and Piore, "Unemployment and the 'Dual Labor Market'"; Piore, *Birds of Passage*; Portes and Bach, "Dual Labor Markets and Immigration."

31. Berger and Piore, *Dualism and Discontinuity*, p. 50.

32. Gary P. Freeman, *Immigrant Labor and Racial Conflict in Industrialized Societies* (Princeton: Princeton University Press, 1979).

33. Leon F. Bouvier, "The Impact of Immigration on U.S. Population Size," in *Population Trends and Public Policy*, Occasional Paper No. 1 (Washington, D.C.: Population Reference Bureau, January 1981).

34. David Heer, "What Is the Annual Net Flow of Undocumented Mexican Immigrants to the United States?" *Demography* 16 (1979): 417–423; Charles Hirschman, "Prior U.S. Residence Among Mexican Immigrants," *Social Forces* 56 (1978): 1179–1201.

35. Campbell Gibson, "The Contribution of Immigration to U.S. Population Growth: 1790–1970," *International Migration Review* 9 (1975): 157–177; Keely, *U. S. Immigration*.

36. See, e.g., Patricia R. Pessar, "The Role of Households in International Migration" (Paper delivered at the Conference on New Directions on Immigration and Ethnicity Research, Duke University, Durham, N. C., May 1981).

37. Charles Keely and Ellen Percy Kraly, "Recent Net Immigration to the U.S.: Its Impact on Population Growth and Native Fertility," *Demography* 15 (1978): 267–283.

38. See Abrams and Abrams, "Immigration Policy"; Ansley J. Coale, "Alternative Paths to a Stationary Population," in *Demographic and Social Aspects of Population Growth*, ed. Charles F. Westoff and Robert Park, Jr. (Washington, D. C.: Commission on Population Growth and the American Future, 1972), vol. 1, pp. 589–603; Cornelius, "Building the Cactus Curtain"; Heer, "What Is the Annual Net Flow?"

39. See Keely, *U.S. Immigration*.

40. Coale, *"Alternative Paths";* Commission on Population Growth and the American Future, *Population and the American Future*, Summary Report (Washington, D. C.: Government Printing Office, 1972); Gibson, "Contribu-

tion of Immigration"; Heer, "What Is the Annual Net Flow?" Interagency Task Force, *Staff Report*; Richard Irwin and Robert Warren, "Demographic Aspects of American Immigration," in *Demographic and Social Aspects of Population Growth*, pp. 167–178; Keely, *U.S. Immigration*.

41. Martin, "Guestworker Programs," p. 42.

42. Cornelius, "Building the Cactus Curtain"; Interagency Task Force, *Staff Report*; Charles Keely et al., *Profiles of Undocumented Aliens in New York City: Haitians and Dominicans* (New York: Center for Migration Studies, 1977); David S. North and Marion P. Houstoun, *The Characteristics and Role of Illegal Aliens in the U.S. Labor Market: An Exploratory Study* (Washington, D.C.: Linton & Co., 1976); Maurice D. Van Arsdol et al., "Non-Apprehended and Apprehended Undocumented Residents in the Los Angeles Labor Market: An Exploratory Study," Population Research Laboratory, University of Southern California, Los Angeles, 1979 (mimeographed).

43. Greenwood, "Economic Consequences of Immigration."

44. David Nunes, "U.S. Puts Number of Illegal Aliens Under 5 Million," *Washington Post*, January 31, 1980, p. A15.

45. Cornelius, "Building the Cactus Curtain"; Freeman, *Immigrant Labor;* Interagency Task Force, *Staff Report;* Philip L. Martin, Mark J. Miller, and Demetrios G. Papademetriou, "U.S. Immigration Policy: The Guestworker Option Revisited," 1981 (mimeographed); Papademetriou, "Rethinking International Migration"; Papademetriou, "U.S. Immigration Policy."

46. Abrams and Abrams, "Immigration Policy"; Cornelius, "Building the Cactus Curtain"; Arthur F. Corwin, ed., *Immigrants—and Immigrants: Perspectives on Mexican Labor Migration to the United States* (Westport, Conn.: Greenwood Press, 1978); Martin, Miller, and Papademetriou, "U.S. Immigration Policy"; Piore, *Birds of Passage;* Jonathan Power, *Migrant Workers in Western Europe and the United States* (Oxford: Pergamon, 1979).

47. For instance, in May 1980, some 66 percent of a national sample of respondents were in favor of halting immigration. Notably, the poll was taken after the Mariel Cubans had begun to arrive on American shores in large numbers. A similar question asked in August 1979 had elicited a 57 percent negative reply. In both cases the respondents were asked their opinion about the immigration of "political refugees." On a question regarding a frequently heard controversial component of immigration policy, e.g., whether it should be unlawful to employ undocumented aliens, 82 percent of the respondents to a 1977 poll answered in the affirmative. The closely related question whether the United States should require all to carry an identification card as a means of controlling employing illegals elicited a negative reply by 50 percent of the same sample. This contrasts sharply with the results of a 1942 poll asking the same question. Sixty-nine percent of that sample were in favor of such cards. In fact, following a well-publicized capture of eight Nazi agents later that year, 72 percent of a subsequent sample also were in favor of identification cards. Opinion on immigration levels has remained fairly steady over the last two decades. In a 1965 poll, 33 percent of the respondents were in favor of decreasing immigration. Thirty-nine percent opted for keeping

immigration at current levels. The figures for the same questions were 42 percent and 37 percent respectively. Of course, disaggregation by income, race, age, education, region, and other similarly relevant factors showed significant variation. See American Institute of Public Opinion, "The Gallup Polls on Immigration," January and July 1942, May 1965, March 1977, August 1979, and May 1980.

48. Cornelius, "Building the Cactus Curtain"; W. Cornelius, "Mexican Migration to the U.S.: Causes, Consequences, and U.S. Responses," Migration and Development Study Group, Center for International Studies, MIT, Cambridge, Mass., 1978; Keely, *U.S. Immigration;* North and Lebel, *Manpower and Immigration Policies;* Papademetriou, "U.S. Immigration Policy"; Portes, "Toward a Structural Analysis"; Michael S. Teitelbaum, "Right Versus Right: Immigration and Refugee Policy in the United States," *Foreign Affairs* 59 (Fall 1980): 21–59.

49. Cornelius, "Building the Cactus Curtain," p. 11.

50. Ibid., p. 22.

51. David S. North, "Comments on Vernon Briggs' Paper" (Paper delivered at the Conference on Border Relations, La Paz, Mexico, February 8, 1980).

52. See also Teitelbaum, "Right Versus Right."

53. Some embryonic attempts in that direction have already begun in the New York and Los Angeles garment industries and, intermittently, in some argricultural areas of the Southwest.

54. Martin, "Guestworker Programs," p. 31.

55. On this, see Wayne A. Cornelius, "The Future of Mexican Immigrants in California: A New Perspective for Public Policy," Working Papers in U.S.-Mexican Relations, no. 6, Program in U.S.-Mexican Studies, University of California, San Diego, Calif., 1981.

56. North and Houstoun, *Characteristics and Role of Illegal Aliens.*

57. Cornelius, "Future of Mexican Immigrants"; Wayne A. Cornelius, "Interviewing Undocumented Immigrants: Methodological Reflections Based on Fieldwork in Mexico and the U.S.," *International Migration Review* 16 (Summer 1982): 378–411.

58. Armando Arias, "Undocumented Mexicans: A Study in the Social Psychology of Clandestine Migrations to the United States" (Ph.D. diss., University of California, San Diego, 1981); Ina R. Dinerman, "Migrants and Stay-at-Homes: A Comparative Study of Rural Migration from Michoachan, Mexico," Monographs in U.S. Mexican Studies, no. 5, Program in U.S.-Mexican Studies, University of California, San Diego, Calif., 1981; Ina R. Dinerman, "Patterns of Adaptation Among Households of U.S.-Bound Migrants from Michoachan, Mexico," *International Migration Review* 12 (1978): 485–501; Sheldon L. Maram et al., "Hispanic Workers in the Garment and Restaurant Industries in Los Angeles County," Working Papers in U.S.-Mexican Studies, no. 12, Program in U.S.-Mexican Studies, University of California, San Diego, Calif., 1981; Richard Mines, "Developing a Community Tradition of Migration: A Field Study in Rural Zacatecas, Mexico, and California Settlement Areas," Monographs in U.S.-Mexican Studies, no. 3,

Program in U.S.-Mexican Studies, University of California, San Diego, Calif.,
1981; Joshua Reichert and Douglas Massey, "History and Trends in U.S.-
Bound Migration from a Mexican Town," *International Migration Review* 14
(1980): 475–491; Joshua Reichert and Douglas Massey, "Patterns of U.S.
Migration from a Mexican Sending Community: A Comparison of Legal and
Illegal Migrants," *International Migration Review* 13 (1979): 599–623; James
Stuart and Michael Kearney, "Causes and Effects of Agricultural Labor Mi-
gration from the Mixteca of Oaxaca to California," Working Papers in U.S.-
Mexican Studies, no. 28, Program in U.S.-Mexican Studies, University of
California, San Diego, Calif., 1981.

59. Alexander L. George, "Case Studies and Theory Development: The
Method of Structured, Focused Comparison," in *Diplomacy: New Approaches in
History, Theory, and Policy,* ed. Paul G. Lauren (New York: Free Press, 1979),
pp. 43–68.

60. Thomas Bailey and Marcia Freedman, "Immigrant and Native-Born
Workers in the Restaurant Industry," Conservation of Human Resources,
Columbia University, New York, 1981 (mimeographed).

61. Roger Waldinger, "The Sweatshop Labor Market: Immigration and
the Dilemmas of Union Regulation in the Garment Industry" (Ph.D. diss.,
Joint Center for Urban Studies of MIT and Harvard Universities, in progress).

62. Maram et al., "Hispanic Workers in the Garment and Restaurant
Industries in Los Angeles County."

63. Eleanor Glaessal-Brown, "The Role of Blue-Collar Migrants from
Columbia in New England Labor Markets for Light Manufacturing Industry"
(Ph.D. diss., MIT, 1982); Richard W. Cuthbert and Joe B. Stevens, "The Net
Economic Incentive for Illegal Mexican Migration: A Case Study," *Interna-
tional Migration Review* 15 (1981): 543–551.

64. Van Arsdol et al., *Non-Apprehended and Apprehended Undocumented
Residents.*

65. Demetrios Papademetriou and Nicholas DiMarzio, "Profiling Unap-
prehended Undocumented Aliens in the New York Metropolitan Area: An
Exploratory Study," Interim Report, Center for Migration Studies, New
York, 1982.

66. David C. Gregory, "A. U.S.-Mexican Temporary Workers Program:
The Search for Co-determination," in *Mexico and the United States,* ed. Robert
H. McBride (Englewood Cliffs, N.J.: Prentice-Hall, 1981), pp. 158–177;
Keely, *U.S. Immigration;* Miller and Yeres, "Massive Temporary Worker Pro-
gramme"; Edwin Reubens, "Aliens, Jobs, and Immigration Policy," *The Public
Interest* 51 (1978): 113–134; Edwin Reubens, "Temporary Admission of
Foreign Workers: Dimensions and Policies," National Commission for Man-
power Policy, Washington, D.C., 1979.

67. Miller and Yeres, "Massive Temporary Worker Programme," p. 35.

68. See also Martin, Miller, and Papademetriou, "U.S. Immigration Policy."

69. Briggs, "Foreign Labor Programs," p. 24.

CHAPTER 2

Comings and Goings in U.S. Immigration Policy

Elizabeth Midgley

"America is a nation of immigrants." That characterization is the starting point for many a discourse on immigration policy, a resonant allusion to an important basis of political equality in America. The ancestors of everyone (even the Indians) came from somewhere, and for some purposes that is enough said. But not for an understanding of the evolution of immigration policy in the United States. Attitudes, practices, and laws have been much affected by important changes in the number and sources of newcomers.

At the beginning, there was not much variety by present-day standards. In 1790, almost 80 percent of the white population was of British stock, while another 12 percent was of German or Dutch origin.[1] Immigration did not change that condition until well into the nineteenth century. In the half-century from 1780 to 1830, immigration contributed only about 6 percent of the country's population growth,[2] and it came from the same sources as the population of the Revolutionary era. Aristede Zolberg estimates that in 1830 some 95 percent of white Americans were "highly fertile English-speaking Protestants, Americans of several generations' standing."[3] African involuntary migrants were disregarded as an element in the national culture. The ethnic deadlock was loosened somewhat in the mid-nineteenth century. Among the British, Catholic Irish came to outnumber immigrants from England. Germany and Scandinavia became important sources of immigrants. The hunger for manpower, joined with the libertarian principles of the new nation, brought the

The author would like to thank the Alfred P. Sloan Foundation and the American Enterprise Institute for support during the preparation of this chapter.

immigrants a generally favorable reception in a fluid, confident new society. Merle Curti has observed:

> The very presence of so many ethnic groups early inspired the conviction that the American people were becoming a blend, entirely unlike people in any one of the European lands that sent immigrants to our shores. . . . "We can boast," declared DeWitt Clinton in 1814, "of our descent from a superior stock. . . . I refer to our origin from those nations where civilization, knowledge, refinement have erected their empire. . . . The extraordinary characters which the United States have produced may be, in some measure, ascribed to the mixed blood of so many nations flowing in our veins."[4]

Two generations after Clinton, Oliver Wendell Holmes asserted in 1892, "We are the Romans of the modern world, the great assimilating people."[5] Celebrating the centenary of the Republic, Bayard Taylor voiced confidence in the integrating power of the nation:

> Fused in her candid light,
> To one strong race all races here unite.[6]

Never mind that the Chinese and Africans were not invited to the party. The poet marveled at the union of the ethnic strains he knew and loved.

The centenary can be taken as a dividing point. During the 1880s, the change in the number and origin of immigrants became so sharp that it gave rise to the appellation "the new immigration," which was used to designate the influx that took place between 1883 and 1914. The motives of the migrants were not different from the motives of those who had come before. Mostly they were uprooted by economic forces: the collapse of the peasant economy, the rise of the factory system, mounting population pressures. But the migration was much bigger, its sources were different, and a significant part of it was transient. In the quarter-century between 1890 and 1914, some 15 million people entered the United States, and during the years around the turn of the century, about one-third of the growth of the U.S. population came from immigration.[7]

The shift in national origins can be seen by comparing the homelands of the immigrants who came in 1882 with those of the entrants of 1907, two peak years of immigration. Of those arriving in 1882, 87 percent came from northern and western Europe, and 13 percent from the countries of southern and eastern Europe. In 1907 the proportions were reversed: 19 percent and 81 percent.[8] Suddenly, it seemed, Russians, Poles, Ruthenians, Rumanians, Croats, Serbs, Slovenes, Dalmatians, Hungarians, Bulgarians, Italians appeared. The "new" immigrants returned to their homelands more commonly than did earlier comers.[9]

Woodrow Wilson was writing his *History of the American People* as the change was taking place.

> Immigrants poured steadily in as before, but with an alteration which students of affairs marked with uneasiness. . . . Now there come multitudes of men of lowest class from the south of Italy and men of the meanest sort out of Hungary and Poland, men out of the ranks where there was neither skill nor energy nor any initiative of quick intelligence; and they came in numbers which increased from year to year, as if the countries of the south of Europe were disburdening themselves of the more sordid and hapless elements of their population.[10]

John Higham, preeminent student of the defensive nationalist American reaction to immigration, described the unsettling qualities of the newcomers a half-century later:

> Italian, Slavic and other peasants from beyond the Alps lived much closer to serfdom than did the folk of northwestern Europe; and the Jews from Russia and Rumania were seeing a world outside of the ghetto for the first time. By western European standards, the new immigrant masses were socially backward and bizarre in appearance.[11]

Turning Against Foreigners

The waves of strangers put American faithfulness to the cosmopolitan and universalistic ideals of the Revolution to a new test, and the country failed the test. Though it lived on not far below the surface of political life, the ideal of a nationality that could encompass all tribes and peoples was not effective in law and politics from the 1890s until the New Deal.

Before the last decade of the nineteenth century, antiforeign antagonisms were mainly aspects of antiradical and anti-Catholic movements. They were aimed at the ideas—anarchism, "popery," socialism—more than at foreignness itself. Social reformers and trade unionists who saw peril in increasing immigration were critical of the number of immigrants joining the labor force and the conditions of life and work in the great cities.

It was not until the 1890s that ineradicable foreignness became the issue, that racism came to play a decisive role in attitudes toward immigration. The cultural differences between the "old" immigration and the "new" were transformed in the minds of many into immutable hereditary distinctions. Darwinism led proponents of the notion of Anglo-Saxon superiority to dwell on the challenge to survival from other peoples. The new science of genetics captured the imagination of nonscientists with its demonstration of the transmission of characteristics down the generations regardless of conditions external to the organism. Pseudoscientists converted natural-scientific discoveries into bogus theories of human development and propagated them entertainingly. By the decade of 1905–1914, when an average of a million people a year were admitted by immigration officers, the old faith in the ability of America to amalgamate any and all comers was considerably weakened.

Immigration from China and Japan and immigration from Europe were always thought of differently. No one thought the same rules ought to apply to both, and each group was the target of different sets of antagonists. The distinction was persistent: "In the twentieth century William Randolph Hearst perpetuated this old Californian combination of sympathy for European immigration and hatred for Oriental."[12]

The first arrivals from the East, in 1850, were Chinese. Some 330,000 came before the Chinese Exclusion Act was passed in 1882. A small Japanese migration by way of Hawaii was ended by the "Gentlemen's Agreement" of 1907, devised to satisfy a strong popular demand for an end to the movement without insulting the Japanese nation. In the nineteenth century (and much of the twentieth century), Asians were a racial minority expected to keep to themselves and not join the melting pot. The expression of that feeling in immigration law was special racial discrimination against Asians.

The northeastern intellectuals who wanted to cut back immigration shared the old assumption of white supremacy, of course. But the influx that frightened them was not that of Asians but that of unfamiliar kinds of white men. Invidious distinctions between the European tribes had to be invented. In taking up the notion of the innate superiority of northern Europeans—the "great race," as Madison Grant called the "Nordics"—they chose the criterion eventually used for restriction of immigration: national origin. They also thought up the device around which restrictionists rallied for a quarter-century before national origin could be instituted as the measure of the would-be immigrant: the literacy test. That test could accomplish indirectly what they could not muster strength to do directly. The Immigration Restriction League of Boston succeeded in getting a law passed by Congress in 1897 (vetoed by President Cleveland) which excluded anyone unable to read forty words in any language.

Then, although immigration continued to increase, the defensive maneuvers stopped for a time. A long stretch of prosperity and the good feeling engendered by the Spanish-American War revived confidence in the integrating force of the American nation. "Discrimination and withdrawal undoubtedly increased. . . . What did decline was fear . . . that immigration endangered the nation."[13] The opponents of immigration restriction had a breathing spell. Immigrant groups organized themselves to oppose restriction; business, citing the need for unskilled labor, advocated immigration.

But continued immigration was not advocated on the basis of a general public interest. The progressives of the early twentieth century were not mostly hostile to immigrants, but they did not claim a virtue in the maintenance of an open policy. Social workers were concerned with the well-being of the immigrant poor after their arrival, not with creating opportunities for more to come. And the reformers who were sympathetic to immigrants were worried about their numbers, the crowding in urban slums, and the damage the influx might do to trade unions and to workers' wages. No general theory was advanced to rebut the gloomy prognostications of the alienated Bostonian restrictionists, no constructive method was proposed to limit or mitigate the bad side-effects of unlimited immigration.

Yet the opponents of restriction were able to win another round in 1906–1907, even though the West and the South, where the foreign-born had little political power and where race-feeling had long been strong, began to contribute important support for restriction. Proponents of the literacy test hoped to capitalize on an anti-Japanese movement on the West Coast. They failed in significant part because of the dogged opposition of the Speaker of the House, Joe Cannon. No friend of the downtrodden masses, Cannon was responding to the electoral power of the foreign-born and to pressure from business interests.

The Dillingham Commission

The antirestrictionists used their lucky victory to buy time, creating in 1907 an immigration commission that came to be known by the name of its chairman, Senator William Dillingham of Vermont. The report of the Dillingham commission, when it appeared four years later, did

not help them. Its authors shared, sharpened, sanctioned, and reinforced the already widespread popular distinction between the "new"
and the "old" immigration, stressing national particularities rather
than human universalities in the migrant streams, and making comparisons between old and new immigrants that were distinctly un-
favorable to the new.

> The old immigration as a class is far less intelligent than the old. . . .
> Generally speaking they are actuated in coming by different ideals, for
> the old immigration came to be a part of the country, while the new, in
> large measure, comes with the intention of profiting, in a pecuniary way,
> by the superior advantages of the new world and then returning to the
> old country.[14]

In the course of investigating "the general effect . . . of the new
immigration movement upon the people, the industries, and the institutions of the United States," the Dillingham commission collected
a great deal of original data, which was laid out in forty-two volumes
and later used to refute some of the conclusions of the commission.[15]
Four general principles were offered to guide legislation. In the circumstances of the time, they seem remarkably appropriate.

> 1. While the American people, as in the past, welcome the op-
> pressed of other lands, care should be taken that immigration be such
> both in quality and quantity as not to make too difficult the process of
> assimilation.
> 2. . . . Further general legislation concerning the admission of aliens
> should be based primarily upon economic or business considerations
> touching the prosperity and economic well-being of our people.
> 3. The measure of the rational, healthy development of a country is
> not the extent of its investment of capital, its output of products, or its
> exports and imports, unless there is a corresponding economic opportu-
> nity afforded to the citizen dependent upon employment for his mate-
> rial, mental and moral development.
> 4. The development of business may be brought about by means
> which lower the standard of living of the wage earners. A slow expansion
> of industry which would permit the adaption and assimilation of the
> incoming labor supply is preferable to a very rapid industrial expansion
> which results in the immigration of laborers of low standards and
> efficiency, who imperil the American standard of wages and conditions
> of employment.

In particular, the commission recommended that immigrants be encouraged to settle permanently, become citizens, keep their savings in

the United States, and work in agriculture rather than in industry, where, the commission found, there existed an "oversupply of unskilled labor." Immigration should be reduced for that reason, according to the commission, and among the criteria considered—literacy, national origin, wealth, marital status—the commission selected "the reading and writing test as the most feasible single method of restricting undesirable immigration."[16]

Those particular recommendations were congruent with the commission's four principles. One recommendation was not: the exclusion of Chinese and the special restriction on Japanese and Korean immigration. No justification was offered for that recommendation; it did not square with the general propositions.

Despite majority support in Congress for immigration restriction by means of a literacy test, it was six years before the Dillingham commission's recommendations became law. Congressional majorities were available, but both President Taft and President Wilson vetoed the legislation.

> The laws here embodied are not tests of quality or of character or of personal fitness, but tests of opportunity. Those who come seeking opportunity are not to be admitted unless they have already had one of the chief of the opportunities they seek, the opportunity of education. The object of such provisions is restriction, not selection.[17]

Those words of President Wilson accompanied the last veto of immigration restriction that prevailed.

Restrictive Policy and the Quota System

The excitement of the world war created the margin of votes necessary to override Wilson's second veto in 1917. The first general restriction was instituted: Anyone over sixteen not able to read any language was barred. The congressional debate shows beyond doubt that the intention of those who supported the literacy test was to screen out the common people of southern and eastern Europe. In addition the exclusion of Asians except for Japanese was codified. Special barriers against bearers of revolutionary doctrines were set in place. In any case, the world war virtually stopped transatlantic migration for several years.

But it revived. In the year 1921, some 800,000 people entered, and despite the tests imposed in 1917, they were predominantly from

·the "wrong" part of Europe. It became obvious that the literacy test
was not a sufficient barrier. A new study was commissioned by the
House immigration subcommittee, which concluded that immigrants
from southern and eastern Europe had more "inborn socially inadequate qualities" than northwestern Europeans, justifying national origin as the criterion for the selection—and exclusion—of immigrants.[18]

In 1921, the principle of selecting people by reference to the past
origins of the American people was put in law, and in 1924 the formula that was to govern the American system for forty years was
embodied in the Johnson-Reed Act. In the first stage, quotas were to
be fractions of the foreign-born population counted in the census of
1890. Ultimately, the quotas would be apportioned in accordance
with an estimate of the contribution of each national stock to the
entire white population of 1920. The final formula accorded perfectly
with the nationalism and self-satisfaction of America of the 1920s. It
aimed at perserving the perfect mix, the ethnic status quo, in per-
petuity.

To accomplish this, immigration patterns had to be reversed, and
they were. In the years just before World War I, more than 80 percent of immigrants had come from southern and eastern Europe.
When immigration was governed by Congress' design, over 80 percent of the people admitted were from northwestern Europe. Foreign
policy considerations and the desire of southwestern farmers for a
ready supply of compliant labor combined to keep immigration from
the western hemisphere unrestricted.

The system had not been long in place when it began to lose its
charm. With unemployment widespread in the depression years,
there was no call to enlarge the annual limit of 150,000 immigrants.
But the validity of sorting people by geographic origin began to be
more widely questioned. Among America's writers and thinkers,
gloomy "scientific" hereditarianism began to give way to a more
cheerful emphasis on environmental factors in human development.
Some cited the work of the anthropologist Franz Boas, launched two
decades earlier under the patronage of the Dillingham commission,
which demonstrated that national groups changed their physical
characteristics once they were brought into the American environment. By the 1930s there was ample evidence at hand that immigrants
from Italy and Hungary and Russia were not all that different from
immigrants who had come before. Among their number were distinguished and prominent citizens whose achievements were giving the
lie to theories of hereditary inequality of peoples. At the same time,

the closing of the gates had quieted fears of cultural domination by immigrants. The politics of the Democratic party and the ideals of the New Deal were not compatible with ethnic exclusiveness

The waning of prejudice was not enough to make a change in immigration policy. "An America pre-occupied with its own salvation had little sympathy for or interest in immigration."[19] For instance, nothing was done to ease the entry of Europeans persecuted by fascism. The 1924 act contained no special provision for refugees, and none was created. Between 1933 and 1944, fewer than 250,000 refugees were admitted to the United States. Many who sought refuge and were turned away died in forced labor and extermination camps.

A formal break with the national origins system did not come until 1965; indeed, the system was reaffirmed in the McCarran-Walter Act of 1952. But exception after exception was made to the general law, with the result that after World War II the ethnic origins of the newcomers did not fit the old formula on the books. The "War Brides Act" allowed the entrance of nearly 300,000 spouses, fiancées, and children outside the quotas, including Asians who were otherwise barred. Displaced persons, refugees and orphans, and others admitted outside the quotas outnumbered regular admissions,[20] ending the preponderance of northwestern Europeans among migrants to the United States. In the years between 1952 and 1965, when the big British quotas were not entirely used, four times as many Italians were admitted as the Italian quota allowed, forty times as many Chinese and Japanese as those quotas allowed, and so on.[21]

The Swing Against Discrimination

Though the friends of various groups of foreigners were able to gain access for them on an ad hoc basis, the reformers' work of abolishing national origin as the basis of immigration law was hard and long drawn out, complicated by the cold war, and delayed by the energetic defense by a dominant older generation of politicians of the system favoring northern Europeans. They gave up the argument of "Nordic" superiority in public debate, but advocated keeping the preference on grounds of tradition. Congressional reformers did not attack it directly until after their efforts at gradual reform had been rebuffed with the passage of the McCarran-Walter Act of 1952. President Truman did not prevail when he vetoed the measure on the ground that the national origins criterion was unfair and out of date. But he was able to lay the foundation for an eventual frontal assault on the national origins system with the creation of a presidential commission that focused new intellectual ingenuity and liberal political energy on the task. The commission's 1953 report, "Whom We Shall Welcome," found that "the major disruptive influence in our immigration law is the racial and national discrimination caused by the national origins system" and that it should be replaced by a "unified quota system which would allocate visas without regard to national origin, race, creed or color."[22] Although President Eisenhower also called for the replacement of the national origins system with "new guidelines and standards" and favored general revision and liberalization of the law, Congress limited itself to temporary and ameliorative measures. Outright racial discrimination persisted. Although the McCarran-Walter Act had created token quotas for Asians, all immigrants of Oriental ancestry had to be charged against those quotas regardless of their country of birth. Immigration policy tends to follow the temper of the times, and those were not years of innovation in public policy.

Ten years after the publication of "Whom We Shall Welcome," President Kennedy sponsored a bill that embodied the recommendations of Truman's commission. As a senator, John F. Kennedy had advocated liberal admission of displaced persons and refugees. "His personal sympathies," wrote his brother Senator Edward Kennedy in 1966, "reflected a deep personal conviction . . . formed in part through counsel given him by his grandfather, the late Representative John Francis Fitzgerald of Massachusetts. Grandfather believed that fair and just immigration policies, for the people of all nations, were very important to our country, and often expressed this to his grandchildren."[23] A substantial part of John F. Kennedy's initial political support came from associations of the foreign-born favorable to expanded immigration.

As president, Kennedy proposed a bill calling for an end to the national origins system, for preferences for people of accomplishment and needed skills, for the creation of an immigration board as a counterweight to congressional conservatism in immigration matters, and for continued numerically unlimited admission of people from the western hemisphere. Two political liberals, Congressman Emanuel Celler and Senator Philip Hart, introduced it. Hearings had not been held when its author was assassinated in 1963. There was still congressional inertia in immigration matters. The bill, however, was taken up by Kennedy's successor, and in the wake of President Johnson's electoral victory the national origins standard was abolished in the autumn of 1965. Compromises were made along the way. No immigration board was established. Numerical limitation of immigration from the western hemisphere was instituted, won by Senator Sam Ervin and Senator Everett Dirksen, conservatives who cited impending population pressure, over the objections of the administration. The broader authority to admit refugees which President Kennedy had sought was not granted. Less weight was given to occupational achievement and more to family reunification than in the original proposal. The approval of the secretary of labor for the granting of visas to immigrant workers was required.

The liberal supporters of the original bill believed that the compromises with conservatives that President Johnson agreed to were excessive.[24] Other observers thought that his political task was difficult and that he was right to use the momentum of his landslide victory to correct the glaring fault of the existing law while it could be done.[25] In any case, it is plain in retrospect that the biggest element of the compromise—numerical limitation of immigration from the western hemisphere—would almost certainly have to have been enacted eventually.

The Immigration and Nationality Act of 1965 was one of three very important, complementary laws passed early in President Johnson's presidency. The Civil Rights Act of 1964 forbade discrimination in the right to vote and in access to public services, employment, and education on grounds of race, sex, color, religion, or national origin. The Voting Rights Act of 1965 provided a mechanism for ensuring political rights. The Immigration Act of 1965 said that individuals of all races and peoples could become Americans. The cosmopolitan and democratic ideal of nationality enunciated by Tom Paine, Ralph Waldo Emerson, Walt Whitman, and Herman Melville was embodied for the first time in American immigration law.

The law established an annual total of 290,000 places, with separate hemispheric ceilings, to be apportioned in seven categories (see Table 1.1). First claim was given to ties of kinship. Distinction in a field of human endeavor, and possession of skills needed in the United States, came next. A maximum of 20,000 people a year could be admitted by these criteria from any one country. Refugees fleeing Communist countries or from the Middle East were originally included among the seven categories; they were removed, to be treated separately, by the Refugee Act of 1980, and the annual total was reduced to 270,000. For the first time Asians were treated like everybody else. Parents, minor children, and spouses of U.S. citizens would be permitted to enter outside all numerical limits.

Like the 1924 act, the law of 1965 produced several changes in the character of immigration. This was of course intended, but not all the effects of the new system in practice were anticipated. Linguistic diversity of immigrants diminished. The great number of immediate family members entering outside the country ceilings of Mexico, Cuba, and other Spanish-speaking countries of the western hemisphere meant that about 35 percent of all legal immigrants from 1968 to 1977 were Spanish-speaking. That effect of the 1965 act was compounded by illegal immigration.[26]

There was also a big change in the geographic and racial origins of immigrants. Immigration from Europe was replaced first by immigration from Latin America and the Caribbean, then by immigration from Asia. Between 1971 and 1977, some 24 percent came from Europe and Canada, while 31 percent came from Asia and from the southern western hemisphere.

But these long-range effects of the 1965 law were not the changes that drew attention in the years immediately after it was passed. It became plain that, under the new law as under the old, the plan that Congress had laid out did not govern most of the entries to the United States. Refugees, mostly Cubans in the 1960s and Indo-Chinese in the 1970s, far exceeded the numbers allowed for in the seventh preference category of the 1965 law, and the attorney general had to resort repeatedly to his so-called parole authority to admit hundreds of thousands of refugees.

Dealing with Illegal Immigration

Immigration unsanctioned by law also increased and began to attract attention. In the late 1960s, after the termination of the *bracero* farm contract labor program with Mexico, increasing numbers of undocumented Mexican workers came across the border without authorization, in violation of the immigration law. It was thought that the illegal traffic was confined to the agricultural sector, but hearings held in 1969 by Senator Walter Mondale in a Senate labor subcommittee showed that this was not so. Congressman Peter Rodino, chairman of the House immigration subcommittee, became interested in the presence of unauthorized Mexicans in the workplace and held a four-year series of hearings around the nation starting in 1971. He became convinced early that "the illegal alien displaces American workers, depresses wages, [and] burdens the welfare rolls." In 1972 and again in 1973, the House of Representatives passed laws forbidding employment of illegal aliens. But the House measures never became law, for a variety of forces combined to block action in the Senate. The voluntary groups that had supported liberal immigration policies after World War II and had lobbied for the reforms of 1965 were opposed to the legislation, as were civil libertarians, Mexican-Americans, and the Catholic church. Those groups could count on the sympathetic support of Senator Edward Kennedy, leading liberal of the judiciary committee. Agricultural employers feared measures that would have the effect of making farm labor costlier; their interests were protected by Senator James Eastland, the committee chairman. And so no measure to control illegal immigration was considered by the Senate.

In 1975, David North and Marion Houstoun began a research project that indicated an adverse effect of illegal immigration on the pay and working conditions of low-skilled American residents. They set forth the implications for the society at large of toleration of a vulnerable underclass. Never published, their report circulated widely through the good offices of the Department of Labor and had considerable influence.[27] The same year, President Ford established a Domestic Council Committee on Illegal Aliens, which in January 1977 recommended "penalties for employers who knowingly hire aliens not authorized to work," legalization of unauthorized residents who had been living in the United States for a long time, raising the Mexican immigration ceiling, and U.S. support of economic development that would reduce illegal inflows.

The next president chose a secretary of labor who was an academic expert on the role of illegal Mexican workers in the labor market. Thus it was that President Carter, in the first summer of his administration, proposed legislation "to help markedly reduce the increasing flow of undocumented aliens and to regulate the presence of the millions already here."[28] The elements were much the same as those of President Ford's committee. New was a two-tier amnesty scheme. People who could prove residence in the United States before 1970 could become permanent residents; more recent unauthorized residents would be granted a new status in American law: "temporary resident aliens." No assurance was offered that these would be allowed to stay beyond a five-year initial stage. Civil fines would be imposed on employers found to have a "pattern or practice" of employing unauthorized workers. Though the secretary of labor urged it, no universal work permit to demonstrate the right to work was proposed. In any event, the Carter proposals sank without a trace; neither house of Congress held hearings. The House was fed up with the inaction of the Senate, where Senator Eastland continued to block action.

The Select Commission on Immigration
and Refugee Policy (SCIRP)

But President Carter did leave a mark. In his message proposing
legislation on illegal immigration, Carter had announced his intention
of creating a task force with the executive branch to review the entire
field of immigration policy. The next year, as the task force was being
organized, Congress outflanked the president, moving to create a
commission in which it would have greater weight than the executive
branch. In the proposed Select Commission on Immigration and
Refugee Policy (SCIRP), four members were to come from the jud-
ciciary committee of the House and four from the Senate committee;
the president's men would be the secretaries of state, justice, labor,
and health and human services. In addition, the president would
name four public members and designate one of them chairman. The
chief purpose of the authors of the bill was to win support for measures to control immigration occurring outside the limits established
by Congress, that is, illegal immigration and large refugee flows.

Remarks on the House floor and the language of the bill showed
the concerns of the sponsors. The "paucity of hard data . . . on the
impact of immigration, both legal and illegal," was the first
justification offered by the immigration subcommittee chairman,
Congressman Joshua Eilberg, as he introduced the bill creating the
commission. The bill also called upon SCIRP to "assess the social,
economic, political and demographic impact of previous refugee programs and review the criteria for and numerical limitations on, the
admission of refugees to the United States."[29] The bill passed without
difficulty in July.

If the pattern of the past decade had been repeated, this House
bill would have been referred to Senator Eastland's committee, where
in all probability it would have died. But Senator Edward Kennedy
saw that it was held at the majority leader's desk and, two months
later, got Eastland's consent that it go directly to the floor for approval. In September 1978, Kennedy had his own reasons for supporting the establishment of SCIRP. The changes he sought in
refugee legislation, broadening the definition of a refugee and for-
malizing the executive-legislative consultation process, had not yet
been embodied in the Refugee Act of 1980. Nor had he gained replacement of hemispheric immigration ceilings with one worldwide
ceiling. And Kennedy had also failed to win enactment of measures to
enlarge the number of Mexicans to be admitted. He correctly judged
that a select commission might recommend them.

In May 1979, SCIRP held its opening meeting in the Capitol. The Senate sent two Republicans, Senators Charles Mathias (Md.) and Alan Simpson (Wyo.), and two Democrats, Senators Edward Kennedy (Mass.) and Dennis DeConcini (Ariz.). From the House there were Congressman Peter Rodino (N.J.) and Congresswoman Elizabeth Holtzman (N.Y.), Democrats, and Congressmen Robert McClory (Ill.) and Hamilton Fish (N.Y.), Republicans. Secretary of State Cyrus Vance, Attorney-General Benjamin Civiletti, Secretary of Labor Ray Marshall, and the Secretary of Health and Human Services, Patricia Harris, represented the executive branch. The public members were Joaquin F. Otero of the Brotherhood of Railway and Airline Clerks, Judge Cruz Reynoso of the California Court of Appeals, Rose M. Ochi of the office of the mayor of Los Angeles, and Reubin O'D. Askew, former governor of Florida, designated chairman. But before long, Askew was shifted to another appointment by the president, and a delay ensued.

Askew's successor, who saw SCIRP through to its final votes in January 1981, was the Rev. Theodore Hesburgh, former chairman of the Civil Rights Commission and president of Notre Dame University. He and the staff director of SCIRP, Dr. Lawrence Fuchs, played decisive parts in framing the questions considered by the commission and formulating its recommendations. In his fifteen years on the Civil Rights Commission, Father Hesburgh had won a reputation for strong commitment to political justice, equality, and enforcement of the law. Dr. Fuchs, a political scientist from Brandeis University, had written about the history of ethnic relations in America and the culture of the American family. His appointment was suggested by President Carter's commissioner of immigration, Leonel Castillo, who had known Fuchs when both men were officials of the Peace Corps in the early 1960s. Father Hesburgh and Dr. Fuchs shared an affectionate regard for the immigration of the past hundred years and were inclined to refer to the benefits of immigration when the opportunity arose.

One of the first issues to appear in SCIRP deliberations was the question of what research would be commissioned. At the first working meeting, held in October 1979 before a sizable audience, Dr. Fuchs distributed a proposed research agenda, introducing it by contrasting the good intentions of the new commission with the record of the Dillingham commission, which, he reminded the audience, had prepared the ground for the national origins quota law. It would be impossible to determine the precise number of illegal aliens in the United States or to obtain "totally accurate" information on their

characteristics, he told the commissioners, and so no such efforts
would be undertaken. Instead, he proposed research on legal immigration, acculturation and family structure of immigrant groups, and
the like.

Senator DeConcini responded that he would find it difficult to
proceed without data on the number of illegal immigrants, and
Senator Kennedy spoke of the desire of Congress for "definitive information" on the subject. He noted a seeming discrepancy between
the issues of policy that the commission had identified as critical and
the proposed research agenda. Joaquin Otero, the trade unionist, said
with some heat that the issue of illegal immigration was not getting
sufficient study. Pressed hard by the commissioners, Dr. Fuchs promised a review of existing data on numbers of illegal immigrants, and
new research on the impacts of illegal immigration and refugee
flows.[30]

In the fifteen months remaining to SCIRP, however, no research
on the impact of illegal immigration or refugee flows was undertaken.
Later, in October 1979, experts on illegal immigration were brought
together to discuss research that could be undertaken under the auspices of the commission to guide its recommendations. A panel of
social scientists was retained to review the proposals. It reported that
there was not enough time for studies of methodological rigor yield-
ing final results before the end of the commission's term.

But the SCIRP staff did not want to use less rigorous approaches
or to commission studies on illegal immigration with preliminary
findings to be completed at a later date. These early decisions not to
look for new evidence meant that when the commissioners voted in
December 1980 and January 1981, it was without benefit of systematically gathered information about the numbers, characteristics, and
impacts of unsanctioned migrants in the United States. About the
only improvement of the basis of knowledge on the subject was a new
estimate of the stock of unauthorized aliens, based on previous
studies (". . . below 6.0 million, and maybe substantially less, possibly
only 3.5 to 5.0 million").[31]

If science was lacking, a great deal of miscellaneous information
and opinion was pressed upon the commission in the dozen public
hearings held across the country. "In the hearings the Select Commission has held and in the letters it has received," the final SCIRP report
stated, "one issue has emerged as most pressing—the problem of
undocumented/illegal migration. . . . The message is clear—most U.S.
citizens believe that the half-open door of undocumented/illegal migration should be closed."[32]

During the year and a half that the commission was meeting, events had a way of overtaking its deliberations. In American cities, violent demonstrations by Iranian students for the Islamic revolution of Ayatollah Khomeini drew attention to the fact that neither the Immigration Service nor the State Department had any way of knowing how many Iranian students and visitors were in the United States or where they might be. The administration's decision to deport Iranians who had violated the terms of their visas was conspicuously frustrated. In April and May 1980, thousands of undocumented Cubans arrived in Florida in small boats sent largely by friends and relatives to bring them to U.S. shores. The unsanctioned migration of Haitians to the United States by sea also increased. The Carter administration policy changed from week to week, reflecting the changing character of the influx and divisions within the administration about what to do. At the start, the Justice Department warned Florida boat owners that they would be subject to fines and loss of their licenses if they brought unauthorized entrants from Cuba. Then, on May 5, apparently stung by criticism that he was unsympathetic to anti-Communist Cubans, President Carter spoke of providing "an open heart and open arms to refugees seeking freedom from Communist domination and from the economic deprivation brought about by Fidel Castro and his government."[33] When it became clear that the Cuban government was releasing criminals and forcing boat owners to take them along, efforts to halt the flotilla were revived, but the effort failed. Some 125,000 Cubans and 10,000 Haitians came in before the year was out.

Further controversy arose when the administration decided not to invoke the new Refugee Act of 1980 to govern resettlement of the Cuban arrivals. The author of the act, the president's political rival, Senator Edward Kennedy, argued that its provisions met the situation at hand, but the Carter administration did not want to apply them to entrants who had come directly to the United States without previous clearance. Consequently, there were several months of uncertainty about how the Florida authorities would be compensated for expenditures made in coping with the rush of people. In the fall of 1980, the administration sponsored and Congress passed legislation authorizing payments to state and local authorities for social service, education, and medical costs equal to what was provided for entrants officially arriving as refugees.

Public sentiment against refugee and migrant flows was sharpened by these events. In early June 1980, the Roper public opinion organization sought reaction to the statement that 60,000 Cuban refugees had arrived, that more were on the way, and that most were "middle-class people dissatisfied with Castro's government." Sixty-three percent of the respondents agreed with the view that "we shouldn't have accepted as many Cubans" as had already entered. Only 11 percent agreed that "the entry of the Cubans would turn out to be a good thing for the future of this country," and 57 percent thought it "would be a bad thing."[34]

In the 1980 elections, bad feeling about refugees hurt incumbents, notably President Carter. The Cubans and Haitians were unsanctioned entrants. But he could not send them back, and his powerlessness compounded the damage done to his public image by the success of the Iranian revolutionaries in holding U.S. hostages in Teheran. Florida's seventeen electoral votes went to his opponent. Residents of Arkansas were displeased that army camps in their state were used as repositories for the Cubans. In August, the underdog candidate for governor, Republican Frank White, launched a series of television commercials blaming his opponent, Governor Bill Clinton, for the detention of 15,000 Cubans at Fort Chaffee, drawing attention to the fact that other incumbent governors had kept the refugees out of their states. White won by a substantial margin.

SCIRP had intended to steer clear of 1980 electoral politics by taking its final votes on recommendations in August, before the start of the 1980 campaign. But the schedule slipped, and the final votes were not taken until well after the election. At the end of the Ninety-Sixth Congress, one commissioner who had lost her seat withdrew from the commission before the voting was complete. Eight of the remaining fifteen members and the staff director had been appointed by the defeated president; they knew that their report would be received by a president who had named none of the authors. The shift of the Senate majority in January 1981 from the Democrats to the Republicans meant that the commission's leading expansionist member, Senator Kennedy, would be replaced by its leading restrictionist, Senator Simpson, as the most powerful member of the Senate judiciary committee in immigration matters. Observers of SCIRP meetings noticed that, naturally enough, the commission staff and the watching press paid greater heed to Senator Simpson's views after the election than before it.

The last votes of SCIRP were taken in January, and its final report and recommendations sent to President Reagan and Congress on February 27, 1981. SCIRP called for an increase in legal immigration, enforcement measures to deter illegal immigration, and an amnesty for most unsanctioned residents already in the country. The ceiling on "numerically limited" immigration would be raised from the current 270,000 a year to 350,000; in addition, there would be 100,000 extra visas a year for five years "to allow backlogs to be cleared." Numerically umlimited immigration would also be increased, by allowing new categories of relatives of U.S. citizens to enter without limit. The commission backed Senator Kennedy's old proposal that spouses and minor children of permanent resident aliens be placed under a worldwide limitation instead of under separate country ceilings. No changes were recommended in the procedures for setting levels of admission and admitting refugees prescribed in the Refugee Act of 1980.

The commission recommended deterring illegal immigration by better border enforcement and by penalties on employers who knowingly employed unauthorized immigrants. By a vote of 8 to 7, it also recommended "some system of more secure identification" of workers that would let employers tell whom they could lawfully hire so that they could be held responsible for their actions. The commissioners were unable to agree on any description of what that system might be. In addition to a general reluctance to make new inroads on individual freedom, there were specific objections to concrete proposals. Father Hesburgh favored improving the social security card to make it counterfeit-resistant and requiring employers to inspect it before hiring any individual, native or foreign, but he was stymied by the unremitting opposition of the secretary of health and human services. Use of the social security card or number, Mrs. Harris said, would "encourage forgery and misuse of social security numbers, thereby endangering our record-keeping system."[35] The secretary of labor had proposed a computer system that would let employers check workers' status with technology similar to that used by retail establishments to check the validity of customers' credit cards. The high cost of establishing such a system frightened off some potential supporters. Thus the recommendation on worker identification, long a sticking point in the immigration debate, was so vague that it was almost meaningless. The commission endorsed enforcement by federal officials at the borders rather than in the interior of the country; in effect, the burden of improving interior enforcement was placed on employers. State and local police would be prohibited from detaining suspected unlawful immigrants who had not otherwise violated the law. Proposals for an enlarged temporary foreign worker program were rejected.

SCIRP recommended a one-time amnesty for people illegally resident in the United States before January 1, 1980, to start after "appropriate enforcement measures" had been instituted. The length of residence that would entitle an alien to legalization was left to Congress to decide.

The final report, written by Father Hesburgh and the commission staff, amplified the ninety-odd recommendations of the commissioners. Taken together, they were a call for the perfection of the existing immigration system and a defense and extension of the principles of the 1965 act and the Refugee Act of 1980.

LEGAL IMMIGRATION

Legal immigration, running above 400,000 a year, excluding refugees, was within reasonable bounds, SCIRP concluded, and could safely be somewhat increased. In his introduction, Hesburgh sympathetically reviewed arguments for greatly increased immigration. He did not reject them on the merits. "This is not the time for a large-scale expansion in legal immigration . . . because the first order of priority is bringing undocumented/illegal migration under control while setting up a rational system for legal immigration." A "more cautious approach" was recommended, to "bring the benefits of immigration to the United States without exacerbating fears—not always rational—of competition with immigrants."

The heavy emphasis in existing law on *kinship* as the chief criterion for awarding immigration visas was endorsed and increased by the commission's recommendations.[36] At the time the report was written, over 80 percent of immigrants who were not refugees were entering by virtue of a kinship tie to a citizen or permanent resident. That proportion would be increased by the SCIRP proposals. Under existing law, spouses, parents, and minor unmarried children of citizens could enter without limit. SCIRP would add adult unmarried children and grandparents of adult citizens to that list. The addition of 100,000 visas a year for five years, recommended by SCIRP to help clear the visa backlogs, would also chiefly increase the immigration of kinfolk, since it was in the preference categories for relatives that the largest backlogs of applicants for visas existed.

As we have seen, the 1965 act reserved no places for immigrants on the basis of national origin. Foreigners qualified for immigration to the United States by virtue of kinship ties, occupational criteria, or refugee status—not national origin. But that did not mean that the chances of applicants qualified under one or another preference would be equal in fact as well as in principle. The annual ceiling of 20,000 immigrants entering under the preference system from one country meant that applicants in popular categories from countries of high demand for visas had to wait longer for admission than people similarly qualified from countries of low demand. For example, a citizen of France whose naturalized American brother petitioned for his admission would receive an immigration visa as soon as the necessary proofs had been examined, whereas a similarly qualified citizen of Korea would wait for many years. The unequal wait of equally qualified applicants resulted from the effort to prevent predominance of one nationality among immigrants. Backlogs were the result.

SCIRP recommended allowing the kinship principle to operate more freely by removing the interference of the nationality ceiling with immigration of close kin of permanent resident aliens. It suggested that spouses and minor children of permanent resident aliens be exempted from the country ceilings and admitted on a first come, first served basis in a consolidated worldwide category. The practical effect would be that the spouses and minor children of, for instance, Mexican and Philippine resident aliens in the United States would leave slow-moving national queues (which would be abolished) and join a new world queue, with place assigned by the date of petition for admission. They would move along as fast as the kin of, say, a citizen of Ghana or Liechtenstein. The Mexicans and Filipinos would move more quickly than in the old system; the Liechtensteiners and Ghanaians, who would not have waited at all under the old rules, would lose the advantage of being from a country of low demand for U.S. immigration visas and cool their heels along with everybody else. In the end, more people from countries with large numbers of permanent resident aliens living in the United States would be admitted than in the old system. Lawful Mexican immigration, in particular, would be increased.

REFUGEE ADMISSIONS

SCIRP endorsed the salient feature of the Refugee Act of 1980, that the number and sources of refugees admitted are determined by the executive branch after consultation with Congress. To "require Congress to legislate refugee numbers each year is not realistic," it said.

ILLEGAL IMMIGRATION

SCIRP's recommendations aimed at cutting back illegal immigration were, for the guiding intelligences of the commission, also part of the effort to protect—and indeed expand—legal immigration to the United States. They did not oppose it on the grounds on which it is deplored by its chief opponents. A continuing influx of low-skilled illegal aliens, labor advocates say, creates a black labor market that depresses the earnings of low-skilled workers, prevents change and rationalization of jobs in the secondary labor market, displaces legal workers, and causes a more unequal distribution of income.[37] Their numbers, characteristics, and illegal status all have worrisome effects, according to this line of thinking. Demographic and environmental considerations are cited by another set of opponents of illegal immigration—the Federation for American Immigration Reform, the Environmental Fund, and Zero Population Growth. Elected officials and state and local governments worry about drains on public resources by unauthorized residents. Father Hesburgh and Dr. Fuchs did not accept any of these lines of argument. "Debates about the size and impact of illegal migrants were uninformed by reliable data and characterized by extreme rhetorical statements," wrote Dr. Fuchs in his first report to Congress.[38] The SCIRP final report, although it alluded to an unquantifiable "displacement of some U.S. workers and the depression of some U.S. wages," concluded: "There is almost no consensus [among researchers] regarding the impact of illegal immigration on U.S. society. . . . The research findings and theoretical arguments with regard to the impact of undocumented/illegal immigration upon the U.S. economy and social services are inconclusive. . . ." The demographic and environmental arguments against sizable immigration were dismissed in the section on legal immigration.

> At present there is no agreement as to what is the most desirable population for the United States. . . . Some representatives of environmentalists . . . have argued that any increase in U.S. population (such as immigration) will have a deleterious effect. . . . Other environmentalists believe that immigration to the United States has a net positive effect on the use of the world's resources . . . and little, if any, negative impact on U.S. society. The Commission has found no conclusive answers in this debate.

And "most studies indicate that undocumented/illegal aliens do not place a substantial burden on social services," according to the report.[39]

Why, then, the recommendation of measures to cut down illegal immigration? For the authors of the SCIRP report, there was only one reason for combating illegal immigration: Illegality has pernicious effects in and of itself. In the summer of 1980, after the Cuban and Haitian influx and the adverse reaction to it, Father Hesburgh wrote:

Now undocumented aliens come to the United States in large numbers by land and sea. There is no question that many of them are ambitious, hardworking seekers of opportunity and freedom. But by permitting our laws to be flouted, we bring immigration policy as a whole into disrespect and . . . undermine respect for law. . . . This must not happen. The world and the United States will be a much poorer place if legal immigration is cut back because we failed to gain control over undocumented/illegal migration.[40]

In the final report as well, the illegality of illegal immigration was the only feature that could be unambiguously deplored:

This illegal flow, encouraged by employers who provide jobs, has created an underclass of workers who fear apprehension and deportation. Undocumented/illegal migrants . . . cannot or will not avail themselves of the protection of U.S. laws. Not only do they suffer, but so too does U.S. society. Most serious is the fact that illegality breeds illegality.[41]

TERMINAL HESITATION

When the House and subcommittees held hearings on the SCIRP report and recommendations in May 1981, Senator Simpson invited Father Hesburgh to identify any deficiencies in the select commission's work. Hesburgh replied that the commission had failed to "bite the bullet" on the question of worker identification, that is, it had failed to recommend measures with a prospect of containing illegal immigration. That failure was nothing new. The Nixon-Ford administration had recognized and studied the problem, had seen the grave political difficulties, and had left its recommendations at the door of President Carter. President Carter, at the urging of his secretary of labor, gave the matter high priority. But his set of remedies did not include a new or improved form of worker identification. Opposition from his own social security administration, from Secretary of Health, Education, and Welfare Joseph Califano, from Mexican and other Latin American groups, from civil libertarians, and from employer groups combined to defeat the secretary of labor's proposal of an identification document for all workers.

Exactly the same arguments and political forces operated on the select commission. To have had a chance at overcoming them and winning support for an attack on illegal immigration, the chairman and staff would have had to make a broadly based, well-documented showing of its deleterious effects. They avoided that, and arguments that, for the sake of law and order, control of immigration had to be regained did not persuade the unconvinced of the necessity to adopt a novel, even radical, remedy. An analysis of the reports of the select commission and of its staff leads one to the conclusion that it was an anxiety to protect immigration in general from restriction that caused the chairman and executive director to make so narrow a case against the illegal variety.

Immigration Policy in the Reagan Administration

When President Reagan assembled a task force of his own early in 1981 to review the SCIRP proposals, there was great public interest in its deliberations. In the preceding year, the debate among SCIRP's commissioners, its public hearings and report, the unwelcome influx of Cubans and Haitians, and doubts about the wisdom of letting in large numbers of Indo-Chinese refugees had combined to form a sense that something had to be done and would be done about immigration and refugee policy. Influential publications like the *New York Times* and *Foreign Affairs* had helped put the matter on the public agenda; many politicians returned to Washington in 1981 believing that their electorates expected action from them.

During the spring and summer of 1981, the task force consulted experts and interest groups and deliberated on the policy choices open to the new administration. The interested public became privy to the negotiations within the administration, mainly through the well-informed reports of Robert Pear in the *New York Times*. The proposals of the new administration became known gradually; only in October were they incorporated in proposed legislation.[42]

The view of the Nixon-Ford and Carter administrations that immigration outside the law was excessive and needed to be curbed was shared by the Reagan administration, and the remedy of penalizing employers of unauthorized workers was also accepted. The reluctance of the Reagan advisers to resort to that means was shown by the exemption of small employers from the penalties and the rejection of any new means of worker identification. Legalization of the status of unauthorized residents who entered the country before 1980 was proposed. As in President Carter's proposal, it would take the form of an inferior status for a period of time before permanent resident status was finally granted. Increased quotas were to be granted for Mexico and Canada, as previous administrations had proposed. One entirely new element was introduced: a temporary foreign-worker program. Early in the administration, Martin Anderson, head of President Reagan's Domestic Council, had proposed a big program— 500,000 to 750,000 workers a year from Mexico with a free run of the labor market. Judging from Reagan's remarks during the campaign and in a television interview in his sixth week in office,[43] the president would have viewed that as a good solution to the problem of the illegal flow across the border. But after listening to views of the representatives from the justice and labor departments, his task force did not recommend it. Instead the advisers agreed on a scaled-down "pilot" program of 50,000 a year. The president's friend Governor Bill Clements of Texas, an advocate of a big program, expressed dissatisfaction with the small experiment but was persuaded to support it as a modest start.

In the Reagan bill, the administration, influenced by the large number of unauthorized Haitians landing on the coast of Florida during the spring, went beyond the SCIRP recommendations in requesting authority for special powers if needed to prevent large unauthorized flows of migrants.

In his second year in office, President Reagan's economic policy difficulties made it look less likely that he could launch a great political initiative for his version of immigration reform. His important southwestern supporters demanded that they be assured a ready supply of labor at all times. Their price for stricter enforcement and tighter control of immigration was the temporary foreign-worker program that the president had included in his 1981 proposal. But unemployment was high and threatening to remain so, and the electorate was anxious. In those circumstances, the president could not be confident that Congress would enact a temporary worker program. The argument that there were many available jobs that resident workers would not accept was hard to make when unemployment was high. Legalization of the unauthorized immigrants already in the country was also less likely to be acceptable when times were hard; and civil libertarians and Mexican-Americans could not be expected to accept penalties on the employers of unsanctioned workers without the quid pro quo of legalization. Without the instrument of fines on employers, the administration could not attack Mexican illegal immigration. But for many in the Reagan camp, it was no unmitigated evil in any case.

President Reagan could achieve considerable limitation of immigration in other areas without legislation. He was already announcing smaller quotas of refugees from Indochina. Congress had shown itself willing, even determined, to give him more money for the enforcement functions of the Immigration and Naturalization Service. Perhaps the way the government suppressed the flow of Haitians in late 1981 was a portent: halting of boats, apprehension and internment of the unauthorized entrants—all without new laws.

From the standpoint of Congress, comprehensive reform was difficult to achieve, but one man in a key position wanted to try it: Senator Alan Simpson, whose interest in immigration reform had not ended with the disbanding of the select commission. When he took charge of the Senate subcommittee on immigration he was a new actor among the old antagonists in immigration controversies, full of knowledge and interest and enthusiasm for his subject, confident that he was in a position to make a historic contribution to the solution of a vitally important national problem. An engaging and able politician, whose father had also served as senator from Wyoming, he was well able to express sophisticated notions in colorful western colloquialisms and to meet his expansionist opponents in friendly disagreement. He appeared at many gatherings of immigration controversialists, cheerfully offering his metaphor of the three-legged stool to symbolize the elements of immigration reform that he regarded as primary: enforcement of the law at the borders and internally, penalties on employers who persistently employed unsanctioned immigrants, and better worker identification.

Sometimes, for all his charm and intelligence, to the listener familiar with the ethnic rivalries and bitter antagonisms of the past, he could seem an innocent treading on dangerous ground:

> My concern [is] that we exercise caution in the number of immigrants, especially those whose cultural backgrounds may seem more different or more foreign to the bulk of our people than have past immigrants seemed to the majority population at those times. . . . I do believe that it is important for new immigrants to become Americans in the fullest sense, . . . adopting not only our obvious political values but our social public values, which may be the source of the political values, things like fair play, compassion, consideration for others. . . . If our values change as a result of immigration, can we reasonably assume that the true freedoms and the things that we have that are dependent upon those values will survive the change?[44]

In March 1982, Senator Simpson offered a bill jointly with the chairman of the House immigration subcommittee, Congressman Romano Mazzoli of Kentucky. It contained the elements of a consensus built up over the previous six years: legalization, employer penalties, bigger quotas for the immediate neighbors. But it was better calculated to restrain illegal immigration than the Reagan bill, or the select commission's proposals, had been. According to this proposal, a new federal system of worker identification for all members of the labor force would be instituted, facilitating the employers' task of establishing the legitimacy of prospective employees. User fees would supplement the budget of the Immigration and Naturalization Service. A new infusion of temporary foreign workers was not proposed.

The Simpson-Mazzoli bill proposed, in addition, a new curb on the growth of lawful immigration— that is, to include the spouses, children, and parents of citizens under the higher ceiling that was to be set. Further growth in that rapidly expanding category would have to be at the expense of immigrants of less preferred status. Refugees, however, would remain outside the general statutory ceiling.

Nondiscrimination was the call of the reformers of the 1950s and 1960s; the spirit animating them was expansionist. Curbing unplanned migration was the ambition of the reformers of the 1970s and 1980s; the spirit animating them was restrictionist. The pendulum had swung.

Notes

1. Stephan Thernstrom, ed., *Harvard Encyclopedia of American Ethnic Groups* (Cambridge: Harvard University Press, 1980), p. 479.

2. Simon Kuznets, *Modern Economic Growth*, quoted by Aristede R. Zolberg in "Contemporary Transnational Migrations in Historical Perspective," Paper prepared for the Rockefeller-Ford-Johnson Foundation Conference, Williamsburg, Va., August 1981, p. 11.

3. Ibid.

4. Merle Curti, *The Roots of American Loyalty* (New York: Columbia University Press, 1946), p. 71.

5. Quoted by Merle Curti, *The Growth of American Thought* (New York: Harper & Bros., 1946), p. 233.

6. Quoted by John Higham, *Strangers in the Land: Patterns of American Nativism 1820–1925*, 2d ed. (New York: Atheneum Publishers, 1978), p. 12.

7. Thernstrom, *Encyclopedia*, p. 476, Table 1.

8. See U.S. Bureau of the Census, *Historical Statistics of the United States: Colonial Times to 1970* (Washington, D.C.: Government Printing Office, 1975). These years chosen by Maldwyn Jones, *American Immigration* (Chicago: University of Chicago Press, 1960), p. 179.

9. Michael J. Piore, *Birds of Passage: Migrant Labor and Industrial Societies* (New York: Cambridge University Press, 1979), pp. 149–153.

10. Woodrow Wilson, *A History of the American People* (New York: Harper & Bros., 1901), 4: 212–213.

11. John Higham, "American Immigration in Historical Perspective," *Law and Contemporary Problems* (Duke University School of Law), 21 (Spring 1956): 219.

12. Higham, *Strangers in the Land,* p. 365.

13. Ibid., p. 110.

14. U.S. Immigration Commission, *Reports of the Immigration Commission: Abstracts,* 61st Cong., 1st sess. (Washington, D.C.: Government Printing Office, 1911), 1:14.

15. See Isaac A. Hourwich, *Immigration and Labor,* rev. ed. (New York: B. W. Heubsch, 1922); Oscar Handlin, *Race and Nationality in American Life* (Boston: Little, Brown & Co., 1957); Paul A. Douglas, "Is the New Immigration More Unskilled Than the Old?" *Publications of the American Statistical Association* 26 (1918–1919): 393–403.

16. Immigration Commission, *Reports,* p. 48.

17. Henry Steele Commager, ed., *Documents of American History* (New York: F. S. Crofts, 1934), p. 282.

18. Quoted in Oscar Handlin, "Memorandum Concerning the Origins of the National Origin Quota System," *Hearings Before the President's Commission on Immigration and Naturalization,* 82d Cong., 2d sess. (Washington, D.C.: Government Printing Office, 1952), p. 755.

19. Higham, *Strangers in the Land.*

20. Marion T. Bennett, *American Immigration Policies,* quoted in *U.S. Immigration Law and Policy: 1952–1979,* Report prepared at the request of Senator Edward M. Kennedy, Chairman, Committee on the Judiciary, U.S. Senate, 96th Cong., 1st sess. (Washington, D.C.: Government Printing Office, 1979), p. 24.

21. Calculation by Aristede R. Zolberg, "The Main Gate and the Back Door: The Politics of American Immigration Policy, 1950–1976" (Paper delivered at the Council on Foreign Relations, Washington, D.C., April 1978), p. 19.

22. Commission on Immigration and Naturalization, "Whom We Shall Welcome," quoted in *U.S. Immigration Law and Policy: 1952–1979,* p. 13.

23. Edward M. Kennedy, "The Immigration Act of 1965," *Annals of the American Academy of Political and Social Science* 367 (September 1966): 138.

24. See Abba P. Schwartz, *The Open Society* (New York: William Morrow & Co., 1968), p. 124.

25. See Edward P. Hutchinson, *Legislative History of American Immigration Policy, 1798–1965* (Philadelphia: University of Pennsylvania Press, 1981), pp. 366–379.

26. For a discussion of this and other trends in migration, see Michael S. Teitelbaum, "Right Versus Right: Immigration and Refugee Policy in the United States," *Foreign Affairs* 59 (Fall 1980): 21–59.

27. David S. North and Marion P. Houstoun, *The Characteristics and Role of Illegal Aliens in the U.S. Labor Market: An Exploratory Study* (Washington, D.C.: Linton & Co., 1976).

28. August 4, 1977. Text in *Congressional Quarterly Almanac* 33 (1977): 43E.

29. *Congressional Record* (daily ed.), July 18, 1978, p. H6852.

30. Account of meeting from author's notes.

31. Select Commission on Immigration and Refugee Policy, *U.S. Immigration Policy and the National Interest,* Final Report, March 1, 1981 (Washington, D.C.: Government Printing Office, 1981), p. 36. Hereafter referred to as SCIRP, Final Report.

32. Ibid., p. 35.

33. *Time,* May 19, 1980, p. 14.

34. Survey by the Roper Organization, *Roper Report* 80–6, June 5–12, 1980.

35. SCIRP, Final Report, p. 333.

36. See the analysis of Barry Chiswick, "Guidelines for the Reform of Immigration Policy," in *Contemporary Economic Problems 1981: Demand, Productivity, and Population,* ed. William Fellner (Washington, D.C.: American Enterprise Institute, 1981).

37. See the discussion in David S. North and Alan Lebel, *Manpower and Immigration Policies in the United States* (Washington, D.C.: National Commission for Manpower Policy, 1978); *Industrial and Labor Relations Review* 33 (April 1980); *Illegal Aliens: Analysis and Background,* prepared for the use of the Committee on the Judiciary, U.S. House of Representatives (Washington, D.C.: Government Printing Office, 1977).

38. Select Commission on Immigration and Refugee Policy, *Semiannual Report to Congress, March 1, 1980* (Washington, D.C.: Government Printing Office, 1980), p. 1.

39. SCIRP, Final Report, pp. 41, 37, 98–99, 38.

40. SCIRP, *Second Semiannual Report to Congress* (Washington, D.C.: Government Printing Office, 1980).

41. SCIRP, Final Report, pp. 41–42.

42. H.R. 4832, 97th Cong., 1st sess., October 22, 1981.

43. Interview with Walter Cronkite, CBS News, March 4, 1981.

44. *Joint Hearings Before the Subcommittee on Immigration and Refugee Policy of the Senate Committee on the Judiciary and Subcommittee on Immigration, Refugees, and International Law of the House Committee on the Judiciary,* 96th Cong., 1st sess., May 7, 1981 (Washington, D.C.: Government Printing Office, 1981), pp. 541–542.

CHAPTER 3

Immigrants and the Labor Market: Historical Perspectives and Current Issues

Walter Fogel

Over 50 million immigrants have entered the United States since 1820. Most stayed permanently and managed to improve the quality of their lives, or at least provided better ones for their children. Immigration stands as a mighty testament to the strength of human aspirations and to mankind's capacity for achievement. The United States rightfully celebrates its immigration tradition, but it should not lose sight of the uneven economic significance of immigration to various categories of its citizenry. The distributional effects of immigration policy stir controversy that can be resolved only by first reaching a balanced understanding of the untoward as well as the beneficial economic effects of immigration.

Immigration has brought to the United States not only large numbers of people but also diverse kinds in terms of national origins, who do not necessarily have uniform effects upon the labor market. Until the 1980s, if slaves are excluded, over 90 percent of all people admitted to the United States came from northern or western Europe. The ethnic composition of immigration changed greatly, however, toward the end of the nineteenth century when people of southern and eastern Europe descent represented almost two-thirds of controlled immigration between 1890 and 1920. A second major change in immigrant composition began in the 1920s with the onset of massive immigration from Mexico. A third major change occurred in 1965, when barriers to Asian immigration were lessened. The Asian share of immigrant admissions, which stood at only 2 percent prior to 1965, rose to one-third of the total immigration in the 1970s.

The sheer volume of immigration over the years suggests that the

Table 3.1   *The Foreign-Born U.S. Population and Labor Force, 1850–1970*[a]

Year	Foreign-Born Population (in thousands)	Percentage of Total Population	Foreign-Born Labor Force (in thousands)	Percentage of Total Labor Force
1850	2.2	9.7	—	—
1860	4.1	13.2	—	—
1870	5.6	14.0	2.7	21.6
1880	6.7	13.3	3.5	20.1
1890	9.2	14.6	5.1	26.1
1900	10.3	13.6	5.8	23.0
1910	13.5	14.7	7.8	24.0
1920	13.9	13.2	7.7	21.2
1930	14.2	11.6	7.4	17.4
1940	11.5	8.8	5.8	12.3
1950	10.3	6.9	4.8	9.2
1960	9.7	5.4	4.2	6.3
1970	9.6	4.7	4.2	5.1

Source: U.S. Bureau of the Census, *Census of Population* (Washington, D.C.: Government Printing Office, various years).
[a] Labor force data for 1890–1950 are for white people only.

historical contributions of immigrants to the growth and development of the United States are inseparable from that growth and development itself. As portrayed in Table 3.1, the foreign born comprised a sizable component of the U.S. labor force throughout the nineteenth century and well into the twentieth. Between 1890 and 1920 the foreign-born percentage of the U.S. labor force stood between 20 and 26 percent. Aliens comprised a larger fraction of the labor force than of the total population because most were of labor-force age and they included a relatively large number of males in a time when males were much more likely than females to enter the labor force outside the home.

The Historical Context

Then as now, immigrants tended to settle in large cities and consequently composed a much larger proportion of the work force of such cities than of the nation as a whole. Near the turn of the century, for example, foreign-born men were a majority of the male labor forces of Buffalo, Chicago, Detroit, Jersey City, Milwaukee, Minneapolis, New York, Portland, San Francisco, and Scranton.[1]

The occupational distribution of the foreign born similarly has been concentrated. Early in this century, when foreign-born people represented nearly one-quarter of the labor force, almost half of all unskilled laborers and nearly two-fifths of all service and factory workers came from abroad. By way of contrast, aliens were employed as craft workers and managers (largely as small proprietors), in equal proportion to their relative numbers in the labor force, while relatively few immigrants were found in white-collar or farm occupations.[2] Foreign-born workers were especially numerous in a few occupations. In 1910, for example, they comprised four-fifths of all tailors and at least half of all bakers, mine and apparel operatives, and laborers in manufacturing, transportation, and utilities. Concentrations of immigrants were also found in certain industries. An extensive congressional investigation in 1909 concluded that "the greater proportion of the wage earners at the present time engaged in manufacturing and mining are of foreign birth."[3] Foreign-born workers were found to be 58 percent of all workers in iron and steel manufacturing, 61 percent in meat packing, 62 percent in bituminous coal mining, and 69 percent in cotton mills.

As the number of immigrants was reduced by legislation in the 1920s, the occupations of foreign-born people became more like those of native-born workers. By 1950, when foreign-born workers amounted to approximately 9 percent of the total labor force, they comprised not more than 13 percent of any of the major occupational categories, with the exception of the services, where they represented nearly 20 percent of all employees.[4] To some extent, the large immigrant proportion of service workers in that year resulted from increased immigration from the western hemisphere. Characteristically, immigrants from the western hemisphere had relatively little schooling or job training, and with employment growing slowly for low skilled manual workers, they frequently turned to service jobs, where formal hiring requirements were minimal.

Officially, the relative size of the work force's foreign-born component has declined steadily since 1920, to about 5 percent in 1970. The census, however, does not count significant numbers of aliens, principally those who have not been lawfully admitted. Even so, the relative numbers of foreign born in the work force are currently near or at all-time lows. Relative autarky characterizes the U.S. labor force now by comparison with the past.

Between 1921 and 1965, when the current immigration law was revised, annual legal immigration averaged 220,000, well below the 590,000 annual average for the peak period of immigration, 1880–1920. The impact of immigration on the labor market during the period after 1921 was slight, because the numbers admitted relative to the growing population were small and the occupational mix of immigrants became similar to that of the native population, so that new immigrant entrants to the labor force were well dispersed throughout U.S. job markets. The enactment of the Immigration and Nationality Act of 1965 increased immigration and changed its composition, but the impact on the labor market of those admitted under the law continued to be slight, as sanctioned immigrants contributed less than 10 percent of new labor force entrants after 1965.[5]

A special kind of immigration stands as an exception to the conclusion that, after World War I, lawful immigration had little effect on U.S. job markets. A contract farm labor program with Mexico, popularly called the *bracero* program (see Chapter 4), did have a substantial impact on farm labor wages and working conditions in the United States. The design of the *bracero* program attempted to protect the wages and employment prospects of U.S. farm workers who were locally available. However, it became increasingly evident that the presence of Mexican contract workers did have adverse effects on the wages and job prospects of both local and migrant U.S. agricultural workers.

Aside from its adverse impacts on farm labor markets, the *bracero* program was significant for two reasons. First, it set in motion a heavy flow of illegal immigrants from Mexico during the early 1950s, a flow that was stopped only by means of paramilitary deportations carried out by the U.S. Immigration and Naturalization Service in the mid-1950s. Second, labor flows once authorized under the *bracero* program became illegal immigration after the program ended and continue today at much increased levels. The unsanctioned immigration of the 1960s was heavily oriented toward the needs of U.S. agriculture, with seasonal migration of Mexican nationals to farm areas of the United States and subsequent return migration to Mexico, much as the practice had been under the prior *bracero* program.

ECONOMIC CONTRIBUTIONS OF IMMIGRATION

Unquestionably, immigration to the United States was a major factor in the economic development and growth of the country as measured by increases in national product. The most fundamental contribution was to labor supply. Immigration augmented the supply of native labor, thereby raising the value of natural resources and stimulating investment in capital. Increases in labor supply cost the American economy very little, since most of the costs of developing the immigrant labor did not fall on it but rather were borne by nations from which the immigrants came.

Immigrants stimulated capital investment by supplying the labor necessary for profitable returns on investments in factories, mines, and railroads. They brought some capital with them, and their migration encouraged foreign investors to seek profitable employment of their capital in the United States. Immigration not only stimulated capital growth in this country but also fostered the development of technically advanced capital. Technical skills were brought by the immigrants in some instances, and the constant arrival of new workers, most of whom were not highly skilled, made possible the continual expansion of factories and other kinds of production units which incorporated the most advanced kinds of production processes.

The continual arrival of immigrants to the United States also fostered and maintained a spirit of economic achievement which aided the development of the nation. One immigrant group after another began life in this country in humble circumstances, struggled for advancement, and eventually achieved it, carrying the nation to new economic heights in the process.

Per Capita Income. The effect of immigration on per capita welfare, usually measured by average income, is not as clear-cut as the effects on total product or income. It is, of course, possible for the former to rise, fall, or stay the same while national income is increasing. Nonetheless, a general consensus exists among students of the question that immigration did increase per capita incomes in the United States throughout the nineteenth century and into the twentieth, perhaps up until World War I.[6] The per capita increases occurred because the United States was a large country and the population increases brought about by immigrants allowed economies of scale to occur in production processes, thereby increasing output per worker. They occurred also by means of immigrant-stimulated investments in technologically advanced capital.

At least by the second decade of the twentieth century, however, most economies of production which could result from population increases had been exploited, and with a much larger population in the United States than in the prior century, immigration itself was no longer a major stimulant to innovative capital investment. Furthermore, as gains in agricultural productivity began to release more and more workers for nonfarm employment, low-skilled immigrants who dominated late nineteenth- and early twentieth-century immigration, increasingly began to "substitute" for low-skilled resident workers.

Since early in the twentieth century, then, immigration has probably not increased average per capita income, although it has continued to enhance the growth of national income. This conclusion has
been reached on both theoretical and empirical grounds.[7]

Distributional Impacts. Even while contributing to economic growth,
and regardless of whether per capita income is also increasing, immigration can have vastly different economic impacts on different parts
of the population. Generally, it has increased returns to owners of
capital and natural resources, including land, and has benefited consumers to the extent of their consumption of the goods and services
produced by immigrants. On the other hand, it has hurt resident low-
skilled workers who had no alternative but to compete with immigrant labor.

The effects of immigration have also varied within the labor
force, in accord with the extent to which immigrant workers have
been "substitutes" for, or "complements" to, resident workers. The
resident workers for whom immigrants substituted had their earnings
and employment prospects adversely affected by the presence of immigrants, unless the stimulative effects of immigration on national
income produced general increases in the demand for labor. When
immigrant-induced increases in labor demand were sufficient, some
unskilled resident workers were able to make occupational advances—on the shoulders of immigrants, so to speak. Many unskilled
resident workers were not able to advance, however, because they
suffered from schooling and training deficiencies or from job discrimination.

Resident skilled and supervisory labor tended to have its productivity directly enhanced by immigrant augmentations to this country's
unskilled labor supply. These complementary effects were greatest in
periods of economic growth accompanied by labor shortages. The
entry of low-skilled immigrants made possible the continued growth
of skilled and supervisory jobs.

The exact incidence of these various distributional impacts during the course of U.S. history has not been assessed, but some conclusions have been reached. One is that the large and continuing
immigration of relatively low-skilled workers to the United States
which occurred between 1890 and the eve of World War I prevented
increases in the real earnings of unskilled and manufacturing workers
during this period, despite the substantial increases in worker productivity (output per man-hour) which took place at the same time.[8]

The other side of the wage effect was that the same waves of immigration which kept unskilled wages low also enabled many resident and earlier immigrant workers to move up the occupational ladder. The meatpacking industry in Chicago exemplified this phenomenon. The first employees of this industry, in the late nineteenth century, were immigrants from Great Britain, Germany, and Ireland. But, as the U.S. economy grew, these groups moved either into white-collar and supervisory jobs within Chicago meatpacking or to comparable jobs in other industries. In either event, the unskilled jobs they left were filled with new immigrants from Italy, Poland, the Baltic nations and other countries, and each of these groups also experienced subsequent upward job mobility.[9]

Group effects aside, however, those individuals who for one reason or another were not able to move out of unskilled jobs in Chicago meatpacking and comparable industries had their job security as well as wages adversely affected by the continuing influx of immigrant labor. And this continuing influx of immigrant labor was partially responsible for the fact that both wages and job security in many such industries remained unsatisfactory until the advent of World War I.

Immigrant labor in the late nineteenth and early twentieth centuries not only kept unskilled wages low but also prevented or delayed improvement in the economic welfare of people who were potentially competitive with immigrant workers. Many of these people were underemployed in agriculture, with incomes below poverty levels, and many were black. The high degree of substitutability which existed between immigrants and underemployed resident workers is shown by the comparative absence of immigration to the South, where many of the underemployed resident workers lived. It is also illustrated by the fact that substantial migration of blacks to northern industrial centers did not take place until World War I sharply reduced immigration to this country.[10] It is a safe conjecture that the economic progress of the black population of the United States would have been more rapid in the absence of the immigration that occurred from 1870 to 1915.[11]

Labor Relations. The dean of American industrial relations, Sumner Slichter, assessed the impact of immigration on early twentieth-century industrial relations as follows:

> To the abundance of cheap immigrant labor are primarily attributable the two outstanding features of American Labor Policy before the war [World War I]—the tendency to adapt jobs to men rather than men to jobs, and the policy of obtaining output by driving the workers rather than by developing their good will and cooperation.[12]

Slichter went on to argue that immigrant workers were very docile, largely because their language difficulties and limited knowledge of American culture and institutions made the possibility of a job loss especially fearful. Furthermore, "employers were able to prevent concerted resistance to drive methods by mixing workers of different and often antagonistic nationalities."[13]

Immigration to the United States did delay the development of enlightened personnel administration and the growth of labor organizations in large-scale industry, even though many immigrants brought with them predilections for such organizations. These predilections, obtained in many cases through experience with labor organizations in Europe, were insufficient in the absence of job-security safeguards and the presence of the vast cultural and language differences that characterized immigrant work forces in many industries.[14]

A Historical Assessment. The successful absorption of millions of immigrants is certainly one of the positive themes of U.S. history. The development of these immigrant peoples and their contributions to the life of this country are synonymous with the growth and development of the nation itself. The economic growth to which immigration contributed mightily brought widespread economic opportunities for millions of Americans and much of the basis for the high standard of living that most enjoy today.

While a broad view of U.S. history necessarily produces great praise for immigration, a perspective which is more detailed as to time and place indicates that immigration, besides its contribution to economic growth, was often the source of much pain and suffering in the resident population as well as among immigrants themselves. Immigration frequently added to an already adequate supply of unskilled resident workers, thereby adversely affecting those who were least well off in American society. Late nineteenth- and early twentieth-century immigration lowered unskilled wages, exacerbated unemployment, increased the inequality of income in the nation, retarded the development of modern industrial relations practice, and heightened ethnic tensions in industrial areas. Immigration also slowed economic advancement for blacks and others who did not enjoy accessibility to the jobs that opened up with the expansion of northern industrial centers.

This list of costly effects does not destroy the broad conclusions that immigration was a positive influence on the United States and that it contributed greatly to the building of the nation, but it should lead to the realization that negative as well as positive impacts were associated with this movement of people and, most important for contemporary policy, that immigration could have been "done better." Control of the arrival of immigrants on these shores would have done much to reduce the suffering of immigrants and residents alike. Control of the number of entrants and the timing of their arrival would have been a substantial improvement on the laissez-faire system that existed, inordinately influenced as it was by land promoters, transportation companies, manufacturers, labor contractors, and others who stood to benefit from a sheer increase in the nation's population.

It would be well to keep in mind this balanced assessment of prior immigration as we turn to the contemporary scene.

Contemporary Labor Market Processes and Immigration

If the characteristics of U.S. labor markets are examined broadly from a social-welfare point of view, it is evident that most of the 105 million people who now comprise the labor force at any one time are reasonably well off with respect to their employment security, wages and benefits, and working conditions. This is not to say that among these reasonably well-off workers there are not thousands, even millions, of people whose jobs in one way or another are unsatisfactory to them. The economic wealth and development of the country have provided generally satisfactory wages and working conditions. And generally adequate protections against individual inequities are provided by government, unions, and private personnel policies.

There are, however, segments of the labor market and labor force where these conclusions do not hold. Parts of the labor market encompass jobs that, at least for adult workers, do not provide satisfactory wages, working conditions, or job security. Millions of workers or potential workers are attached to these unsatisfactory jobs in some fashion, because they are employed in them, because they are unemployed but will eventually take one of them, or because if they some time enter the labor force it will be to take one of these jobs. Most of the workers who are attached to these job markets suffer from one or more of the conditions that constitute labor-market failures from a societal point of view: low wages, inadequate protections of labor standards, unemployment, and welfare dependency.

There is no need to belabor this dichotomized representation of the labor market for present purposes. The genesis of the idea is to be found in the work of Peter Doeringer and Michael Piore.[15] Many of its details, for example, the relative size of the two segments, are not readily ascertainable. Neither can the labor market dichotomy be defended as literally accurate. Surely it would be more accurate to represent the attractiveness of jobs along a continuum, from best to worst, rather to place them on either side of a separation between two segments. Nonetheless, this exposition device of segmenting the labor market is useful because it captures the fundamental truth that only a small fraction of the labor market does not function satisfactorily from a social-welfare standpoint, and it facilitates useful discussion of certain labor-market processes. One of these processes is the employment of immigrant workers. For simplicity's sake, the Doeringer-Piore terms "primary" and "secondary" will be used not only to distinguish between the two segments but also to refer to the jobs, workers, and employers encompassed by each.

Before turning to the subject of contemporary immigrant employment patterns, it is necessary to note the kind of immigrants under discussion. If current immigration to the United States were at the level anticipated under the existing immigration law (400,000 to 500,000 per year), there would be little need for concern about its labor market or any other effects. And there would be little sentiment for change in immigration policy. The number of immigrants would be small enough, and their occupations would be sufficiently like those of the resident population (including everyone but recent immigrants), that they would be absorbed into the American economy and society without adverse impacts, although existing policy could well be amended to include provisions for reducing entry in recession years and expanding it in periods of rapid growth.

Unsanctioned immigration and, to a much lesser extent, refugee admissions change all that. Although the numbers can only be guessed at, the belief is widespread that the annual numbers of unlawful entrants is two or more times as large as the number of non-refugees admitted under immigration law, and nearly all unsanctioned immigrants enter the labor force. Because of the presumed numbers and the high concentration of unsanctioned immigrants in low-wage, manual-job markets, some economists believe that these immigrants are having substantial effects on these markets and on the resident workers who are attached to them, or who would be in the absence of immigrants. It should be understood, then, that even though reference at times is simply made to "immigrants," an issue arises over their labor market effects only because existing U.S. immigration law is not adequately enforced.

IMMIGRANT EMPLOYMENT

Although many immigrants admitted under the preference procedures of immigration law are quickly employed in the primary job
sector, most refugees and nearly all unsanctioned immigrants can
obtain employment only in the secondary sector. There they compete
with resident workers for the available jobs, causing some of the latter
to be unemployed. The presence of these immigrant workers acts as a
kind of subsidy to employers in the secondary market, since employers are assured of obtaining labor even though they offer only
low wages and substandard working conditions.

The employment allocation process is not complex. The resident
workers available for employment in the secondary sector are those
who cannot obtain jobs in the primary sector (excess supplies of labor
are available to many, if not most, primary-sector jobs). They tend to
be without trained skills and demonstrable histories of stable employment. In short, they are workers the primary sector doesn't want.
Some of them are capable of stable, productive work effort, but many
are unwilling to provide it for the low pay offered by most employers
in the secondary labor market.

Employers in the secondary sector tend to operate labor-
intensive processes. Consequently, the cost of labor is very important
to them. The cost of labor is determined by the wage rate and the
productivity of the workers employed. Labor costs can be reduced
either by lowering the wage rate or by improving the productivity of
the work force. The former is usually not possible because secondary
market wages are often already at the statutory minimum. Or wage
rates are established in competitive labor markets, so that individual
employers must pay the market wage or go without workers.

There is greater opportunity for secondary employers to reduce
or hold down labor costs by concentrating on the productivity of
workers. Improved supervision, planning, and management in general may be able to improve worker productivity. But the major variable affecting productivity is usually worker quality and performance.
Employers seek workers who will put considerable effort into their
jobs, who will show up for work every day at the established hours,
and who do not cause trouble with other workers or supervisors.
There can never be enough workers with these characteristics for
most employers—worker quality could almost always be better than it
is from the employer's standpoint.

In the United States in the 1980s the reality is that only a minor proportion of secondary market workers possess the characteristics employers prize. Many of those who do are students, housewives, and semiretired workers, who maintain a comparatively brief attachment to the secondary labor market and who, while willing to work for low pay for a time, will not often take jobs that are dirty or physically demanding. Few resident workers who are both productive and reliable apply for the worst secondary labor market jobs—those with both low pay and undesirable working conditions.

If wages were to rise for secondary jobs (relative to those for other jobs), employers would be able to hire better-quality workers. More students, retired workers, and housewives would be attracted by the better wages. Whether lower labor costs would follow is strictly an empirical matter. If productivity gains from hiring better-quality workers were proportionately greater than the increases in wages necessary to attract them, labor costs would fall. But there is no reason to believe this would occur, and the fact that secondary-market employers rarely raise their relative wages suggests that it would not. Instead, higher wages would raise rather than lower labor costs.[16]

Thus, secondary employers continually look for better-quality workers to hold down their labor costs. One source of such workers, discovered by U.S. employers during the labor shortages of the mid-1960s, is the immigrant population, principally those who have not been lawfully admitted. The need for income, the lack of alternatives to secondary jobs, and the fear of deportation all make the unsanctioned immigrant something close to an ideal worker for many secondary jobs—he is productive, reliable, and docile.

Beginning with the mid-1960 labor shortages, U.S. employers made increasing use of illegal immigrants. At first they were employed chiefly in agriculture and in service occupations in the largest cities, especially Chicago, Los Angeles, New York, and Washington, D.C. Their use spread to smaller cities and to other occupations, however, as employers became aware of immigrant availability and potential immigrants learned of the jobs available in the United States.[17]

It is important to understand that immigrants are not the only source of labor to which employers in secondary markets can turn. They are simply in many instances the best source, in the sense of output produced at the going wage, which is often the statutory minimum.[18] However, nearly all local labor markets that employ immigrants also employ at least a few resident workers in the same or similar jobs. Furthermore, jobs that principally employ immigrants in the large cities exclusively employ resident workers in some middle- and smaller-sized cities of the north.

LARGE CITIES

Unsanctioned immigrant workers are employed in the secondary labor markets of all large cities in the United States and in many middle- and smaller-sized cities as well. There are, however, smaller cities in the North which do not employ immigrants or employ very few in relation to the number of residents. The North-South difference, of course, results from the fact that the predominant flows of immigrants enter the United States through the southern and, to a lesser extent, eastern borders of the country. It seems likely that the attractiveness of unsanctioned immigrant workers will eventually lead to their pervasive employment throughout the nation. Since this has not yet occurred, it is useful to examine why it has not, for the light that it sheds on the phenomenon of immigrant employment.

The principal factors that explain the incidence of unsanctioned immigrant employment appear to be the availability of immigrant workers and the relative quality of the available resident labor supply. Unsanctioned immigrant workers are much more readily available in large cities than in smaller ones. They tend to settle in large cities because they are less likely to be detected and more likely to be given support by their countrymen who have formed earlier settlements. It is more difficult in a variety of ways for an illegal Hispanic worker, for example, to settle in a small northern city than to settle in a place like Chicago, Los Angeles, or New York, all of which have large Hispanic communities.

The quality of the resident labor supply is the other important variable, because quantity is rarely a problem. If an adequate supply of productive and reliable resident workers is available at prevailing wages, there is little incentive to employ immigrants, particularly if wages are already at or just above the statutory minimum.

In retrospect, it is evident that, in the mid-1960s, changes in the availability of both immigrant workers and resident workers occurred in big cities, bringing about the ultimate dominance of the former in big-city secondary labor markets. Greater numbers of unsanctioned immigrants became available at that time for two reasons.

First, termination of the contract labor program with Mexico in 1964 set off a replacement stream of illegal entry. Initially, this inflow was small and directed to southwestern agriculture, but it grew rapidly and spread to service and other low-wage jobs in large cities throughout much of the nation. Second, a less recognized increase in illegal entry, to large East Coast cities, occurred in the last half of the 1960s, hand in hand with increases in lawful immigration from North and South American nations. Lawful immigration from the North American nations other than Canada and Mexico had been only 309,000 over the decade from 1956 to 1965. This figure increased to 817,000 during the years 1967–1976.[19] Increases were particularly large from the Caribbean nations of Barbados, Jamaica, and Trinidad and Tobago, rising from 22,000 in the first period to 207,000 in the next.

All these nations gained their independence in the 1960s. As colonies, their immigration had been restricted to 200 people a year by U.S. immigration law. When this numerical limit no longer applied, lawful immigration surged dramatically. But the pent-up demand could not be satisfied by this means alone, in part because would-be immigrants who were not relatives of U.S. citizens or resident aliens could be admitted only after obtaining "labor certification" from the U.S. Department of Labor, and such certification was not easily obtained. Consequently, illegal entry mushroomed. The growing settlements of sanctioned immigrants from the Caribbean and other North and South American nations which now existed facilitated this illegal inflow.

The second factor affecting immigrant employment, the quality of the available resident labor supply, may also have changed in the 1960s. The ethnicity of big-city populations—particularly their central cities, where many secondary jobs existed—was in transition during the 1960s (as it had been for some time), from predominantly white to black, Hispanic, and, to a lesser extent, Asian. There is no evidence indicating that this ethnic change affected the quality of labor available in big cities one way or another. Regardless of the absence of evidence from social scientists, employer perceptions of the quality of workers available for secondary employment probably worsened in the 1960s.

Social protest erupted violently among blacks in 1965 with the Watts riots and spread to other minority populations. The increased militancy of young blacks and Hispanics during the 1960s may have reduced their perceived value as employees in the eyes of big-city secondary employers.[20] It is also likely that the increased social militancy of young blacks and Hispanics made them less willing to take unattractive secondary jobs, either out of a group resolve not to do the white man's dirty work or because of individual preferences.[21]

Regardless of these hypotheses, it is a fact that big-city secondary employers increasingly turned to illegal immigrants as minority youth and inner-city unemployment rose during the 1970s.[22] The most plausible explanation for that apparent anomaly is that secondary employers found illegal immigrants to be superior to *any* resident workers—black, Hispanic, or the small number of whites still available. However, a perception of young minority workers as unreliable and a reluctance by these workers to take menial, poorly paid jobs may have contributed to the anomaly as well.

SMALL CITIES

In some middle-sized and smaller cities of the North, primarily white resident workers hold secondary labor market jobs such as food and lodging work, refuse collection, and manual labor. High school and college students, new entrants to the labor force, and older workers who cannot get better jobs are the sources of labor supply. Why are the jobs that in the big cities are filled by immigrants held by resident workers in the smaller cities? The answer appears to be that employers in the big cities have discovered that unsanctioned immigrants are superior to the available resident workers, while in the small cities resident workers satisfactorily perform the secondary jobs and immigrant workers are not so readily available.

Both the availability of immigrants and the quality of resident workers, then, contribute to the locational differences, but the former is more important. The combination of extreme need for income and fear of deportation make the illegal alien an extraordinarily motivated and cooperative worker, overcoming any language or schooling limitations such people may also possess. Consequently, it is likely that they will be employed increasingly in the smaller northern cities in place of resident workers, although this replacement will be constrained by the reluctance of illegal immigrants to live in small cities of the North.

The quality of the resident labor supply as seen by secondary employers is undoubtedly better in small cities than in large cities. This should not be surprising. More workers in the small cities are products of upwardly mobile families who continue to strive for and anticipate success, while many inner-city residents of big cities, especially blacks, look back upon debilitating labor market and social experiences. Furthermore, shifting locational preferences, including a desire to escape big-city woes, are now bringing an increasing supply of educated, middle-class workers to smaller cities and towns. Yet, the quality of the resident work force is secondary to the availability of illegal immigrants. Few resident workers are going to labor as hard and persistently for low pay on unattractive jobs.

Labor Market Effects of Immigration

BROWNSVILLE: AN ILLUSTRATIVE CASE

There is not much disagreement among economists on the short-run impacts of immigration. Immigrant labor will enable the economy to grow faster, increasing returns to capital and wages to the skilled resident workers whom they complement. At the same time, there is some substitution of immigrants for unskilled residents, and wage rates for unskilled labor fall, at least in relative terms.

Many lay people are inclined not to take these conclusions seriously unless it can be shown that they are based on actual experiences rather than logic, particularly the conclusions that illegal immigrants lower the wages and employment of unskilled resident workers. Empirical verification is easily obtained by talking with and following the fortunes of distinguishable groups of residents who must compete with the immigrants,[23] but that kind of evidence does not add up to the measured impacts some people seem to require. Recently, some systematic evidence from an intensive examination of a small border city by Michael Miller has become available.[24] It provides an unusual illumination of a wide range of effects of immigrant labor.

The city Miller studied was Brownsville, Texas, located next to the U.S.-Mexico border, across from the city of Matamoros, Mexico. A great supply of immigrant workers is available in Brownsville: There are workers in Matamoros who lawfully commute each day to jobs in the U.S. city, lawful Mexican immigrants who have settled in the Brownsville area, and a seemingly limitless number of people who cross the border illegally.

Until the late 1960s, Brownsville was a sleepy city. Its population of 53,000 in 1970 was characterized by very low average income (51 percent of the national family average) and a high percentage of inhabitants of Mexican origin (over three-quarters of the total population). However, rapid economic growth began in the late 1960s, spurred initially by Mexico's Border Industrialization Program, which provided incentives for U.S. manufacturing plants to locate in the border region of Mexico, and subsequently by the discovery by U.S.

entrepreneurs of the cheap labor available in Brownsville. Since 1967, forty-two U.S. corporations have located in Matamoros, and many of them have also established "twin plants" in Brownsville. In addition, considerable industrial development occurred in Brownsville independently of the Mexican border program, in metal fabrication, shipbuilding, petrochemical processing, and oil-equipment manufacturing, among other industries. Between 1966 and 1978, Brownsville's population grew to 80,000, over 100 firms established operations in the city, 8,000 industrial and 5,600 nonindustrial jobs were created, and 7,000 housing units, 8 shopping centers, and 3 country clubs were built, to cite just some of the city's spectacular growth statistics.

This growth, much of it induced by the availability of immigrant labor, provided enhanced opportunities for profits to manufacturers, merchants, landowners, builders, and developers. It also provided higher incomes, as median family income rose from 51 percent of the U.S. average in 1970 to 60 percent in 1978. The higher incomes, however, went principally to new residents who moved to the city to take skilled and professional jobs. This was especially true of new Anglo residents, whose median household income in 1978 was $20,000, nearly twice the average for all residents.

There are other indications that the immigrant-induced growth did not benefit the least skilled of Brownsville's population. Although the proportion of the city's population living in households with poverty level incomes declined in the 1970s, the absolute number of such persons rose from 24,000 to 30,000. Unemployment, most of it among people of Mexican origin, also rose, from 7.0 percent to 10.5 percent over this period, and doubled in absolute numbers. Wage rates for all types of manual and service labor remained low throughout the period of rapid growth. Only 42 percent of the respondents to a survey indicated satisfaction with the availability and quality of employment opportunities in the city. Many respondents blamed the gloomy employment situation on competition from Mexican labor living in Matamoros.

Unions, never very successful in Brownsville, were unable to organize the city's expanding work force in the 1970s. Efforts failed in the fishing industry and in city government, and the United Steelworkers Union was decertified by Brownsville's largest employer, Marathon LeTourneau, after the company defeated a 1977 strike by hiring replacements for striking workers. Marathon's wage history also illustrates the impacts of a readily available labor supply. When the firm began Brownsville production in the early 1970s, it paid its welders $10.00 an hour. After it began to train local workers in the mid-1970s and to recruit welders from Monterrey, Mexico, its top wage for welders had dropped to $6.50 an hour by 1979.

Because it is small enough that most of its economic aspects could be comprehended by a social scientist, Brownsville aptly illustrates the effects of a highly elastic supply of immigrant (or any other kind) labor. The availability of this cheap labor was an important contribution to the economic growth of the city, although that growth was highly uneven. Large profits were undoubtedly made in industry, commerce, and land development, and many new jobs were created, enabling some of the resident population to move up the occupational structure. But much of the blue-collar and service work force did not benefit from the growth. Competition from immigrant labor prevented improvements in job security and wages, and the ability of these workers to bargain collectively with employers probably declined.

UNRESTRICTED IMMIGRATION: A BURDEN
FOR THE UNDERPRIVILEGED

Migrants who move from one country or region to another make labor cheaper in the receiving area and also provide buyers for goods, services, and land. That is why the owners of capital and land so strongly support immigration. Skilled workers, and those with the ability to advance occupationally, may also benefit from the economic expansion that immigration brings. Unskilled workers will suffer harm from their immigrant competitors unless the former possess the abilities and have access to the means for job-upgrading.

It is the latter effect which requires control of immigration, regardless of whether national policy is to be liberal or conservative in terms of numbers of people to be admitted. It is unconscionable for the United States to permit immigration practices that harm the poorest people in the resident population while providing benefits for most others, including particularly large benefits for the owners of capital and land. Illegal immigration has produced these kinds of impacts over the last ten years.

The current flows of unsanctioned immigrants amount to nearly unrestricted movement of low-skilled workers between sending countries and the United States. It is ironic that "free entry" from abroad prevails in the lowest-paid U.S. labor markets, while nearly all the better-paid occupations are protected from entry by qualified foreigners. Licensing, examinations, union, and other requirements ensure that large numbers of immigrants will not be able to enter the professional and other skill occupations, even if foreigners who qualify for them were willing to risk illegal entry, which is not often the case. One must conclude that the political powerlessness of the unskilled accounts for this anomalous imbalance.

Unrestricted immigration of low-skilled workers can produce an ever-expanding layer of resident workers who are frequently, if not permanently, unemployed or out of the labor force. These resident workers either are not as valuable to employers as immigrants, so that they cannot get hired, or they prefer to survive on some combination of welfare programs, family support, episodic income-producing activity, and sporadic employment, rather than hold permanent employment in a secondary job. Already, it seems likely that the nonworking resident population has grown as a result of the unsanctioned immigration of the last decade. Witness the rise in unemployment and withdrawal from the labor force of minority males, the group most hurt by unsanctioned immigration, during the 1970s.

Many American leaders apparently wish to ignore the fact that current flows of unsanctioned immigrants undercut social policy aimed at improving the welfare of the poor and the least skilled. Unsanctioned immigration undercuts labor standards, such as overtime-pay requirements for more than forty hours of work a week, because unsanctioned immigrants cannot press for their enforcement. It also undercuts the statutory policy of giving workers the choice of whether to organize and bargain collectively with their employers because illegal aliens are hardly in a position to make this choice when their employers oppose it. Government training programs for the disadvantaged are undercut by illegal entry because immigrants fill the jobs that would otherwise be available for successful trainees and because the immigrant labor supply lowers the wage for jobs available to trainees. Similarly, the statutory minimum wage is undercut by increasing labor supply to the extent that many market equilibrium wage rates fall below the statutory level, making it possible for employers to pay below that level and still attract enough workers. Finally, policies to reduce welfare dependency are undercut because illegal entry helps keep wage earnings low on many jobs that, with higher earnings, would provide welfare recipients with greater incentive for self-sufficiency.

More generally, the nearly unrestricted current flows of unsanctioned immigrants exacerbates the job and income problems of blacks, Hispanics, and other secondary-market workers by reducing the number of jobs available to them and by reducing the wage for those jobs that are available to them. It makes no sense from a social policy standpoint to passively watch unemployment and the number of labor-force dropouts in central cities climb to disastrous levels, while at the same time unsanctioned immigrants take an ever-growing number of nearby jobs. More of these jobs need to go to the unemployed residents of big cities; for this to occur, the jobs need to provide better wages and working conditions. This can happen only if the supply of unsanctioned immigrants is cut off.

THE NEED FOR REFORM

Many policy proposals have been put forward during recent years of debate over immigration, but all except one are premature. The United States needs to regain control over immigration before it can deal intelligently with various proposals such as expanded immigration levels, special quotas for Mexico, amnesty for unsanctioned aliens, and a temporary worker program. The ease with which unsanctioned immigration can now occur must first be remedied.

The last two federal administrations, one Democratic and one Republican, have agreed that immigration control requires legislation that prohibits employment of illegal aliens. There simply is no other way to reduce the flow of unlawful immigration; it is not feasible to block the borders or track down people who enter on tourist visas. A prohibition on employment of illegal aliens must be enacted and means of enforcing this ban discovered. The latter may mean self-enforcement by employers, the requirement that workers present evidence of lawful residency, or the requirement of a work card or number that irrefutably establishes the possessor's eligibility for employment. Once control is regained, other immigration issues can be dealt with.

Despite its intrinsic importance, the labor market should be subordinate to other considerations in the development of policy. Concern for refugees, family unification, cooperation with neighboring countries, population policy, and internal social policy are all more important for informing immigration policy over the long run. Furthermore, it is not clear that the United States, as the wealthiest nation on earth, should rely upon immigration for solutions to its labor market problems.

When labor-market considerations are brought into immigration policy, in connection with a temporary worker program, for example, the welfare of those at the bottom of the job structure should be given more weight. That recommendation may not be taken seriously in this current phase of deference to the wishes of the wealthy. Nonetheless, heed should be taken of it, not only out of concern for justice, but also because the poor may yet have something to do with the future of this nation.

Notes

1. *Reports of the Immigration Commission* (Washington, D.C.: Government Printing Office, 1910), 1: 151.

2. Edward P. Hutchinson, *Immigrants and Their Children, 1850–1950* (New York: John Wiley & Sons, 1956), p. 202.

3. *Reports of the Immigration Commission*, 1: 493.

4. Hutchinson, *Immigrants and Their Children*, Appendix.

5. Author's estimate based on data presented in David S. North, *Immigrants and the American Labor Market* (Washington, D.C.: Department of Labor, 1974), pp. 18–22.

6. Joseph J. Spengler, "Some Economic Aspects of Immigration into the United States," *Journal of Law and Contemporary Problems* 21 (Spring 1956): 236–255.

7. Ibid.; Peter J. Hill, "The Economic Impact of Immigration into the United States" (Ph.D. diss., University of Chicago, 1970).

8. Paul H. Douglas, *Real Wages in the United States, 1890–1914* (Boston: Houghton Mifflin Co., 1930); and *Reports of the Immigration Commission*, 1: 540–541.

9. Walter Fogel, *The Negro in the Meat Industry* (Philadelphia: Industrial Research Unit, Wharton School of Finance and Commerce, University of Pennsylvania, 1979), pp. 17–43.

10. Spengler, "Some Economic Aspects," p. 250; Melvin W. Reder, "The Economic Consequences of Increased Immigration," *Review of Economics and Statistics* 45 (August 1963): 221–230.

11. Brinley Thomas, *Migration and Economic Growth*, 2d ed. (New York: Cambridge University Press, 1973), chap. 18.

12. Sumner H. Slichter, "The Current Labor Policies of American Industries," *Quarterly Journal of Economics* 5 (May 1929): 393.

13. Ibid., pp. 394–395.

14. Harry A. Millis and Royal E. Montgomery, *Organized Labor* (New York: McGraw-Hill Book Co., 1945); *Reports of the Immigration Commission*, 1: 530–538.

15. Peter B. Doeringer and Michael J. Piore, *Internal Labor Markets and Manpower Analysis* (Lexington, Mass.: D. C. Heath Co., 1971), chap. 8.

16. On this point, see Michael J. Piore, *Birds of Passage: Migrant Labor and Industrial Societies* (New York: Cambridge University Press, 1979), pp. 97–98.

17. Walter Fogel, *Mexican Illegal Alien Workers in the United States* (Los Angeles: University of California, Institute of Industrial Relations, 1978), pp. 82–88.

18. Ibid., pp. 89–91.

19. U.S. Immigration and Naturalization Service, *Annual Report* (Washington, D.C.: Government Printing Office, various years).

20. Piore, *Birds of Passage,* pp. 161–163.

21. Ibid.

22. For example, the unemployment rate for black males, age twenty to twenty-four, rose from an average of 8.4 percent during the last five years of the 1960s to an average of 20.5 percent in the last half of the 1970s. Labor-force participation rates for this group fell between the two periods from 87.3 percent to 78.6 percent of the population. U.S. Bureau of Labor Statistics, *Handbook of Labor Statistics,* Bulletin 2070 (Washington, D.C.: Government Printing Office, 1980), pp. 15, 70.

23. For a convincing example with respect to California farm workers in the *bracero* era, see Ernesto Galarza, *Merchants of Labor: The Mexican Bracero Story* (Charlotte, N.C.: McNally & Loftin, 1964).

24. Michael V. Miller, "Economic Growth and Change Along the U.S.-Mexico Border: The Case of Brownsville, Texas," Working paper, University of Texas at San Antonio, Human Resources Management and Development Program, 1981. The factual material that follows is based on Miller's paper.

CHAPTER 4

Nonimmigrant Labor Policy: Future Trend or Aberration?

Vernon M. Briggs, Jr.

Throughout much of the history of the United States, the employment of foreign workers as a supplement to the available domestic
labor force has been a recurrent public policy issue. Nonimmigrant
workers should not be confused with illegal immigrant workers.
Nonimmigrant workers are allowed legal entry and access to the
American labor market; illegal immigrants are not. As a result, the
legislative and administrative actions that have authorized nonimmigrant programs have generally been shrouded in controversy. The
subject of concern has centered both upon the economic effects that
nonimmigrant workers have on working conditions for citizen workers and on the special restrictions often imposed on nonimmigrants
which would be both unfair and often illegal if applied to citizen
workers.

If examined individually at different points in history, the nation's nonimmigrant labor policy would seem to be the result of ad
hoc reactions to events of their time. If studied over the long run,
however, it would seem that there are patterns to these programs and
policies. Recognition of these themes and characteristics is essential to
any effort to evaluate the efficacy of contemporary nonimmigrant
policy as well as any future proposals of a similar nature that assuredly will occur.

The subsequent discussion of nonimmigrant labor policy adopts
a broad definition of the term, for in addition to those initiatives that
bear the imprimatur of being legally called nonimmigrant programs,
there are other policies that have in the past or still do function in an
identical manner. A thorough understanding of the topic requires
that they too be included.

93

Policy Development: The Pre-1952 Experience

CONTRACT LABOR

The initial effort to establish by law the right of American employers
to hire foreign labor to work in the United States was the Contract
Labor Act of 1864. It was also known as the Act to Encourage Immigration, which indicates that it was linked more permanently to efforts to increase the supply of labor than most subsequent policy
enactments. Passed during the height of the Civil War, the Contract
Labor Act was ostensibly designed to respond to wartime labor shortages experienced by manufacturing and railroad construction interests in the North. The act allowed private employers to recruit foreign
workers and to pay their transportation expenses to the United States.
The enlisted workers entered into legally binding contracts in which
they would pledge their wages for up to twelve months to the employer who paid these transportation costs. In addition, they were
often induced into signing contracts for additional years of work to
pay the cost of their maintenance during the initial year.

The Civil War, with its mandatory conscription of young men,
had caused labor shortages to occur at the same time that war-related
production needs increased the demand for labor. President Abra-
ham Lincoln, in a message to Congress in late 1863, urged that a new
law to encourage immigration be passed. The Contract Labor Act was
enacted within a month. It was designed primarily to attract unskilled
workers. A number of private labor-recruiting firms had earlier
sought unsuccessfully to have the government subsidize their
activities. With the new law, these private firms—especially the American Emigrant Company—entered into a very profitable undertaking.
These companies received fees both from the employers for whom
they contracted workers and from the steamship lines who
transported the recruits from Europe to the United States.

Opposition to the Contract Labor Law from existing worker organizations began at once. In some instances, the new immigrants
became involved in labor disputes as strikebreakers. When the war
ended in 1865, the economy slipped into a serious recession that
lasted from 1866 to 1868. Organized labor—especially the newly
formed National Labor Union (NLU)—blamed the new law for the
unemployment and the depressed wages that existed in the postwar
period.[1] The NLU began a move to repeal the act which succeeded in
1868. The use of contract labor continued, however, because the
practice itself had not been banned.

Throughout the 1870s and early 1880s, immigration increased, even though there were prolonged periods of economic recession from 1873 to 1879 and from 1884 to 1886. The existing labor organizations of this era—the Knights of Labor, as well as a number of independent craft unions—became openly hostile to the prevailing public policies that favored tariff restrictions to protect industrialists while permitting new immigrants to enter and to compete freely with citizen workers for jobs. As a result of the lobbying efforts by labor groups who feared adverse competition in the labor market, as well as by groups who had concerns about the changing racial composition of the population, the first legislation to restrict immigration was enacted. The Chinese Exclusion Act was promulgated in 1882, while other acts in 1875 and 1882 sought to exclude criminals and paupers from immigration. It was in this context that the Alien Contract Labor Law of 1885 and its amendments of 1887 and 1888 were adopted. These laws sought explicitly to prohibit any person or business enterprise from assisting financially or encouraging in any way the immigration of aliens under the terms of any contracts or agreements. A fine of $1,000 per violation was set.

The alien contract laws were significant because they were the first statutes designed to restrict immigrants from Europe who were capable of self-support.[2] Such restrictions were politically palatable only in that they demonstrated a need for "a specific protection against a definite recognized evil"[3]—the "evil" being a form of artificial immigration used by employers for the primary purpose of undermining existing labor organizations: contract labor.

Even after passage of the 1885 law and subsequent amendments, the practice of contracting for foreign labor continued. The courts' liberal interpretation of the law perpetuated the tradition of an open border policy for Europeans.[4] As a result, contract workers continued to be a factor in labor disputes despite the ban on the practice. One notable encounter involved the use of sixty-two Scottish stonecutters who were contracted to build the mammoth state capitol building for the state of Texas. The stonecutters were recruited in Scotland in 1885 and had their transportation expenses paid to Austin, Texas, after the union workers of the Granite Cutters International boycotted the project. As a study of that dispute concluded: "It was not the scarcity of American stonemasons, however, which necessitated the importation of alien labor, but the conditions under which the Capitol Syndicate required their stonemasons to work."[5] By the time the case came to court in 1889, the work by the contract workers had been completed and they had scattered. The contractor was found guilty, but only a token penalty was assessed.

We do not know how many people entered the United States

under contract agreements. There were, however, almost four hundred suits filed by the federal government over violations of the Alien Contract Labor Act.

Technically speaking, the contract labor era does not represent a nonimmigrant program. The practice of contract labor belonged to an era that preceded the formulation of a nonimmigrant policy. But contract labor embodied a number of the characteristics of subsequent nonimmigrant programs. Indeed, many of the contract workers had no intention of settling in the United States. As with many immigrants in the latter half of the nineteenth century, contract workers usually came without their families, and they often returned to their homelands after their period of work in the United States.[6]

A "TEMPORARY" FARM WORKER PROGRAM

Only months after the United States enacted the most restrictive immigration legislation in its history up until that time—the Immigration Act of 1917—the first publicly organized foreign labor program was initiated.[7] In response to strong pressure from the large agricultural employers of the Southwest, Congress included in the act of 1917 a provision that would allow entry of "temporary" workers from western hemisphere nations who were "otherwise inadmissible." The statute allowed the secretary of labor to exempt such people (Mexicans in this instance) from the head tax and literacy requirements applied to all immigrants. In May 1917, with the nation officially at war with Germany, a "temporary" farm worker program for nonimmigrant workers was instituted. The scope of the program was expanded to allow some Mexican workers to become engaged in nonfarm work. When the program was announced, so were rules and regulations to govern temporary worker employment. Ostensibly, these measures were designed to protect both citizen workers and Mexican workers, as well as to assure that the Mexicans returned to Mexico after their work was completed. But, as has become the pattern, "these elaborate rules were unenforced."[8]

National defense considerations initially justified the secretary of labor's relaxation of the ban on nonimmigrant labor. Nonetheless, the program, which has been called "the first *bracero* program," was extended until 1922, well after the war had ended.[9] It was terminated for several reasons: First, its rationale as a national defense policy could no longer be maintained; second, organized labor contended that the program undermined the economic welfare of citizen workers; and third, many people believed that there were no labor shortages but only greedy employers who wished to secure economic gains from being able to secure cheap and docile workers. During the program's life span, 76,862 Mexican workers were admitted to the United States, of which only 34,922 returned to Mexico.[10]

BORDER COMMUTERS

Before 1917, there were virtually no restrictions placed on immigrants (except those from Asia) who wished to work in the United States. In 1917 and 1921, temporary restrictions were imposed on immigration, and shortly afterward the Immigration Act of 1924 established the first permanent numerical restrictions on immigration. People from the western hemisphere, however, were not included in the quotas established by the act. The act did require all people entering the United States to be either "immigrants" or "nonimmigrants." "Immigrants" were defined as all entrants except those designated as "nonimmigrants," who are visiting the nation temporarily "for business or pleasure." For a short interval, workers who lived in Mexico but commuted to jobs in the United States were classified as "nonimmigrant visitors" and were free to cross the border "for business." As a result of an arbitrary administrative decision by immigration officials in 1927, however, the status of these people was changed to "immigrants." Subsequently, in 1929, the U.S. Supreme Court acknowledged that it is "amiable fiction" that the commuters live in the United States. But it still upheld the administrative decision with the famous ruling that "employment equals residence," thereby avoiding the permanent residency requirement of the immigration statutes.[11]

Border commuters are a subgroup of a larger immigration classification known as resident aliens. Resident aliens are foreign-born nationals who apply for permission to live and work in the United States on a permanent basis. They can retain their original foreign citizenship. After a period of five years, they may apply at any time to become citizens, or they may remain resident aliens indefinitely. A substantial number of resident aliens never elect to become naturalized citizens.

There are two types of resident aliens. The larger group is made up of those who live and work on a permanent basis in the United States. The other resident alien group works regularly in the United States but resides permanently in either Mexico or Canada. This latter group are called "commuters" or, more commonly, "green-carders" (because the identification card issued to all resident aliens was originally green in color; it is now blue). The important distinction is this: all commuters are "green-carders," but most "green-carders" are not commuters.

To clarify the diverse labor market effects of various categories of commuters, it should be noted that there are also two types of commuting "green-carders." One crosses the border on a daily basis. The other works in the United States on a seasonal basis. Generally speaking, the daily commuter is the one whose presence is felt in the border economy of the United States—especially the southern border. Seasonal commuters usually move farther inland and return home to Mexico only during the off-season of the industry in which they are employed. The regional impact of the seasonal commuter is diluted by their employment in jobs that are scattered all over the nation. The daily commuters, on the other hand, are much more concentrated. Accordingly, their impact on the local labor market is significant. One study in 1970 aptly described the daily commuter as "this generation's *bracero*."[12]

Because Mexico and the United States are in quite different stages of economic development, commuters from Mexico are often willing to work for wages and under employment conditions that a person who must confront the daily cost of living in the United States on a permanent basis finds impossible to accept. Thus, the commuter has a real income advantage. Also, commuters often act as strikebreakers in labor disputes along the border and accordingly are one factor that explains the scarcity of unions in the region. A study in 1970 placed the number of daily commuters from Mexico at 70,000 people.[13] This would mean that roughly one out of eleven people employed in 1970 in the U.S. counties along the borders was a commuter. A work force of this magnitude exerts a tremendous impact on these U.S. border communities.

The question of whether a "green-carder" must reside in the United States has been the subject of extensive controversy. Since the Immigration Act of 1965 was passed, it has been charged that the prevailing law actually forbids the practice of commuting, since the reentry rights of a resident alien are limited to a person who is "returning to an unrelinquished lawful permanent address."[14] Before 1965, the Immigration and Naturalization Service (INS) reasoned that any commuter who had been accorded the "privilege of residing permanently" was always entitled to enter the country. The Immigration Act of 1965, however, altered the previous statutory language. The amended language restricted informal entry to "an immigrant lawfully admitted for permanent residence who is returning from a temporary visit abroad."

Accordingly, one legal scholar has concluded: "No distortion of the English language could result in a finding that the commuter was entering the United States after a temporary visit abroad to return to his principal, actual dwelling place. Rather, the commuter was simply leaving this foreign home and entering the United States to work."[15] He argued that since 1965 the status of border commuters is "not merely lacking in statutory authority" but "actually prohibited."

In November 1974, however, the U.S. Supreme Court rejected this position by upholding the INS position that daily and seasonal commuters are lawful permanent residents returning from temporary absences abroad.[16] In essence, the court said that it was not going to overthrow fifty years of administrative practices by judicial decree.

It is true that commuting resident aliens could simply move across the border and live in the United States if they wished or were forced to do so. In this sense, they have legal rights that far exceed those of nonimmigrant workers. Yet as long as they live outside the United States but work within the United States, commuters function in the labor market in a manner that is identical to that of nonimmigrant workers.

"VISITOR WORKERS"

There is another more pernicious form of nonimmigrant workers whose status, unlike that of commuting "green-carders," is not debatable. It is simply illegal. It too involves thousands of people along the southern border region, who pass through the border checkpoints to jobs in border towns of the United States. They are not citizens of the United States, nor have they any claim to citizenship. For lack of a better name, they can be called "visitor workers." Technically, these people are part of the group called nonimmigrants as defined in the Immigration Act of 1924.

The phenomenon of "visitor workers" arises because citizens of Mexico living permanently in Mexican border towns are accorded special privileges to enter the United States at will. These Mexican citizens can request an I-186 card from the INS. Because the card is white, its bearers are known as "white-carders." The I-186 card is for persons known as "legal visitors" or "border-crossers." The bearer of the card can remain in the United States for up to seventy-two hours on any single visit and is restricted to a radius of twenty-five miles of the border, but he is forbidden to seek employment or be employed anywhere in the United States.

In fact, however, there is little to stop a "white-carder" from working, and many do. For this reason they constitute a form of nonimmigrant labor, although they are seldom mentioned in the discussion of the topic. Prior to January 1, 1969, a white card was valid for only four years. Since that time, however, the cards are no longer dated. As a result, no expiration date appears on the card. The INS claimed that the renewal procedures were too time-consuming and costly. The result is that many Mexican citizens regularly cross the border to work within the border perimeter.[17] Given the immense number of people who cross the border checkpoints each day, as well as pressure to expedite the flow, little can be done by border officials to police the prohibition against working which is supposedly a condition for receipt of the I-186 card.

Exactly how many "white-carders" there are is a mystery. The INS reports that over 2.2 million cards were issued in the Southwest region between 1960 and 1969.[18] There is no reliable estimate of how many have been issued since then. How many of these "white-carders" abuse their visiting privileges by seeking employment is unknown. The fact that the statistics of "green- and white-carders" are either vague or completely unknown was labeled "astonishing" by the comprehensive Mexican-American Study Project conducted in 1970.[19]

THE BRACERO PROGRAM (THE MEXICAN LABOR PROGRAM)

With the advent of World War II, the military manpower requirements of the United States and its related manufacturing labor needs led to assertions that another labor shortage existed in the agricultural sector. The growers of the Southwest had foreseen these developments before the Pearl Harbor attack in 1941. They made two historic decisions. First, the pool of cheap labor in Mexico was to be tapped to fill the manpower deficit; second, the federal government was again to be the vehicle of deliverance.[20]

The initial requests of U.S. growers in 1941 for the establishment of a contract labor program were denied by the federal government. By mid-1942, however, the U.S. government had come to favor the program, but the government of Mexico balked at the prospect of a formal intergovernmental agreement. The unregulated hiring of Mexican citizens by foreign nations is prohibited by Article 123 of the Mexican Constitution of 1917. Moreover, in the 1940s the Mexican economy was flourishing; Mexican workers feared they might be drafted; there were bitter memories of the efforts to "repatriate" Mexican immigrants (both legal and illegal entrants) in the 1930s; and there was knowledge of the discriminatory treatment accorded people of Mexican ancestry throughout the Southwest.

Negotiations between the two governments, however, resulted in a formal agreement in August 1942. The Mexican Labor Program, better known as the "*bracero* program," was launched. Mexican workers were supposed to be afforded numerous protections with respect to housing, transportation, food, medical needs, and wage rates. Initiated through appropriations for Public Law (P.L.) 45, the program was extended by subsequent enactments until 1947. *Braceros* were limited exclusively to agricultural work. Any *bracero* found holding a job in any other industry was subject to immediate deportation. When the agreement ended on December 31, 1947, the program was continued informally and without regulation until 1951. In that year, under the guise of another war-related labor shortage, the *bracero* program was revived by P.L. 78. The legislation was extended on three separate occasions, until the program was unilaterally terminated by the United States on December 31, 1964.

Under P.L. 78, only Mexican workers could be contracted for work in the United States. Employers were required to pay the prevailing agricultural wage, provide free housing and adequate meals at a reasonable charge, and pay all transportation costs from the work site to the government reception centers near the border. As was the case before, these requirements often were not met.[21] The workers were also exempt from both social security and income taxes, which meant that they received more income than would a citizen worker employed at the same gross wage rate.

In Mexico, the national government determined the allocation process for workers to be chosen from among its states. The state governments, in turn, made similar decisions for their cities and other political subdivisions. Understandably, the Mexican government had sought to spread out the job opportunities geographically rather than set off a mass internal migration to the border region. Unfortunately, however, there were far more applicants than available slots. Hence, corruption in the allocation process became widespread at the local level. Potential workers were often forced to pay a *mordida* (i.e., a bribe, or literally, "a bite") if they wished to be chosen.

The *bracero* program demonstrated well how border policies can adversely affect citizen workers in the United States—especially, in this case, the Chicanos, who composed the bulk of the southwestern agricultural labor force. Agricultural employment in the Southwest was removed from competition with the nonagricultural sector. At the program's peak, almost 500,000 *braceros* annually were working in

the agricultural labor market of the Southwest. The availability of
Mexican workers significantly depressed existing wage levels in some
regions, modulated wage increases that would have occurred in their
absence, and sharply compressed the duration of the employment
period for which many citizen farm workers could find jobs.[22] Citizen
farm workers simply could not compete with *braceros*. Employers
found *braceros* especially appealing since these workers were virtual
captives, totally subject to the unilateral demands of employers. The
anomalous dependency of *braceros* led to extensive human abuse by
employers. Most of the provisions for the protection of wage rates
and working conditions for the *braceros* were either ignored or cir-
cumvented.[23] The *bracero* program was also a significant factor in the
rapid exodus of rural Chicanos between 1950 and 1970 to urban
labor markets, where they were often poorly prepared to find employment and housing.[24]

THE WEST INDIES LABOR PROGRAM

Following the precedent set by the Mexican *bracero* program in 1942,
a similar nonimmigrant program was set up to recruit workers from
the British West Indies. The governments of the British West Indies
(including Jamaica, St. Lucia, St. Vincent, Dominica, and Barbados)
and the Bahamas entered into an intergovernmental agreement with
the U.S. government in April 1943 pertaining to the supply of agricultural workers. This set the foundation for the British West Indies
Program (BWI program). The BWI program was designed to respond to concerns voiced by employers along the entire East Coast
that they too were experiencing wartime manpower shortages. Since
many of the BWI workers spoke English, they had some advantage to
employers over the Mexican workers in the *bracero* program.

The original BWI program was established largely on the basis of
informal memorandums of understandings, but it drew its legislative
authority from the aforementioned provisions of the Immigration
Act of 1917, which permitted the admission of temporary workers
from the western hemisphere. Like the *bracero* program, it too was
formalized on the basis of P.L. 45 from 1943 through 1947. Although
their aggregate number was small—about 24,000 a year—when compared to the *bracero* program, BWI workers were substantial in the
particular agricultural labor markets in which they were employed.[25]
Eleven East Coast states participated in the program, but Florida was
by far the largest recipient. In addition, the BWI program differed
substantially from the Mexican program in that, during the war years,

employment of BWI workers was also permitted in nonagricultural work. In 1945, for instance, there were 16,000 BWI workers employed outside agriculture (mostly in foundaries, food processing, and lumber).[26]

From 1947 to 1952, the BWI program was reconverted into a contract-labor program as permitted under the temporary-worker provisions of the Immigration Act of 1917. The contracts were made on a tripartite basis between U.S. employers, the foreign workers, and the governments of the participating nations of the West Indies. The U.S. government was not a direct participant. The travel and recruitment expenses were paid entirely by the U.S. employers. These workers were employed only in agriculture.

A review of the BWI program in 1951 by the president's Commission on Migratory Labor condemned the administration of the program. In particular, it attacked the lack of "vigilance for the protection of living and working standards" of the workers.[27] Whereas the same report was critical of the adverse wage effects of the Mexican program on citizen workers in the Southwest, it did not make a parallel contention about the wage effects of the BWI workers.

During the legislative debate over the continuation of the *bracero* program in 1951, the BWI program was specifically included in the original draft of what was to become P.L. 78. But because East Coast employers—especially those in Florida—specifically requested that the BWI workers not be included in the pending bill, the language was changed to say that only "agricultural workers from the Republic of Mexico" were to be permitted. These employer groups preferred to keep the BWI program as it was. Hence, BWI workers were excluded from the legislation, and the program continued as a temporary labor program as permitted under the Immigration Act of 1917.

Policy Development: The Immigration and Nationality Act of 1952

In 1952, the nation's immigration law was significantly recodified and revised by the Immigration and Nationality Act of 1952 (also known as the McCarren-Walter Act). This statute did maintain the principle of previous legislation whereby all people entering the nation must be classified as either immigrants or nonimmigrants. But the concept of nonimmigrants became infinitely more complex. Twelve classes of nonimmigrants are specified. These classes are, in turn, subdivided into a number of subclasses. An unofficial convention has evolved whereby the individual classes and subclasses are identified by the letters and numbers of the section of the act that created them. Several of the classes cannot work in the United States (e.g., visitors for pleasure or aliens in transit); others can work in the United States, but their work has little or no impact on the U.S. labor market (e.g., foreign ambassadors, officials of international organizations, or representatives of foreign news media); and there are those who do work directly in the labor force.[28] It is this last group that has relevance for present purposes.

Among the nonimmigrants who work among the regular labor force, there are several classifications whose numbers are small and who are free to change jobs at will. They are not contractually linked to employers. Among these are foreign students who may legally work (F-1 workers) if they receive permission from the INS. There is little labor-market controversy about this group. Most of the other nonimmigrants are under some binding contractual obligation to their employers. Among these are H-1 workers (people of distinguished merit and ability such as opera singers, actors, and various professionals); J-1 workers (people who are exchange visitors in various international programs); and L-1 workers (people who are intracompany transferees of multinational corporations). Most of these workers are in white-collar occupations or other highly skilled jobs.

The H-2 program for "other temporary workers" has generated most of the controversy over the years. In quantitative terms, the largest number of H-2 workers was in 1969, when 69,288 workers were admitted. Since then, the number has declined steadily to around 23,000 a year at the end of the 1970s. Within the H-2 classification, the largest single occupation has generally been farm workers.[29] As the size of the overall program has declined, the proportion of the total who are agricultural workers has risen to over one-third the annual number of H-2 workers.

The nonagricultural H-2 workers are highly dispersed in their occupational makeup. The largest segment of the nonagricultural group is composed of professional and technical workers. These are generally people "of lower status than those entering on H-1 visas or as exchange visitors."[30] The largest number of these are writers, artists, and entertainers, followed by athletes and musicians. The remainder of the H-2 workers are largely various white-collar and skilled workers.

Supposedly, H-2 workers can be admitted only "if unemployed persons capable of performing such service or labor cannot be found in this country."[31] It is up to the Department of Labor to decide whether citizen workers are actually available. In making its determination, a system of adverse wage rates and working conditions was devised. These wage rates and working conditions are set by regulations issued by the Department of Labor. They must be met by any employer who seeks to hire foreign workers under the H-2 program. The intention of the requirements is to avoid depressing existing work standards. The final entry decision, however, resides not with the Department of Labor but with the Department of Justice. Negative admission decisions by the former are frequently overruled by the latter.

It should also be noted that H-2 workers do not pay social security taxes, which means that the employer does not deduct the tax from the employee's wage and that the employer does not have to match the tax, as he does in the case of citizen workers. H-2 workers are also exempt from unemployment-compensation taxes on employer payrolls. Hence, an employer may secure H-2 workers at wage costs below those that must be paid to citizen workers, even when the nominal wage rates are the same to both.

Although many nonagricultural workers enter under contractual terms that tie them to specific employers, their wages and working conditions are not controversial and they are not seen as any particular threat to citizen workers. Instead, they tend to reflect rather than influence their respective labor markets. The same cannot be said for the agricultural H-2 workers or for the use of the entire H-2 worker program in the territories of Guam and the Virgin Islands. These cases require special mention.

AGRICULTURAL H-2 WORKERS

The H-2 program in agriculture incorporates all the undesirable features of the *bracero* program. The workers are totally dependent upon the employers. Eligibility to be chosen for the program often depends upon one's contacts with governmental officials. It is often considered a privilege to be selected. Corruption in the selection process is rampant in most of the source countries. If chosen, the worker can be assured only of the opportunity to return again if his work and attitude please the American employer, because the employer may "request by name" a set proportion (usually 50 percent) of a year's H-2 workers to return the next year. In effect, this means that the workers compete with one another on terms that are very favorable to the employer. If any part of the worker's demeanor is unsatisfactory to the employer, the worker may be deported without an appeal. Given this system, "it is little wonder that H-2 aliens are 'hard working and diligent.' "[32]

During the late 1970s and early 1980s, four rural industries on the continental United States used H-2 workers primarily:[33] the sugarcane industry in Florida (using BWI workers); the apple industry in a number of eastern states (using BWI workers); the woodcutting industry in Maine (using Canadians); and sheepherding in the western states (using Peruvians and Mexicans). In addition, there have been several small programs involving row-crop harvesting in isolated rural border areas of Texas in which Mexican workers have been admitted as H-2 workers. The users of H-2 workers may seem to be incidental industries. Nonetheless, they all have powerful and influential political lobbies, as the Department of Labor has regularly found when it has tried to tighten the regulations governing H-2 availability.[34]

Although several countries serve as sources of agricultural H-2 workers, about 90 percent of their annual numbers are from the British West Indies (predominately from Jamaica). Their current employment status as H-2 workers represents a continuation of the BWI labor program. As previously indicated, employers of BWI workers resisted the move in 1951 to include their workers under P.L. 78, which extended the *bracero* program. As a result, the BWI workers were assumed into the H-2 program that began in 1952. Throughout the 1950s, the use of BWI workers increased, but when compared to the coexisting *bracero* program the BWI program was dwarfed in size. Consequently, the BWI program escaped the close scrutiny leveled on its southwestern counterpart. Also, again compared to the *bracero* program, there was virtually no involvement of the U.S. government in the administration of the BWI program.

When the *bracero* program was phased out in the early 1960s, however, attention of the government turned to the BWI program, for despite their differences in legislative authorization, the programs were so similar that the same arguments that led to the termination of the *bracero* program seemed to apply to the BWI program. Reflecting the tone set by the civil rights movement, the Department of Labor began to issue more restrictive regulations in the early 1960s for all H-2 workers. The restrictions prompted a congressional effort in 1965 to shift the labor-certification and wage-setting authority of the H-2 program from the Department of Labor to the Department of Agriculture.[35] This employer-backed initiative sought to facilitate temporary foreign worker entry but was narrowly defeated.

In 1977, "major and very controversial revisions in the regulations" for H-2 workers were proposed by the Department of Labor.[36] The thrust of these regulations was further restriction of the H-2 program. In August 1977, however, a district court ordered the Department of Labor to admit 5,000 apple pickers—mostly Jamaicans—despite opposition from the Department of Labor.[37] The secretary of labor at the time said that the court's order "undermines my fundamental responsibility to approve the importation of temporary foreign workers only when domestic workers are unavailable."[38]

The employers of H-2 agricultural workers have contended that the major alternative to H-2 workers is illegal immigrants. There are already illegal immigrants involved in East Coast agriculture, but the incidence is seen by employers to be less than has been the case in agriculture in the Southwest. The East Coast employers claim that the termination of the *bracero* program in the Southwest led to the widespread use of illegal immigrants in that region.[39]

THE H-2 PROGRAM ON GUAM AND THE VIRGIN ISLANDS

One recent study of nonimmigrant labor programs concluded that, while the number of H-2 workers in the American labor force is small, these workers have had "severe impacts on micro labor markets,"[40] and their experiences make "good social science laboratories."[41] The extensive use of the H-2 program on both Guam and the Virgin Islands provides precisely that opportunity for insight.

The Virgin Islands Labor Program. The Virgin Islands were purchased by the United States from Denmark in 1917. They are an unincorporated territory, and the native-born islanders are U.S. citizens. Until 1938, islanders were allowed to travel freely in search of employment. In 1938, however, the immigration acts of 1917 and 1924 were applied to the islands. All aliens who resided in the islands as of 1938 were deemed to be legal resident aliens. The needs of the United States for unskilled civilian labor in order to build fortifications on St. Thomas to defend the Panama Canal during World War II attracted large numbers of illegal workers from the French and British islands. These workers were initially allowed to stay, and later efforts to force them to leave proved unsuccessful.

With the Immigration and Nationality Act of 1952, the groundwork was laid for the formalization of a process that had already begun. Beginning in 1956, a temporary worker agreement was reached between the United States and the representatives of the government of the nearby British Virgin Islands. In 1959, it was geographically extended to include the many islands of the British, French, and Dutch West Indies.[42] These agreements limited employment of H-2 workers from these areas in the agricultural and tourist industries.

By the early 1960s, however, H-2 workers were permitted to take "any job."[43] Furthermore, the jobs ceased being of a temporary nature and became permanent jobs. By the end of the 1960s, "alien labor constituted roughly half of the Virgin Islands labor force,"[44] or 13,288 persons out of a total labor force of 27,000. One explanation for the increasing dependence on H-2 workers was that the wage rates in many of the occupations in which they worked were too low relative to the extremely high cost of living on the islands to attract citizen workers.[45] By this time, the problems of housing, education, and social conditions for H-2 workers had become so "terrible" that the H-2 workers had become "the biggest single problem" on the islands.[46] It was even feared that if there was a change in status from H-2 workers to resident aliens (which would entitle them to become naturalized citizens in five years), the native-born population could lose political control of the islands.

In 1970, the immigration statutes were amended to allow the spouses and children of nonimmigrants (called H-4s) to join the H-2 workers. The effect of this seemingly humane gesture to allow family reunification was not foreseen on the Virgin Islands. The number of H-4 persons reached 30,000 by the mid-1970s. The aforementioned housing and social problems were all exacerbated. The island government sought to exclude the children of H-2 workers from attending public schools, but a federal court intervened to stop the practice.[47]

By this time, it was obvious that "the non-immigrant aliens virtually determined the prevailing wage in many occupations."[48] The Department of Labor issued indefinite labor certifications to these H-2 workers and allowed them to change jobs freely. There would in effect no longer be any effort made to see if citizen workers were available. Procedures were established whereby the nonimmigrants could become resident aliens and eventually citizens if they wished, thus dropping all pretense of the existence of a temporary work program.

The temporary worker experience on the Virgin Islands has led to resentment of the H-2 workers by the citizen population and to discrimination against them. This seemed inevitable in view of the fact that the program fostered the development of a "two-tiered labor market" that has made the island's "economy dependent upon foreign labor in spite of relatively high unemployment."[49]

The Guam Labor Program. Guam was ceded to the United States in 1898 as part of the treaty ending the Spanish-American War. Citizenship to residents of Guam was extended in 1950, while the Immigration and Nationality Act of 1952 was the first immigration statute to apply to Guam.

Only after the recapture of Guam from Japan in 1944 did Guam became the major military center it remains today. World War II left Guam's economy devastated. During the rebuilding process, many island residents sought jobs with the federal government because the private economy had been virtually destroyed. It was against this backdrop that efforts began to import nonimmigrant labor for a wide variety of jobs. In May 1947, workers from the Philippines and other islands were hired for short-term contracts. The authority for the programs was merely an exchange of intergovernmental notes.[50] No attempt was made to reconcile this program with existing immigration laws until 1953, when the INS accepted the Navy's contention that foreign workers were needed for defense purposes and granted blanket H-2 status to all such workers. In March 1957, H-2 workers employed in Guam could get an initial permit for six months with the maximum possibility of extension set at three years.

Meanwhile, a "triple-wage system" developed on the island: a high wage for "statesiders," a medium wage for natives of Guam, and a low wage for H-2 workers.[51] Criticism of the "slave wages" paid to H-2 workers and of the extensive racketeering among labor recruiters in the Philippines began to mount. Consequently the INS announced in 1958 that the program for nondefense employers would be phased out. A total of 791 workers were affected. Despite protests from many business groups, a three-year phaseout of the nondefense-related H-2 worker program began in March 1959.

In 1960, the INS decided that the H-2 defense worker program should also be phased out. It feared that the H-2 program was becoming a permanent part of the Guam economy and that few efforts were being made to train citizen workers for the jobs that H-2 workers held. In its place, however, nonimmigrant workers continued to be admitted under the separate parole authority given the attorney general to admit persons temporarily for "emergency reasons" deemed to be in the public interest.[52] Thus, to meet the requests of defense contractors and the military on the island, nonimmigrants from the Philippines were again admitted. The practice continued until 1975. A second parole program was also instituted in 1962 for temporary workers to do reconstruction work after the island was hit by two severe typhoons in 1962 and 1963. This program was terminated in

May 1970, when it was decided that the H-2 program was more appropriate for construction workers than the parole procedures.[53]

The revival of the H-2 program came in response to employer
claims of labor shortages in light of expanding tourism and growth in
the island's population. The government of Guam also sought H-2
workers as a means of developing new industries, especially in agriculture and fishing. Recognition of the long-existing problem of
noncompliance by H-2 workers with the terms of their admission did
not appear until the 1970s,[54] when a 1977 Department of Labor
report labeled the labor-market conditions on Guam "abysmal."[55] By
1976, there were 4,293 H-2 workers in a civilian labor force of 26,910.
It was of greater importance that H-2 workers composed 82 percent
of people employed in construction, 47 percent of those employed in
agriculture, and 15 percent of those in manufacturing.[56] With
reference to working conditions, the report is resplendent with examples of worker abuse by employers and by labor recruiters. It also
details the inability of the Department of Labor to enforce existing
labor standards in an environment in which many workers are completely beholden to their employers. The H-2 workers, in these circumstances, have become preferred workers for employers. Citizen
workers cannot compete with them on these terms. Hence, citizens
often became unemployed or underemployed. As the report noted,
"alien workers constitute such a large proportion of the work force
that the wages at which they are certified are the prevailing wage
rates."[57] It noted that the wages and working conditions were not set
by a free market but are the result of government policies.

Nonimmigrants and Illegal Immigration

In addition to the various nonimmigrant programs of both the past
and the present, there are millions of illegal immigrants who have
simply bypassed the complexities of the existing immigration laws. It
is necessary to mention the topic of illegal immigration during a discussion of nonimmigrant labor policy for two reasons. First, illegal
immigrants constitute a totally unregulated nonimmigrant labor program. Officially, illegal immigrants are unsanctioned, but because the
immigration policy of the United States is so blatantly tolerant of their
presence, it can be argued that they are unofficially both condoned by
the government and welcomed by many employers. Certainly, any
nation that has a policy placing no penalties on employers for hiring

illegal immigrants, that gives voluntary departures back to their homelands to 95 percent of those who are apprehended, and that has an immigration enforcement agency chronically underfunded and understaffed can hardly be taken seriously in its claims to oppose illegal entry.

The second reason for raising the issue of illegal immigration is that a number of proposals to address that problem have included various nonimmigrant programs among their array of policy solutions. Hence, not only have the questions of illegal immigration and nonimmigrant policy been intertwined in the past, but there are also many suggestions being made that would increase the relationship in the future. A sampling of these suggestions warrant review.

PROPOSALS FOR NEW NONIMMIGRANT PROGRAMS

One such proposal draws from the experience in western Europe with foreign worker programs[58] and assumes that the United States has a demand for "cheap and industrious"[59] unskilled workers. Under this plan, a Mexican worker could get a visa to cross the border and find any job within three months. If a nonseasonal job is found, the worker would request a contract for up to twelve months. At the end of the period, the contract could be renewed "on the spot." If only seasonal contract work is found, the worker must return to Mexico, but he could be requested by name the following year. If a Mexican cannot find work after three months or for a full season, he or she must return to Mexico or face deportation.[60]

While in the United States, the worker would be accorded all economic and social rights. Nonseasonal workers could be joined by their families when their first contract was renewed. For seasonal workers, family reunification would be possible at the latest after two consecutive seasons in the United States. Following five years of continuous residence, the worker could apply for permanent resident alien status. Stiff penalties would be placed on employers who hire illegal immigrants, as well as on illegal immigrants who were apprehended, but no further changes would be made in the existing immigration system.

Another proposal for "a temporary labor program" would permit foreign workers to be employed "in regions and sections" identified by the U.S. Department of Labor "as in need of labor."[61] The decision would be made after consultation with employers and labor unions.[62] Temporary workers could be granted immigrant status if they could find work for a set period of time. The basis of this plan is that "if a worker worked here, he could build up some rights to settle."[63] Family members would be able to accompany the temporary immigrants and would be entitled to all social programs available to citizen workers. This proposal includes additional recommendations for enforcement of existing labor laws and sanctions against employers of illegal immigrants.

A third proposal focuses on the existing H-2 program and recommends the instituting of a "new" H-2 program[64] by enlarging the existing program "in certain jobs" for periods of one year, with renewals of up to three years. After this period, the H-2 worker would have to leave the country and join the pool of job-seekers back in his country. The next cohort of job-seekers would not be admitted until the preceding group departed as scheduled.

This "new" H-2 program would be limited to the expansion of "those jobs of low skill, low paid work which currently are often filled by undocumented aliens and are not very attractive to American unemployed workers."[65] In order to avoid the local social pressure associated with Europe's guestworker programs, dependents of the foreign workers should be excluded.[66] This requirement should be made clear to all applicants for H-2 permits, and those who cannot accept this condition "should not volunteer for the program."[67] Furthermore, the Department of Labor should "conduct an outreach program in the source countries" to "ensure that appropriate types and numbers of persons are recruited" that will "meet the actual needs of U.S. labor markets."[68] The wage rates would be set by the Department of Labor to be at "comparative wage minimums" to those paid to domestic workers. As such, these established rates could be used to "sustain present labor standards," and they could be gradually raised in order to be attractive to more citizen workers.

The proponents of this program realize that if this proposal is intended to absorb the jobs currently held by illegal aliens, it would have to enroll "hundreds of thousands" of H-2 holders a year[69] and could easily overburden the existing administrative capability of the appropriate government agencies. The thrust of this proposal is also designed for workers from Mexico, although, unlike the first proposals, it does not restrict it to them.

Many of these alternatives were responding to a Carter administration initiative in 1977 for comprehensive immigration reform.[70] Although denying any interest in a *bracero* program, the administration felt that an expanded temporary work program might meet the needs of some employers while not adversely affecting citizen workers.

In response to the Carter proposals for immigration reform, Congress passed legislation that established a commission to study all dimensions of the nation's immigration policy. The Select Commission on Immigration and Refugee Policy was formed in early 1979 and issued a comprehensive report on March 1, 1981.[71] Included within its discussion of nonimmigrant issues were recommendations pertaining to the H-2 program. Acknowledging that the H-2 program has been the source of criticism, the commission still concluded that "a continuation of the program is necessary and preferable to the institution of a new one."[72] Several suggestions were made to streamline the administration of the program. It recommended that employers be required to pay both social security and unemployment compensation payroll taxes on all H-2 workers in order to remove "inducements to hire H-2 workers over U.S. workers,"[73] and it concluded that there should be no new temporary worker program as part of any strategy to combat illegal immigration.[74]

By the time the commission issued its report, the Carter administration was no longer in office. The Reagan administration responded to the report by forming a review committee called the Task Force on Immigration and Refugee Policy, which was chaired by the attorney general. The task force released its response on July 30, 1981.[75] In its report, no mention was made of the H-2 program, but it did propose that an "experimental temporary worker program for Mexican nationals" be established.

AN ASSESSMENT OF THE "NEW" ROLE
OF NONIMMIGRANT LABOR POLICY

It should be apparent from the review of the evolution of nonimmigrant labor policy that its use to combat illegal immigration is a departure from its historic role. The renewed interest in nonimmigrant worker programs is not based on the existence of a demonstrated need in the labor market. Unemployment rates in the United States have consistently ranked among the highest of any of the Western industrialized nations. Moreover, the unemployment rates among Hispanics, blacks, women, and youth far exceed the national aggregate unemployment rates. All the proposals for new nonimmigrant labor programs are designed exclusively for recruiting more workers for unskilled and semiskilled occupations in primarily low-wage industries. These are precisely the same labor markets in which those citizen workers with the highest unemployment rates are already disproportionately found. No one is suggesting that there be a foreign-worker program to supply more workers for white-collar occupations. Such proposals would lead to charges of a "brain drain" from source nations, and the domestic opposition of these privileged and protected workers in these labor markets could be counted upon to kill any such idea at the moment of its conception. It is because these programs may benefit the privileged of our society while adversely affecting only opportunities for the less fortunate and the least politically organized that such proposals are even given serious consideration.

There is no evidence that citizen workers will not do the work that nonimmigrants and illegal immigrants do. This fundamental point is asserted without empirical evidence to support it, usually by those who support new or expanded nonimmigrant work programs.[76] No one can cite a single occupation or industry—including farm work—in which the vast majority of present workers are not U.S. citizens. Hence, it cannot be the *type* of work that makes nonimmigrant and illegal immigrant workers attractive. Rather, it is the prevailing wage rates and working conditions that determine worker availability. Each year thousands of people apply for the privilege of collecting garbage in New York City and San Francisco, but they do not do so in many other communities. Why the difference in worker supply? It is because garbage collectors in these two cities are highly paid, unionized, and enjoy liberal fringe-benefit packages. The same can be said of applicants for apprenticeship positions in the building, machinist, and printing trades. Supply always exceeds demand, although the jobs are often dirty, dangerous, and physically demanding. Again, it is not the type of job but the associated economic benefits that explain why applicants seek such jobs in such great numbers. For the contentions of the advocates of nonimmigrant worker programs to be valid, they must be willing to argue that there will be too few citizen workers available no matter what the wages or benefits associated with certain occupations in the American economy. Certainly no one can seriously argue this point when it is refuted everyday by millions of low-wage citizen workers who are already working in all the same industries for which nonimmigrant workers are sought.

As every student of elementary economics knows, it is impossible to separate the employment effects from the wage effects whenever there is a change in the supply of labor. Hence, the presence of nonimmigrant workers would affect not only job opportunities but also wage levels in any given labor market. It is these wage effects that are part of the attractiveness of illegal immigrants to American employers. Employers are able to obtain workers at less cost than would be the case in their absence. This does not mean that most employers exploit these workers by paying wages below the federal minimum wage. Rather, it merely means that their presence serves to mitigate pressures that would otherwise increase wages in certain low-wage labor markets over time. New or expanded nonimmigrant labor programs could be expected to have exactly the same dampening effect on wage movements.

The real reason nonimmigrant labor programs have persisted long after their initial justifications (which were usually associated with wartime labor shortages) had passed and new programs are sought by employers is more subtle. It rests upon experience that shows that nonimmigrant workers can be expected to be more docile in their demands than citizen workers. Citizen workers know that they have job entitlements, which include minimum-wage protection but also extend into a number of other areas, such as overtime pay provisions, safety requirements, equal employment opportunity protection, and collective bargaining rights. If foreign workers are available, an employer can often escape these additional employee entitlements. Even though foreign workers (and illegal immigrants too, for that matter) may technically be covered by these work standards, their presence creates a situation in which these safeguards cannot be guaranteed in practice. Since the enforcement mechanisms of most of these laws are based largely upon employee complaints or actions, the foreign workers are likely to be reluctant to do anything about abuses for fear of losing their jobs, even if they know their rights. Given the job alternatives available in their native lands, they may not even perceive that the violations are being exploitative.

Thus, even if the wage rates an employer must pay are identical for foreign workers and for citizen workers, the foreign workers will be preferred. It is the knowledge that nonimmigrant workers will be less likely to make demands for job rights or to join unions that makes them highly prized.

Another flaw in these proposals is their intended size. A foreign worker program will not help to reduce illegal immigration unless the program involves a significant number of people, at least 500,000 to 750,000 a year. The larger the program, however, the greater the adverse impact on citizens. On the other hand, a small-scale program will not be a deterrent to illegal entry. There must be some limit on the size of the program, but what will stop others who are not selected from coming, or others whose period of work has expired but who wish to remain from staying? A new or expanded nonimmigrant labor program does not resolve any of the current problems with the nation's immigration policies, and it adds a host of new ones.

Moreover, most of the discussions of the need for more nonimmigrant workers assume that the program would be a bilateral arrangement with Mexico. But times have changed in both Mexico and the United States. Indeed, it is no accident that the momentum for immigration reform began in the 1960s and 1970s, when there was heightened domestic interest in civil rights and the eradication of poverty. The point is that illegal immigrants are streaming into the United States from almost every country in the world. President Jimmy Carter's message accompanying his immigration proposals stated that sixty countries are "regular" sources of illegal immigration.[77] Fifteen countries have been identified as the *major* source countries of illegal immigrants.[78] Although about 90 percent of the illegal immigrants apprehended annually are from Mexico, this figure results from the concentration of INS enforcement efforts on illegal entrants in the Southwest. It is doubtful that Mexicans compose as much as 60 percent of the total stock of illegal immigrants in the United States. The non-Mexicans generally enter the country with proper documents but overstay their visas. Many of these people faced economic deprivation and political persecution in their own country that are worse than conditions confronting Mexicans. In fact, compared to many other countries in the Caribbean, Central America, and South America, economic life in Mexico is considerably better.[79] Many of these other countries in the Caribbean—such as Haiti, the Dominican Republic, Jamaica, Barbados, and Trinidad—have large black populations. All of them, and others that could be cited, are regular sources of "visa abusers." In many instances, the question is not why so many of them seek entry into the United States but why any of them stay behind, given the bleak futures that confront them. The same can be said of many Asians from Hong Kong, Korea, the Philippines, and Malaysia, which are also major sources of illegal immigration. Hence, it is unlikely that any foreign-worker program could be (or should be) restricted to workers from Mexico. If it was, it would be seen as an unfair, or even racist, proposal, and it would have nothing to offer as a solution to the equally difficult problem of illegal entry from other nations of the world.

Let History Sound a Tocsin Warning

Nonimmigrant labor policy in the United States is an aberration. The nation has a complex body of immigration law that presumes to regulate the conditions under which people from other nations can enter the United States. Every person who legally enters the nation is classified as being either an immigrant or a nonimmigrant. The nonimmigrant group is essentially the residual of all categories of entrants who are not specifically given immigrant status. Accordingly, it is not really surprising that nonimmigrant labor policy seems to be composed of makeshift arrangements that rationalize exceptions from the basic immigration statutes.

Indeed, some features of nonimmigrant labor policies are not only logical but also beneficial to the economy and the quality of life of the nation. Foreign students sometimes need jobs to supplement inadequate stipends provided by their own governments; soccer and hockey fans wish to see a higher grade of sports performance than American players can provide, so foreign players are allowed to play for American teams; opera stars and rock bands from abroad are allowed to perform for American audiences in the name of cultural diversity; visiting professors from abroad add to the quality of many university programs; and the growth of multinational corporations has required the stationing of foreign executives to administer their enterprises. These examples, as well as numerous others, suggest that nonimmigrant labor policy provides a realistic and desirable flexibility to what would otherwise be a rigid immigration system.

Yet within the broad dimensions of nonimmigrant labor policy there has also been a programmatic history that is not so easy to rationalize. It has usually involved the employment of workers who are less skilled and less talented than available citizen workers but who are, nonetheless, similar in employment capabilities to certain segments of the American labor force. In these instances the sanguine attitude surrounding nonimmigrant labor policy is challenged, for as the history of these endeavors reveals, there has been a persistent theme of misuse and abuse of these programs. Because these nonimmigrant workers are unskilled and from relatively impoverished backgrounds, they are often easy prey for corrupt selection processes over which the United States has little control. Once in the United States, these workers are often subject to working conditions that they may perceive to be desirable (relative to the alternatives in their homelands) but that affect the attractiveness of the jobs to citizen workers. To the degree that the prevailing working standards tend to

reflect the presence of the nonimmigrant workers in their specific
labor markets rather than those of the general labor market, citizen
workers gravitate elsewhere and become less available. Employers
soon not only become dependent on nonimmigrant workers but also
come to prefer nonimmigrants.

As a predictable consequence, these nonimmigrant programs for
less-skilled and less-talented workers are consistently implemented
under the guise of being temporary worker programs, but in fact they
become long-term sources of labor supply. They become an in-
stitutionalized phenomenon that exerts a narcotic influence on all
parties who become involved in the employment process. Employers,
foreign workers, and source countries become addicted to the programs. The original rationale for their existence becomes lost in the
reasoning process that justifies their continuation.

Nonimmigrant worker programs in low-wage industries are of
interest to employers primarily as a means of either reducing their
costs of production or enhancing their control over their workers.
Nonimmigrant low-wage workers are attractive because of their dependency upon their employers. Citizen workers who compete with
these nonimmigrant workers find that their existing work conditions
usually either become frozen or decline. Under few circumstances will
they improve. Efforts to establish unions are thwarted or, at a minimum, made more difficult.

There are other pernicious long-run effects of nonimmigrant
labor programs in low-wage industries. Namely, when workers come
from economically less developed countries to the United States, they
are made aware of opportunities that for many were beyond their
imagination. The relatively higher wages and broader array of job
opportunities will induce many to find ways to remain. Rather than
being an alternative to illegal immigration, nonimmigrant labor in the
past fostered the phenomenon. To the degree that such programs
have contributed to illegal immigration, it is generally the citizen
workers who are least capable of defending themselves in the competition for jobs that bear the brunt of the competition. It is not surprising, therefore, that among the strongest voices in opposition to
proposals to expand temporary worker programs have been those
from groups most closely associated with the protection of opportunities for low-wage workers.[80]

Nonimmigrant labor policy has played a long and often controversial role in American immigration policy. It will continue to do so,
especially if any of the suggestions to include within various immigration reform packages a new or expanded nonimmigrant worker pro-

grams are taken seriously. Extant nonimmigrant labor programs of the nation are in need of extensive reform.[81] Such is especially the case for H-2 workers in low-wage industries. Despite their relatively small scale (when compared to the size and effects of the flows of legal immigrants, illegal immigrants, and refugees), the influences of nonimmigrant labor policies have at times been significant and sometimes even perverse.

Notes

1. Joseph G. Rayback, *A History of American Labor* (New York: Free Press, 1966), p. 120.
2. Philip Taft, *Organized Labor in American History* (New York: Harper & Row, 1964), p. 305.
3. Ibid.
4. Samuel P. Orth, "The Alien Contract Law and Labor Law," *Political Science Quarterly* 22 (March 1907):60.
5. Ruth Allen, "The Capitol Boycott: A Study in Peaceful Labor Tactics," in *Chapters in the History of Organized Labor in Texas* (Austin: University of Texas, 1912), p. 46.
6. Michael J. Piore, *Birds of Passage: Migrant Labor and Industrial Societies* (New York: Cambridge University Press, 1979), pp. 149–150.
7. George C. Kiser and Martha Woody Kiser, *Mexican Workers in the United States: Historical and Political Perspectives* (Albuquerque: University of New Mexico Press, 1979), chap. 1.
8. Ibid., p. 10.
9. The term *bracero* is a corruption of the Spanish word *abrazo*, which means "arm." Literally, the term means "one who works with his arms."
10. George C. Kiser, "Mexican American Labor Before World War II," *Journal of Mexican American History* 2 (1972):130.
11. *Karnuth v. Albro*, 279 U.S. 231 (1929).
12. David S. North, *The Border Crossers: People Who Live in Mexico and Work in the United States* (Washington, D.C.: Trans-Century Corporation, 1970), p. 72.
13. Anna-Stina Ericson, "The Impact of Commuters on the Mexican-American Border Area," *Monthly Labor Review* 93 (August 1970):18.
14. Sheldon L. Greene, "Public Agency Distortion of Congressional Will: Federal Policy Toward Non-Resident Alien Labor," *George Washington Law Review* 40 (March 1972):442, citing 8 C.F.R. 211.1(b)(1)(1971).
15. Ibid., p. 443, citing 8 U.S. 65 (1974).
16. *Saxbe v. Bustos*, 419 U.S. 65 (1974).
17. For example, see the discussion in Gilberto Cardenas, "Manpower Impact and Problems of Mexican Illegal Aliens in an Urban Labor Market" (Ph.D. diss., University of Illinois, 1976), p. 31.

18. Senate Committee on Labor and Public Welfare, Subcommittee on Migratory Labor, *Hearings on Migrant and Seasonal Farmworker Powerlessness*, 91st Cong., 1st and 2d sess., May 21, 1969, pt. 5A, p. 2145.

19. Leo Grebler, Joan W. Moore, and Ralph Guzman, *The Mexican American People* (New York: Free Press, 1970), p. 73.

20. Ernesto Galarza, *Merchants of Labor: The Mexican Bracero Story* (Charlotte, N.C.: McNally & Loftin, 1964); Richard Craig, *The Bracero Program: Interest Groups and Foreign Policy* (Austin: University of Texas Press, 1971); and Carey McWilliams, *North from Mexico* (New York: Greenwood Press, 1968), pp. 265–267.

21. Galarza, *Merchants of Labor*, chaps. 8–16.

22. President's Commission on Migratory Labor, *Migratory Labor in American Agriculture: Report* (Washington, D.C.: Government Printing Office, 1951), pp. 56–59.

23. Galarza, *Merchants of Labor*, chaps. 12, 13, 15, 16, 17.

24. Vernon M. Briggs, Jr., *Chicanos and Rural Poverty* (Baltimore: Johns Hopkins University Press, 1973), p. 29.

25. Senate Committee on the Judiciary, Subcommittee on Immigration, *The West Indies (BWI) Temporary Alien Labor Program: 1943–1977* (Washington, D.C.: Government Printing Office, 1978), p. 8.

26. Ibid.

27. President's Commission on Migratory Labor, *Migratory Labor*, p. 58.

28. David S. North, *Nonimmigrant Workers in the U.S.* (Washington, D.C.: New Trans-Century Foundation, 1980), chap. 1.

29. Edwin P. Reubens, *Temporary Admission of Foreign Workers: Dimensions and Policies*, Special Report no. 34 (Washington, D.C.: National Commission for Manpower Policy, 1979), p. 15.

30. Ibid.

31. 8 U.S.C. sec. 1101 (a)(15)(H)(ii) (1952).

32. Philip L. Martin and David S. North, "Nonimmigrant Aliens in American Agriculture" (Paper delivered at the Conference on Seasonal Agricultural Labor Markets in the United States, Washington, D.C., January 10, 1980), p. 20.

33. Ibid., pp. 11–12.

34. Ibid., p. 9.

35. U.S. Senate, *The West Indies Program*, p. 25.

36. Ibid., p. 26.

37. *Frederick County Fruit Growers Assoc., Inc., v. Marshall*, Civil no. 77-0104(H) (W.D. Va., filed August 30, 1977).

38. U.S. Senate, *The West Indies Program*, p. 36.

39. Ibid., pp. 37–40.

40. North, *Nonimmigrant Workers*, p. 27.

41. Ibid., pp. 29–30.

42. House Committee on the Judiciary, Subcommittee on Immigration, Citizenship, and International Law, *Nonimmigrant Alien Labor Program on the*

Virgin Islands of the United States (Washington, D.C.: Government Printing Office, 1975), pp. 5–6.

43. Ibid., p. 15.

44. Ibid.

45. Ibid., p. 16.

46. Ibid., p. 17.

47. Ibid., pp. 33–34 (the case was *Hosier* v. *Evans*, 314 F. Supp. 316 [Virgin Islands, 1970]).

48. Ibid., p. 36.

49. Mark J. Miller and William W. Boyer, "Foreign Workers in the U.S. Virgin Islands: Lessons for the United States" (Paper delivered at the 1980 meetings of the American Political Science Association, Washington, D.C.), p. 18.

50. House Committee on the Judiciary, Subcommittee on Immigration, Citizenship, and International Law, *The Use of Temporary Alien Labor on Guam* (Washington, D.C.: Government Printing Office, 1979), p. 4.

51. Ibid., p. 13.

52. Sec. 212 (d) (5) of the Immigration and Nationality Act of 1952.

53. House Committee on the Judiciary, *Use of Temporary Labor*, p. 25.

54. Ibid., p. 49.

55. Cover letter from Walter J. Haltigan, regional administrator to Floyd E. Edwards, administrator of the U.S. Department of Labor, which accompanied report entitled "Guam Alien Labor Situation," San Francisco, California, May 16, 1977, p. 1.

56. Ibid., p. 18 of the report.

57. Ibid., p. 40 of the report.

58. W. Roger Böhning, "Regularizing Undocumentados," World Employment Programme, Working Paper No. 36 (Geneva: International Labor Organization, 1979).

59. Ibid.

60. Ibid.

61. Charles B. Keely, *U.S. Immigration: A Policy Analysis* (New York: Population Council, 1979), p. 60.

62. Ibid.

63. Ibid., p. 61.

64. Edwin Reubens, *Temporary Admission of Foreign Workers: Dimensions and Policies,* Special Report No. 34 of the National Commission for Manpower Policy (Washington, D.C.: Government Printing Office, 1979).

65. Ibid., p. 59.

66. Ibid.

67. Ibid.

68. Ibid.

69. Ibid., p. 60.

70. Office of the White House Press Secretary, "Message of the President to Congress on Illegal Immigration," Washington, D.C., August 4, 1977, p. 6.

71. Select Commission on Immigration and Refugee Policy, *U.S. Immigration Policy and the National Interest,* Final Report, March 1, 1981 (Washington, D.C.: Government Printing Office, 1981).

72. Ibid., p. 227.

73. Ibid., p. 228.

74. Ibid., p. 45.

75. U.S. Department of Justice, "U.S. Immigration and Refugee Policy," Washington, D.C., July 30, 1981.

76. See Böhning, "Regularizing Undocumentados"; Wayne A. Cornelius, *Mexican Migration to the United States: Causes, Consequences, and U.S. Responses* (Cambridge: MIT Center for International Studies, 1978); and Piore, *Birds of Passage,* chap. 2.

77. Office of the White House Press Secretary, "Message of the President," August 4, 1977, p. 7.

78. Domestic Council of the White House, "Preliminary Report of the Domestic Council Committee on Illegal Immigrants," December 1976, p. 39. (This report was subsequently made the final report of the committee.)

79. Calvin P. Blair, "Mexico: Some Recent Developments," *Texas Business Review* 51 (May 1977): 98–103.

80. Labor Council for Latin American Advancement, "Declaration of Albuquerque and Employment Action Program," Conference Report of the National Conference on Jobs for Hispanics, August 1979, p. 10.

81. For a thorough review of needed reforms in all forms of nonimmigrant labor policy, see North, *Nonimmigrant Workers,* pp. 169–172.

CHAPTER 5

Immigration Debate
and Demographic Policy

Ellen Percy Kraly

Concern over the demographic impact of immigration to the United States has had a long history. In the last quarter of the nineteenth century, the immigration of Asians was banned because of the effect of Asian workers on domestic labor conditions, particularly along the West Coast, and perhaps more important because of the implications of further Asian immigration for ethnic composition. Francis Walker, chief of the U.S. Bureau of the Census during this period, suggested that native fertility was declining as a result of concern that the massive influx of "alien" cultures created a bad social environment in which to raise children. Moreover, the concentration of southern and eastern European immigrants in northeastern urban industrial centers at the turn of the century was a factor in mounting popular support for the immigration quota acts of the 1920s. Historically, these issues, economic conditions, ethnic composition, and regional concentration, are all facets of the *social demographic impact* of immigration on U.S. society, economy, and polity.

Similar issues show contemporary life. Advisory groups such as Zero Population Growth and the Environmental Fund are concerned not simply with the impact of immigration on U.S. population growth but also with the effect of legal and illegal immigration on working conditions of U.S. labor and on the cost of national, state, and local services. Response in Miami and Puerto Rico to the influx of Cuban refugees has taken the form of racial and ethnic conflict. Officials from New York City have argued that the number of illegal or undocumented immigrants should be included in 1980 census counts in order to secure federal funds appropriate for the social and economic support of the de facto metropolitan population.

Clearly the relationship between immigration and national population dynamic is a component of broader national social and economic processes. The purely demographic issues, however, have yet to be resolved. The consequences of both overall international migration to and from the United States and immigration of specific groups—such as aliens admitted for permanent residence, refugees, and undocumented aliens—for national population size, growth, and composition have yet to be determined.

This chapter is intended to clarify the discussion of the role of immigration in U.S. population dynamics. The historical impact of international migration on national demography will be examined in order to illustrate traditional analytic issues. Contemporary issues focus on the consequences of international migration streams for U.S. population growth, age structure, and ethnic composition. The anticipation of future demographic impacts of immigration policy is tentative; problems in conceptualization and measurement of "demographic impact" are underscored. Here we present areas of demographic research needed for immigration policy analysis by demonstrating weaknesses of existing methodology and available data. Speculations about policy analysis in this substantive area emphasize the need for explicit national policy goals concerning immigration and population.

The Old "A Nation of Immigrants" Bit:
Problems of Analysis

Historical analyses of the role of immigration in U.S. demography have had to deal with the problem of defining who is an immigrant or alien and who is a native. Of course, the philosophical or political implication of the choice of any particular definition, for example, "new" versus "old" immigrant stock, is the distinction between who is "more" American and who is "less" American. The issue of definition is critical in analyses of the contribution of immigration to national population growth because the United States is truly a nation of immigrants. Even if one considers the population of American Indians as the original citizens of the newborn nation, the growth and redistribution of the nation's population can be almost totally attributable to immigrants (and here we include slaves from Africa) and their descendants.

The historical impact of immigration on U.S. population and society has been measured in a variety of ways. Many studies have relied on the concept of nativity or lifetime migration. The population of people of foreign birth has been used to represent the immigrant component of the national population. This population excludes children of immigrants and people who were born in the United States but have resided for a significant length of time outside the country. Table 5.1 presents these data for the United States, based on census counts from 1850 to 1970.[1] These data present stock data on population composition according to nativity. People who emigrated or have not survived to the time of the census are excluded from these census counts.

Table 5.1   *Total and Foreign-Born U.S. Population, 1850–1970*

Year	Total Population, Number	Foreign-Born Population	
		Number	Percent
1850	23,191,876	2,240,535[a]	9.7
1860	31,443,321	4,096,753[a]	13.0
1870	38,558,371	5,567,229	14.4
1880	50,155,783	6,679,943	13.3
1890	62,947,714	9,249,547	14.7
1900	75,994,575	10,341,376	13.6
1910	91,972,266	13,515,886	14.7
1920	105,710,620	13,920,692	13.2
1930	122,775,046	14,204,149	11.6
1940	131,669,275	11,594,896	8.8
1950	150,697,361	10,347,395	6.9
1960	179,323,175	9,738,091	5.4
1970	203,211,926	9,619,302	4.7

Source: U.S. Bureau of the Census, *Historical Statistics of the United States: Colonial Times to 1970,* Bicentennial Edition, pt. 2 (Washington, D.C.: Government Printing Office, 1975), series A 91–104 and 105–118.

[a] White foreign-born population only.

Interpretation of such data must be made with care. Data on nativity allude only to the social and economic consequences of lifetime migration such as geographic concentration and ethnic influence. Moreover, these data do not speak to the issue of the contribution of immigration to national population growth. Analyses of the historical role of immigration in national population dynamics have used a variety of methodologies representing diverse perspectives on the process of immigration.

Table 5.2 *Components of U.S. Population Change, 1940–1978*

| Year | Total Population Change | | Components of Population Change (percent) | |
	Number (in thousands)	Percent	Natural Increase	Net Civilian Immigration
1940–1944	7,713	100.0	92.6	7.4
1945–1949	11,369	100.0	89.8	10.2
1950–1954	13,452	100.0	89.4	10.6
1955–1959	14,789	100.0	89.3	10.7
1960–1964	13,837	100.0	87.5	12.5
1965–1969	10,625	100.0	80.3	19.7
1970–1974	8,899	100.0	79.8	20.2
1975–1978	6,783	100.0	78.5	21.5

Source: U.S. Bureau of the Census, *Current Population Reports*, Series P-25, no. 802, Population Estimates and Projections (Washington, D.C.: Government Printing Office, 1979), Table 1.

One straightforward approach to assessing the impact of immigration on national population dynamics analyzes the components of population growth—that is, the apportioning of population change among births, deaths, and net immigration during some period of time. Table 5.2 presents historical data on the proportion of population growth due to net immigration to the United States. In recent decades the proportion of population growth resulting from migration has been increasing, while overall growth of the population has been decreasing.

This type of analysis has several important shortcomings. First, the statistical concept of "net immigration" requires data on international migration *to and from* the United States of both aliens and U.S. citizens. National data have been available historically only for alien immigration and for alien emigration between 1907 and 1957; the migration patterns of U.S. citizens are not represented in these official statistics. (This point will be discussed more fully below.) Second, this analytic approach disregards the magnitude of total change in population; net immigration may account for a very large proportion of a very small amount of total population growth. Third, the partitioning of the three demographic processes disregards the interrelationships among the volume of births, deaths in the United States, and the net flow of immigrants. Charles Keely describes this critical conceptual issue:

Combining births and deaths into natural increase and immigration and emigration into net migration presupposes that only native-born are among those who died and that only foreign-born emigrated. This is clearly an unwarranted assumption. In short, to measure the effect of immigration on population growth requires a partitioning of the deaths and emigration components into native and foreign-born.[2]

Formal demographic studies by Campbell Gibson, and Simon Kuznets, and Ernest Rubin, among others, consider the role of immigration in U.S. population growth in terms of the other demographic processes, mortality and fertility.[3] For example, Gibson has estimated the contribution of immigration to the historical growth of the U.S. population by taking into account the mortality and fertility of foreign-born immigrants in a decade. The general approach is to estimate the "end-of-a-period population attributable to the population present at the beginning of a period."[4] Gibson's results include estimates of the contribution of net immigration to population change during each decade between 1790 and 1970 and an estimate of the contribution of immigration to the size of the U.S. population in 1970:

> The estimated 35.5 million net immigrants of the 1790–1970 period contributed an estimated 98 million to the 1970 population. Most of these immigrants came to the United States before the first World War and experienced much higher fertility than is presently occurring in the United States or than seems likely in the forseeable future.[5]

The work of Gibson has made an important contribution to the general discussion of the role of immigration in U.S. population dynamics by considering the subsequent demographic characteristics of immigration streams—that is, fertility and mortality—as an important component of "impact." As important, however, is the presentation of the details of the methodology used, implicit and explicit assumptions, and biases inherent in the available data. For example, Gibson makes clear that the population attributable to immigration does not represent an ethnic group:

> Estimates of the population attributable to immigration since a specified date refer not to actual individuals, but rather to their *numerical equivalent,* due to the "reproductive mixing" of persons resident at a specified date (and their descendants) with persons immigrating subsequently (and their descendants).[6]

Thus, an important conceptual, if not politically important, point is made. Moreover, Gibson points out the limitations of available data on emigration and intergenerational fertility change of U.S. natives and the foreign-born.

In sum, Gibson's historical work speaks to general theoretical and methodological issues that remain of critical interest to social and policy scientists working in this area. Let us proceed to illustrate these issues within a contemporary context.

The Demographic Impact of Contemporary Immigration Policy

Contemporary discussion of the relationship between U.S. immigration and demographic policies includes a number of policy relevant themes.[7] There is, for instance, increasing demand by policymakers for information on the social-demographic characteristics and consequences of such specific groups of migrants as undocumented or illegal migrants and refugees. Federal interest focuses on the relationship between immigration streams and specific sectors of domestic social and economic policies such as social security programs, tax revenues, local labor market conditions, and growth in industrial sectors. Finally, concern is mounting over the consequences of contemporary patterns of immigration for ethnic relations and stratification in the United States. Demographers, however, have yet to resolve the essential demographic characteristics of immigration, whether defined broadly or specifically. Policy-relevant research in this area must begin by assessing basic demographic impacts of migration such as population growth and composition.

The Commission on Population Growth and the American Future sought to consider the relative advantages of positive net population growth for standard of living and quality of life in the United States.[8] Research supporting the discussion and recommendations of the commission concerned both the impact of alternative levels of population on national economic and social life and the feasibility of achieving a stationary population. In the latter regard, Ansley Coale prepared an important theoretical statement concerning the effect of immigration on population growth.[9] Coale was able to conclude that existing levels of immigration to the United States were *consistent* with the path to a stationary population.

> Thus, we find that continued migration at the levels that we are now experiencing would require only a slight further reduction in the fertil-

ity of the American population. The stationary population that would result would be about eight percent bigger than it otherwise would, and it would also have a slightly older age composition. It is not true that continued immigration at current, fairly substantial levels implies indefinitely continued growth of the American population.[10]

Coale's surprising conclusions played an important role in the recommendations on immigration agreed upon by the commission:[11] "The Commission recommends that immigration levels not be increased and that immigration policy be reviewed periodically to reflect demographic conditions and considerations."[12]

The popular belief had been that any net additions to the population through immigration when natural increase was zero would result in an exponentially growing population. Using formal demographic techniques, Coale was able to show that age structure of both fertility behavior and immigrant streams was a critical variable in the analysis of the long-term effect of immigration on annual population growth. Coale calculated the population of foreign-born people implied by constant age-specific rates of immigration. The size of the national population would be increased by this foreign-born population. A stationary national or total population could be achieved if recent levels of net immigration are maintained and if national fertility levels remain near replacement. Coale's line of reasoning has been rigorously extended by Thomas Espenshade, Leon Bouvier, and Brian Arthur, who demonstrate that a stationary population results from *any* stable pattern of below-replacement fertility given a constant (positive) pattern and level of annual immigration.[13]

Coale's research has served as a basis for subsequent research in this area. Coale, and subsequently Espenshade et al., have developed theoretical formulations concerning the role of international migration in population dynamics. Consistent with the peripheral status of immigration studies in the American demographic community, however, the significance of Coale's commission paper, now a decade old, goes largely unnoticed.[14]

Coale's analysis considers stable population dynamics—that is, the interrelationships among age-specific rates of fertility, mortality, and net immigration which remain constant over time.[15] Given positive net immigration at stable age-specific rates, the fertility of native-born women must compensate both for incoming migrants and for births occurring to foreign-born women in order to maintain a stationary population. This adjustment in native fertility is required to maintain a constant annual number of births, a characteristic of a stable population. The number of births produced by the foreign-born population is dependent upon the level and age pattern of immigrant fertility and size of the foreign population. Constant age-specific levels of annual net female immigration imply a stationary population of foreign-born females.

It is this stationary population of the foreign-born which increases the ultimate size of the national stationary population. The size of the stationary population P_t, in the absence of net immigration, is equal to the average life expectancy at birth, e_0, times the annual number of births, B_t. With positive net annual immigration in the form of constant age-specific levels of immigration, the stationary population would be increased in the following way:

$$P_t = e_0 B_t + FB_t \qquad (1)$$

where FB_t is the size of the stationary population of foreign-born people. According to Coale's calculations, levels of annual net immigration as of 1972 imply a national stationary population that would be about 8 percent larger than the population in the absence of net immigration.

The size and structure of the foreign-born female stationary population is the basis for Coale's method of calculating the reduction in native-born fertility necessary to assure a constant level of annual births. Coale's methodology accommodates variable levels of immigration and variable fertility characteristics of the foreign-born population. The model thus does not assume any singular pattern or trend in fertility among immigrant groups.

The following equation allows Coale to calculate the fertility of native-born women necessary to maintain a stationary population given positive net immigration:

$$R_n = 1.0 - (B_f/I)(I/B_t)(T_f/2.11) \qquad (2)$$

where

  R_n is the net reproduction rate of native-born women,
  B_f is the annual female births occurring to foreign-born women,
  I is the annual number of female immigrants,
  B_t is the total annual female births, and
  T_f is the total fertility rate of foreign-born women.

One can see that in the absence of annual immigration R_n will be equal to 1.0. By applying an age-specific fertility schedule to the foreign-born female population, Coale calculates B_f. For his empirical analysis, Coale assumed 3.6 million births in the stationary population, or B_t, to be equal to 1.756 million female births. However, the value of B_t serves only to construct the ratio representing the level of annual immigration in relation to a U.S. stationary population and has no impact on the model in and of itself. Similarly, the value of I, while assumed as 223,000 in Coale's empirical example, has relevance for the model only in the form of the ratio, I/B_t, indicating the level of immigration relative to births. The recent levels of annual net immigration relative to total annual births in the stationary population and replacement-level fertility of the foreign-born imply a native fertility level only slightly below replacement, 1.97 births per woman.

Coale bases his conclusions on empirical examples of native fertility and recent alien immigration to the U.S. Espenshade et al. have developed a general model role of immigration in stable population dynamics. These demographers have shown that any constant level and age pattern of annual immigration is consistent with the attainment of a national stationary population when native fertility is below replacement. The situation holds for all levels and age patterns of below-replacement fertility. The work of Coale and of Espenshade et al. presents both a theoretical statement on the role of international migration in stable population dynamics[16] and a methodology by which to assess the demographic consequences of current patterns of international migration. While the concept of stable population exists as an ideal type, its usefulness as an analytic tool is clear in the capacity to focus on particular policy variables, in this case immigration and fertility.

These formal demographic analyses use empirical examples of annual immigration to calculate the size of the ultimate U.S. stationary population. Accordingly, we must consider the issue of the availability of data for the empirical analysis of the demographic impact of immigration. The issue of data on international migration is not specific to formal analyses, such as that of Coale; it is general to research on the consequences of immigration for social, economic, and demographic structures.

The statistical concept adopted by Coale is that of net civilian immigration used by the U.S. Bureau of the Census in its series of population projections. Net civilian immigration includes alien immigration with the addition of citizens born overseas, citizens returning, net Puerto Rican migration, an estimate of the combined emigration of native and foreign born and of refugees. However, as in Coale's commission paper, the generic term "immigration" is used for net

Table 5.3 *Recent Average Annual Alien Immigration, Emigration, and Net Alien Immigration and Estimates of Recent Annual Net Civilian Immigration, by Sex and Age, United States, 1975 (numbers in thousands)*

Age	Immigration[a] Number	Emigration[b] Number	Net Immigration Number	Net Immigration Percent	Estimated Annual Net Civilian Immigration Number	Estimated Annual Net Civilian Immigration Percent
	Average Annual Alien				*Estimated Annual Net Civilian Immigration*	
	Total Population					
All ages	377.4	113.1[c]	264.4	100.0	400.0	100.0
0–4	31.4	1.8	29.6	11.2	53.8	13.5
5–9	34.2	1.5	32.6	12.3	33.9	8.5
10–14	32.0	10.5	21.5	8.1	34.4	8.6
15–19	36.7	7.4	29.2	11.0	40.4	10.1
20–24	50.7	5.8	44.9	17.0	56.2	14.1
25–29	57.5	7.2	50.3	19.0	65.3	16.3
30–34	40.3	14.8	25.6	9.7	39.9	10.0
35–39	26.7	13.5	13.2	5.0	23.8	6.0
40–44	19.1	8.8	10.3	3.9	16.5	4.1
45–49	14.2	7.4	6.8	2.6	12.0	3.0
50–54	10.1	5.4	4.6	1.7	9.6	2.4
55–59	8.6	5.1	3.5	1.3	7.5	18.8
60–64	6.6	4.8	1.8	0.7	4.7	1.2
65–69	4.7	4.4	0.3	0.1	1.0	0.3
70–74	2.6	4.8	−2.2	−0.8	0.5	0.1
75+	2.2[d]	9.8[e]	−7.6	−2.9	0.5	0.1
	Female					
All ages	201.2	66.5	134.7	100.0	212.6	100.0
0–4	15.6	1.0	14.6	10.8	27.0	12.7
5–9	16.8	0.0	16.0	11.9	16.8	7.9
10–14	15.9	5.0	10.9	8.1	17.1	8.0
15–19	20.0	3.8	16.2	12.0	21.7	10.2
20–24	32.6	4.1	28.5	21.2	34.8	16.4
25–29	30.0	6.5	23.5	17.4	33.6	15.8
30–34	19.7	8.7	11.0	8.2	19.5	9.2
35–39	13.2	6.5	6.7	5.0	21.1	9.9
40–44	9.8	4.4	5.4	4.0	8.8	4.1
45–49	7.5	3.5	4.0	3.0	6.6	3.1
50–54	5.6	2.9	2.7	2.0	5.7	2.7
55–59	4.9	3.0	2.0	1.5	4.6	2.2
60–64	3.9	3.2	0.7	0.5	0.8	1.4
65–69	2.7	2.2	0.6	0.4	0.3	0.4
70–74	1.6	3.0	−1.4	−1.0	0.3	0.1
75+	1.4[d]	7.9[e]	−6.5	−4.8	0.4	0.2

(continued)

civilian immigration and can lead to interpreting the concept as net alien immigration. The estimate of net civilian immigration used in the projection series of the Bureau of the Census and used by Coale has been 400,000 annual net immigrants (the age structure of net immigration assumed by the bureau has varied in the projection series), a level which is strikingly close to annual numbers of aliens admitted for permanent resident status. Thus, the effect of what should be interpreted as a hypothetical level of net civilian immigration, a demographic concept, is usually interpreted as a result of annual gross alien immigration, a legal concept.

The importance of conceptual clarity was demonstrated by Keely and Kraly in their analysis of the effect of net alien immigration on U.S. population growth and the path to a stationary population.[17] They sought to refine the concept of "immigration" by relating estimates of annual alien immigration and alien emigration. The resulting estimate of annual net alien immigration was then incorporated into projections of the U.S. population consistent with the Bureau of the Census series. Similarly, Coale's analysis was replicated using the refined statistical concept.

The analysis of net alien immigration hinges on the incorporation of data on alien emigration. Data on emigration from the United States are not collected by the federal government.[18] However, through demographic analysis of stock data available from the decennial census and flow data on alien immigration collected by the U.S. Immigration and Naturalization Service (INS), estimation of the emigration of foreign-born persons has been possible. Robert Warren and Jennifer Peck, demographers at the U.S. Bureau of the Census,

---

Sources: Charles B. Keely and Ellen Percy Kraly, "Recent Net Alien Immigration to the U.S.: Its Impact on Population Growth and Native Fertility," *Demography* 15 (August 1978), Table 3; U.S. Bureau of the Census, *Census of Population: 1970,* Vol. 2: Subject Reports, PC(2)-1A, *National Origins and Language* (Washington, D.C.: Government Printing Office, 1973); U.S. Bureau of the Census, *Census of Population: 1970,* Vol. 2: Subject Reports PC(2)-1C, *Persons of Spanish Origin* (Washington, D.C.: Government Printing Office, 1973).

[a] Average 1969–1973.
[b] Average 1960–1970.
[c] Alien emigrants 0–4 years are estimated by assuming the same ratio between age-groups 0–4 and 5–9 years as that displayed in the native emigrant population, as estimated by Robert Warren, U.S. Bureau of the Census, personal communication, March 16, 1976.
[d] People not reporting age are included in the 75+ age-group.
[e] Alien emigrants 75–79 and 80–84 years in the original data are assumed as the open age-group, 75+ years.

134   ELLEN PERCY KRALY

Table 5.4 *Projections of U.S. Population, Assuming Selected Estimates of Annual Net Immigration, 1975–2050 (numbers in thousands)*

| | Projections of the U.S. Population | | |
| | U.S. Bureau of the Census, 1975[a] | | Revised |
Year	Series II-X	Series II	Estimates
1975	213,448	213,448	213,448
1980	220,386	222,495	221,797
1985	229,323	233,793	232,357
1990	237,830	244,887	242,673
1995	244,726	254,557	251,528
2000	250,044	262,815	258,934
2005	254,814	270,688	265,914
2010	259,936	279,071	273,367
2015	264,996	287,522	280,863
2020	268,887	294,898	287,268
2025	271,071	300,613	292,002
2030	271,836	304,929	295,331
2035	271,877	308,537	297,943
2040	271,701	311,949	300,351
2045	271,708	315,571	302,961
2050	272,172	319,673	306,044

Source: Charles B. Keely and Ellen Percy Kraly, "Recent Net Alien Immigration to the U.S.: Its Impact on Population Growth and Native Fertility," *Demography* 15 (August 1978), Table 4.

[a] The Series II Projections assume the "most realistic" trends in fertility which are intermediate to other projected fertility trends. Series II-X assumes zero net immigration; Series II assumes an annual level of 400,000 net alien immigration and the age distribution by sex shown in Table 5.3. These total population figures are those resulting from the replication of U.S. Bureau of the Census projections. Percentage differences between the displayed population figures and published totals for each year are generally less than 0.5 percent.

have estimated foreign-born emigration from the United States during the decade 1960–1970 using INS immigration data in relation to decennial census tabulations.[19] The estimation procedure combines a component method of measuring population change with survival techniques. Essentially, the foreign-born population in 1960 is "survived" to 1970, while annual immigration during the decade is incorporated. The extent to which the resulting foreign-born population of 1970 differs from that enumerated in the 1970 census of population provides an estimate of foreign-born emigration during the dec-

Table 5.5 Projected Population Growth Between 1975[a] and Specified Year and Proportion of Growth due to Immigration, Assuming Selected Estimates of Annual Net Alien Immigration, 1980–2050 (numbers in millions)

Year	Projected Net Civilian Immigration (U.S. Bureau of the Census)			Estimated Net Alien Immigration (Keely and Kraly)	
	Series II-X	Series II			
	Population Growth	Population Growth	Proportion due to Immigration[b]	Population Growth	Proportion due to Immigration
1980	6.9	9.0	23.3	8.3	16.9
1985	15.9	20.3	21.7	18.9	15.9
1990	24.4	31.4	22.3	29.2	16.4
1995	31.3	41.1	23.8	38.1	17.8
2000	36.6	49.4	25.9	45.5	19.6
2005	41.4	57.2	27.6	52.5	21.1
2010	46.5	65.6	29.1	59.9	22.4
2015	51.5	74.1	30.5	67.4	23.6
2020	55.4	81.5	32.0	73.8	24.9
2025	57.6	87.2	33.9	78.6	26.7
2030	58.4	91.5	36.2	81.9	28.7
2035	58.4	95.1	38.6	84.5	30.9
2040	58.3	98.5	40.8	86.9	32.9
2045	58.3	102.1	42.9	89.5	34.9
2050	58.7	106.2	44.7	92.6	36.6

Source: Charles B. Keely and Ellen Percy Kraly, "Recent Net Alien Immigration to the U.S.: Its Impact on Population Growth and Native Fertility," Demography 15 (August 1978), Table 5.

[a] N = 213,448.
[b] For example, Series II for 1985: 20.3 − 15.9 ÷ 20.3 = 21.7%.

ade. Using this technique, Warren and Peck have estimated that approximately 1.065 million people of foreign birth emigrated from the United States between 1960 and 1970.[20]

Keely and Kraly combine these results with data on average annual alien immigration from 1969 to 1973 to produce estimates of recent annual net alien immigration. These data are shown by age and sex in Table 5.3. The final column of Table 5.3 presents the estimate of net civilian immigration used in the Census Bureau projections for comparison.

The effect of refining the concept of immigration to net alien immigration is presented in Table 5.4, in which population projections incorporating estimates of net civilian immigration and net alien immigration are compared. The proportion of population growth from 1975 to 2050 as a result of immigration in the selected projection series is given in Table 5.5.

The results of Keely and Kraly's analysis are obvious: Lower annual net immigration implies a significantly smaller national population over the course of seventy-five years and a smaller proportion of growth due to immigration. The importance of the research rests not so much in the actual numbers, however, but in the demonstrated effect of the refinement of statistical concepts. This point is similarly illustrated theoretically by replicating Coale's methodology using the revised estimates of net alien immigration.

Different assumptions about the annual level and age structure of net immigration result in different relationships of the foreign-born population to the national stationary population. Table 5.6 shows the size and age structure of the ultimate foreign-born female population implied by the estimates of annual female immigration adopted by Coale for his analysis. Similarly, the foreign-born female populations implied by the Census Bureau's 1975 estimates of annual female immigration and by our revised estimates of net female alien immigration are also shown. A comparison of the three foreign-born populations indicates that both estimates of the Bureau of the Census, that published in 1970 and adopted by Coale and that published in 1975, imply ultimate foreign-born populations larger than that implied by the revised estimates of recent net alien immigration. The ultimate foreign-born population derived from the Census Bureau estimates of 1975 is 47.1 percent larger than that implied by the revised estimates.

The stationary population of foreign-born people will increase the size of the national stationary population. Using Equation 1 Coale's estimates of annual net immigration imply a national popula-

Table 5.6   *Ultimate Foreign-Born Female Population Implied by Estimates of Annual Net Female Immigration and Percent of Total Population, by Age (numbers in thousands)*

| | Implied Ultimate Foreign-Born Female Population | | | |
| | Net Civilian Immigration (U.S. Bureau of the Census, 1975) | | Net Alien Immigration (Keely and Kraly) | |
Age	Number	Percent	Number	Percent
All ages	11,228	100.0[a]	7,636	100.0[a]
0–4	67[b]	0.6	36	0.5
5–9	176	1.6	113	1.5
10–14	261	2.3	180	2.4
15–19	357	3.2	247	3.2
20–24	498	4.4	358	4.7
25–29	667	5.9	487	6.4
30–34	797	7.1	571	7.5
35–39	872	7.8	612	8.0
40–44	917	8.2	638	8.3
45–49	945	8.4	653	8.5
50–54	958	8.5	658	8.6
55–59	955	8.5	650	8.5
60–64	928	8.3	626	8.2
65–69	864	7.7	580	7.6
70–74	750	6.7	500	6.5
75+	1,216	10.8	745	9.7

Source: Charles B. Keely and Ellen Percy Kraly, "Recent Net Alien Immigration to the U.S.: Its Impact on Population Growth and Native Fertility," *Demography* 15 (August 1978), Table 6.

[a] Figures may not add to 100.0 due to rounding.

[b] The age distribution is not exactly that published by Coale (Ansley J. Coale, "Alternative Paths to a Stationary Population," in U.S. Commission on Population Growth and the American Future, *Demographic and Social Aspects of Population Growth*, vol. 1 of the Research Reports, ed. Charles Westoff and Robert Parke, Jr. [Washington, D.C.: Government Printing Office, 1972], p. 601). A replication of Coale's analytic procedure revealed slight errors in the originally published figures. The age distribution above is correct, having been verified analytically and through computer simulation. Coale has offered a further refinement of his model in communications with the authors. The refinement affects exposure time to the assumed mortality schedule for each age-group. The effect of this conceptual refinement has no impact on the age schedules presented.

tion that is about 8.4 percent larger than the population in the absence of immigration. The 1975 Census Bureau immigration estimates imply a foreign-born population of approximately 11.2 million, which would increase the size of the national stationary population by 8.5 percent. The revised estimates of net alien immigration result in an ultimate foreign-born population of 7.6 million, implying a national stationary population 5.8 percent larger than that without positive net immigration.

The implications of annual immigration for native fertility required for a national stationary population are illustrated in Table 5.7 for the selected estimates of annual net immigration. These results are based on Equation 2. Each set of the estimates, shown in panels A, B, and C of the table, indicates a unique level of fertility of the native-born population necessary to accommodate immigration and still maintain a national stationary population. Let us assume the level of annual immigration relative to annual births (I/B_t) to be 0.05. Let us also assume that the level of fertility of foreign-born women is at replacement, a total fertility rate of 2.11. Under these assumed immigration parameters, the estimates of annual immigration adopted by Coale, panel A, imply a net reproduction rate of 0.974 and a total fertility rate of 2.06 of native-born women required for a stationary population. Similarly, 1975 Census Bureau estimates of annual immigration, panel B, indicate a net reproduction rate of 0.970 and a total fertility rate of 2.05. The level of native-born fertility indicated by the revised estimates of annual net alien immigration implies a net reproduction rate of 0.966 and a total fertility rate of 2.04 (panel C). A careful comparison of the three panels of Table 5.7, then, indicates that the revised estimates of annual net alien immigration require the largest adjustment in the level of native-born fertility necessary for a national stationary population when the ratio of immigration to total births and foreign-born fertility is held constant.

Coale's model of requisite fertility for the maintenance of national stationary population considers the level of annual immigration a variable. What varies in the above comparison when the amount of immigration is held constant (i.e., the level of immigration is assumed to be 5 percent of total births) is the age distribution of the stationary foreign-born female population. A comparison of the age structures of the foreign-born populations (Table 5.6) indicates that the proportion of females within the childbearing age-groups implied by the revised net alien immigration estimates is relatively larger than either of the Census Bureau estimates. As a result, if both the ratio of immigration to total births and the fertility of the foreign born are held constant, the foreign-born population implied by the revised estimates will produce the greatest number of births. Consequently, native fertility would have to be adjusted to the greatest degree, given the age structure of the revised immigration assumptions.

Can Demographers Speak to the Issue of Ethnicity?

The theoretical work of Coale is an elegant foundation for research evaluating the role of international migration in national population dynamics. This formal analysis, like analyses of the components of population change, however, considers the "immediate" effect of im-

Table 5.7 *Fertility of Native-Born Women Required to Produce a Stationary Population as Implied by Selected Estimates of Annual Net Immigration*

Annual Female Migrants Relative to Annual Total Female Births	Total Fertility of Foreign-born Females	Fertility of Native-Born Women for Stationary Population	
		Net Repro-duction Rate	Total Fertil-ity Rate
A. U.S. Bureau of the Census, 1970			
0.00	—	1.000	2.11
0.05	2.11	0.974	2.06
	2.50	0.969	2.04
0.10	2.11	0.948	2.00
	2.50	0.938	1.98
0.15	2.11	0.922	1.95
	2.50	0.907	1.91
B. U.S. Bureau of the Census, 1975			
0.00	—	1.000	2.11
0.05	2.11	0.970	2.05
	2.50	0.965	2.03
0.10	2.11	0.940	1.98
	2.50	0.929	1.96
0.15	2.11	0.910	1.92
	2.50	0.894	1.89
C. Revised Estimates			
0.00	—	1.000	2.11
0.05	2.11	0.966	2.04
	2.50	0.960	2.03
0.10	2.11	0.932	1.97
	2.50	0.920	1.94
0.15	2.11	0.899	1.90
	2.50	0.880	1.86

Source: Charles B. Keely and Ellen Percy Kraly, "Recent Net Alien Immigration to the U.S.: Its Impact on Population Growth and Native Fertility," *Demography* 15 (August 1978), Table 7.

migration on population growth. The effect of migration occurs only
at entry (or exit) from the population, and thus subsequent offspring
of migrants are accounted to the native population. Migration is conceptualized as a flow event. The longitudinal impact of migrants as a
stock population of ethnics or descendants of immigrants is not considered.

Empirical studies such as that of Campbell Gibson and that of
Simon Kuznets and Ernest Rubin,[21] on the other hand, conceptualize
migration in a markedly different manner. These studies assume that
all descendants of an immigrant stream constitute an "effect" or "impact" of migration. Leon Bouvier's series of population projections
calculated for the U.S. Select Commission on Immigration and Refugee Policy illustrates well this perspective on demographic consequences.[22] He has projected the national population under different
assumptions of the level and age structure of annual net immigration
and levels of national and ethnic fertility (i.e., the fertility of immigrants and their native-born descendants). Bouvier concludes that
during the next century approximately 40 percent of national population size will be attributable to post-1980 immigrants and their descendants.

In this type of analysis, a migrant and his subsequent issue never
cease to be alien. There appears to be a critical problem in conceptualization here, with implications for the objective definition of ethnicity and for the scientific grounding of policy relevant discussion of
the role of immigration in U.S. population dynamics. The source of
the problem lies both in existing concepts and theory concerning
migration[23] and in available demographic data and methodology.

Data available from the federal statistical system reflect the limited conceptual development in the area of ethnic studies. Most
official records and forms rely on self-reporting of race, place of
birth, and, more recently, ethnic background or ancestry. The decennial census schedule has asked place of birth of the respondent since
1850. Birthplace of parents was also asked in each census beginning
in 1870. In the 1980 census, the question on parentage was dropped
and replaced with a question on "ancestry." This question exists to
represent the concept of ethnicity, specifically ethnic identification.
The relationship between ethnic identity, basically a subjective concept, and objective characteristics of ethnicity, such as the number of
generations removed from the original immigrant, and relationship
to the immigrant, cannot be determined using available census data.

Again, the use of formal demographic techniques may be useful in addressing the issue of ethnicity. Specifically, stable population analysis has the potential for considering the demographic characteristics of generations of immigrants. We present here an illustration of such an analytic strategy. Ethnicity is essentially a sociological concept, however, and is virgin territory in the application of demographic models.[24] The following approach is meant to provoke discussion and possibly controversy.[25]

We seek to make no assumptions about the definition of the "impact of immigration" by considering alternative definitions of "migrant" and "ethnic." The approach here is to consider the effect of immigration streams defined according to a variable number of generations of descendants or ethnics. The definition of "effect of immigration" thus becomes a variable whose value is to be determined by the policy analyst.

Stable population analysis has the advantage of holding constant several demographic variables in order to summarize the effect on one dynamic component. Also important for our purposes, stable population analysis has the benefit of demonstrating longitudinal effects of existing demographic regimes, such as demographic trends implied by an immigration policy. This can also be viewed as a disadvantage in that the short-term effect of demographic components of change cannot be demonstrated, reflecting a general limitation of stable population analysis: the lack of empirical grounding of research results. The "ideal type" may or may not be a relevant tool in policy analysis.

We have estimated the size of succeeding generations descending from an original immigrant stream. Annual immigration flow from Mexico has been chosen as an illustration and represents an operationalization of immigration policy. The demographic characteristics of the immigration stream, taken together, represent a variable in this analysis. Here we present two schedules of annual immigration, total and net annual immigration from Mexico. These schedules differ in size and age structure of the immigrant cohort. These immigration schedules are assumed to be constant throughout the analysis. Constant annual immigration levels under stable mortality conditions imply a stationary population of foreign-born persons, or first-generation migrants. If fertility is assumed constant within a generation, regardless of year of entry, then the second generation will likewise constitute a stationary population.

The demographic impact of annual immigration is represented by the size and structure of the population of descendants of immigrants, what we have called the ethnic population. How that population is conceptualized or defined in terms of the number of generations constituting an ethnic population is left open.

The *total* immigration model assumes a level of female immigration of 50,000. The age distribution of immigrants is shown in Table 5.8 and is an average of the age distributions of Mexican female immigrants admitted for permanent residence in 1975, 1976, and 1977.[26] The *net* immigration model is derived from an established level and age distribution of Mexican-born female emigrants. The age-specific levels of emigration are adopted from estimates of rates of emigration of total annual female immigrants, 1960–1970, calculated by Robert Warren and Jennifer Marks Peck.[27] The annual level of *net* immigration is estimated at 20,237 and distributed by age as shown in Table 5.8. The *net* immigration model accounts for the emigration of first-generation or original Mexican immigrants only. The immigration of native-born, Mexican-origin females has not been included in this analysis.

These two models of annual migration are held constant in the calculation of the stationary population of first-generation Mexicans in the United States. (The stationary populations have been calculated using the level and pattern of mortality represented by West family level 24 of model life tables prepared by Ansley Coale and Paul Demeny.[28]) Table 5.8 also presents the populations implied by the two migration models, respectively. Incorporating estimates of Mexican emigration results in a stationary population about 18 percent smaller than that implied by assumptions concerning gross annual immigration.

The calculation of subsequent generations of Mexican ethnics requires assumptions concerning fertility. For the sake of simplicity, in this illustration we have made the assumption that fertility change occurs intergenerationally rather than according to birth cohort. Patterns of intergenerational change are considered a variable. This is appropriate given the relative unavailability of data concerning generational fertility[29] (or mortality) for migrants, a point to which we shall return. We have selected eight models of intergenerational fertility change shown in Table 5.9. Two contrasting theories of migrant adjustment have guided the choice of fertility patterns: the assimilation hypothesis and the minority-group hypothesis. The former theory predicts that the social demographic characteristics of immigrants, such as fertility behavior, will converge over successive generations to those of native population. The fertility models operationalized here assume convergence will occur in the first, second, third,

Table 5.8 *Total and Net Annual Immigration for Mexican Females and Stationary Population of First-Generation Mexican Female Immigrants for Total and Net Immigration Models, by Age (numbers in thousands)*

| | Immigration Models | | | | Stationary Populations[b] | | | |
| | Total Annual Immigration | | Net Annual Immigration | | Total Immigration | | Net Immigration | |
Age	Number	Percent[a]	Number	Percent	Number	Percent	Number	Percent
Total	25.0	100.0	20.2	100.0	1,375.4	100.0	1,134.6	100.0
0–4	2.5	9.9	2.4	11.7	6.2	0.5	5.9	0.5
5–9	2.5	10.0	2.1	10.5	18.6	1.4	17.1	1.5
10–14	2.4	9.5	2.1	10.5	30.8	2.2	27.8	2.5
15–19	3.0	12.1	2.5	12.5	44.2	3.2	39.4	3.5
20–24	4.4	17.4	3.4	16.9	62.6	4.6	54.2	4.8
25–29	3.6	14.2	2.6	13.0	22.3	6.0	69.3	6.1
30–34	2.3	9.2	1.7	8.5	96.7	7.0	80.0	7.1
35–39	1.4	5.4	1.0	5.1	105.5	7.7	86.6	7.6
40–44	0.8	3.2	0.6	3.0	110.4	8.0	90.3	8.0
45–49	0.7	2.8	0.5	2.5	113.2	8.2	92.4	8.1
50–54	0.6	1.9	0.4	1.8	114.6	8.3	93.3	8.2
55–59	0.5	1.9	0.4	1.7	114.4	8.3	92.9	8.2
60–64	0.2	0.9	0.2	0.8	111.8	8.1	90.7	8.0
65–69	0.2	0.9	0.2	0.8	105.6	7.7	85.6	7.5
70–74	0.1	0.3	0.1	0.3	94.1	6.8	76.2	6.7
75+	0.1	0.4	0.1	0.3	164.3	12.0	132.9	11.7

Sources: U.S. Immigration and Naturalization Service, *Annual Reports* (Washington, D.C.: Government Printing Office, 1976, 1977, 1978), Table 9; U.S. Bureau of the Census, *Census of Population: 1970*, Vol. 2: Subject Reports, PC(2)-1A, *National Origins* (Washington, D.C.: Government Printing Office, 1973), Table 17; Robert Warren and Jennifer Marks Peck, "Foreign-Born Emigration from the United States: 1960–1970," *Demography* 17 (February 1980), Table 3.

[a] This age distribution is based on an average of age distributions of Mexican female immigrant admission in 1975, 1976, and 1977 and on 1970 census data on age distribution of Mexican-born female residents who immigrated in 1965–1970.

[b] The population projection package "FIVFIV-SINSIN" (Frederic C. Shorter and David Pasta, *Computational Methods for Population Projections: With Particular Reference to Development Planning* [New York: Population Council, 1974]) was used in calculating these populations.

Table 5.9   *Models of Intergenerational Fertility Change*

Fertility Model	Total Fertility Rate in Generation			
	1	2	3	4+
Assimilation hypothesis				
I	4.00	3.25	2.08	2.08
II	3.25	2.08	2.08	2.08
III	2.08[a]	2.08	2.08	2.08
Minority-group hypothesis				
IV	4.00	3.25	2.50	2.50
V	3.25	2.50	2.50	2.50
VI	2.50	2.50	2.50	2.50
VII	4.00	3.25	2.50	1.80
VIII	3.25	2.50	1.80	1.80
IX	2.50	1.80	1.80	1.80
X	1.80	1.80	1.80	1.80
XI	4.00	4.00	4.00	4.00

[a] A total fertility rate of 2.08 constitutes replacement-level fertility for the level and pattern of mortality of West family level 24.

or fourth generations. The minority-group hypothesis postulates continuing differences in social characteristics between the ethnic population and the host population.[30]

A constant level of fertility is assumed for each generation of migrants, depending on the fertility model being considered.[31] Thus, a fertility level is applied to the first-generation stationary population. The result is a constant number of annual births that constitute *second*-generation Mexicans. This constant stream of annual births implies a stationary population. The size of this population is equal to the annual numbers of births, B, times the life expectancy of birth, e_o. The age structure is fixed by the level and pattern of mortality and the intrinsic rate of population growth, which in a stationary population is zero. (For the age distribution of the stationary population, e_o = 77.5 years (West), see Coale and Demeny.[32] Again, a fertility pattern and level is applied to this second-generation population to calculate a constant annual number of births, members of the *third* generation of Mexican migrants. This procedure can be applied to as many generations of ethnics as desired.

In sum, this illustrative analysis allows the definition of a Mexican ethnic population varying from between one (first) and eight genera-

Table 5.10 *Mexican Ethnic Population Size (in millions)*

Generation	Fertility Model[a]										
	I	II	III	IV	V	VI	VII	VIII	IX	X	XI
	Total Immigration										
1	1.4	1.4	1.4	1.4	1.4	1.4	1.4	1.4	1.4	1.4	1.4
2	3.7	3.3	3.3	3.7	3.3	2.8	3.7	3.3	2.8	2.4	3.7
3	7.3	5.1	5.3	7.3	5.5	4.6	7.3	5.5	4.1	3.3	8.1
4	10.9	7.0	7.2	11.7	8.2	6.6	11.7	7.4	5.1	4.1	16.7
5	14.5	8.9	9.1	16.9	11.5	9.2	15.4	9.1	6.1	4.8	33.2
6	18.1	10.8	11.1	23.2	15.4	12.2	18.7	10.6	6.9	5.4	65.0
7	21.8	12.6	13.0	30.8	20.1	15.8	21.5	11.9	7.6	5.9	126.2
8	25.4	14.5	14.9	40.0	25.8	20.2	24.0	13.0	8.2	6.3	244.1
	Net Immigration										
1	1.1	1.1	1.1	1.1	1.1	1.1	1.1	1.1	1.1	1.1	1.1
2	3.1	2.7	2.7	3.1	2.7	2.4	3.1	2.7	2.4	2.0	3.1
3	6.1	4.3	4.3	6.1	4.6	3.8	6.1	4.6	3.4	2.8	6.8
4	9.2	5.9	5.8	9.8	6.9	5.6	9.8	6.3	4.3	3.4	14.1
5	12.3	7.4	7.4	14.3	9.7	7.7	13.0	7.7	5.1	4.0	28.0
6	15.3	9.0	9.0	19.6	13.0	10.3	15.8	8.9	5.8	4.5	54.9
7	18.4	10.6	10.5	26.1	17.0	13.3	18.2	10.0	6.4	4.9	106.6
8	21.5	12.2	12.1	33.8	21.8	17.0	20.3	11.0	6.9	5.3	206.2

[a]The models of intergenerational fertility change are presented in Table 5.9.

146

ELLEN PERCY KRALY

tions of Mexicans. Assuming complete intermarriage, a member of the eighth generation of Mexican migrants is $\frac{1}{256}$ Mexican.

The results of the analysis are shown in Table 5.10. Total ethnic population size is presented in the body of the table according to immigration assumptions, model of intergenerational fertility change, and definition of the ethnic population based on the number of generations included. Thus, if one defines the Mexican ethnic population as first- and second-generation Mexicans (the concept adopted by the Census Bureau between 1870 and 1970) and assumes fertility model II (convergence to replacement-level fertility in the second generation), then the size of the Mexican population is 3.3 million, using gross or total immigration figures, or 2.7 million, using net immigration assumptions.

The results indicate the importance of specifying the empirical content of the concept of ethnicity. The size of the Mexican-origin population increases dramatically as more generations are included in the definition of an ethnic population. For example, consider fertility model III, which assumes replacement-level fertility in all generations. If one defines an ethnic population as including the first three generations of immigrants, then the Mexican origin is 4.3 million, using net immigration assumptions. If the ethnic population is defined as all people of Mexican heritage up to eight generations, then the population will measure 12.1 million, a difference of 300 percent over the narrower definition.

The sensitivity of population size to number of generations included in the concept of ethnicity varies according to assumptions about generational fertility levels. The fertility level of one generation determines the (stationary) size of the next generation. For example, fertility model I assumes replacement-level fertility from the third generation onward. The size of the third generation is 3.6 million people in the total immigration model (7.3 minus 3.7). Thus, the ethnic population will be increased by 3.6 million for each generation beyond the third included in the definition of ethnicity. Fertility model XI implies above-replacement-fertility in all generations, and thus positive growth in the size of generations from one generation to the next. In the case of model XI, the rate of intergenerational population change is constant because fertility level, 4.0, is unchanging. For example, in the total immigration model, generations beyond the first increase in size by about 92 percent from one to the next. Fertility model X illustrates decreasing generation size. The fertility level in model X is 1.8 for all generations, which is below replacement. Thus, generations decrease in size at a rate of approximately 20 percent.

However, the effect of varying definitions of the ethnic population remains clear: the broader the definition of ethnic origin with regard to generation, the larger the size of the ethnic population.

The effect of emigration on the results is also clear. The net immigration model implies a population of Mexican origin which is smaller than the population derived from total immigration. The populations based on total immigration are between 18 and 27 percent larger than population derived from net immigration streams. The magnitude of difference decreases as the definition of ethnic population is broadened to include more generations. It is important to note, moreover, that these results incorporate estimates of the emigration of original or first-generation immigrants only. The calculations of generations of descendants does not account for emigration of native-born persons. To date there are no data on which to base estimates of the emigration of native-born U.S. residents. Thus, the size of subsequent generations of ethnics is overestimated in this analysis in both migration models.

It is difficult to interpret these results in the absence of meaningful data on the demographic characteristics of generations of migrants. The availability of such data would clearly make this formal demographic exercise unnecessary. However, one might compare the research results to available census data on the Mexican population. There were 388,248 females of Mexican birth and 797,534 native females of Mexican parentage residing in the U.S. in 1970.[33] These census data are quite different from the estimates of generation size shown in Table 5.4. According to census data, 1.2 million women of Mexican stock, that is, first- and second-generation Mexicans, resided in the United States in 1970. Estimates of the Mexican population defined as two generations range from 2.0 to 3.1 million women in the net immigration model.

Census data on ethnicity are of limited usefulness because the conceptual content of the self-identity question on ethnic origin is unknown.[34] In 1970, some 2.3 million women identified themselves as of Mexican origin.[35] This is quite close to the estimates of the ethnic origin population implied in fertility models VI and IX, net immigration assumptions, when ethnicity includes two generations. The similarity between the measures of Mexican population size is meaningless, however, given the comparison of direct data on first- and second-generation Mexicans with estimates generated by the model.

The estimation of ethnic population characteristics is based on assumptions that are clearly poor reflections of the past and current

demographic experience of Mexicans in the United States. The results of this analysis, however, are intended not so much to approach
contemporary demographic characteristics of the Mexican population, but to illustrate the long-term implications of a range of stable
demographic trends concerning immigration. In this sense, interpretation of these results for immigration-policy analysis is even more
difficult and is dependent upon how one defines a large or small
ethnic population relative to some optimum total population. Analysis
of these results requires the specification of national policy goals concerning population size, ethnic composition, and age structure.

Continuing Issues in the Demographic Analysis of Immigration

The purpose of the above analysis is not to make predictions about
the size of any particular ethnic population, but rather to illustrate the
usefulness of formal demographic theory for the analysis of the role
of international migration in population dynamics. The research
selected for illustration throughout this chapter demonstrates three
salient issues confronting both the social scientist and the policy analyst. These issues pertain to data, concepts, and analysis.

Following the scientific method, we should begin by discussing
conceptual issues concerning the study of international migration. In
this substantive area, however, demographers rarely collect their own
data. We rely on administrative and secondary sources of data. This is
generally so throughout the world. Data on immigration and emigration are collected by national statistical offices and administrative
agencies. Migration data generally reflect what governments need to
know for the enforcement of laws and policies concerning entry and
exit to and from the country.[36]

The U.S. federal statistical system is a clear example of administrative definition of data on international migration. Nationally available sources of data have been extensively described elsewhere.[37]
Briefly, flow data on immigration to the United States are collected by
the INS and refer to aliens being admitted under the Immigration
and Nationality Act. Annual stock data on aliens in the United States
are also collected by the INS. The U.S. Bureau of the Census collects
detailed social demography information on people of foreign birth
and people living abroad at some specified time before the inquiry in
the decennial census and in selected Current Population Surveys. The
Social Security Administration is increasingly being considered a
source of data on international migrants: place of birth is available for

workers dating from 1937; the application for a social security number (form SS-5) has been revised recently to ask citizenship and visa status.

The collection of data for administrative purposes has resulted in the dearth of data on certain categories of international migrants. The lack of data on emigration was shown above. The international migration behavior of U.S. citizens is virtually unknown. Representing the migration of undocumented aliens in demographic analyses is particularly problematic. The limitations of administrative sources of data make it impossible to represent a demographic conceptualization of the process of international migration by including all people entering and departing the country for a significant length of time.[38]

The lack of information on the demographic experience of immigrants once in the United States has also been illustrated in the selected research. Data on age-specific fertility are available from standard vital registration forms for women of foreign birth, although only selected geographic origins are coded by the National Center for Health Statistics (NCHS). Moreover, annual data on the total foreign-born population do not exist. Analyses of intergenerational fertility change have relied on census data on cumulative fertility of women by age, place of birth, parentage (until 1980), and ancestry. Even less is known about the mortality of immigrants and their descendants. Place of birth is coded for the statistical records derived from death certificates. These data are not tabulated by the NCHS; the quality of the data on deaths occurring to the foreign-born is largely unknown.

Limitations of available data place severe restrictions on how the demographer operationalizes concepts of international migration and assesses demographic impacts. The conceptual issues in this area of research, however, go beyond the demographic definition of a migrant and specification of demographic behaviors. The definition of demographic "impact" (i.e., the choice of salient consequences considered by the demographer) is critical. As illustrated here, analyses of the demographic impact of immigration have focused on effect of present and future streams on the components of population change, intrinsic rate of population and the path to stationary population, and the age and sex structure of the U.S. population. This strict formal demographic definition of "impact" is useful only to a point, however. Ultimately the demographic characteristics of international migration must be related to the significant aspects of the U.S. economic and social structure. Demographers must begin to incorporate their results in analyses concerning the relationships between patterns of international migration to the United States and significant social and economic structures and processes. We have attempted to illustrate this position by considering the population dynamics of ethnic composition. International migration is directly related to areas of public policy including domestic labor and employment conditions, social security and social services, and cultural or ethnic mix.

These areas of public policy are implicitly areas of national demographic policy, that is, demographic policy goals are implicit in national social and economic programs. Herein lies the problem of analyzing the relationship between U.S. immigration and demographic policies: No explicit demographic policy exists in the United States. Zero population growth, or the attainment of a stationary population, has been advocated by some as an appropriate national policy goal, while other voices suggest slow positive growth or no federal intervention. The age structure of the U.S. population is increasingly viewed as a social and economic parameter impinging upon planning for social security, educational and health services, and changes in labor markets. Concern over ethnic composition, in this author's view, is gathering strong momentum throughout the country; references to "we" and "they" and to the absorptive capacity of the United States, as well as concern over the economic impact of immigrants and refugees, reflect the underlying concern over cultural mix and change.

Policy-relevant research in these areas of U.S. demography must derive from national policy goals concerning population size, rate of growth, fertility behavior, age structure, and ethnic composition. Official policies in these areas do not exist in explicit form. In general, the United States lacks an orientation to even short-range national social planning. Bouvier summarizes the problems this poses for analysis of the demographic effect of alternative immigration policies: "Determining the 'best' immigration policy can hardly be accomplished without an overall population policy which includes at least a tentative 'optimum goal'—both as to population numbers and growth rates."[39] The interpretation of results such as those presented in Tables 5.4, 5.5, and 5.10 for the purposes of the analysis of alternative immigration policies is impossible without reference to standards of population size and composition.

This alludes to the development of a theory of optimum population size and structure, a call back to the traditions of positivistic Western thought. A review of Aristotle's *Politics* [40] may not be necessary; one can begin with the noted French demographer Alfred Sauvy.[41]

Whether it is feasible to resolve conflicting social, economic, and political issues to establish national goals concerning population is a current issue in and of itself. The attempt should be made, however, and would require interaction between the policy analyst and the social scientist in the definition of concepts and their interpretation of scientific results. How else are we to address Bouvier's question, "How many immigrants should the United States accept every year?"[42]

Notes

1. The counts of the 1980 national and foreign-born population are preliminary.

2. Charles B. Keely, "The Estimation of the Immigration Component of Population Growth," *International Migration Review* 8 (Fall 1974): 432–433.

3. Campbell Gibson, "The Contribution of Immigration to the United States Population Growth: 1790–1970," *International Migration Review* 9 (Summer 1975): 157–176; Simon Kuznets and Ernest Rubin, *Immigration and the Foreign Born* (New York: National Bureau of Economic Research, 1954).

4. Gibson, "Contribution of Immigration," p. 160.

5. Ibid., p. 177.

6. Ibid., p. 161.

7. See Charles B. Keely, *U.S. Immigration: A Policy Analysis* (New York: Population Council, 1979); Ellen Percy Kraly, "Systems of International Migration Statistics: The United States as a National Case Study" (Ph.D. diss., Fordham University, 1979).

8. U.S. Commission on Population Growth and the American Future, *Population and the American Future* (Washington, D.C.: Government Printing Office, 1972).

9. Ansley J. Coale, "Alternative Paths to a Stationary Population," in U.S. Commission on Population Growth and the American Future, *Demographic and Social Aspects of Population Growth*, vol. 1 of the Research Reports, ed. Charles Westoff and Robert Parke, Jr. (Washington, D.C.: Government Printing Office, 1972), pp. 591–603.

10. Ibid., p. 599.

11. See also Charles F. Westoff, "The Commission on Population Growth and the American Future," in *Sociology and Public Policy: The Case of the Presidential Commissions*, ed. Mirra Komarovsky (New York: Elsevier, 1975), pp. 43–59.

12. Commission on Population Growth, *Population and the American Future*, p. 117.

13. Thomas J. Espenshade, Leon F. Bouvier, and W. Brian Arthur, "Immigration and the Stable Population," *Demography* 19 (February 1982): 125–133.

14. The analytic derivation of his model of migration has not been published by Coale.

15. This discussion is adapted from Charles B. Keely and Ellen Percy Kraly, "Recent Net Alien Immigration to the U.S.: Its Impact on Population Growth and Native Fertility," *Demography* 15 (August 1978): 267–281.

16. Nathan Keyfitz has also used analytic techniques to evaluate emigration as a means of population control. Keyfitz related age-specific rates of out-migration to the intrinsic rate of increase of a population. He concluded that while a sustained pattern of emigration (i.e., negative net migration) will affect the rate of growth, the initiation of a policy of migration is not an efficient population policy. The effect of emigration on growth is directly related to the number of people of reproductive potential who migrate, that is, the number of births averted. Keyfitz was able to demonstrate the proportion of people required to emigrate to achieve a stationary population. In high-fertility societies, this proportion is quite large; often around 50 percent of each birth cohort approaching childbearing years would have to emigrate each year. See Nathan Keyfitz, "Migration as a Means of Population Control," *Population Studies* 25 (March 1971): 71–72.

17. Keely and Kraly, "Recent Net Immigration."

18. Departures of aliens and U.S. citizens from the United States by land and sea carriers are documented by the Department of Transportation from passenger manifests. Demographic analysis of these data has been attempted by Daniel R. Vining, "Net Immigration by Air: A Lower Bound on Total Net Migration to the United States," Regional Science Department, University of Pennsylvania, Philadelphia, 1980.

19. Robert Warren and Jennifer Marks Peck, "Emigration from the United States: 1960–1970" (Paper delivered at the Annual Meeting of the Population Association of America, Seattle, Wash., 1975).

20. Ibid., p. 11.

21. Gibson, "Contribution of Immigration"; Kuznets and Rubin, *Immigration and the Foreign Born.*

22. Leon F. Bouvier, "The Impact of Immigration on U.S. Population Size," Population Trends and Public Policy no. 1, Population Reference Bureau, January 1981.

23. See Sylvia Helen Forman, "Migration: A Problem in Conceptualization," in *New Approaches to the Study of Migration,* ed. David Guillet, Rice University Studies, vol. 62, no. 3 (Houston: Rice University, 1976), pp. 25–35.

24. Espenshade, Bouvier, and Arthur, in "Immigration and the Stable Population," also consider the generations deriving from constant annual net immigration streams. Convergence to below-replacement-level fertility by descendants of migrants is consistent with the maintenance of a national stationary population.

25. This research project was described in a presentation and background paper for the Social Policy Seminar on Immigration, Annual Meeting of the American Sociological Association, Toronto, August 1981.

26. These data are reported by the INS in ten-year age-groups for ages 10 to 79. Census data on age characteristics of female residents of Mexican foreign birth who immigrated during the period 1965–1970 were used to distribute ten-year grouped data into five-year age-groups. These age distributions were then averaged.

27. Rates of emigration are derived from Warren and Peck's estimates of annual immigrant emigration between 1960 and 1970. Age at migration refers to age at the midpoint of the emigration interval 1960–1970. Rates of emigration for age-groups above 60–64 are assumed equal to the rate for the terminal age-group calculated by Warren and Peck. Robert Warren and Jennifer Marks Peck, "Foreign-Born Emigration from the United States: 1960 to 1970," *Demography* 17 (February 1980): 71–84.

28. Ansley J. Coale and Paul Demeny, *Regional Model Life Tables and Stable Populations* (Princeton: Princeton University Press, 1966).

29. The U.S. Bureau of the Census collected data on cumulative fertility for women of foreign birth and foreign parentage until 1980, when the question on parentage was dropped from the decennial census schedule. Other research has been based on social survey data, although generational analysis has usually been limited to first- and second-generation immigrants. See Frank D. Bean, Gary Swicegood, and Thomas F. Linsley, "Patterns of Fertility Variation Among Mexican Immigrants to the United States," Texas Population Research Center Papers, Series 2, no. 2.016, University of Texas at Austin, 1979–1980.

30. For an excellent discussion of the relationship between ethnicity and fertility, see the article by Frank Bean and John Marcum, "Differential Fertility and the Minority Group Status Hypothesis: An Assessment and Review," in *The Demography of Racial and Ethnic Groups*, ed. Frank D. Bean and W. Parker Frisbie (New York: Academic Press, 1978). See also Ronald R. Rindfuss and James A. Sweet, *Postwar Fertility Trends and Differentials in the United States* (New York: Academic Press, 1977).

31. The age pattern of fertility used by Coale ("Alternative Paths") is assumed constant for all fertility levels. This schedule is as follows:

Age of Female	Proportion of Fertility
15–19	0.123
20–24	0.329
25–29	0.272
30–34	0.167
35–39	0.086
40–44	0.024

In order to consider only female births, a sex ratio at birth of 105 has been assumed.

32. See Coale and Demeny, *Regional Model Life Tables and Stable Populations,* p. 72.

33. U.S. Bureau of the Census, *Census of Population: 1970,* vol. 2, Subject Reports, PC(2)-1A, *National Origins and Language* (Washington, D.C.: Government Printing Office, 1973), p. 70.

34. See National Academy of Sciences, *Counting the People in 1980: An Appraisal of Census Plans* (Washington, D.C.: Government Printing Office, 1978), pp. 70–76, for a discussion and critique of the question on ethnicity adopted in the 1980 decennial census.

35. U.S. Bureau of the Census, *Census of Population: 1970,* vol. 2, Subject Reports, PC(2)-1C, *Persons of Spanish Origin* (Washington, D.C.: Government Printing Office, 1973), p. 9.

36. United Nations, Statistical Commission, "National Practices in the Definition, Collection, and Compilation of Statistics of International Migration," ST/ESA/STAT/80/Rev. 1, New York, 1977.

37. E. P. Hutchinson, "Our Statistics of International Migration: Comparability and Completeness for Demographic Use" (mimeograph); Ellen Percy Kraly, "Nationally Available Data on International Migration to and from the United States," Report prepared for the Interagency Task Force on Immigration, Washington, D.C., 1978; Ellen Percy Kraly, "International Migration Statistics: Definition and Data" (Paper delivered at the Annual Meeting of the American Statistical Association, Houston, Tex., 1980); Kraly, "Systems of International Migration Statistics"; Sylvano Tomasi and Charles B. Keely, *Whom Have We Welcomed?* (Staten Island, N.Y.: Center for Migration Studies, 1975).

38. The U.N. Statistical Commission has endorsed the incorporation of international standards concerning the definition, collection, and tabulation of data on international migration by national governments. Recommended definitions of long- and short-term immigration and emigration represent an inherently demographic conceptualization of the process of international migration. International travelers are to be classified according to prior presence in or absence from the countries of arrival and departure and length of stay and purpose of travel in the country of arrival. See United Nations, Statistical Commission, "Recommendations on Statistics of International Migration," ST/ESA/STAT/SER.M/58, New York, 1980.

39. Bouvier, "The Impact of Immigration on U.S. Population Size," pp. 1–2.

40. *The Politics of Aristotle,* ed. and trans. Ernest Barker (London: Oxford University Press, 1971), pp. 58–59, 289–292.

41. Alfred Sauvy, *General Theory of Population* (New York: Basic Books, 1969).

42. Bouvier, "The Impact of Immigration on U.S. Population Size," p. 16.

CHAPTER 6

Immigration and U.S. Foreign Policy

Mark J. Miller and *Demetrios G. Papademetriou*

Economic, foreign, and defense policies define the parameters of the crucible in which statesmanship is tested. Increasingly, the twin issues of immigration and refugee policy are inextricably intertwined with a state's ability to articulate and implement these policies. Especially in light of mounting global economic scarcities and sociopolitical polarization, the international movement of people promises to be one of the most challenging and stubborn policy dilemmas for the international community in the 1980s. International migration already is giving rise to a critical new scarcity—this one measured in terms of willingness to bear the internal sociopolitical and international political costs required to address the migration problem successfully.

Immigration policy in the United States traditionally has been looked upon as a domestic policy issue, a perception apparent in the virtual absence of immigration policy concerns in U.S. foreign policy debate.[1] In fact, until recently, scholarly research on the foreign policy implications of U.S. immigration and refugee policy consisted of a handful of efforts pertaining most notably to immigration as a factor in U.S.-Mexican relations.[2] In the flurry of articles on the theme of U.S. foreign policy priorities in the 1980s, for example, rarely was the immigration issue mentioned, except in reference to U.S.-Mexican relations, and rarer still was the analyst who regarded immigration as a potentially salient foreign policy issue for the 1980s.[3] This disregard for the immigration variable in foreign policy prognostics stood in sharp contrast to more general appraisals of major issues facing the United States in the 1980s, since these almost always listed immigration as a leading issue.

Because of its domestic political salience, the immigration issue could not help but be an important foreign policy issue. The lag in

155

appreciating immigration policy as a component of foreign policy would seem to be a matter of convention, of outdated issue-identification. It also results, however, from analytical traditions in the fields of foreign policy and international relations which tend to obscure or minimize the significance of migration phenomena in world affairs. Underlying assumptions concerning the fundamental nature of foreign policy and international politics have left migration matters outside the traditional focus of foreign policy analysis in much the same way that the foreign policy significance of energy, finance, and political terrorism issues long were underestimated. Since assumptions underlying foreign policy analysis are intimately related to normative and legal aspects of the immigration issue, they doubly merit explication.

High Versus Low Politics

Sovereignty, or the idea that there is a final and absolute authority in a society and none above it, is simultaneously a normative, legal, and analytical concept.[4] Historically, the modern concept of sovereignty developed in response to the breakdown of the divine justification of the medieval political order during the religious wars. Sovereignty provided both a theoretical underpinning and a secular rationale for the emerging European nation-states. It has since been firmly ensconced in the affairs of mankind, as has its progeny, the nation-state, which for over three hundred years now has organized and dominated the affairs of mankind and world politics.

From the time of its full-fledged emergence in seventeenth- and eighteenth-century Europe, the sovereign nation-state has been fated for demise by critics of various ideological persuasions.[5] Yet sovereignty as a politico-legal doctrine remains the unquestioned foundation of world order in the twentieth century. Sovereignty, for all its shortcomings, apparently is indispensable. The existence of multiple sovereign states constantly reinforces the possibility of war and inhibits the enforcement of international law. All expectations of restricting claims of sovereignty, or superseding it, have ultimately proven illusory, because world order in the absence of sovereignty would collapse.

As a politico-legal doctrine, sovereignty connotes the right of each state to exercise full self-determination within its borders. Sovereignty rationalizes the rule of law within nation-states, while condemning these same states to interact in the absence of enforceable law. Hence, the sovereignty concept implies a sharp distinction between the domestic or internal politics of a state and its external or international relations. The concept further implies that states control and are responsible for all kinds of interactions with the outside world, the global environment. The distinction drawn between domestic affairs and international affairs, and the notion of state control over and responsibility for interactions with the global environment, are hallmarks, and underlying assumptions, of the traditional approach to analysis of foreign policy and international affairs. These analytical assumptions corresponded closely to the political reality of Europe before industrialization. However, they appear less and less useful to understanding contemporary politics, both foreign and domestic, although sovereignty remains the undisputed legal foundation of world order.

Since the emergence of international politics as a distinct field of analysis, theories have traditionally been based on the often unstated assumption that sovereign states are the principal actors in international affairs. The corollary of this assumption is that the proper focus of analysis is upon interstate relations, especially upon relations pertaining to the questions of peace and war—the so-called high politics.[6] Central to the "high politics" approach to foreign policy and international political analysis is the belief that purposive actions by governments comprise what is important to understanding world politics. Conversely, nongovernmental contacts among nations are generally deemed to be of lesser significance, because they are not seen as fundamentally influencing the course of world politics. In this scenario, foreign and domestic policy issues are often assumed to be distinct. Domestic political processes are assumed to be largely autonomous and impermeable to external influences.

The high politics approach, with its characteristic focus upon intergovernmental contacts and politico-military security issues, would view international migration as a question of marginal significance to the conduct of a state's foreign policy. The paucity of reflection upon U.S. immigration policy as a foreign policy issue would appear to testify to the continuing influence of high politics assumptions about the nature of foreign policy and international politics. But the high politics approach to analyzing international affairs, which reached its zenith during the 1950s and early 1960s, increasingly has been balanced by an alternative school of analysis, variously called the "low" or "transnational politics" approach. This second way of conceptualizing foreign policy and international affairs is different from the high politics approach, less for its deemphasis of military concerns and formal diplomatic interactions than for its assumptions that foreign policy and international affairs in general can be vitally affected by nonstate (and thus nonsovereign) actors and that nation-states are characterized more by political, economic, and social inter-dependence than by autonomy. For some critics of the high politics orthodoxy, sovereignty and the nation-state are vestigial myths. Both no longer correspond and are ill-adapted to contemporary realities. Those who view international affairs in terms of these outmoded notions lose sight of underlying transnational processes which, to this alternative school of thought, hold the key to true understanding of contemporary global affairs.

International population movements are often organized and regulated by sovereign states since everyone recognizes that a key attribute of sovereignty is the ability to decide who shall enter a country. However, international migration increasingly seems to take place outside the ambit of state control as it mushrooms quantitatively and shifts from the classic East-West axis to a South-to-North flow. The economic, social, and political relationships between states which have arisen as a result of international migration lie outside the focus of the high politics analytical tradition but are highlighted by assumptions concerning the nature of contemporary world politics that are central to the transnational, or low, politics approach. Given the weight of tradition in foreign policy analysis, the significance of immigration issues to U.S. foreign policy obviously is not self-evident, and it re-mains to be demonstrated why the marginal or tangential role tradi-tionally assigned this issue requires reassessment. The key to such an endeavor rests in illuminating the underlying changes in global af-fairs which should propel immigration issues to a prominent place on the U.S. foreign policy agenda.

While it is empirically impossible to prove or disprove whether high politics or low politics more aptly characterizes world affairs (since both foreign policy "models" are pretheoretical, nonfalsifiable constructs), it is appropriate to dwell on the insights and limitations of the two conceptual frameworks, for they generate quite different appreciations of the significance of immigration issues in world af-fairs. It also goes without saying that assumptions concerning the underlying nature of world affairs have normative connotations. The low politics approach inevitably raises questions about the value of sovereignty as a normative or moral construct. Does it still make sense to speak of sovereign prerogatives and rights of sovereignty if the domestic affairs of individual nation-states are inextricably bound up with exogenous influences and if governments are losing control over

and responsibility for significant kinds of societal interactions with the
global environment?

Islands of Wealth and Relative Stability in a Sea of Poverty and Turmoil

Islands of Wealth and Relative Stability
in a Sea of Poverty and Turmoil

It is beyond dispute that the continuing nuclear arms race, with the
attendant risk of nuclear Armaggedon, and the growing socioeconomic and political acrimony between the industrialized North and
the far less developed South fundamentally define contemporary
world politics. It is less evident, however, that the issues of immigration and refugee policies act as significant destabilizing forces in the
already volatile North/South relationship as they feed on and compound the larger issues of Third World poverty, population growth,
hunger, war, and revolution. If these discomfiting trends in the Third
World continue, migratory pressure toward Western democracies
could conceivably threaten democratic life as is known there today. At
a minimum, the essence of immigration policy—the decision to admit
or exclude—will take on acute foreign policy significance, almost regardless of the public strategies adopted to cope with the consequences of North/South disparities.

The conceptual key to grasping the relationship between global
political, economic, and social trends and the foreign policy implications of U.S. immigration policy is the notion of interdependence.
Interdependence can be defined as a relationship of mutual rele-
vancy. It "refers to situations characterized by reciprocal effects
among countries or among actors in different countries."[7]

From the transnational standpoint, the industrial revolution and
its attendant communications and transportation revolutions have
fundamentally altered the socioeconomic and political environment
in which nation-states exist. Whereas the nation-state was relatively
impervious to external influences, it no longer is so today, except in
the most repressive of states National autarky, once a viable economic concept, would have little applicability to the closely interwo-
ven economies of nation-states today. The high degree of current
global economic interdependence has been demonstrated repeatedly
since the Great Depression but most recently, and most starkly, during the oil crisis following the 1973 Arab-Israeli war and the resultant
contagion of "stagflation," or simultaneous economic recession and
inflation, which has affected virtually all non-Communist countries.
Witness also the "rippling effect" of high interest rates and currency

devaluations across most of the world's economies. The inability of
U.S. national policy to control inflation in the 1970s, for example, was
once tellingly explained as follows: "[The] U.S. effort to use price
controls was subverted in large part by exports of controlled goods, in
response to higher prices abroad and the close ties among world
markets."[8]

Global economic interdependence is reinforced by an extensive
global division of labor and the growth of such institutions as the
multinational corporation. Excess industrial capacity in the highly
developed economies of North American and Western Europe has
contributed to the severe imbalance in general economic welfare between North and South, a relationship also rooted in colonialism and
a network of ethnic and cultural dynamics. Post–World War II international labor migrations especially enabled Western European industry to expand through a capital widening process wherein
existing, relatively labor-intensive industrial technologies often could
be utilized or replicated only with an infusion of foreign labor.[9]

The process of economic development is such that it will not
automatically and instantly diffuse its rewards to its many suitors. The
persistant North/South economic gap may indeed reflect unequal
distributions of natural resources along with other endowments (such
as education) and what John Kenneth Galbraith recently termed the
"equilibrium" of and "accommodation" to poverty.[10] However,
underlying this gap is a world economic system that restricts (some
would say prevents) national actors in the South from more than
nominal opportunities to affect their own economic, and often political, fate. Therefore, explanations of international migration which
are anchored on such variables as wage differentials between advanced, industrial states and less-developed countries or on the
micro-motives of individuals are inadequate in that they ignore the
complex dynamics of socioeconomic and political interdependence
which create the conditions for substantial population movements.

The manner in which the enormous socioeconomic disparities
between the advanced and the least developed universes affect international population flows is a subject that must be understood before
immigration becomes a central concern of U.S. foreign policy. Of
course, global economic disparities would not influence the United
States directly and immediately if the world's less favored were im-
mobile. Because of the communications and transportation revolutions, however, they are not. Modern communications generate a
revolution of aspirations which for many in the Third World will lead
to the path of migration. Modern transportation affords all but the

most impoverished the possibility of international migration. The transportation and communications revolutions, hence, have rendered advanced industrial democracies permeable to the determined clandestine migrant as well as to various classes of legal immigrant entrants. At the same time, the very structure and characteristics of advanced industrial democracies make it difficult to opt for and implement the extensive enforcement instruments required to control unregulated or illegal international migration.

Advanced industrial democracies are vulnerable to clandestine migration for many of the same reasons that they are vulnerable to political terrorism. Closed societies do not have immigration problems or fear political terrorism, primarily because citizen rights are sharply circumscribed and police powers and controls on movement are extensive. Just as measures taken to surpress political terrorism can jeopardize fundamental democratic values, so too can measures taken to prevent illegal migration. This is why the prospect for ever greater migratory pressure from the Third World can be said to threaten democratic life as it is known today. Preserving the fundamental values of the United States is, of course, the essential motivation of U.S. foreign policy.

Before turning to consideration of demographic and economic characteristics of advanced capitalist states and their relationship to international migration, the existence of a constellation of "underdevelopment"—related conditions which strengthen the appeal of the emigration alternative—also must be acknowledged. Obvious determinants of emigration such as high birth rates, high unemployment, and extreme underemployment often coexist with extreme forms of ethnic, religious, linguistic, and racial repression which further reinforce the emigration option. Resultant political instability has been exacerbated by irresponsible arms-sales policies by East and West which make it easier for Third World countries to use force in efforts to solve both internal issues and international issues. This situation again not only has roots in the colonial policies of the advanced industrial states but, more important, can be seen as indicator of continuing Third World political dependence on the industrialized states.

Marxists have elaborated on the relationship between "underdevelopment" and emigration in a different manner. To use Marxist idiom, migration is a major structural contradiction in society. Both Marx and his more or less orthodox disciples view emigration as the coerced result of the interdependence and disparities between more economically advanced sectors—cities to Marx, but core/center countries to contemporary neo-Marxists—and less developed sectors, such as rural areas or now so-called periphery countries.[11] The migration process is by definition cumulatively unequal and leads to the weakening of less-developed sectors vis-à-vis the advanced. Migration results from socioeconomic and political dependencies in the dichotomous, exploitative relationship between center and periphery.

According to the Marxist school of analysis, then, international migration is a (structural) process central to both sending and receiving societies, and one of the most important defining features of the contemporary world economy.[12] As such, international migration is seen as an integral part of the capital accumulation process, the driving force of capitalism. Within this broad framework of understanding, the Marxist focus shifts to the historical-structural components of national and global economic relations and to the role of labor in this pantheon. State actors (nation-states) become components of a single, integral totality, "the world capitalist economy [that] simultaneously depends on and recreates conditions for economic inequality worldwide."[13] Migration becomes the tangible response to uneven international (and national) development. The migration decision shifts from the individual to the level of national and international forces and their concomitant class relations. The Marxist approach transforms migration from micro-behavior to macro-social process and from a unidimensional, static event into a historically informed dynamic process that constantly influences—in fact, determines—behavior of individuals and dependent sectors.

In this scenario, emigration is viewed as serving both the interests of "center" capital and the ruling classes of sending societies. The latter's political hegemony is reinforced through emigration's sociopolitical functions: relieving some of the sociopolitical pressures caused by unemployment; providing the necessary capital to "proletarianize" local labor by changing the mode of production from pre-capitalist subsistence to wages for industrial work; helping local elites in their role as middlemen importing industrial goods and exporting raw materials along with complementary industrial goods; and fostering higher aggregate demand due to the buying power of remittances.

Whatever the sociopolitical benefits accruing to the elites of emigration lands, the dominating, center nation as an aggregate benefits more than the dominated, emigrant-sending nation. Since labor migration is "cumulative asymmetric" in terms of what each labor-sending and -receiving nation derives from the process, the gap between core and periphery states is expected to widen. Hence, international migration is seen by Marxists as an integral part of the present global relationship of dominance as a key element in a "vertically integrated system of control and accumulation, production and distribution on a global scale."[14]

However one may choose to interpret the causes of the economic woes and consequent political unrest in the Third World, the forces behind continuing high levels of instability there remain unchecked. The inevitable result will be growing numbers of migrants seeking haven in economically advanced, relatively stable, and politically tolerant Western democracies, especially the United States.

Although the concept of dependency is often reserved for describing the domination of the Third World periphery by the industrial capitalist center, the center-periphery, or North/South, relationship is extremely complex. Analysts cannot delineate the precise nature of economic interpenetration or fully understand all the strands of purported political interpenetration between the two universes. Analysis is further complicated by the realization that the demographic structures of advanced capitalist societies themselves also seem to generate a form of dependency—namely, many advanced capitalist states, in spite of present immigration inflows, are rapidly aging societies that apparently will require a steady infusion of immigrant workers to sustain their economies and social security systems.[15]

The United States is showing signs of following the path of societies like West Germany, where the native German birthrate has fallen beneath replacement level and where only the influx of foreigners has enabled the social security system to remain afloat without fundamental reform. What the French call their demographic insufficiency is or soon may be an appropriate term to describe many advanced industrial societies. Indications are that this demographic trend will increase the saliency of immigration issues, even if advanced industrial states do not opt to recruit massive numbers of foreign workers, as did France and the Federal Republic of Germany. Regardless of public policy, the demographic insufficiency of advanced industrial states seems to generate an influx of foreigners. In the case of West Germany, the foreign population is not considered assimilable, and consequently still is seen as nonpermanent despite the already apparent settling of many *Gastarbeiter*. The demographic trends of advanced capitalist societies may mean that there is no reasonable alternative to authorizing large-scale immigration, a possibility that would place the United States with its immigrant-welcoming tradition at a relative advantage to a country like the Federal Republic of Germany.

As already noted, contemporary Marxist theorists argue that

massive recourse to alien labor has become a structural necessity of advanced capitalism. In addition to the hypothetical effects upon emigrant-sending countries previously considered, foreign labor is seen as functioning as a modern reserve industrial army that cushions capitalism through its booms and busts with foreign labor recruitment and then expulsion. Foreign labor, with its inferior rights, is seen as a work force that stabilizes advanced industrial societies by dividing the working class and otherwise attenuating class conflict.[16] The political function of foreign labor is seen as central to the maintenance of capitalist hegemony, as is its economic function. In this scenario as well, then, advanced industrial society has a need for alien labor that makes immigration and its regulation a vital issue in international relations.

Somewhat akin to the Marxist belief that foreign labor is a structural necessity of advanced capitalist society is the notion of dual or segmented labor markets. Dualist theory attributes immigration to the needs of a segmented labor market whose lower (secondary) segment thirsts for the "type" of labor offered by both regulated but especially unregulated immigration. By "type" of labor, reference is not necessarily to the immigrants' specific skill levels but rather to labor that will occupy low-level jobs in such secondary labor market occupations as waste removal, simple sales and clerical jobs, cleaning, and simple processing and assembling, as well as jobs in declining industries and industrial plants with variable demand patterns (such as textiles) and finally in occupations with seasonal or erratic labor demands (such as harvesting and resort restaurants and hotels).[17] The characteristics of such jobs include low wages, poor working conditions, high instability, inferior social standing, and few opportunities for advancement. The purported general applicability of the segmented labor market notion to all advanced capitalist economies is what approaches dual labor market theory to Marxism.

According to analysts who have applied dual labor market theory to the United States, some indigenous workers—blacks, Hispanics, and largely rural-raised poor whites—still take jobs in the secondary sector. But the reluctance of indigenous workers to move to where the jobs are and, more arguably, the disincentives arising from the possibility of welfare, are seen as holding labor supply below demand even in times of high unemployment. Hence the steady demand for cheap foreign labor, which to several American proponents of the dual labor market theory will inevitably be satisfied by alien migrant workers whether their entry is officially sanctioned or not.[18] Therefore, if foreign labor inflows respond to genuine labor market need, this dependence ensures that immigration issues will intrude into U.S. foreign policy considerations and that the question of regulating the foreign labor flow is bilateral and regional in nature.

In a progressively interdependent world, then, developments in both the Third World and advanced industrial societies indicate that the need to reassess the place of immigration policy in U.S. foreign policy is increasing. Reassessment seems particularly urgent in light of the fact that U.S. immigration matters are subject to immediate hemispheric scrutiny. As success or failure of a nation's foreign policy often hinges on its ability to project a good international image, the United States cannot afford to have its image distorted and blemished by perceptions of an irresponsible and inequitable immigration policy. A central tenet of U.S. foreign policy in the twentieth century has been that the internal order of the United States—liberal, democratic, and capitalist—should provide a model for the rest of the world to follow. Consequently, the image of U.S. domestic politics is tied inextricably to the conduct of U.S. foreign policy. The treatment afforded aliens by modern states has always been a matter of bilateral and international concern, but the development of instant electronic communications has vastly increased the sensitivity of the issue.

The permeability of modern states, the blurring or linkage of foreign and domestic issues, the changes produced by the transportation and communications revolutions, the emergence of non-sovereign, autonomous international actors, the loss of control by presumably sovereign governments over domestic politics and foreign policy—in short, all those general processes which make world politics much more complex than the simplified reality assumed by the high politics school—suggest that U.S. immigration policy fairly redounds with significance for foreign policy. If this is so, can consideration of immigration policy as foreign policy point the way to a strategy that better takes into account foreign policy concerns?

U.S. Immigration Policy as Foreign Policy

The questioning of traditional or classical foreign policy analysis in the 1960s led to a series of efforts to formulate a genuinely scientific approach to foreign policy analysis. The heart of this effort involved the search for taxonomies and classificatory schemes that would lead to the systematic accumulation of evidence and eventually to the generation of empirically testable hypotheses. Despite laudable efforts, the scientific study of foreign policy, when assessed against the canons of the scientific method, remains in a largely preparadigmatic stage.[19] There exists no single model or classificatory scheme with which to analyze U.S. immigration policy as foreign policy. At best, diverse theoretical notions eclectically drawn from the literature on foreign policy analysis can inform such an endeavor.

One way to structure a consideration of U.S. immigration policy as foreign policy would be to break down the general policy area by broad types of migrants concerned: immigrants, illegal aliens, temporary foreign workers, refugees, and visitors. In each case, the foreign policy significance of U.S. policy seems somewhat different, although the five categories are of mutual relevance to one another.

IMMIGRANTS

The United States is the world's preeminent immigration country. The immigration tradition has assumed a privileged place in American myth and national self-image. The notion of the United States as the world's major immigration country is an important positive factor in the image of the United States projected abroad. The significance of this intangible, symbolic factor for foreign policy is perhaps most apparent in comparisons made to the Soviet Union, which has a tradition of emigration rather than immigration. As a foreign policy symbol, the U.S. immigration tradition conjures up an image of national generosity, attractiveness, and, to a lesser extent, ethnic and religious toleration. Although tarnished by past excesses, the immigration-land symbol represents one of the most potent but least appreciated foreign policy assets the United States has.

An untoward consequence of the immigration-land image projected abroad is its magnet effect upon potential migrants worldwide. The image certainly has contributed to the upsurge of illegal immigration. The image itself also makes it more costly, in terms of international opinion, for the United States to undertake deportation and other such severe measures against illegal aliens. Maintenance of authorized immigration levels well below global demand for U.S. visas thus carries international costs that rarely seem to be appreciated in policy formulation. As a result, such measures as deportation, interdiction at sea, and internment entail not only significant enforcement costs but also substantial and less well understood symbolic costs.

The rationale behind the current system of visa distribution (see Chapter 1) also has significant foreign policy implications. The pref-

erence system has been portrayed as fair and nondiscriminatory, in
contrast to the visa-allocation system during the period 1924–1965,
when western hemisphere would-be immigrants had preferential
status and potential immigrants from northern Europe clearly were
more favored than immigrants from southern and eastern Europe.
However, aside from the question of the total size of the allocation
relative to global immigration pressure, the present visa-allocation
system has little flexibility, which limits its potential as a diplomatic
tool. The present visa-allocation system assumes a relatively static
world instead of a world characterized by flux and upheaval. Because
the latter image more closely approximates reality, immigration policy is poorly adapted to its international policy environment. The
20,000-per-country limitation bars any major visa-distribution adjustment dictated by general diplomatic concerns. This problem has been
acutely manifest in U.S. relations with Mexico. Mexican immigration
was numerically unrestricted until 1978, when the 20,000-per-
country visa limitation went into effect. Clearly, the proximity of Mexico and other American states, and the size of the U.S. population of
Mexican descent, warrant special consideration in visa allocations. Yet
little flexibility is possible, and U.S. diplomatic relations with Mexico
and other neighbors to the south are the worse for it. Authorization
of a sizable number of visas to be allocated by the Department of State
or the president in response to diplomatic considerations might make
immigrant-visa allocation a more rational foreign policy tool. However, perceptions of equity are vitally important. Care should be taken
that expressions of preference for one hemispheric neighbor do not
injure relations with another which could expect similar solicitude.

The present visa-allocation system promotes family reunification
and favors the immigration of skilled labor over unskilled labor. As
such, it is not fashioned to diminish pressure from the great mass of
low-skilled and often impoverished workers who seek to better their
lives through immigration to the United States. Surely, not all the
world's aspiring immigrants can be accommodated by the United
States. But the diplomatically troublesome problem of illegal immigration and attendant enforcement measures might be somewhat attenuated if a large number of visas were set aside for the prototypical
economically motivated illegal alien from the Caribbean area. Such a
preference adjustment would respond to the alleged labor market
dependence posited by dual labor market theorists. If illegal immigration does respond to genuine labor market needs (with salaries and
working conditions taken as given), does it not seem likely that the

diplomatically nettlesome problem of illegal-alien employment could be ameliorated through a measure that would in essence legalize a currently illegal inflow?

Several critics of U.S. immigration policy have suggested just such a strategy. But their preference is for the issuance of temporary visas as opposed to permanent resident visas. The advantages and disadvantages of proposals for a massive U.S. temporary foreign worker policy are discussed elsewhere (see Chapters 4 and 10). Suffice it to note here that such proposals are based on the assumption that most illegal aliens desire only temporary employment opportunities in the United States. While this may be warranted, although there is considerable reason to doubt this assumption, the issuance of permanent resident visas to putative temporary migrants in no way prejudices the migrant's right to return home, since the United States does not force permanent residents to become U.S. citizens after a certain length of time. Of course, the legal and employment status of permanent resident aliens is far more secure and less exceptional than that of migrants holding time-limited visas. In fact, since migrants holding permanent resident visas have extensive labor market and civil rights, it would be less likely that they would encounter the degree of discrimination and exploitation reserved for clandestine and temporary workers. It is precisely the treatment of clandestine and temporary workers, in turn, which has repeatedly strained U.S.-Mexican relations in the past.

The generally liberal legal status extended to permanent resident aliens puts the United States in a diplomatically favorable position with regard to an international factor that will be increasingly important to the formulation of U.S. immigration policy: international institutions monitoring treatment of aliens. The international norms for treatment of permanent resident aliens include equal social and economic rights with citizens and public liberties (such as the freedoms of speech and press) but permit restrictions on political participation (most notably the rights to vote and hold office).[20] Further, it is permissible for sovereign states to enjoin aliens against actions tending to disturb bilateral relations and foreign policy in general. International guidelines concerning treatment of aliens also condone the exclusion of aliens from certain kinds of employment in the public sector.

Despite a recent number of court decisions tending to restrict the rights of permanent resident aliens (see Chapter 8), it seems unlikely that U.S. participation in such institutions as the United Nations and the International Labor Organization (ILO) will be troubled by criticism over U.S. treatment of permanent resident aliens. Instead, the focus of criticism by these two institutions concerns the plight of illegal aliens. Before broaching the topic of illegal aliens and U.S. foreign policy, a final remark concerning the foreign policy implications of permanent resident aliens is in order.

Although lacking the right to vote and hold office, resident aliens can have an effect upon the conduct of U.S. foreign policy. This possibility was dramatically manifested during the demonstrations by pro- and anti-Shah Iranians on U.S. soil. Many of the demonstrators were students, but many undoubtedly held permanent resident status as well. International migration has always involved the spatial diffusion of homeland political passions and rivalries to countries of immigration. Hence, the fact that Iranian residents in the United States became an autonomous nonnational political factor affecting the conduct of foreign policy is not exceptional. Rather, it is part of a perceptible global trend.[21] Democracies such as the United States may seek to deport politically troublesome aliens, but permanent resident aliens enjoy civic rights similar to citizens, and it is very difficult in a democratic society to restrict alien rights without jeopardizing or restricting citizen rights as well. The sheer enormity of the administrative task and the adverse publicity of enforcing restrictions on large numbers of dissident or otherwise disruptive permanent resident aliens would usually seem to outweigh the foreign policy gain from silencing them.

What constitutes disruption of foreign policy or the public order is open to wide, even arbitrary, interpretation. In this situation it would seem better for the U.S. government to err on the side of toleration, as the United States did during its most trying international crisis with Iran (notwithstanding the order for all Iranian students to report to the Immigration and Naturalization Service). The Iranian demonstrators episode was but one example of a general transnational trend toward diffusion of Third World politics to advanced industrial democracies. As a result of massive international migration, political upheaval in the Third World will not be contained there; it will become a disruptive force in Western industrial democracies as well.

The spatial diffusion of homeland-oriented political activity to the United States takes a variety of forms, however, not all of which are disruptive. Increasingly, foreign electoral campaigns are waged on U.S. soil, as witnessed by Ecuadorian presidential candidate Jaime Roldós's, taking to the hustings in New York City, where over 200,000 of his compatriots live, in 1978.[22] Similarly, Italian parliamentary candidates vied for absentee votes on U.S. soil during the 1980 Italian general election.[23] The electoral weight of an expatriate community's vote on U.S. soil is perhaps most significant in the case of Israel, which may have up to 500,000 citizens living in the United States out of a total population of less than 4 million.[24] Foreign election campaigns, political fund-raising, party and trade-union organization, alien organizations taking public positions on international issues, and alien military training aimed at overthrowing homeland regimes represent diverse but increasingly prevalent forms of alien political participation despite their restricted status in the United States. One consequence of this trend again seems clear: Immigration-related matters will loom larger in the conduct of U.S. foreign policy.

ILLEGAL ALIENS

Adoption in 1975 of ILO Convention 97, pertaining to migrants in abusive conditions, and of the U.N. Economic and Social Council resolution, pertaining to measures to improve the situation and ensure the human rights and dignity of all migrant workers, underscores the international political ramifications of illegal migration. By definition, massive illegal migration takes place outside the ambit of governmental control, but the logic of sovereignty shoulders governments, especially in receiving countries, with diplomatically sensitive responsibilities. Illegal immigration illustrates well how a transnational process operating outside governmental control can become a significant factor in the foreign affairs of sovereign states. Illegal immigration blurs traditional distinctions between domestic policy and foreign policy to the point that domestic policy toward illegal aliens is almost indistinguishable from foreign policy. Domestic policy areas pertaining to education, social services, or housing, for example, now have foreign policy significance in spite of the internationally recognized fact that these policy matters fall under the sovereign jurisdiction of the United States.

   The process of illegal immigration makes potentially significant international actors out of ordinary policemen, workers, judges, or employers. This potentiality is most vividly apparent in cases of mistreatment of illegal aliens by private citizens. Abusive acts that in no way are condoned by the U.S. government nevertheless can undermine foreign policy, as witnessed time and again by cases where Mexican nationals are abused. The vulnerability of illegal aliens to private discrimination and exploitation becomes a foreign policy problem because aliens are involved, even if their residency is not officially sanctioned.

Some critics would question whether it is accurate to regard illegal immigration as unsanctioned immigration in the first place. To many observers, the U.S. government has tolerated illegal immigration through its lack of energetic border control and controls at the workplace. Officially restrictive immigration policy has been undermined by a de facto immigration policy that encouraged millions of illegal aliens to enter. Some would argue that this unofficial policy was motivated by foreign policy considerations as much as by employer interests. For Mexico and other Caribbean area states, illegal immigration is thought to function as a safety valve for unemployed workers who otherwise might become a factor of sociopolitical unrest. From this perspective, a U.S. crackdown on illegal immigration could have untoward diplomatic consequences beyond the question of equity to illegal aliens who, through their labor, have built up a stake in U.S. society and therefore should not be deported. A sudden rupture in illegal employment possibilities in the United States would be likely to destabilize countries that U.S. foreign policy seeks to stabilize.

The view that illegal immigration serves important but unofficial U.S. foreign policy goals through its alleged safety-valve function represents one of the relatively few examples where U.S. immigration policy is popularly linked to the conduct of U.S. foreign policy. Unfortunately, the nature of the linkage may be misunderstood. There is little doubt that the labor forces of Mexico and other Caribbean nations have become somewhat dependent on employment opportunities in the United States over the years. The extent to which this dependency promotes or detracts from economic development and political stability in the countries of out-migration is unclear. Hence, it is far from certain that enforcement measures taken to curtail illegal immigration would undercut stability in Caribbean-area countries and thereby disserve U.S. foreign policy interests. Of course, U.S. policy options are not limited to enforcement alone. An effort to curtail illegal immigration through beefed-up enforcement could conceivably be accompanied by increased immigration quotas or foreign aid that could substitute for the alleged safety-valve effect of illegal immigration.

The plight of millions of illegal aliens in the United States already is a festering foreign policy problem as well as a domestic policy problem. If steps are not taken to curb illegal alien entry more effectively, global conditions are such that the problem could reach crisis proportions. There would seem to be a real danger that relative governmental inaction would be followed by overreaction. Massive deportations of illegal aliens who have established roots in the United States, if at all administratively feasible, would have extremely deleterious effects upon U.S. foreign relations. The right of the United States to deport aliens might not be questioned, but the humaneness and equity of such a policy would. The most appropriate strategy for the United States to follow would involve close U.S. adherence to ILO Convention 97, which elaborates a humane policy for dealing with illegal aliens. A major feature of Convention 97 is the inclusion of severe sanctions against employers of illegal aliens. Unfortunately, the disinclination of the United States to ratify ILO instruments concerning migrant workers in the past has been a measure of its disregard for the foreign-policy implications of immigration matters.

Better border enforcement, employer sanctions, national identity cards, and other measures that, when followed in concert, hold out the prospect of appreciably diminishing illegal immigration without violating the rights of aliens should be considered a foreign policy priority for two major reasons. First, a high incidence of clandestine immigrants in democratic societies poses a several challenge to democratic ideals. Failure to control illegal-alien entry over the long run will lead to charges of human rights violations unless these individuals are permitted adjustment of status. Second, measures taken to stem the inflow of illegal aliens would be enhanced by bilateral and regional cooperation. Unilateral solutions will solve neither bilateral problems nor global ones. Defining immigration policy as a foreign policy issue encourages a realistic approach to finding long-term solutions to the illegal-alien problem.[25]

TEMPORARY FOREIGN WORKERS

A policy that would permit a large number of aliens to enter the United States to perform temporary services of labor has been touted as a boon to U.S. foreign policy.[26] The arguments made on behalf of this assertion are threefold and always resemble the following.

A massive guestworker, or temporary foreign worker, policy would substantially reduce illegal immigration by giving legal status to foreign workers who would otherwise come illegally. Therefore, an important source of strain in U.S. relations with Mexico, among other countries, would be attenuated. However, the United States would continue to function as an economic safety valve to Caribbean-area countries now staggering from unemployment and high rates of de-

mographic growth. Hence, the U.S. foreign policy goal of strengthening the stability of non-Communist regimes in the Caribbean area
would be served. Concomitantly, the same Caribbean-area countries
would receive an infusion of worker wage remittances, which would
help sustain workers' dependents and perhaps spur economic development. Thus, a massive temporary foreign worker program is
seen as serving the diplomatic, national security, and foreign economic assistance goals of U.S. foreign policy.

The temporary foreign worker policy idea has attracted considerable support in the United States and abroad. The government
of Mexico regretted the unilateral U.S. decision to terminate the *bracero* program in 1964.[27] Since at least 1973, various Mexican officials
have hinted that they would like to see some sort of bilateral temporary foreign worker program resumed.[28] However, the diplomatic
signals sent by Mexico have been mixed. Officially, a return to a
bracero-like program would be unthinkable for Mexico because of the
abuses tolerated under the 1942–1964 program.

Criticism of the proposed temporary foreign worker program on
foreign policy grounds has been just as intense as the program's advocacy. Critics point out that the assumption that illegal immigration will
be reduced by a temporary foreign worker policy is unwarranted on
historical grounds. During the first twelve years of the *bracero* program, apprehensions of undocumented Mexican workers rose dramatically. Most historians now agree that the *bracero* program actually
spurred illegal immigration.[29] Temporary worker policy appears to
have had a magnet effect upon illegal aliens in the U.S. Virgin Islands
as well.[30] At a minimum, a large-scale temporary foreign worker policy and massive illegal immigration were not mutually exclusive in the
past. Hence, the critics doubt that a temporary foreign worker policy
would substantially alleviate bilateral tensions stemming from illegal
immigration. Indeed, they fear that a temporary foreign worker program might become a supplementary source of strain in bilateral
relations above and beyond the problem of illegal immigration.

In support of the argument that such a program might harm
rather than promote improved bilateral relations with Mexico, the
critics once again turn to the historical record. Besides spurring illegal
immigration, the *bracero* program period was characterized by U.S.-
Mexican friction over the implementation and administration of their
bilateral labor program.[31] Mexico resented shortcomings in U.S. protection of Mexican workers' rights. The historical lesson to be drawn,
according to temporary worker program critics, is that despite the
best intentions and the granting of extensive formal protections to

alien workers, much can go wrong in the administration of these policies, and any shortcomings will likely complicate bilateral relations.

Other foreign policy arguments in favor of a temporary worker policy are likewise questionable. To the contention that such a program would shore up sending countries politically and economically, the critics respond that a temporary foreign worker policy may undercut political stability over the long run by forestalling necessary reforms. Such a program would be likely to spur the revolution of expectations which many experts on political development regard as destabilizing. Further, it is argued that worker remittances may be as likely to distort, and even inhibit, overall economic development as foster it.

The critics of a temporary worker policy do not dispute the positive role of remittances in the balance-of-payments situation of the countries of worker origin. This role is indeed significant. Their difficulty with the alleged beneficial effect of remittances begins when one examines (a) whether such funds are placed into productive use and (b) the broad socioeconomic impact of such uses on the sending societies. Research in actual remittance usage by Mediterranean-area migrant workers shows investment in housing and land purchases as accounting for between two-thirds and three-quarters of all remittances. The remainder tends to go toward purchasing consumer goods, retirement of debts, and other family-centered activities. Only a small fraction of the total goes toward investment in productive activities—mostly toward the purchase of agricultural equipment and the financing of service sector activities (opening of small stores, garages, or purchasing buses and taxis). The problem is that most of these activities are prototypical examples of clashing individual and societal goals. Migrants utilize their earnings in a manner essentially consistent with their goals for emigration. Yet, such spending behavior has unintended, and often serious, negative consequences.

For instance, investments in housing distort the real estate market and are responsible for serious inflationary pressure in the building sector. (Although such activity does generate significant employment opportunities for sending countries and does have helpful multiplier effects, its intermittent character has few lasting economic advantages.) Further, the propensity to purchase consumer goods with relative abandon in a limited market is responsible for broad demand-pull and, gradually, cost-push inflation along the entire economic structure of the country. The increasing pressure for luxury imports to satisfy the substantial consumption appetites of emigrant families for advanced services and products often leads to similar behavior by nonmigrant households—the latter having had their consumption aspirations raised via the demonstration effect of remittances. Finally, a corollary to these changing consumption patterns is the inflation of the economic and psychological value of foreign products (and the concomitant depression of that of domestic goods) and the increasing allocation of foreign currency reserves to import such products.[32]

Ultimately, the critics' argument boils down to the following. Temporary foreign worker programs have not worked very well in the past, either in the United States or Europe, and a massive new temporary foreign worker program would seem to entail much greater foreign policy risks than possible advantages. A temporary-worker policy probably is incompatible with the democratic values that U.S. foreign policy professes to defend around the world.

REFUGEES

In recent years, the refugee policy of the United States has sparked significant political controversy focused on the effect of refugees upon U.S. society. One casualty of this often acrimonious debate has been a balanced perspective on the international dimensions of U.S. refugee policy. The debate over refugee policy is usually framed in terms of domestic economic and political impacts, with little regard for international considerations. U.S. refugee policy is a multifaceted foreign policy issue that almost certainly will increase in salience on the U.S. foreign policy agenda as the world's army of refugees, numbering almost 17 million in 1981, continues to swell.

Refugee policy, as such, is relatively novel for the United States (see Chapter 9). In 1938, when President Franklin Roosevelt proposed the Évian Conference to attempt to ameliorate the plight of Jewish refugees fleeing Nazi persecution through international cooperation, U.S. foreign policy was hamstrung by U.S. immigration law restrictions. Instead of taking the lead in granting haven to European Jewish refugees, the United States set an example unfortunately followed by most other countries as well. Virtually nothing was done for Jewish refugees by the United States until after the end of the war.

United States entry into World War II brought the age of isolationism to an end. The United States became a founding member of the United Nations and an active supporter of the U.N. adjunct, the U.N. High Commission on Refugees (UNCHR). Yet the United States continued to lack a refugee policy per se. In 1952, the Immigration and Nationality Act contained a provision defining refugees as those fleeing Communism and the Middle East. However, there was no institutional arrangement for regular refugee entry.

Despite the ad hoc nature of refugee admissions throughout most of the post–World War II period, refugee admissions and aid given to refugees in Third World countries had already become significant components of U.S. foreign policy. Refugee admissions were an integral part of U.S. opposition to Communism, while U.S. support for the UNHCR and such agencies as the United Nations Works Relief Agency was based on both humanitarian and *Realpolitik* considerations. Refugees from Castro's Cuba became an ill-fated military instrument of U.S. foreign policy at the Bay of Pigs.

The United States debacle in Vietnam catapulted refugee policy to the center stage of U.S. foreign policy. In the closing weeks of the war, a huge, U.S.-organized airlift of Vietnamese out of that strife-torn land underscored the near total inadequacy of the refugee provisions of existing U.S. immigration law. The continuing out-migration of Vietnamese after the fall of South Vietnam, often in perilously overcrowded and inadequately supplied boats, was viewed with sympathy and concern by the United States, which saw in this exodus a massive rejection of Communism. The groundswell of sympathy and support for Vietnamese "boat people," as well as the immediacy of the newest Cuban refugee debacle, were instrumental in the passing of the Refugee Act of 1980, which laid the groundwork for a comprehensive, as opposed to an ad hoc, U.S. refugee policy.

Premier Fidel Castro's pledge in early 1980 to allow Cubans to emigrate triggered a mass exodus toward the United States. After initially hailing the emigration, the U.S. government felt compelled to reassess its stance when the size and composition of the flow became evident. Castro's act came to be regarded as a hostile action that threatened U.S. sovereignty.

The dramatic events of March and April 1980 climaxed the emergence of a new brand of international politics—migration politics. Even the most obdurate analysts of the high politics school had to recognize that the refugee crisis brought immigration questions to the forefront of U.S. foreign policy. The Cuban influx came to be regarded as a formidable policy instrument in the hands of a hostile regime. Meanwhile, reports from the Far East suggested that the United States was encouraging a refugee outflow as part of a deliberate policy to undercut the Communist regime of newly reunified Vietnam.[33] Already, in the early 1970s, the Jackson-Vanik amendment to the Trade Act of 1974 linking the grant of most-favored trade status to the Soviet Union with the Soviet acquiesence to Jewish emigration had figured prominently in superpower relations.

Officially, U.S. refugee policy is humanitarian and apolitical in nature. The United States is the single largest contributor to the UNHCR,[34] but foreign policy considerations clearly influence U.S. refugee policy. Despite redefinition of the refugee concept, the United States has been more prone to accept right-wing refugees than left-wing refugees. Thousands of Nicaraguans were granted haven in the United States following the victory of the Sandinistas. There is now considerable evidence that the Nicaraguan exiles are engaging in military training on U.S. soil in the hopes of counterrevolution.[35] At the same time, thousands of Salvadorans fleeing civil war are denied refugee status.[36] Determination of the legal status of the two nationality groups seems to hinge closely on the nature of U.S. relations with the respective governments.

Whereas Immigration and Naturalization Service officials on duty in Southeast Asia charge that large numbers of Vietnamese emigrants granted refugee status actually are economically motivated migrants who can prove no well-founded fear of presecution, Haitian emigrants almost always are denied refugee status.[37] The grant of refugee status to Haitians would be inconsistent with U.S. foreign policy toward that Caribbean nation. In fact, U.S. friendship for the Duvalier regime often seems to impinge upon determination of refugee status in the case of Haitians. There is mounting evidence that U.S.-Haitian cooperation in sea interdiction of migrants, along with harsh treatment of the migrants if they get to the United States, has undercut middle-class support for the regime.[38] Hence, a restrictive policy motivated in part by United States support for the Haitian dictatorship may in the end backfire and be counterproductive to the fundamental goal—maintenance of the Duvalier regime—being pursued.

Refugee policy considerations affect virtually every facet of U.S. foreign policy. Aid given in one context may help a friendly government, while in another context refugee aid may serve to undermine an opposing government. The United States does not recognize the concept of economic refugees and attempts to draw a sharp distinction between bona fide political refugees and those fleeing poverty. Legitimate fears of inundation by a tidal wave of economic refugees dictate a more thorough reappraisal of linkages between refugee phenomena and other aspects of U.S. foreign policy such as conventional arms sales, political interference, and economic policies such as trade, investment, tariffs, and quotas. U.S. foreign policy has directly and indirectly helped generate the huge contemporary refugee fluxes

that currently are seen as so potentially threatening. Yet refugee flows
still tend to be regarded as transitory eruptions upon the world scene
which are the result of circumstances of the moment instead of as a
persistent, growing, transnational phenomena.

In Haiti, like El Salvador, U.S. foreign policy plays a central role
in encouraging or discouraging refugee flows over the short term and
the long run. One wonders if migration from Haiti and El Salvador
would be such grievous problems in the 1980s if the United States had
not supported tyranny in those two countries over the preceding
decades.

VISITORS

This final category of migrants consists mainly of students and tourists. Again, in this instance, decisions to grant or deny entry to the
United States have multiple and diverse implications for U.S. foreign
policy.

The granting of visas to foreign students has traditionally been
seen as an important way to promote friendship and goodwill for the
United States abroad. Presumably, foreign students will undergo a
process of political socialization during their sojourns and return
home with positive impressions of U.S. democracy. Foreign-student
education also promotes the U.S. foreign policy goal of diffusing
technical knowledge and, implicitly, a predisposition toward Western
ideas about the development of Third World countries. Finally, and
in light of the projected severe declines in U.S. college enrollments,
many U.S. educators are predicting increased foreign student enrollments in the decades ahead.

Foreign students can have direct and indirect impacts of
significance to U.S. foreign policy. The mobilization of Iranian students in the United States and Western Europe into the anti-Shah
movement played an important role in the overthrow of that former
linchpin of U.S. Middle Eastern policy. Students abroad comprise an
elite whose oppositional political activities can complicate U.S. bilateral relations. Such students may become a domestic and international source of criticism of the conduct of U.S. foreign policy. In
theory, open debate and criticism of U.S. foreign policy serves and
enhances the policymaking process. But the fact that aliens are
criticizing U.S. foreign policy on U.S. soil often magnifies the effect of
the criticism, thereby making foreign students possibly significant
transnational pressure groups affecting U.S. foreign policy.

Advanced industrial democracies are open societies. They cannot be otherwise. Business, family life, education, the arts, medicine, and many other aspects of contemporary society all involve international travel. International tourism is a major industry in most advanced industrial democracies, and the United States is no exception. Every day, thousands of tourists, businessmen, and relatives enter the United States. The foreign policy significance of this inflow can at times be major.

Decisions to deny applications for visitor visas sometimes have political repercussions. For many years, former and current members of Communist parties abroad were regularly denied visas. This practice, originally justified on security grounds, has repeatedly sparked domestic and international criticism of the United States.[39] Efforts to curb visa abuse (overstay) by tightening up screening procedures at U.S. embassies has resulted in frayed relations with several U.S. allies, including the Philippines, Korea, and Greece.[40] More recently, visa applications have been scrutinized from the angle of combating international terrorism. Palestinian Arabs, many of whom have document problems (no passports) because of their technically alien status in their countries of sojourn, have had an especially difficult time obtaining visitor visas. U.S. concern over possible terrorist entry has increased the sense of injury commonly felt by Palestinians against the United States at a time when the United States has been trying to court sympathy with the so-called "moderate silent majority" of Palestinian Arabs.

The Reagan administration declared combating international terrorism to be its top foreign policy priority. Yet, when the administration publicly announced that a five-man terrorist "hit team" had been directed to assassinate President Reagan, the Immigration and Naturalization Service was hardly capable of preventing the clandestine entry of this alleged squad into the United States. A critical component of U.S. antiterrorism policy would seem to be the ability to monitor alien entries to and departures from the United States. But thus far the United States has not had that capability.

The linkage between U.S. antiterrorist policy and U.S. immigration policy underscores the theme of U.S. permeability to nonnational international political actors and its significance to U.S. foreign policy. The United States can influence international politics by decisions it makes on whom to allow in. However, the loss of control over events and the heightening of unpredictability as a result of international travel are perhaps more crucial foreign policy concerns.

Toward an Immigration Policy
More Relevant to Foreign Policy

The domestic political focus of U.S. immigration policy is to be explained primarily by the way it is formulated. Traditionally, U.S. immigration policy has been the virtual preserve of the Congress. The
executive branch, including the Department of State, has largely de-
ferred to Congress in this issue area. Interest groups oriented to
domestic considerations exert decisive influence. Foreign policy considerations carry little weight, since support for domestic interests
carries at least the expectation of rewards, electoral or otherwise, for
members of Congress. Consequently, foreign policy considerations
are less likely to be articulated in the making of immigration policy.
Ethnic interest groups sometimes express international concerns, but
their influence is generally limited to the narrow objective of securing
easier access to the United States for members of the nationality or
ethnic group abroad.

Given the pluralistic nature of public policymaking in the United
States, are the foreign policy concerns of U.S. immigration policy
condemned to subservience to domestic pressures? Does the policymaking system eschew the possibility of a more foreign policy relevant
immigration policy, or alternatively of a foreign policy that is more
concerned with immigration? We hope not.

The question is not whether foreign-policy-relevant change in
U.S. immigration policy will come, but when and how it will come.
Three major scenarios seem likely. First, immigration policy can stand
as is and be slowly overwhelmed by the events and forces that already
have prompted cries of alarm. The likely outcome of such a policy
choice would be a radical policy departure in the form of immigration
restriction, which would seek to seal off the United States from international migratory pressures. The foreign policy consequences of
such a departure would be severe. The United States would be be-
traying its national heritage and international image. A new kind of
isolationism in the realm of immigration policy would be a form of
negative, defensive adaptation to changed national and internatioual
circumstances. Immigration policy in this scenario would not be a
constructive instrument of U.S. foreign policy but rather a kind of
Maginot Line disguising national vulnerability and policy weakness
with the illusion of impregnability.

A second scenario could result from a continuing inability of the
United States to adapt to changing world circumstances as manifested
in increasing global migratory and refugee pressures. An essentially

laissez-faire approach to the immigration issue might result in fundamental alteration of U.S. society. A substratum, or underclass, of illegal aliens, overstayers, visitors, and so on, would grow, and an uneasy *modus vivendi* might be found. But the United States would no longer be a modern democracy; instead, it would resemble the political order of the Greek city-state democracies—a population of citizens ruling over a population of helots, or slaves.

Between the extremes of the two scenarios sketched above lies a discernible third option: constructive response to the global immigration problem. The key to this response is creative and farsighted diplomacy. The United States remains capable of absorbing large numbers of immigrants, many more than presently authorized. But as a democracy it must meet the global migration challenge on its own terms, which means a more liberal immigration policy instead of a massive temporary worker policy. The United States cannot possibly accommodate all immigration and refugee entry demands, so the key to its strategy must be to reduce or attenuate those underlying problems that have given rise to massive international migration, namely, hunger, war, and poverty.

Such an effort would require a fundamental reordering of U.S. foreign policy. For instance, the U.S. could no longer spare international efforts to bridge the North-South gap, as it did by its unconstructive participation in the Cancún Conference held in Mexico in late 1981. Some observers may feel that redirecting U.S. foreign policy toward increased economic and development assistance to the Third World and away from military aid betrays utopian idealism. It does not. Such a redirection of U.S. foreign policy is dictated by a rational calculation of the national interest. A fortress America bristling with draconian immigration laws and harsh measures against illegal workers is as unacceptable in terms of U.S. democratic traditions and values as is the scenario of the United States as a modern Athens or Rome—always wary of a new Spartacus.

U.S. foreign policy in this century has always been posited on the belief that U.S. national interests will ultimately be served best when other countries espouse democratic forms of government. Democratic order, however, can flourish only in societies that do not have crushing poverty. Hence, the United States must move with determination to alleviate massive global disparities in economic well-being, as a means of strengthening its own security. A sure consequence of a failure to accomplish this will be a global immigration crisis that will haunt the rich and imperil democratic order as we know it today.

Underlying any initiatives in this regard must be the realization that international migration has deep historical roots and is permanently grounded as an integral component of the global political economy. As such, the "solution" to the immigration "problem" must be forged on an international level, as a result of decisions made not only by individuals and socioeconomic and political groups within single national entities, but also through conflict and compromise across national boundaries. The United States must not be found wanting in this endeavor.

Notes

1. See Interagency Task Force on Immigration Policy, Departments of Justice, Labor, and State, *Staff Report* August 1979, pp. 279–296.

2. For example, Richard B. Craig, *The Bracero Program, Interest Groups, and Foreign Policy* (Austin: University of Texas Press, 1971).

3. A notable exception would be Michael S. Teitelbaum, "Right Versus Right: Immigration and Refugee Policy in the United States," *Foreign Affairs* 59 (Fall 1980): 21–59.

4. Francis H. Hinsley, *On Sovereignty* (London: C. A. Watt, 1966).

5. This is a theme found in Francis H. Hinsley, *Power and the Pursuit of Peace* (New York: Cambridge University Press, 1968).

6. The classic expositions of the "high politics" approach are found in Hans J. Morgenthau, *Politics Among Nations: The Struggle for Power and Peace,* 5th ed., rev. (New York: Alfred A. Knopf, 1978), and Raymond Aron, *Peace and War: A Theory of International Relations,* 1st ed. (Garden City, N.Y.: Doubleday, 1966).

7. Robert O. Keohane and Joseph S. Nye, *Power and Interdependence: World Politics in Transition* (Boston: Little, Brown & Co., 1977), p. 8.

8. James A. Nathan and James K. Oliver, *United States Foreign Policy and World Order* (Boston: Little, Brown & Co., 1981), p. 3.

9. Emilio Reyneri, "The Impact of the Migrant Workers Inflow and the Position of Europe in the International Division of Labor: From Old Benefits to New Problems" (Revision of paper delivered at the Conference of Europeanists, Washington, D.C., October 23–25, 1980), pp. 15–18.

10. John K. Galbraith, *The Nature of Mass Poverty* (Cambridge: Harvard University Press, 1979); the "equilibrium" of poverty refers to the inability of impoverished countries to gain more than marginal increases in wealth and escape from the cycle of poverty. The result of this inability is that people "accommodate" themselves to low living standards and are reluctant to take the substantial risks required to change their condition.

11. See, e.g., Stephen Castles and Godula Kosack, *Immigrant Workers and Class Structure in Western Europe* (New York: Oxford University Press, 1973), and Manuel Castells, "Immigrant Workers and Class Struggles in Advanced Capitalism: The Western European Experience," *Politics and Society* 5: 33–66.

12. Demetrios G. Papademetriou, "Rethinking International Migration: A Review," *Comparative Political Studies,* forthcoming.

13. Alejandro Portes and John Walton, *Labor, Class, and the International System* (New York: Academic Press, 1981), p. 4.

14. Helga Hveem, "The Global Dominance System: Notes on a Theory of Global Political Economy," *Journal of Peace Research* 10 (1973):319–340.

15. See Jean-Marie Dupont, "Pourquoi?" *Le monde,* January 22, 1976, pp. 1, 30, and Kenneth McLennan and Malcolm Lovell, Jr., "Immigration Reform: An Economic Necessity," *Journal of the Institute for Socioeconomic Studies* 6 (Summer 1981): 38–52.

16. André Gorz, "Immigrant Labor," *New Left Review,* no. 61 (May–June 1970): 28–31.

17. See Michael J. Piore, *Birds of Passage: Migrant Labor and Industrial Societies* (New York: Cambridge University Press, 1979).

18. David Gregory and Wayne Cornelius argue that the choice was not between more or less immigration but rather between authorized and illegal immigration. See, e.g., Gregory's testimony before the Senate Subcommittee on Immigration on October 22, 1981.

19. Thomas S. Kuhn, *The Structure of Scientific Revolutions* (Chicago: University of Chicago Press, 1964).

20. See Société Française pour le Droit International, *Colloque de Clermont-Ferrand: Les travailleurs étrangers et le Droit International* (Paris: A. Pedone, 1979).

21. Mark J. Miller, *Foreign Workers in Western Europe: An Emerging Political Force* (New York: Praeger, 1981).

22. David Vidal, "200,000 Ecuadoreans Share Hope in the Future," *New York Times,* July 19, 1979, p. B2.

23. Robin Herman, "Votes in '80 Italian Election Sought by Brooklyn Visitor," *New York Times,* January 15, 1979.

24. Drora Kass and Seymour Martin Lipset, "America's New Wave of Jewish Immigrants," *New York Times Sunday Magazine,* December 7, 1980, pp. 44ff.

25. See Select Commission on Immigration and Refugee Policy, *U.S. Immigration Policy and the National Interest,* Final Report, March 1, 1981 (Washington, D.C.: Government Printing Office, 1981), pp. 19–34.

26. See, e.g., David D. Gregory, "A U.S.-Mexican Temporary Workers Program: The Search for Co-determination," and Wayne A. Cornelius, "Legalizing the Flow of Temporary Migrant Workers from Mexico," both in Select Commission on Immigration and Refugee Policy, *Staff Report,* 1981, Appendix F.

27. Joyce Vialet, ed., *Selected Readings on U.S. Immigration Policy and Law* (Washington, D.C.: Government Printing Office, 1980), p. 260.

28. Tad Szulc, "Foreign Policy Aspects of the Border," in *Views Across the Border: The United States and Mexico,* ed. Stanley Ross (Albuquerque: University of New Mexico Press, 1978), pp. 236–238. See also *New York Times,* February 11, 12, and 19, 1979.

29. Joyce Vialet, *Temporary Worker Programs: Background and Issues* (Washington, D.C.: Government Printing Office, 1980), pp. 42–43.

30. Mark J. Miller and William W. Boyer, "Foreign Workers in the U.S. Virgin Islands: Lessons for the United States," Select Commission on Immigration and Refugee Policy, *U.S. Immigration Policy and the National Interest,* Final Report, March 1, 1981, Appendix F of Supplement (Washington, D.C.: Government Printing Office, 1981), pp. 250–279.

31. Vialet, *Temporary Worker Programs,* pp. 32–56.

32. Demetrios G. Papademetriou, "Emigration and Return in the Mediterranean Littoral: Conceptual, Research, and Policy Agendas" (Paper delivered at the First European Conference on International Return Migration, Rome, Italy, November 1981).

33. Patrick Smith, "Pull Factor Gets the Push," and Richard Nations, "The Saigon Cowboys Will Not Give Up," both in *Far Eastern Economic Review,* July 17, 1981: 26–28 and 32.

34. Bernard D. Nossiter, "Worldwide Work of U.N. Agency Seems Endless," *New York Times,* October 15, 1981, p. A6.

35. Robert Lindsay, "Foes of Nicaragua Regime Train in California," *New York Times,* January 18, 1982, p. A1.

36. Frank C. Kiehne, "Deported to El Salvador," *New York Times,* February 3, 1982, p. A27.

37. John Tenhala, "Boat People Flee Haiti to U.S.," in *1980 World Refugee Survey* (New York: U.S. Committee for Refugees, 1980), pp. 52–54.

38. William Paley, "Haiti Increasingly Unstable," *Manchester Guardian Weekly,* January 24, 1982, p. 7.

39. For a recent incident, see Michael T. Kaufman, "Two Visa Disputes Annoy and Intrigue India," *New York Times,* February 11, 1982, p. A10.

40. See, e.g., Interagency Task Force, *Staff Report,* pp. 293–94.

CHAPTER 7

Treating the Causes: Illegal Immigration and U.S. Foreign Economic Policy

Sidney Weintraub

It is commonplace to state that U.S. policy should treat the causes of illegal immigration and not the symptoms.[1] This is an unexceptionable viewpoint for the long run, or else dealing with symptoms will be perennial. Most of the underlying causes of international migration are not amenable to U.S. policy: proximity, kinship, differences in economic opportunity, and the structure of societies which generates migrants and refugees. What U.S. policy can do is contribute to economic development in sending countries so that the push factors may be reduced, if not now then over time. "Contribute" is a key word, since the United States cannot direct development programs of other countries. This chapter discusses the feasibility and potential consequences of a U.S. approach to immigration issues that seeks to deal explicitly with causes.

The discussion will be of U.S. foreign economic policy. It will not deal with political policy, or human rights actions, or even domestic economic policy, to the extent that these can be separated from foreign economic policy. U.S. political policy can stimulate or discourage migrant flows, as witness the causes and consequences of refugee flows to the United States from Southeast Asia. Human rights policies can encourage people to migrate, as U.S. policy did when it linked most-favored-nation tariff treatment for the Soviet Union with greater freedom of emigration. When the U.S. economy is stagnant, there is less incentive to migrate here in search of a job than when the economy is booming and the pull factors are heightened. This immigration outcome, however, is and must be a side effect of domestic

185

economic policy. On the other hand, aid, trade, and investment policies can be manipulated to some extent to take immigration considerations into account.

First I will examine briefly some of the relevant theories, those dealing with migration, trade, investment, and development generally, and seek to find points of confluence among these theories, which usually are examined in isolation by specialists from different disciplines. The central part of the chapter will look specifically at current U.S. foreign economic policy in order to speculate on changes that could be made to diminish incentives for out-migration from developing, sending countries and to assess whether the potential results are worth the effort. A final section will summarize the conclusions of this examination. The chapter takes no position on whether migration is good or bad for either the sending or the receiving country. It assumes that the United States would like to stanch the inflow of illegal aliens, a position stated by both the Carter and Reagan administrations.

Theoretical Considerations

The most comprehensive theories of migration focus on structural features in both sending and receiving societies and their complementarity, that is, on reinforcing incentives for exodus from one country and entry into another.[2] The incentives to leave one country for another relate to employment possibilities, whether jobs occupy a person's full working energy day in and day out, season in and season out, the opportunities for upward economic mobility (can an underemployed farm worker aspire to owning his own farm, or his own house after moving to the city?), and the limits to personal and professional satisfaction. All people do not have these aspirations to the same degree; a skilled researcher is more apt to focus on professional satisfaction as a basis for emigration than an uneducated farmhand. Not everybody who fits into one of these categories does, in fact, leave his country. It takes personal initiative to migrate. It also generally requires information, reliable or otherwise, about what awaits one at the other end. The motivation to emigrate cannot be explained solely in terms of economics, since personal characteristics, cross-country networks, and other social considerations play a large role, but neither can it be explained without economics.

The empirical evidence demonstrates that people who emigrate to another country come not from the poorest groups of the sending society but from the middle spectrum, or more accurately for illegal migrants, from the lower end of this middle group.[3] A similar phenomenon exists for countries; those with substantial out-migration are not the very poorest but rather the middle-income category of developing countries.[4] Intuitively, this conforms with what one would expect from a comprehensive socioeconomic explanation for migration. Personal initiative and a reasonable degree of information about what can be expected in the country of destination is more likely to exist among persons above the subsistence level than among those whose full attention must be devoted to survival.

This is a significant point, and one to which I shall revert, because it means that increased economic opportunity in the sending country may not translate immediately into reduced emigration. It may lead to the reverse. The fewer the number of people living in absolute poverty in a society, the greater the proclivity to seek fortunes somewhere else, in urban rather than rural areas within a country, or out of the country.

Distance makes an obvious difference in explaining the origin-destination combination in international migration, particularly for illegal immigrants who may intend to be only sojourners or temporary workers outside their own country. The cost to migrate is one reason for this. For the United States, illegal immigration comes mostly from nearby places, such as Mexico, the Caribbean, Central America, and northern South America (see Tables 7.1 and 7.2). The earliest attempts to theorize rigorously about migration gave pride of place to geography along with economics, as was natural when transportation was relatively more costly and certainly more time-consuming than it is today.[5] Over time, the influence of proximity was reinforced by habits of migration and by the networks established in the proletarian diasporas that developed in receiving countries.[6] Geography still counts, but so do other circumstances that helped bring these networks into existence, such as prior colonial relationships (France and Africa, the United Kingdom and South Asia, the United States and the Philippines) and previous efforts to contract for temporary labor, such as the U.S. *bracero* program with Mexico and the guestworker programs in Europe. The explanatory power of distance also must be tempered by standard economic analysis of opportunity cost.[7]

There is overwhelming evidence that "temporary" migration is a myth, not for all who migrate under short-term contracts or with short-term intentions, but for a significant proportion of such people. This has been amply demonstrated in Europe,[8] and it is the expected

Table 7.1 *Principal Countries Sending Migrants to the United States as Measured by Absolute Number of Expulsions from the United States and Expulsions per 100,000 Population*[a]

Sending Country	Absolute Annual Expulsions	Annual Expulsions per 100,000 of Population
Mexico	834,700	1,212.1
Antigua	168	236.6
St. Kitts-Nevis	[b]	204.3
Belize	217	149.7
Bahamas	271	128.4
El Salvador	4,892	114.8
St. Lucia	[b]	89.6
Dominica	[b]	88.5
Barbados	208	80.3
Guatemala	3,097	49.5
Trinidad and Tobago	409	42.7
Jamaica	743	34.7
Guyana	[b]	31.4
Canada	5,034	21.9
Dominican Republic	1,066	20.9
Honduras	627	19.1
Ecuador	1,316	18.5
Costa Rica	354	17.5
Nicaragua	345	15.3
Panama	217	12.6
Greece	1,073	11.7
Hong Kong	422	9.5
Colombia	2,071	8.5
Haiti	369[c]	7.0
Chile	576	5.5
Peru	809	5.1
Israel	265	2.8
Taiwan	392	2.4
Venezuela	235	1.8
Argentina	449	1.7
Poland	512	1.5
Philippines	590	1.3
Portugal	111	1.1
United Kingdom	551	1.0
Spain	224	0.6

Source: Milton D. Morris and Albert Mayio, *Foreign Policy Aspects of Immigration,* a study by the Brookings Institution for the Employment and Training Administration (Washington, D.C.: U.S. Department of Labor, 1980), Tables 3-6 (pp. 3–25), 3-7a (pp. 3–31), and 4-1 (pp. 4–5).

[a] Based on average expulsions for 1975–1977 per 100,000 population of sending country.
[b] Total of the four countries is 566.
[c] This is understated if recent refugee flows are taken into account.

Table 7.2 *Population and Income Data for Main Countries Sending Migrants to the United States*

Sending Country	Population, Mid-1979[a] (in thousands)	Population Growth Rate, 1970–1978 (percent)	Gross National Product Per Capita, 1979[a] (dollars)
Mexico	67,621	3.3	1,590
Guatemala	6,825	2.9	1,020
El Salvador	4,424	2.9	670
Honduras	3,565	3.4	530
Nicaragua	2,587	3.3	660
Costa Rica	2,163	2.5	1,810
Panama	1,858	2.7	1,350
Belize	131	1.0	1,030
Antigua	74	1.3	1,070
St. Kitts-Nevis	50	0.9	780
St. Vincent	106	2.2	490
St. Lucia	122	2.2	780
Dominica	79	1.2	410
Barbados	253	0.6	2,400
Bahamas	231	3.6	2,780
Trinidad and Tobago	1,152	1.2	3,390
Jamaica	2,184	1.7	1,240
Dominican Republic	5,286	3.0	990
Haiti	4,963	1.7	260
Guyana	843	1.7	570
Ecuador	8,068	3.3	1,050
Colombia	26,122	2.3	1,010
For comparison			
United States	219,773	0.8	10,820
Puerto Rico	3,415	2.6	2,970

Source: 1980 World Bank Atlas (Washington, D.C.: World Bank, 1981), pp. 18–20.
Note: Data on the islands of the eastern Caribbean are labeled as tentative in source.
[a]Preliminary.

outcome if one accepts the structural explanations for migration discussed above. If the forces that first motivated migration remain in existence, there will be pressure to repeat the process or, because of the complexity of round trips repeated periodically, for the migrant to stay put in his or her new country. There are emotional and social ties that attract a migrant home, and many do go home, some repeatedly year after year, but many do not. Geography, trip time, trip cost, and the ease of reentry into the receiving country are all relevant to whether a migrant stays put. A Mexican is more likely to come for work in the United States and then go home for a time than a Colombian, but the competing attractions between staying and going will not always lead a Mexican to go home again. The proof of this is that there are millions of Mexicans living illegally in the United States.

A corollary question to that which asks whether U.S. foreign economic policy can inhibit emigration from countries whose people tend to come to the United States is whether U.S. policy can encourage the return of people who came with the intention of staying only temporarily. The new outflow of people from Puerto Rico to the United States was about 40,000 per year in the 1950s and early 1960s. U.S. economic policy toward Puerto Rico was then altered, and the direction of the net human flow was reversed in the late 1960s and early 1970s by a return flow of close to this number from the United States to Puerto Rico.[9] Is this replicable elsewhere? There are special circumstances in the U.S.-Puerto Rican relationship that do not apply to migrants from other countries, mainly the freedom to come and go. During the past four years, because of the high unemployment in Puerto Rico and the legislated cuts in the U.S. budget affecting programs in Puerto Rico, there has been a renewal of the net flow to the mainland.[10]

The three broad areas of foreign economic policy which the United States can manipulate are in the conduct of foreign trade, investment, and aid. Measured in dollar-flow terms, trade is the most important instrument (see Table 7.3). This is particularly true in relations with Mexico, which the evidence indicates sends more illegal migrants to the United States than all other countries combined.[11]

Trade theory is in an unsettled state, perhaps equally so with migration theory. Most textbooks stress the Heckscher-Ohlin approach, which seeks to explain the direction and content of trade by the relative endowments of different countries of different factors, especially labor and capital. This has been refined from earlier versions to take the heterogeneity of labor into account (and, indeed, the heterogeneity of capital as well). U.S. exports may embody more labor than U.S. imports,[12] but technical skills of the labor in U.S. exports are of a higher quality. If this is an accurate explanation of trade flows among countries, one would expect developing countries to have a comparative advantage in products that embody a high proportion of relatively unskilled labor and relatively less capital than would be the case for U.S. production and exports. Lower-quality cotton textiles,

Table 7.3   *U.S. Trade with, Investment in, and Bilateral Concessional Aid to Main Migrant-Sending Countries (in millions of dollars)*

Sending Country	U.S. Exports (1980)	U.S. Imports (1980)	U.S. Investment (end 1979)	Bilateral Economic Aid[c] (USFY 1979)[d]
Mexico	14,885.8	12,519.5	4,575	—
Guatemala	548.4	435.0	221[a]	24.8
El Salvador	268.2	427.3	111[a]	11.4
Honduras	373.7	418.8	202[a]	29.1
Nicaragua	247.3	211.1	121[a]	18.3
Costa Rica	493.6	356.4	143[a]	17.9
Regional/Central America	—	—	—	2.8
Panama	688.5	329.5	2,756	21.2
Belize	51.9	59.7	8[a]	—
Bahamas	391.5	1,381.8	2,081	—
Jamaica	302.1	383.0	[b]	18.4
Dominican Republic	786.8	785.9	244[a]	52.8
Haiti	303.8	251.7	16[a]	24.8
Leeward and Windward Islands	148.6	34.5	[b]	[e]
Barbados	134.1	95.6	23[a]	[e]
Regional/Caribbean	—	—	—	26.8
Trinidad and Tobago	673.6	2,378.3	851[a]	—
Guyana	95.7	119.8	24[a]	8.5
Colombia	1,708.4	1,240.5	885	—

Source: U.S. Bureau of the Census, Department of Commerce, *U.S. General Imports: World Area by Commodity Groupings,* FT155/Annual 1980 (Washington, D.C.: Government Printing Office, 1981); U.S. Bureau of the Census, Department of Commerce, *U.S. Exports: World Area by Commodity Groupings,* FT455/Annual 1980, (Washington, D.C.: Government Printing Office, 1981); *Survey of Current Business* 60 (August 1980): 27; and Agency for International Development, Latin American and Caribbean Bureau, internal tables.
[a] End 1978.
[b] Data suppressed in source to avoid disclosure of individual companies.
[c] Economic-aid figures are the total bilateral commitments for development assistance, P.L. 480 (food for peace program), economic support funds, and other, mainly disaster relief and Peace Corps.
[d] Aid figures have been highly variable in recent years as a result of U.S. attention in the Caribbean basin. Many individual country aid levels have increased since fiscal year 1979; others, such as Nicaragua, have decreased.
[e] Aid to the small islands in the eastern Caribbean is distributed by intermediary institutions under the Regional/Caribbean program. Regional/Central American aid is in addition to aid shown for the individual countries.

apparel, shoes, electronic componentry which requires much hand labor, and simple engines are among the products for which these conditions apply. These are precisely the products assembled in the border industries in Mexico (the *maquiladora*) and in similar plants in other developing countries. U.S. trade policy could, in theory, affect employment positively in developing countries that send migrants by permitting unrestricted imports of these products or, even more so, by giving preferential treatment to such imports from *only* these countries. I will return to this theme in the next section because such preferential treatment has in fact been proposed by the U.S. government, even though it represents a sharp departure from the U.S. trade policy of most of this century.

The product-cycle theory of trade does not discard the Heckscher-Ohlin approach, but it focuses on the learning process that trade engenders. This genre of theories would show a typical product cycle along the following lines: product innovation in an economically and technologically advanced country, production for the home market, then exports, in due course investment in the former export market for its home consumption, then competition in other export markets, and finally the loss of competitiveness in the originating country. This cycle has been demonstrated for several industries, such as office machinery, many consumer durables, and currently the automotive industry.[13] The production functions, that is, the mix of factor use, may not remain stable as the cycle proceeds. Indeed, one would expect a producer to take advantage of the relatively cheaper labor in production processes in developing countries, and the evidence is that this in fact occurs. One complaint of developing country economists is that it does not take place enough, that production processes are transferred from high-wage to low-wage countries without adequate modification. Again, as with Heckscher-Ohlin, U.S. stimulation of this product-cycle process, such as by encouragement of U.S. investment in migrant-sending developing countries and by keeping open access to the U.S. market for products in which the cycle has led to a loss of U.S. competitiveness, should lead to employment creation outside the United States.

Much trade, perhaps a quarter or more of total world trade, takes place today among related parties. Related party trade between Mexico and the United States is about 45 percent of the total. Related party trade between the U.S. and Central America and the Caribbean is also substantial.[14] Much of the trade between affiliated parties is not in final products but in components. Trade generated by assembly plants in Mexico, the Caribbean, and Central America takes place mostly within the same industry. Components are sent outside the United States for the addition of value using relatively cheap labor, and then reimported into the United States by paying duty only on the value added abroad. It is hard to know whether this system increases employment abroad. It apparently does, since the very intent is to use cheap foreign labor; and it could be that complete elimination of U.S. tariff and nontariff barriers on the products involved in this trade would lead to establishment of all production steps in these industries in low-wage countries.[15]

Freedom of trade can be a partial substitute for freedom of factor movements, but the substitutability is not perfect.[16] In addition, there are "real world" impediments to this substitutability. Trade is not free, and many of the most serious trade barriers today affect products in which developing countries have a comparative advantage. The multifiber arrangement, for example, contains import quotas on trade in textiles and wearing apparel. Tariff levels are higher for labor-intensive finished products than for the components of these products, to deliberately encourage labor use in the home rather than the exporting country. These significant policy matters will be taken up in the next section.

The distortion of factor use comes not only from protection by the importing country but also from protection and incentives by the developing country. Mexico's development model encouraged the substitution of capital for labor by such devices as minimum wages, making labor relatively expensive, and exoneration from otherwise high tariffs for the importation of capital equipment, making capital relatively cheap. The Mexican development model encouraged labor emigration,[17] and there is little that U.S. trade policy can accomplish to counter this in the face of the overwhelming dominance of Mexican policy on events in Mexico.

This is an appropriate point on which to shift to investment theory and its relevance to migration issues. Here again there is a theoretical world which, as with trade theory, has some relevance, and a practical world which has even greater relevance. Classical theory, based on competitive markets and freedom of capital movement, would result in investment moving to locations in which comparative advantages would be optimized, and over time there would be a tendency for wages (and product prices) to equalize across countries. It was evident to the early theorists that this perfect world market did not exist; much of the difference ascribed to domestic as opposed to international economics was based on the greater freedom of factor movement (particularly labor, but also capital) within rather than between economies. Many economies are so primitive in terms of infra-structure and availability of trained manpower that they are not suitable locations for many kinds of investment.

Practical considerations further dilute this competitive model. Developing countries often provide incentives, such as tax holidays and import protection, to attract foreign direct investment. They also impose limitations on foreign direct investment in terms of percent-age of foreign ownership or sectors of permissible foreign invest-ment, or require minimum levels of domestic components to be incorporated in final products. The market for capital movement is not free, but it is not absolutely controlled either. Mexico, for exam-ple, has stringent laws about acceptance of foreign direct investment, but this investment is nevertheless substantial. U.S. investment is par-ticularly significant in the *maquiladora* industry, where limitations on percentage of foreign equity positions do not apply. The countries of Central America and the Caribbean have some restrictions on foreign investment, but their stance is more one of seeking such investment in the interest of job creation.[18]

From the viewpoint of limiting emigration, the key issue is the number of additional job opportunities created in migrant-sending countries from foreign investment. For a populous country like Mex-ico, the additional jobs that can be created from foreign investment must be marginal. For example, in 1980, new foreign direct invest-ment in Mexico was $963 million and domestic investment was the equivalent of $45.7 billion.[19] For the countries of the eastern Carib-bean, whose populations are small but whose unemployment and underemployment rates are high, additional manufacturing or as-sembly plants can be more significant to the total economy.

One question that arises with respect to job creation from foreign investment or from increasing job opportunities in rural areas, by whatever means, or in urban areas to which rural populations are moving, is whether the short-term result of more jobs deters or stimu-lates emigration. The answer is unclear.[20] In the long term, however, there is no question but that opportunities must exist at home in order to keep people with initiative at home.

It is not trade theory as such, or investment theory, that is the heart of the matter with respect to the creation of opportunities that would constitute counterpressures to out-migration incentives, but rather how these aspects of economics fit into total development pro-grams of migrant-sending countries. Mexico's employment problem, its highly unequal distribution of income, and the pressures these problems create for rural to urban migration and for out-migration, are the result of a complex of measures that shape the entire Mexican economic and social structure. The same is true for the countries of the Caribbean and Central America. For the smaller Caribbean islands, development problems are both more complex than for the larger countries and simpler. They are simpler in that opportunities must be created for fewer human beings; they are more complex in that the means to create these opportunities are less available.

Development theory is infinitely more complex than any of its parts, such as those dealing with trade and investment, because it deals with an entire national environment. Dealing with the parts has gone through fashions, one of beliefs firmly and devoutly held only to change as experience has been negative. In Latin America and the Caribbean, which is the appropriate region for concentration in an essay dealing with illegal migration to the United States, the theoretical emphasis in the 1950s and early 1960s was on import substituting industrialization (ISI). This came about practically when the great depression of the 1930s wiped out much of Latin America's earnings from the export of nonmanufactured goods; and if these goods were to be had, domestic industries had to be created. ISI also was fostered by theories promulgated by the Economic Commission for Latin America, which saw industrialization as the only escape for Latin America's structural problems.[21] Practically all of Latin America's industries were created behind high protective walls, and most of the industries turned out to be noncompetitive in world markets. In the stress on ISI, agriculture tended to be neglected, and consequently production suffered.

The theory began to be modified in the late 1960s and 1970s. In most of Latin America today, export promotion is equally important as import substitution, indeed, much more so in many countries.[22] Export promotion is given much lip service in Mexico, but the emphasis remains on import substitution and protection of domestic industries at almost any cost. Agricultural production is now stressed in all Latin American development models, whereas in the past it was seen mostly as a source of resources to build industry and the source of cheap products to fill the bellies of politically active urban residents.

The shift to export promotion means, however, that protectionism in export markets can extract a heavy toll on development programs. It is not accurate to state that past protectionism in industrial countries has fundamentally impeded development programs of emigrant-sending countries, since those countries that embarked reasonably early on promoting exports have in fact been able to penetrate markets. This is particularly true for the newly industrializing countries of Asia, such as South Korea, Taiwan, and Hong Kong. The concern, rather, is that the current atmosphere of relatively low growth and high unemployment in the industrial countries will not only lead to rejection of past programs of importing "temporary" labor, but also compound this problem by rejection of imports from developing countries. This may be the primordial trade issue of the early 1980s; it is being so touted by the most respected international economic organizations.[23]

The U.S. and other aid programs, both bilateral and multilateral, must work within the development framework established by aid-receiving countries. U.S. bilateral aid provides little direct assistance to industry. Instead it focuses on alleviation of poverty and stimulation of agriculture. If it is true that the first migration response to the elimination of poverty is to move to urban centers or out of the country, this emphasis will have the short-term result of exacerbating the illegal immigration problem of the United States. The bilateral U.S. aid program also focuses on family planning and population problems, and over time this should relieve some of the pressure to emigrate from those countries with currently high rates of population growth.[24] This will take time, of course, since the decline in population growth rates will not affect potential migrants for another fifteen to twenty years.[25]

The different economic instruments available to the United States are not equally applicable to all migrant-sending countries. Mexico receives no bilateral aid from the United States. It does receive nonconcessional aid from the World Bank and the Inter-American Development Bank, to both of which the United States contributes. However, these gross official capital flows to Mexico amount to hundreds of millions of dollars each year, whereas Mexico's gross foreign-exchange receipts from borrowing in private capital markets amount to billions of dollars and receipts from the export of goods and services to about $30 billion currently.[26] Thus, for Mexico, the country sending most illegal migrants to the United States, U.S. aid policy is irrelevant and even the actions of the multilateral development banks are marginal. But U.S. trade policy can have some significance, at least in theory.

Most Central American and Caribbean countries, however, are recipients of U.S. aid, and aid is undoubtedly the most flexible instrument of U.S. foreign economic policy vis-à-vis these countries. U.S. trade and investment policies are significant as well because durable and attractive economic opportunities in these countries must be based on domestically inspired production of goods and services.

It is now possible to summarize the interaction of the various theoretical considerations, those relating to migration, trade, investment, aid, and development generally—but tempering pure theory with practical considerations. Four points merit stress:

1. There is an obvious difference between the effects on migration in the short and long run from increased domestic job opportunities and higher incomes. By itself, this point hardly needs mentioning, but it is worth emphasizing that the duration of the short run can be quite short. It took Japan not much more than a decade after World War II to transform itself from a labor-surplus country to a labor-shortage country. The same was true for South Korea and Taiwan in the 1960s and 1970s. Hong Kong finds itself short of much labor despite continued refugee inflow. In each country cited, jobs were created as a result of total development programs. It is possible, in other words, for policy to have an impact on out-migration pressures in a relatively brief period.

2. The desire to emigrate seems to increase as a person raises his or her income from the lowest end of the income ladder, but there is a point on this ladder when the emigration pressure diminishes. This was evident in South Korea and in Puerto Rico. What this implies is that if a country wishes to lower the incentives for emigration, there is no escape from development programs that create domestic job and social mobility opportunities. Things may get worse before they get better in terms of emigration pressure, but the evidence is that they do get better at a certain point.

3. The case of Puerto Rico is instructive because it shows that it is possible to reverse the incentives from out-migration to return migration. This case is not really useful as a model for other countries, however, because of the special circumstances in its relationship with the United States. This relationship included tax privileges for Puerto Rico, free entry for all its export products, and a level of budgetary transfers in the billions of dollars, none of which is likely to be repeated to the same extent in U.S. relations with other countries of the Caribbean and Central America, or Mexico. The other unique aspect of the case of Puerto Rico is that the migrant could come and go; a decision to return to Puerto Rico was not irrevocable, since legal entry to the United States could be repeated over and over again.

4. Finally, a point made earlier should be restated, namely, that U.S. foreign economic policy can play some part in diminishing emigration incentives, but this inevitably will be a peripheral role, U.S. foreign economic policy cannot compensate for an inadequate domestic development policy in migrant-sending countries.

Policy Options for the United States

How can the United States help reduce emigration pressures in sending countries? Suggestions to the U.S. government for dealing with causes of emigration usually are phrased in the most general terms: give more aid, reduce trade barriers. A few people have made more specific proposals. Jorge Bustamante of Mexico has suggested setting up units for agricultural production, processing of agricultural products, and establishment of assembly plants using mostly Mexican inputs, in the rural areas of Mexico from which most emigration originates.[27] The idea is to encourage intensive use of labor in places where labor otherwise leaves. Bustamante further suggested that the United States should accept unrestricted importation of products from these areas and use the agricultural output in the U.S. food-for-peace program.[28] Wayne Cornelius has made a similar suggestion of targeting job-creation activities in the main sending areas of Mexico by use of public works projects, double-cropping, and other techniques.[29] Cornelius does not pretend that such action would absorb all the additions to the Mexican labor force over the next decade or more. Some aspects of what Cornelius suggests are in fact being carried out under the PIDER project (Integrated Rural Development Program), an extensive undertaking covering many of the main sending areas in Mexico which is being financed by the Mexican government with the assistance of the World Bank and the Inter-American Development Bank. The intent is to create job opportunities, in agriculture and otherwise, in rural areas.

Creating employment opportunities in Mexico should have a favorable long-term impact in reducing pressures to emigrate, but it is simplistic to think that migratory patterns are static or that creating job opportunities in areas that currently send most migrants will have a decisive impact on total Mexican migration. Francisco Alba, also a Mexican, makes the proper point that the employment problem in Mexico is global and not just in the areas of emigration.[30] Human beings are mobile, and the need is to create jobs—and not merely jobs in places where people now depart from Mexico to seek work in the United States. The Mexican border-industry program is a good paradigm of the global nature of employment. These assembly plants have helped create more than 100,000 jobs along the U.S.-Mexican border, filled not by men most prone to migrate, as had been hoped, but mostly by young women, who have not been the main problem in emigration from Mexico.[31] In the process, the border area attracted many men who learned the ropes of migration. While the border-industry program has been of value to Mexico in augmenting exports and in creating many jobs, it has to some extent increased the pressure for emigration by the prime emigrating group of young men.

In early 1982, the U.S. government proposed a major program for dealing with economic issues in the Caribbean basin (i.e., for countries in and abutting the Caribbean, including Central America and northern South America). The objective is to forge a cooperative program of assistance by the United States, Canada, Mexico, and Venezuela, each donor country focusing on recipient countries of its choice in the manner it deems best.[32] The motive of the U.S. government seems to be primarily to strengthen the security of the region against infiltration from Cuba or from internal pro-Communist pressures, but the means will be largely economic, including aid, trade, and investment incentives. One objective will be to foster job creation in the target countries and thereby reduce emigration pressures. The programs proposed by the U.S. administration are quite precise, involving tax benefits and trade preferences for Caribbean basin countries which will not be extended to other developing countries.[33]

TRADE

Mexico sent 63 percent of its merchandise exports, by value, to the United States in 1980.[34] The percentage was typical for recent years, even though the composition of Mexico's exports is changing as petroleum grows in relative importance. Other individual migrant-sending countries rely as much as Mexico on the U.S. market, but the percentages are lower both for the Caribbean and for Central America, upward of 30 percent for the former and 50 percent for the latter.[35] In all cases, the U.S. market is significant and U.S. trade policy is therefore highly germane.

Table 7.3 gives the absolute level of U.S. merchandise trade in 1980 with the individual migrant-sending countries. The figures are large for the more populous countries and insignificant in U.S. terms for the smaller countries of the eastern Caribbean. This does not necessarily mean that U.S. trade policy is irrelevant for the latter, since a small concession by the United States (for instance, the liberal admission of goods from a new processing or assembly plant) can have an important effect on employment in countries with small labor forces. It is not just U.S. policy regarding merchandise trade that can have an impact on the economies of these countries, but also U.S.

policies with respect to their earnings from services, such as tourism. Increased earnings from exports of goods and services can create jobs directly and indirectly by helping to finance development programs.

U.S. merchandise trade concessions can take two broad forms: the reduction of tariffs or the reduction of nontariff barriers. These reductions can be granted either on a most-favored-nation (MFN) basis (i.e., by treating all foreign countries alike) or on a preferential basis.[36] With the major exception of the general system of preferences (GSP), which provides preferential treatment for specific imports from all developing countries, unconditional MFN has been the cornerstone of U.S. trade policy since the 1920s. The rationale for this policy is that the United States has worldwide trade and political interests and that optimizing these is not compatible with special preferential treatment for some countries. The European Economic Community (EEC) is less rigorous in its adherence to the unconditional MFN principle, and in addition to its GSP program for all developing countries, it grants special preferences to developing countries in Africa, the Caribbean, and Asia (ACP countries), which are signatories of the Lomé agreement with the EEC. A question that arises, therefore, is whether the United States might emulate the EEC and provide special trade preferences to the main migrant-sending countries. I will deal in order with the issues raised in this paragraph.

In successive rounds of negotiations in the General Agreement on Tariffs and Trade (GATT), most U.S. tariff rates have been reduced to what are generally trivial levels, at least nominally.[37] However, tariff rates tend to remain higher for labor-intensive products than for capital-intensive products, and higher for semimanufactures than for raw materials, and in turn higher for finished manufactures than for semimanufactures. The general U.S. tariff pattern (and that of other countries as well) is that rates are higher the more value is added to a product. The motive is to add as much value at home as possible, that is, to protect domestic labor. This escalation of tariffs has been a major complaint of developing countries. Escalation magnifies effective protection from tariffs, since duties are levied not only on the value added abroad but on the total value of the product, which therefore incorporates protection on materials that otherwise could have been imported with low or nil duties.[38] When all the tariff reductions granted in the recent round of multilateral trade negotiations (MTN) are in effect in 1987, U.S. tariffs on products of interest to developing countries will average between 7.5 and 10.3 percent for finished manufactures, between 3.3 and 6.1 percent for semimanufactures, and between 0.5 and 1.4 percent for raw materials.[39] In other words, there is considerable scope for lowering U.S. tariff rates further on products of particular interest to developing countries. The reason these rates were not lowered further in the MTN was because some domestic industries and some domestic labor were being protected. It follows, therefore, that the potential is low for unilateral lowering now of these rates for the benefit of migrant-sending countries.

In addition, lowering of the post-MTN rates on an MFN basis is apt to be of scant benefit to most migrant-sending countries. Other than Mexico, these countries are not formidable world competitors in the trade in manufactured goods. Indeed, even Mexico can hardly compete in most products on an even basis with South Korea, Taiwan, Hong Kong, and other newly industrializing countries, let alone with the industrial countries. In sum, the scope for benefiting the countries that send most migrants to the United States from across-the-board MFN duty reductions is insubstantial.

The same is true for those nontariff barriers that affect developing countries generally, particularly those in textiles and apparel. U.S. imports of these products from some of the migrant-sending countries are restrained under various international and bilateral agreements, but they are also limited when imported from more competitive producers, particularly those in Asia. A general lifting of these import restrictions would benefit the latter countries most.

In order to pinpoint the benefit to the migrant-sending countries and retain the MFN principle, product selectivity is necessary in lowering U.S. trade barriers. For example, Mexico would be the main beneficiary from lowering the high U.S. seasonal duties on tomatoes and other fresh vegetables. Even though the duty on rum was lowered by 20 percent in the MTN, it will remain higher than the U.S. duty on scotch. Lowering it further would benefit mainly several Caribbean basin countries; the protection is kept high to protect rum production in Puerto Rico and the Virgin Islands.

An examination of the currently dutiable imports by the United States from Caribbean basin countries other than Mexico shows a concentration in four commodity categories: wearing apparel, meat and meat products, tobacco and cigars, and rum. The first two also are burdened by U.S. nontariff barriers.

One must conclude that the scope for MFN duty reductions by the United States, pinpointed by product, for the benefit of Caribbean basin countries other than Mexico is insignificant, certainly in terms of creating enough new jobs or generating enough new revenue to reduce emigration pressures. This is so mainly because the

export potential of these countries is limited, but also because of
protectionist pressure by U.S. interests that would be adversely affected by trade liberalization. The scope for benefiting Mexico by
MFN duty reductions on particular products is more substantial, but
still not overwhelming because of Mexico's general lack of competitiveness in manufactures. As will be noted below, many of Mexico's exports to the United States already benefit from some form of
special treatment by the United States.

One legal point deserves mention. The authority in the current
U.S. trade law permits the executive branch to reduce duties by a
further 20 percent on an MFN basis, but only if some reciprocity is
received from the countries that will be the main beneficiaries of these
reductions.

The scope for cuts in U.S. nontariff barriers which would lead to
export increases by Caribbean basin countries, rather than other
countries, is greater than in the tariff field. The United States operates a program to restrain meat imports in years when there is domestic oversupply (i.e., when supply would drive prices below some
arbitrarily set level). The Central American countries and some of the
Caribbean countries, particularly the Dominican Republic, are meat
exporters. Import restraints are not in effect each year, but when they
are these can reduce earnings by the exporting countries. If the
United States eliminated these restraints, the principal beneficiary
countries would be Australia and New Zealand, but some migrant-
sending countries also would benefit. However, not too many jobs
would be created, since cattle-grazing is not a labor-intensive occupation.

The manufacture of apparel, however, is labor-intensive. Elimination of U.S. quotas on an MFN basis is not likely, and even if it
occurred, this would not benefit most the main migrant-sending
countries. However, since these quotas are established by the United
States on a country-by-country basis, there is leeway for greater
generosity than now exists in the allowable level of U.S. imports from
the migrant-sending countries. This could create more employment
in the sending countries. Such a step could not be taken without
opposition from affected domestic interests, but the quantities of extra imports in the particular apparel categories involved need not be
great in terms of the total U.S. market.

Such extra generosity to migrant-sending countries in the setting
of import quotas would be discriminatory. This points up the dilemma of using trade policy to limit emigration from the main migrant-sending countries: trade policy works best in this respect when

it departs from the MFN principle. This sets up a conflict between two objectives, maintaining the principle of nondiscrimination in international trade versus taking some economic policy measures that might inhibit emigration to the United States. U.S. abandonment of the MFN principle would be a clear cost; the extent of the benefit of inhibiting emigration would be uncertain. It is not obvious, either, that the United States could limit special trade preferences to Caribbean countries without facing irresistible pressure for comparable treatment from other developing countries not included in the Lomé agreement with the EEC.

There is no satisfactory way to avoid this dilemma and still benefit the migrant-sending countries through preferential treatment. In theory, one could "graduate" those developing countries that are most competitive in international trade from the GSP system. In 1980, the five largest beneficiaries of the U.S. GSP program (Taiwan, Hong Kong, South Korea, Mexico, and Brazil) captured 60 percent of the benefits.[40] If they and other newly industrializing countries were graduated, this could, in theory at least, benefit less competitive countries. There are two problems with this "solution": It would eliminate Mexico, the main migrant-sending country, and there would be no assurance that the Caribbean basin countries would be the main beneficiaries. Another technique to attenuate the extent of the dilemma would be not to graduate countries for all products but to graduate countries only for particular products, which was done for one product coming from Hong Kong in 1981.[41] This would require finding products in which migrant-sending countries could compete if all competitors were eliminated from preferential tariff treatment in the U.S. market just for those products. There are few such products which migrant-sending countries, other than Mexico, produce. Most of these products were listed earlier when discussing reduction of U.S. barriers on an MFN basis; for many of these products, such as apparel, the issue is not preferential tariff treatment but preferential quotas.

Mexico deserves unique attention in this trade discussion because it is this field of U.S. foreign economic policy—and, indeed, only in the trade field—in which U.S. policy manipulation is relevant. In 1980, U.S. GSP imports from Mexico were $509 million, making Mexico the fourth largest beneficiary of this system.[42] In addition, U.S. imports from Mexico in 1980 from *maquiladora* plants were $2.3 billion, about half of which represented value added in Mexico and half components originally sent from the United States.[43] In other words, the major portion of Mexico's exports of manufactures to the

United States already receives special treatment. This must be coun-
terbalanced by restrictive U.S. trade practices affecting Mexico, such
as those cited above on tariff escalation and nontariff barriers. What is
not clear, however, is how much Mexico would benefit in the short
term from a reduction of U.S. trade barriers on an MFN basis. Not
much, the evidence would lead one to believe. This, in turn, leads one
to conclude that U.S. trade policy measures designed to augment
employment opportunities in Mexico would be marginal unless they
were specially preferential. This is not likely to be done on a nonrecip-
rocal basis. Indeed, Mexico was excluded from the preferential treatment for the Caribbean basin cited earlier. Creating trade
opportunities really requires internal measures by Mexico.

INVESTMENT

As with trade, the critical requirement in using U.S. foreign direct
investment policy to influence job creation in migrant-sending countries is to be able to pinpoint the effect of policy. Trade policy, as
noted above, is a blunt instrument in this respect unless the primacy
of global considerations is compromised in favor of regional interests.
The same is true for investment policy. In both cases, therefore, if
used to affect migration problems, policy would have to depart from
theoretical optimization from comparative advantage or allowing the
market to maximize the marginal efficiency of capital, and have to
depart as well from an MFN concept which has suited the United
States because of its global interests.

Broadly stated, U.S. investment policy purports not to influence
the country distribution of investment and seeks to eliminate both
impediments and incentives to investment imposed by foreign governments. Ideally in all countries, but practically among the industrial
countries, the objective of U.S. policy is for foreign investors to be
given the same treatment as domestic investors, or national treatment
as it is called.[44] In practice, there are departures from this pristine
policy. Some sectors in the United States are legislatively closed to
foreign investors (such as in the defense industry, nuclear energy,
some transportation, and use of federally owned land). There are also
programs to encourage foreign direct investment in low-income developing countries. The Overseas Private Investment Corporation
(OPIC) provides political risk insurance and related services for investment in developing countries. OPIC does not operate in Mexico,
and its legislation requires that it give preferential treatment to low-
income countries (those with per capita income of $520 or less in 1975

dollars) and restrict its activities in countries with per capita income of $1,000 or more in 1975 dollars. As Table 7.2 shows, this leaves most of the Caribbean basin countries in the nonpreferential area. This restriction no longer fits U.S. priorities in this region. OPIC can and does drum up business, but for the most part its role is passive; it can provide services when private investors planning to make investments in developing countries come to it.

U.S. trade policy encourages foreign investment in at least three ways, although not necessarily to any particular country. The first way is by the GSP program, which gives duty-free treatment to U.S. imports of specific products produced in beneficiary developing countries. The second way is through limitations on textile and apparel imports by country, which often encourages U.S. investors to find new countries for investment and thus obtain new quotas for products at their ceilings when exported from the earlier country of investment. The third way is by imposing import duties only on the value added abroad for components shipped from the United States, which has been significant in the establishment of assembly plants in Mexico and the Caribbean basin generally.

What further steps can be taken by the United States to promote investment in the main migrant-sending countries and to shape this investment in as labor-intensive manner as possible consistent with the production possibilities for that industry? OPIC can actively seek to promote its services for investment in these countries, and this could have some minor effect. Investment treaties can be negotiated with these countries, under which the rules of the game are spelled out for U.S. investors in order to provide some assurance of stability of treatment by the host country and for avoidance of double taxation. This too can have some impact, but if past experience with such treaties is any guide, not very much. More dramatically, these treaties could provide for exemption or sparing from U.S. taxes of profits remitted from investments in these countries, in partial emulation of what was done in Puerto Rico.[45] This would be a wholesale departure from the professed U.S. policy of neutrality in shaping the direction of foreign investment and almost certainly would be resisted on this ground, as well as out of fear of setting a precedent for similar demands by developing countries in other regions.

In sum, there are distinct limits to the degree that U.S. international investment policy can be manipulated to direct labor-creating investment specifically to the major migrant-sending countries. There is no great reluctance by U.S. investors to go to Mexico, as evidenced by the large amount of U.S. investment already there.[46] The main limitation is that imposed by Mexico. There is greater reluctance to invest in what are seen as more turbulent countries in Central America and the Caribbean because of political risks and the small size of the domestic market. The various investment-stimulating measures discussed above presumably would apply to these countries. OPIC could, in theory, influence the labor-intensity of such investments when its services are sought, but there are limitations on how much government officials can or should dictate production processes in private investment. The natural inducement to setting up an assembly plant in Central America or the Caribbean is to reduce labor costs so that official interference to maximize the use of labor may not be needed.

Because of its large population, foreign investment can have only a marginal impact on employment in Mexico. At the other extreme, because of the small absolute sizes of the labor forces in many Caribbean islands, just a few plants processing local products or assembling components shipped from the United States can have a significant effect in lowering unemployment or underemployment. This would lead one to conclude that if the United States does depart from the principle of neutrality in foreign investment policy, this should be directed primarily at countries with small labor forces. It is unclear how much emigration-inhibiting effect such measures will have, but they could help provide a domestic employment alternative to emigration—although not necessarily for the population that actually emigrates but rather for their womenfolk who stay home in any event.

As with development generally, U.S. policy can have some impact on creation of jobs and opportunities in other countries—the smaller the work force of the country, the greater the impact—but domestic opportunities are created mostly by national policies.

AID

Aid is a more flexible instrument than trade or international investment policy. Bilateral assistance can be directed to particular countries and shaped with specific objectives in mind, without violating other principles based on the total U.S. national interest. National flexibility is reduced when aid is provided through multilateral channels, although not completely eliminated since the United States does have an important voice in shaping the policies of the multilateral aid agencies.

Bilateral aid is not now used with immigration issues in mind. The major criteria shaping the direction of U.S. bilateral aid are security interests (which explain the large amount of aid provided in the Middle East) and the poverty of recipient countries, since countries with higher per capita incomes have greater theoretical maneuverability in their allocation of resources. However, the current focus on U.S. security interests in the Caribbean basin dovetails with the idea of inhibiting emigration pressures, since both require creation of greater economic and social opportunities in the countries of the region.

U.S. foreign assistance policy has gone through phases (perhaps "fads" would be a more accurate word), with emphases in turn on technical assistance, large infrastructure projects, general balance-of-payments assistance, then eschewing the last two in favor of small projects, appropriate technology, and a focus on basic human needs or the alleviation of absolute poverty. Sector concentration has shifted from transportation, irrigation, and communications, when infrastructure aid was in vogue, to agricultural and rural development, health, family planning and population control, and to some extent education, when infrastructure assistance lost favor in the U.S. bilateral program. The current emphasis on security may not be consistent with a basic human needs approach since political agitation for change rarely comes from people who must devote all their energies to survival. Helping to raise people out of absolute poverty is likely to stimulate emigration pressure, as indicated earlier. In addition, most people living in absolute poverty are in South Asia and Africa, not in the Caribbean basin, and the emigration-inhibiting objective for the United States must focus on the Caribbean basis.

These considerations would argue for a U.S. aid policy that favors bilateral over multilateral programs, since this provides greater control over the direction and content of programs; greater concentration on nearby regions than on distant regions, and hence lesser concentration on relative economic need as measured by per capita incomes; and giving more attention to total development programs of recipient countries and the extent to which they deal with job creation, rather than concerning itself primarily with how the U.S. aid program affects the poor majority in the recipient countries. Such emphases in the bilateral program would leave the objective of reducing or eliminating absolute poverty to the multilateral institutions.

In other words, international development ideology would be subordinated to some degree to national security and immigration considerations. This may be deplored or applauded, depending on one's philosophic outlook. But this shift in emphasis, which already is occurring, does permit use of the aid instrument with more potential

effect on immigration issues than is possible through other instruments of foreign economic policy.

What is occurring is that the total level of U.S. foreign aid is
declining from earlier levels, and more resources are being devoted to
the countries of the Caribbean and Central America within this diminishing total.[47] Foreign aid generally constitutes a small proportion
of a recipient country's gross national product (GNP), around 1 to 2
percent for countries with larger GNPs and up to about 5 percent for
countries with lower GNPs.[48] Distribution of foreign aid normally has
had a small-country bias, that is, aid received per capita tends to be
higher in less-populous countries than in more-populous ones. By
focusing more resources on countries with small populations and low
GNPs, the impact of U.S. programs in these places is enhanced. In
this respect as well, aid can be a relatively powerful instrument of U.S.
foreign economic policy in dealing with immigration issues.

Conclusions

U.S. immigration policy is normally shaped not with foreign policy
considerations in mind but rather to satisfy perceived domestic pressures.[49] This would be true, as well, in seeking to use foreign economic policy measures to reduce pressures for migrants to come to
the United States without our prior consent. The foreign economic
policy steps would be the tools, but the curtailment of unwanted immigration would be the objective. The United States may or may not
be correct in wanting to curtail this immigration, but that is the stated
intent of the current administration.

It would be desirable for the United States to reduce import
barriers in the interest of a more efficient international division of
labor, regardless of the impact on immigration. Over time, such reduction of trade barriers should reduce emigration pressures in other
societies. The issue under discussion here, however, is not the
efficiency of freer trade but how to have a reasonably direct impact on
emigration to the United States from the manipulation of U.S. trade
policy. This requires some targeting of trade measures to benefit the
countries that send most immigrants to the United States, namely,
Mexico and the countries of the Caribbean and Central America. To
have its greatest impact in accomplishing this, the reduction of trade
barriers would have to be preferential, by giving benefits to Caribbean
basin countries not granted to other countries. Even then, the total
impact on the trade of these countries, and the impact on inhibiting

emigration, are uncertain. The direction of the outcome seems clear enough—more exports by these countries would create more jobs and greater economic opportunity at home—but not its quantitative extent or its permanence.

The cost of such special preferences also seems clear enough in that it would compromise U.S. worldwide trading interests and lead to a clamor for equal treatment from other developing countries who consider themselves firm allies of the United States. Special regional preferences by the United States would have the effect of creating a sphere of influence (which may exist in any event) to match the preferential trading relationship that exists between the EEC and Africa, or more broadly under the Lomé agreement, between the EEC and the ACP countries.

Foreign investment policy similarly would have to be targeted to the main migrant-sending countries for maximum impact in attaining the objective of reducing the pressure to emigrate to the United States. This, like trade policy, would entail departure from a globalist principle of official neutrality in directing investment flows, although departures from this principle already exist. As with trade policy, the migrant-inhibiting result of directed investment incentives is uncertain, whereas the departure from previous policy would be clear.

The use of foreign aid to achieve the objective of reduced pressure to emigrate to the United States is more flexible than using either trade or investment policy. By its very nature, the direction of bilateral foreign aid can be pinpointed wherever the United States wishes without violating other national objectives. There would be a cost, however, in that the international development motive of U.S. aid would be further compromised in favor of regional objectives. The job-creating and emigrant-inhibiting effect of aid so used would be uncertain, but probably less uncertain than with use of either the trade or investment instrument.

Bilateral aid policy cannot be used with any effect in Mexico because Mexico neither needs nor seeks such aid. Neither does Mexico want official U.S. government encouragement of private companies to invest in Mexico. For all practical purposes, therefore, the only U.S. foreign economic policy instrument that is relevant for seeking to curtail emigration pressure from Mexico is trade policy. A general lowering of U.S. trade barriers would help Mexico to some extent, but probably not significantly if this were done on an MFN basis. And it is not likely to be done preferentially for Mexico in the absence of some reciprocity.

It is worth stressing once more that national development policies are critical for determining the push factors for emigration. There are countries that in recent decades have been able to turn around a labor-surplus situation to one of labor shortage in a relatively brief time. The U.S. contribution to these turnarounds was to provide aid, to not restrict the flow of U.S. investment, and to keep the U.S. market reasonably open for imports. The self-help capacity is greater for the more populous migrant-sending countries than for the tiny, island countries, where external help can play a more decisive role.

The general conclusion of this study is twofold: A general admonition to the U.S. government that the way to deal with emigration problems is to provide more aid and admit more imports is of little use, since general statements do not make the necessary correlation between policy instrument and impact on migrant-sending countries. And the United States has economic means to mitigate emigration pressures in the main sending countries, but only marginally and usually at a cost in terms of other national interests.

Notes

1. Those who favor minimum U.S. restrictions on migrant inflow, or the legalization of foreign-worker programs, such as Jorge A. Bustamante and Wayne A. Cornelius, have suggested generous U.S. aid and trade programs as a long-term solution to push factors. So have those who wish to restrict entry of foreign workers, such as Vernon M. Briggs and Philip L. Martin. The specific suggestions of some of these authors will be discussed below.

2. See Alejandro Portes, "Toward a Structural Analysis of Illegal (Undocumented) Immigration," *International Migration Review* 12 (Winter 1978): 469–484.

3. See, e.g., David S. North and Marion P. Houstoun, *The Characteristics and Role of Illegal Aliens in the U.S. Labor Market: An Exploratory Study* (Washington, D.C.: Linton & Co., 1976); and David S. North, "Worker Migration: A State-of-the-Art Review," Paper prepared for the Bureau of International Labor Affairs, U.S. Department of Labor, 1979.

4. North, "Worker Migration," p. 7; and U.S. Agency for International Development/International Development Cooperation Agency, "The Relationship of U.S. Aid, Trade, and Investment to Migration Pressures in Major Countries of Origin," in Select Commission on Immigration and Refugee Policy, *U.S. Immigration Policy and the National Interest,* Final Report, March 1, 1981, Appendix B of Supplement (Washington, D.C.: Government Printing Office, 1981), p. 13 (hereafter referred to as SCIRP, Final Report, Appendix B).

5. See E. G. Ravenstein, two articles each entitled "The Laws of Migration," *Journal of the Royal Statistical Society* 48 (1885): 167–227, and 52 (1889):

241–301. Robert Sayers and Thomas Weaver, "Explanations and Theories of Migration," in *Mexican Migration,* ed. Thomas Weaver and Theodore E. Downing (Tuscon: University of Arizona, Department of Anthropology, 1976), pp. 10–29, review migration theories.

6. The phrase "proletarian diasporas" is from J. A. Armstrong, "Mobilized and Proletarian Diasporas," *American Political Science Review* 70 (June 1976): 393–408.

7. Mildred B. Levy and Walter J. Wadycki, "What Is the Opportunity Cost of Moving? Reconsideration of the Effects of Distance on Migration," *Economic Development and Cultural Change* 22 (January 1974): 198–214. This econometric study of migration within Venezuela concludes that the explanatory power of distance on migration is reduced by taking monetary reward into account and that the "economic approach to migration within the traditional framework of rational choice is valid" (p. 211).

8. Scores of studies document European problems with the temporariness of "temporary" workers. Only a few will be noted: W. R. Böhning, "Temporary or Permanent: This Is the Question," and Friedrich Heckman, "Temporary Labor Migration or Immigration? 'Guest Workers' in the Federal Republic of Germany" (Both papers prepared for a World Peace Foundation conference on Temporary Labor Migration in Europe: Lessons for the American Policy Debate, Elkridge, Md., June 12–14, 1980); Mark J. Miller and David J. Yeres, "A Massive Temporary Worker Programme for the U.S.: Solution or Mirage?" Working paper for Migration for Employment Project, World Employment Programme, International Labor Organization, Geneva, November 1979; Philip L. Martin, "Germany's Guestworkers," *Challenge* 24 (July–August 1981): 34–42, and "Guestworker Programs: Lessons from Europe" (Report prepared for the Joint Economic Committee, U.S. Congress, June 1979). See also Joyce Vialet and Barbara McClure, *Temporary Worker Programs: Background and Issues,* S. Rept. 55-752, 96th Cong. 2d sess., prepared for the Select Commission on Immigration and Refugee Policy (Washington, D.C.: Government Printing Office, 1980), pp. 95–99 and annotated selected bibliography, pp. 121–144.

9. *Economic Study of Puerto Rico,* vol. 2, report to the President by the Interagency Task Force coordinated by the U.S. Department of Commerce (Washington, D.C.: Government Printing Office, 1979), p. 591.

10. *New York Times,* July 25, 1981, p. 1.

11. Mexicans make up about 90 percent of apprehensions of illegal aliens in the United States by the Immigration and Naturalization Service, but the U.S. government has estimated that Mexicans make up only 60 percent of aliens who stay illegally in the United States; see U.S. Department of Justice, *Preliminary Report: Domestic Council Committee on Illegal Aliens* (Washington, D.C.: Government Printing Office, 1976), pp. 132, 133.

12. This is the Leontiev paradox, which is taught to all university students studying trade theory.

13. G. C. Hufbauer, "The Impact of National Characteristics and Technology on the Commodity Trade in Manufactured Goods," in *The Technology*

Factor in International Trade, ed. Raymond Vernon (New York: Columbia University Press for the National Bureau of Economic Research, 1970), pp. 145–231, deals with both the Heckscher-Ohlin and product-cycle theories.

14. Percentages of U.S. related-party to total imports in 1979 were: Mexico, 46 percent; Central America, 23 percent; and the Caribbean, 59 percent. U.S. International Trade Commission, "Background Study of the Economies and International Trade Patterns of the Countries of North America, Central America and the Caribbean," Washington, D.C., February 1981, p. 163.

15. Marina v.N. Whitman, "International Trade and Investment: Two Perspectives," Essay in international finance no. 143, International Finance Section, Princeton University, July 1981, contains a discussion of intra-industry trade, especially in the automotive industry.

16. Some of the theoretical limitations to perfect substitutability are discussed in Louka T. Katseli-Papaefstratiou, "Trade Flows and Factor Mobility," in SCIRP, Final Report, Appendix B, pp. 33–70.

17. See Francisco Alba, "Mexico's International Migration as a Manifestation of Its Development Pattern," *International Migration Review* 12 (Winter 1978): 502–513.

18. Incentives to attract and limitations on foreign direct investment in Mexico and Caribbean and Central American countries are summarized in International Trade Commission, "Background Study," pp. 65–76.

19. Data are from the Bank of Mexico. The foreign direct investment figure comes from the preliminary balance-of-payments accounts and therefore measures capital inflow for direct investment and not the total investment by foreign companies. The domestic figure comes from preliminary national income accounts for public sector and private sector fixed direct investment, converted from pesos at the rate of 22.95 pesos to the dollar.

20. This point, that it is not clear whether development programs and job creation lead to a corresponding fall in out-migration pressures, is made in Nelle W. Temple, "Migration and Development: A Preliminary Survey of the Available Literature," in SCIRP, Final Report, Appendix B, p. 205.

21. The seminal document was Raúl Prebisch, *The Economic Development of Latin America and Its Principal Problems* (New York: U.N. Commission for Latin America, 1950); published in Spanish in 1949.

22. Colombia began a program of promoting nontraditional exports in the late 1960s, as did Brazil. The southern cone countries, especially Chile and Uruguay, shifted policy in the 1970s to emphasize export promotion.

23. See *IMF Survey* 10, no. 15 (August 3, 1981): 1; *World Development Report, 1979* (Washington, D.C.: World Bank, 1979), pp. 20–28; and *International Trade 1979/80* (Geneva: General Agreement on Tariffs and Trade, 1980).

24. Mexico'a annual population growth has declined from about 3.3 percent in the mid 1970s to what is now believed to be less than 3 percent.

25. Clark Reynolds, "Labor Market Projections for the United States and Mexico and their Relevance to Current Migration Controversies," Stanford

University, Food Research Institute, July 6, 1979, argues that even the highest economic growth projections will leave Mexico with surplus labor for decades (p. 31). Dilmus D. James and John S. Evans, "Conditions of Employment and Income Distribution in Mexico as Incentives for Mexican Migration to the United States: Prospects to the End of the Century," *International Migration Review* 13 (Spring 1979), state that there is little reason to expect the pressure to migrate from Mexico to diminish in the near future (p. 19).

26. The World Bank approved $300 million in loans to Mexico in the bank's fiscal year 1980 (World Bank, *Annual Report, 1980,* p. 120). According to World Bank document EC-181/802, "Foreign and International Bond Issues, Publicized Eurocurrency Credits," Mexico's borrowing in 1980 from bond issues and Eurocurrency credits was $5.3 billion (p. 40), of which $5 billion were Eurocurrency credits (p. 7). This does not include loans from banks in the United States and other countries. Mexico's current account receipt figure is from the Bank of Mexico's *Informe Anual 1981,* p. 153.

27. Jorge A. Bustamante, "Emigración indocumentada a los Estados Unidos," *Foro Internacional* 18 (January–March 1978): 430–463.

28. The latter is a naive suggestion for two reasons. The most important is that labor-intensive agricultural production does not normally involve grains, which Mexico can ill afford to export in any event, precisely the products needed in U.S. P.L. 480 (food for peace) programs. The other is that P.L. 480 is supported in the United States to deal with U.S. agricultural surpluses, and that the constituency that supports this program is not likely to want to prejudice its operation in the interest of Mexican production.

29. Wayne A. Cornelius, "Mexican Migration to the United States: Causes, Consequences, and U.S. Responses," Migration and Development Study Group, Center for International Studies, Massachusetts Institute of Technology, Cambridge, Mass., 1978, p. 99.

30. Francisco Alba, "Industrialización sustitutiva y migración internacional: El caso de México," *Foro Internacional* 18 (January–March 1978): 478.

31. Mitchell A. Seligson and Edward J. Williams, *Maquiladoras and Migration: Workers in the Mexican–United States Border Industrialization Program* (Austin: University of Texas Press for the Mexico-United States Border Research Program, forthcoming).

32. See the article by Alan Riding in *New York Times,* June 23, 1981, p. 2.

33. These "special" preferences would be in addition to the "general" preferences the United States provides to developing countries from all regions.

34. *Comercio Exterior* 31 (March 1981): 357.

35. U.S. International Trade Commission, "Background Study," p. 136.

36. In a similar manner, the United States could increase the duty-free allowance for returning tourists on either a MFN or a discriminatory basis. Or the United States could permit expenses of Americans to be deducted from income taxes for attending conventions in Caribbean countries.

37. Thomas R. Graham, "The Impact of the Tokyo Round Agreements

on U.S. Export Competitiveness," Center for Strategic and International Studies, Georgetown University, Washington, D.C., 1980, states that U.S. tariff levels on industrial products (excluding petroleum), when the results of the Tokyo Round are in effect, will be 7.0 percent on a simple average basis and 4.4 percent when weighted by MFN imports (p. 22).

38. The *maquiladora*, or border industries, flourish in part because there is provision in the U.S. tariff schedule (in sections 806.30 and 807.00) for payment of U.S. duty only on the value added abroad for products originally shipped out of the United States containing U.S. components.

39. Agency for International Development/International Development Cooperation Agency, "The Relationship of U.S. Aid, Trade, and Investment to Migration," p. 31. A range of tariff levels is given, since the figures depend on whether the average is calculated on a simple basis or weighted by trade. Products of export interest to developing countries were defined as those exported by developing countries and those for which they requested concessions in the MTN.

40. Press release, Office of the U.S. Trade Representative, March 19, 1981.

41. Ibid. The product was eyeglass frames and mountings, and parts thereof.

42. Office of the U.S. Trade Representative, computer printout.

43. U.S. International Trade Commission, "Tariff Items 807.00 and 806.30, U.S. Imports for Consumption, Specified Years 1966–1980," June 1981, pp. 13, 26.

44. Two statements on U.S. international investment policy can be found in U.S. Department of State, *Bulletin* 81 (July 1981): by Robert Hormats, assistant secretary of state for economic and business affairs, p. 27; and John T. McCarthy, deputy assistant secretary for economic and business affairs, pp. 30–32.

45. See the letter to the editor by Richard L. Bolin, director, Flagstaff (Arizona) Institute, *Wall Street Journal,* July 20, 1981.

46. The book value of U.S. direct investment in Mexico was $4.6 billion at the end of 1979, three-quarters of which was in manufacturing. Most U.S. investment in Caribbean-basin countries is in the Bahamas and Bermuda, but this is mostly in finance and insurance and designed with U.S. tax purposes in mind and not job creation. The same is generally true in Panama. Other than in Mexico, the amount of U.S. investment in manufacturing in the Caribbean basin is low in terms of total U.S. overseas investment. See U.S. International Trade Commission, "Background Study," p. 30.

47. As stated earlier, Mexico receives no bilateral concessional aid.

48. Agency for International Development/International Development Cooperation Agency, "The Relationship of U.S. Aid, Trade, and Investment to Migration," p. 29.

49. Joyce Vialet, "U.S. Immigration Policy: The Western Hemisphere," Congressional Research Service of the Library of Congress, report no. 80-69 EPW, 1980, p. 32.

CHAPTER 8

The Rights of Aliens: National and International Issues

Elizabeth Hull

While the poor we may have with us always, perhaps the migrant and the homeless and the displaced we shall have with us as well. For millennia, new lands have been settled by those seeking conquest, opportunity, a promised land, by those fleeing famine, persecution, or poverty. They arrive as "strangers in the land," "aliens," whose very status conjures up images of people who are peculiar and out of place. They are looked upon with suspicion and often with hostility, and perceived as emissaries of unfriendly nations whose presence within the host country could contaminate it culturally and compromise it civically.

Almost alone among nations, the United States was settled and developed by immigrants; notwithstanding this fact, however, Americans traditionally have greeted newcomers with only half-open arms. Periods of fulsome generosity have alternated with ones of xenophobia and intolerance. Other countries throughout history have treated their noncitizens according to local custom; in some places they enjoyed official hospitality, in others they were treated as virtual outlaws, entitled to few if any of the rights and privileges conferred upon nationals.

Responsibility for the Protection of Aliens

Although states rarely felt free to treat them with absolute license, aliens began to receive protection only with the expansion of trade and commerce in the latter Middle Ages. At this time, mercantilism was merging into capitalism, and modern nation-states were developing and then expanding, sending their envoys into "uncivilized"

215

territories overseas in quest of land and riches. The success of these ventures depended upon the treatment these envoys received, and hence it was essential to evolve a doctrine for the protection of foreign nationals that would be respected throughout the developed nations, but above all throughout their colonial outposts.

Emerich de Vattel, writing in the nineteenth century, conceived this doctrine, and by the last half of the nineteenth century and certainly by the beginning of the twentieth century it had become a central tenet of international law. According to Vattel's theory, the state is an entity comprised of both the sovereign and its citizens and possesses the right to protect its citizens whenever they are present in foreign territory. It follows that an injury to an alien is perforce an injury to the state of which he is a national:

> Whoever ill-treats a citizen indirectly injures the State, which must protect that citizen. The sovereign of the injured citizen must avenge the deed and, if possible, force the aggressor to give full satisfaction or punish him, since otherwise the citizen will not obtain the chief end of civil society, which is protection.[1]

This doctrine was predictably a popular one among the major international actors; as Judge Philip C. Jessup noted, it provided "adequate protection for the stranger, to the end that travel, trade, and intercourse may be facilitated."[2] That is to say, Vattel's doctrine was popular because it promoted the self-interest of industrializing states. Although perhaps unintended, his theory also fostered a second and benign consequence: the development of customary international law for the protection of aliens.

While many international tribunals continue to perpetuate the myth that injury to a foreign national is in fact an injury to his state, in increasing numbers jurists agree with the Mixed Claims Commission in *United States* v. *Germany*: "[Such myths] must not be permitted to obscure the realities or blind us to the fact that the ultimate objective of asserting the claim is to provide reparation for private claimants."[3] In practice, moreover, tribunals frequently assess compensation in terms of the injury suffered by the individual national.

As it became firmly embedded in customary law, Vattel's doctrine resulted in a paradox: A home state was obliged to protect the fundamental rights of aliens within its territory, but it retained the right to treat its own nationals with complete discretion. Particularly during the twentieth century, Vattel's doctrine has also resulted in controversy, perhaps as heated as any other in international law.

THE INTERNATIONAL MINIMUM STANDARD
AND EQUALITY OF TREATMENT

While few countries deny that a state is obligated to provide foreign nationals with protection, they disagree adamantly over the breadth and character of this protection. Generally speaking, the older and economically developed countries, such as the United States, subscribe to the so-called "international minimum standard," according to which the state is obliged to observe certain "universal principles of justice" in the treatment of aliens and their property, regardless of whether it bestows the same benefits on its own nationals and even if such treatment is inconsistent with its own law.

Speaking in 1910, then U.S. Secretary of State Elihu Root provided what has become an oft-quoted defense of the "international minimum standard":

> There is a standard of justice, very simple, very fundamental, and of such general acceptance by all civilized countries as to form a part of the international law of the world. The condition upon which any country is entitled to measure the justice due from it to an alien by the justice which it accords to its own citizens is that its system of law and administration shall conform to this general standard. If the country's system of law and administration does not conform to that standard, although the people of the country may be content or compelled to live under it, no other country can be compelled to accept it as furnishing a satisfactory measure of treatment to its citizens.[1]

While historically the weight of "established" opinion has favored the "international minimum standard," the ardor of those who subscribe to the "equality of treatment" or "national treatment" standard has not diminished, and they accordingly aver that aliens may demand no more from a state than treatment equal to that which it accords its own nationals. In the early part of the twentieth century, these spokesmen were mainly from Latin America, but recently they also include representatives from the Communist countries and the postcolonial states of Africa and Asia.

Opposition to the "equality of treatment" standard has been long-standing and intense. Most developed nations consider this standard no more than a pretext by which derelict nations can avoid responsibility for their mistreatment of foreign nationals, while simultaneously preventing intervention from the injured sovereign. Those advocating the "equality of treatment" standard, however, regard its alternative with no less aversion; postcolonial and Communist coun-

218 ELIZABETH HULL

tries frequently consider the "international minimum standard" an imperialistic tool, utilized in the past by stronger states to exploit the weaker, remaining today as an irritant calculated to exacerbate tensions between citizens and aliens. Latin Americans, in particular, have long sought recognition as equal participants in the international arena and have resented the suggestion that their domestic law is inferior to that of "civilized nations" or that its system of justice does not comport with minimum international standards. Latin Americans have accordingly endorsed the so-called Calvo Doctrine, which, in addition to providing the "equality of treatment" standard with theoretical underpinnings, posits that any remedy to which an injured alien is entitled is determined solely by municipal law.[5]

Partisans of both standards remain steadfast, and consequently jurists have had difficulty determining many of the rules of international law that are applicable to foreign nationals. This fact notwithstanding, the "international minimum standard" has triumphed, as evidenced by the widespread recognition it has received in practice. Its victory, however, has not been unsullied. There is still confusion and controversy regarding its content and, more fundamental, some question whether the standard even retains independent vitality given the recent emergence of human rights norms that are intended to be of universal applicability.

THE "DENIAL OF JUSTICE"

States may agree to treat aliens according to a "national minimum standard," but the meaning of this phrase is neither self-evident nor clarified by jurists, whose language is frequently less legal than metaphysical: States are admonished to observe "universal standards of justice" or to abide by "the established standards of civilization." Perhaps this obfuscation is at least functional, if not intentional, because jurists usually disagree regarding all but the "core" rights protected by this standard. They do agree that the standard is violated whenever state practice constitutes a "denial of justice"—a term in itself the essence of imprecision. Nevertheless, practitioners and legal scholars have shown no reluctance to define what they believe constitutes a "denial of justice."

In 1926, in *United States* v. *Mexico*,[6] Commissioner F. K. Nielson provided an expansive definition: "I consider that a denial of justice may, broadly speaking, be properly regarded as the general ground of diplomatic intervention";[7] a subcommittee of the League of Nations recommended a definition considerably more narrow: A denial of justice is conduct that "consists in refusing to allow [aliens] . . . easy access to the courts to defend those rights which the national law accords them."[8] In 1929, the Harvard Draft Convention similarly concentrated on the centrality of the judicial proceeding, arguing that deficiencies in procedural due process constitute a denial of justice for an alien.[9]

Burns H. Weston and associates have summarized the conduct that international tribunals have most frequently adjudged to constitute a denial of justice: (1) any treatment of an alien that violates international law; (2) treatment of an alien that departs from generally accepted standards of substantive law; (3) treatment of an alien that departs from generally accepted standards for the conduct of legal proceedings; (4) failure to provide an adequate domestic remedy for an injury to an alien for which the state has international responsibility.[10]

As the U.S. Supreme Court pointed out over ninety years ago in *United States* v. *Arizona*, "the law of nations requires every national government to use 'due diligence' to protect a wrong being done within its dominion to another nation with which it is at peace, or to the people thereof."[11] While the obligation to prevent the commission of acts injurious to foreign nationals does not similarly obligate a state to suppress all harmful conduct by private parties, a state does assume international liability if it thereafter fails to take reasonable steps to apprehend and punish the wrongdoer or if it metes out punishment grossly inadequate in light of the injury inflicted upon the alien.

A. H. Roth enumerates a series of substantive rights to which aliens are entitled, among which are the right to have their legal capacity recognized by the receiving state, respect for and protection of their life, property, and personal and spiritual liberty "within socially bearable limits," and equality of commercial treatment among counterparts whenever aliens are permitted to undertake economic activity.[12] Finally, aliens are entitled to treatment that is generally evenhanded, meaning that a state is derelict if it differentiates without a reasonable ground between either aliens and nationals or between aliens of different nationalities.[13]

EXPROPRIATION OF PROPERTY

One issue in international law provokes debate that is both heated and acrimonious: whether, or to what extent, a state is obliged to compensate foreign nationals for the expropriation of their property. This has become a salient question as new states have cast off their colonial moorings and as socialist tenets have spread. Consequently, the debate typically pits industrialized, capitalist states against developing, socialist ones, whose respective economic and political assumptions are sharply divergent. Members of both factions agree that a state is liable under international law whenever its expropriation of an alien's property violates treaty obligations; in general, members also agree that under some circumstances expropriation may occur. They disagree in a fundamental sense, however, over the nature of these circumstances.

Capitalist states maintain that expropriators must observe "international minimum standards"; more specifically, as Secretary of State Cordell Hull noted in 1938, they must provide affected aliens with "prompt, adequate, and effective compensation."[14] Although Hull's terms are laden with ambiguity, his formula has received widespread acceptance: noncapitalist states deny, of course, that they are bound by any "international minimum standard"—particularly one they had no share in establishing; on the contrary, they are entitled to determine in reference to their own needs the circumstances and conditions of expropriation. While their view is commanding increasing support in the United Nations, it engenders such intense opposition from most developed states that at least in the foreseeable future it will continue to lack the status of customary international law.

Citizen Rights Versus Noncitizen Rights

When there is a reasonable basis for the difference, states are not prohibited from distinguishing between citizens and aliens, regardless of whether they adhere to an "international minimum" or "equality of treatment" standard. As noted above, however, the distinction must bear a reasonable relation to the different obligations and loyalties that a state might expect from its nationals, on the one hand, and from its guests, on the other. That is to say, the distinction must be a rational one in light of the legitimate interests of the state.

Nations frequently distinguish not only between citizens and aliens but also between various classes of aliens—a practice that comports with international law as long as the distinctions are reasonable and consistent with applicable treaty provisions. For instance, while all people within the territorial jurisdiction of the United States are protected from the arbitrary deprivation of life, liberty, and property, there remain a wide spectrum of rights and government services to which individuals are entitled only as they approach citizenship.

At one end of this spectrum is the immigrant, or resident alien, who is admitted on a permanent basis, permitted to settle and work anywhere in the United States, and eligible for citizenship after living there for five years.[15] Resident aliens enjoy most, although not all, rights accorded citizens.[16]

Midway on the spectrum are nonimmigrant aliens, such as tourists, businesspeople, and students, who are admitted only "for such time and under such conditions as the Attorney General may by regulations prescribe."[17] On the assumption that nonimmigrants owe obligations and allegiance to their home country, while in the United States they are rarely accorded either government largesse or the privileges of citizenship. A recent court case demonstrates, moreover, that as long as its actions are reasonable the federal government may discriminate against nonimmigrant aliens on the basis of their nationality without violating either domestic or international law.

In 1979, the U.S. attorney general required Iranian students and teachers present in this country to report to the Immigration and Naturalization Service to verify their visa status.[18] Although the students challenged this action on the ground that they were being unfairly singled out on the basis of their nationality, the Court of Appeals for the District of Columbia sustained the government's action. Given the crisis then under way in Iran, such a distinction was "an element in the language of diplomacy."[19] The court held, in addition, that this or similar distinctions could be made in response either to particular diplomatic agreements or to specific relations that prevail between the United States and another country. The president or attorney general was therefore entitled to withdraw privileges from visiting Iranians as reciprocity for the treatment of Americans in Iran.

Finally, at the far end of the spectrum are so-called illegal, or undocumented, aliens—those individuals who enter the country without authorization or who, once here, violate the terms of their visas.[20] While the status of nonimmigrant aliens is relatively settled, the courts in this country are still determining to what extent both resident and undocumented aliens are entitled to constitutional protection.

The system used by the United States for classifying noncitizens is similar to that instituted by most other nations, which similarly restrict certain activities either to citizens or to permanent resident aliens. Under international law, nations may permit only the latter to own property, important natural resources, and domestic corporations, or they may impose various conditions whenever such property is owned by foreign nationals.

Individual states in this country historically have forbidden resident aliens to hunt, fish, own property, bear arms, or receive public largesse.[21] Until recently the Supreme Court routinely sustained these policies, reasoning that they were defensible both under international law and in light of the so-called "public interest" doctrine. According to this doctrine, as guardian of its citizens a state is obliged to regulate the public fisc and to conserve the land and its resources, and to this end might discriminate against noncitizens.[22]

Closely aligned and often indistinguishable from the "special public interest" doctrine is the theory that a country, under its police powers, possesses the authority to confine to citizens occupations that it considers harmful, sensitive, or susceptible to abuse—on the rationale, as a Rhode Island judge once expressed it, that "aliens as a class are naturally less interested in the state, the safety of its citizens, and the public welfare."[23]

Armed either with their ample police powers or with the "special public interest" doctrine, states traditionally have restricted to citizens a multitude of activities and a large proportion of lucrative, competitive, or licensed professions. Such restrictions are legitimate under international law, and most nations impose similar restrictions on their noncitizens. The U.S. Supreme Court recently indicated for the first time, however, that when applied to resident aliens the bulk of these restrictions may not be legitimate under domestic constitutional law.

In 1971, the Supreme Court held, in *Graham* v. *Richardson*,[24] that state practices conditioning welfare payments upon citizenship or long U.S. residency were unconstitutional, in part because a state could have no "special public interest" in limiting to citizens the expenditure of tax revenues to which aliens had contributed.[25] More important, the Court declared that legislative classifications based on alienage, like those based on race or national origin, were "inherently suspect" and therefore subject to close judicial scrutiny. Finally, the Court noted that aliens deserve particular solicitude from the judiciary because they can neither vote nor hold public office, and are consequently unable to rely on the political process to protect their interests.

While the Court's holding in *Graham* applied only to resident aliens and only to state, as opposed to federal, legislation, its implications were nonetheless enormous. Hereafter states would be permitted to discriminate against resident aliens only if such discrimination furthered "compelling interests" that could be achieved by no alternate means. This is a difficult standard to satisfy, and in a series of cases postdating *Graham*, the Court invalidated state statutes that permitted only citizens to work for the civil service,[26] to practice law,[27] to do civil engineering,[28] or to receive state educational loans.[29]

Even while issuing these rulings, however, many members of the Court were apparently troubled by *Graham*'s potential impact on the country's federal system: *Graham* implicitly challenged on constitutional grounds most state laws that distinguish between citizens and noncitizens, cumulatively hundreds in number, and states howled in protest each time one of their statutes was toppled. Perhaps for this reason, shortly after rendering its opinion in *Graham*, the Court seized upon a tenet in international law by which to carve out an exception to its broad ruling.

International law permits countries to exclude aliens from participation in their so-called political, or decision-making, processes, on the theory that the acts of voting, serving on a jury, and holding public office intimately affect the character and needs of the political community. Accordingly, in a 1973 case, the Supreme Court observed that a state has the power "to preserve the basic conception of a political community" and might therefore restrict to citizens those who hold "state elective or important nonelective executive, legislative, and judicial positions . . . or who otherwise participate directly in the formation, execution, or review of broad public policy."[30]

On the authority of this doctrine, a large number of state policies that discriminate against resident aliens have withstood constitutional challenge. The Court reasoned, not surprisingly, that a state might limit to citizens those eligible to vote[31] or hold high public office,[32] since both activities closely affect the political community. Recently, however, states have been allowed to exclude aliens from activities whose relationship to this community is nowhere as obvious. For instance, New York was permitted to bar noncitizens from serving as police officers on the ground that in the exercise of their "plenary discretionary powers" these officers perform functions that intimately affect the political climate.[33] Similarly, a New York statute that prohibits noncitizens from teaching in the public schools was sustained, this time on the rationale that teachers are transmitters of civic virtue and consequently in an optimal position to influence the character and values of the citizenry.[34]

In January 1982 in *Cabell* v. *Jones Chavez-Salido*, its last case to date on the subject, the Supreme Court sustained a California statute that requires all those categorized as "peace officers" to be citizens—a category that subsumes more than seventy different occupations, including cemetery sextons, furniture and bedding inspectors, and toll service employees. The district court had invalidated the statute, reasoning that at least some of these positions could not affect the political community, no matter how "liberally" this community is viewed. The Supreme Court disagreed, however, and upheld the California law on the ground that "broad leeway" should be accorded the states in determining what positions do and do not affect the political community and hence might be confined to citizens.

Underlying these statutes is a premise that supposedly had been laid to rest in *Graham* v. *Richardson:* that aliens as a class are characterized by divided allegiance and conflicting loyalties. By upholding these statutes, the Court tacitly acknowledged this premise; moreover, by allowing states to exclude aliens from activities only tenuously related to official policymaking, the Court has suggested that the "political community" doctrine is an elastic one, with no readily discernible limiting principle.

The Court's holding in *Graham*, as Justice Thurgood Marshall once predicted, may be "swallowed up by exceptions,"[35] but as long as it is not formally overruled, it still prevents individual states from subjecting resident aliens to the baldest forms of discrimination. No such legal restrictions bind the federal government, however, and it can and does discriminate against noncitizens in myriad ways—limiting their acess to many occupations and social services and otherwise depriving them of the full range of legal rights available to citizens.

The U.S. Supreme Court invariably has upheld federal policies when they have been challenged on constitutional grounds, most recently sanctioning one such policy that limits Medicare benefits to citizens and only certain resident aliens.[36] Whether or not the Court's action represents sound constitutional interpretation, it is consistent with a principle well established in international law: While countries are prohibited from imposing gratuitous liabilities upon anyone within their territory, they are not required to provide even long-term resident aliens with the largesse they make available to their own citizens.

On the theory that such rights inhere in sovereignty, international law vests every nation with power to regulate the admission, exclusion, or expulsion of aliens and the conditions of their entry and residence. These powers are virtually absolute, and they are exercised in a manner that is arbitrary, frequently discriminatory, and often harsh.

Since the U.S. Constitution vests the Congress with authority to establish "an uniform rule of naturalization,"[37] the Supreme Court readily concluded that federal law in this area preempted any conflicting state legislation. The Court has displayed no similar willingness to overturn federal legislation that relates even peripherally to immigration and naturalization, however, reasoning that the political branches of the federal government are vested, by the Constitution and as an attribute of sovereignty, with "plenary powers" in this area; moreover, the Court fears that by "meddling" it may restrict the maneuverability of the executive and legislative branches both domestically and in foreign affairs.[38]

As a consequence of such logic, the Supreme Court and by extension most lower courts have virtually abdicated their responsibility toward the noncitizen who is victimized by unfair or discriminatory federal policy—even when this policy involves "political questions" or foreign policy in only the most attenuated sense. Perhaps in no other area of the law has judicial abdication been as complete. While the Supreme Court has from time to time required that noncitizens be accorded at least minimal procedural rights, it has not once in its history invalidated federal practices on substantive grounds.

In the past the Supreme Court upheld federal policy that discriminated on the basis of a prospective immigrant's race[39] and political views,[40] and recently it approved an admissions scheme that discriminated on the basis of both gender and legitimacy.[41] On another occasion, a long-term resident alien returned to the United States after a brief trip abroad, whereupon Congress excluded him from the country. The high court not only affirmed Congress' right to do so, but also recognized Congress' further authority to exclude him without a hearing, on the basis of undisclosed information.[42] In a related case, the Supreme Court explained its rationale: "Whatever the procedure authorized by Congress is, it is due process as far as the alien denied entry is concerned."[43]

In deference to principles time-honored in international law, the Supreme Court similarly explained that "the right of a nation to expel or deport foreigners, who have not been naturalized or taken any steps toward becoming citizens of the country, rests upon the same ground [as the power to exclude] and is as absolute and unqualified."[44] Courts in the United States, as in most countries, continue to hold that even long-term resident aliens can be deported on any grounds that the political branches deem fit, and regardless of whether such deportations bear any relation to the country's security or welfare.[45]

As a consequence, the Supreme Court did not interfere during

"Operation Wetback" in 1954, when residents of Mexican ancestry, including many who were U.S. citizens, were rounded up and returned to Mexico. The Court was similarly acquiescent during the McCarthy period, upholding every challenge to a deportation order that was authorized under the Alien Registration Act of 1940—even those banning resident aliens and naturalized citizens for membership in the Communist party that had terminated before the passage of this act. Justice Robert Jackson defended the Court's action by invoking a familiar "reasons of state" argument: "That aliens remain vulnerable to expulsion after long residence is a practice that bristles with severities. But it is a weapon of defense and reprisal confirmed by international law as a power inherent in every sovereign state."[46]

In most countries with a sizable immigrant population, there is still controversy over the extent to which resident aliens are entitled to the rights and privileges of citizenship; this controversy is comparatively insignificant, however, when compared to the controversy aroused when the rights and privileges in question are those of undocumented aliens.

CAN ILLEGAL ALIENS HAVE RIGHTS?

Every nation is prohibited by international law from subjecting any human being to wanton suffering, and in addition most nations have entered into bi- or multilateral agreements in which they pledge to accord named rights to specific classes of people. Beyond these generally vague and self-enforcing covenants, however, the protection provided most undocumented aliens depends largely upon the prevailing values in the host countries and the political clout of the sending countries.

In recent years, the United States has absorbed more immigrants than all other countries combined,[47] and the resulting strain may account for the popular indignation and even alarm that is focused on undocumented aliens, whose political powerlessness and clandestine existences render them natural scapegoats. As a result, these migrants are the targets of both legal and extralegal discrimination.

The courts in this country have had scant opportunity to rule on the constitutionality of official practices that discriminate against undocumented aliens. This is understandable, given the latter's reluctance to expose themselves by maintaining a lawsuit. Predictably, the bulk of cases that have come before the judiciary involve alleged procedural inadequacies in deportation proceedings, which are already under way.

Past litigation has established that undocumented aliens are entitled at least to minimal due process, and recently the Supreme Court reaffirmed this fact:

> There are literally millions of aliens within the jurisdiction of the United States. The Fifth Amendment, as well as the Fourteenth Amendment, protects every one of these persons from deprivation of life, liberty, or property without due process of law. . . . Even one whose presence in this country is unlawful, involuntary, or transitory, is entitled to that constitutional protection.[48]

Ordinarily, "due process" for undocumented aliens is satisfied as long as they are afforded, prior to deportation, notice of the grounds for their expulsion, an opportunity to rebut the charges against them, and an administrative hearing conducted according to established standards of fairness. On the theory that a deportation is a civil rather than criminal proceeding, however, even long-term resident aliens are denied many rights that are deemed essential in a criminal trial: For instance, indigent defendants in deportation proceedings are denied court-appointed attorneys;[49] since the constitutional prohibition against ex post facto laws does not apply in civil actions, they may be expelled from the country for past activity that was legal when undertaken;[50] defendants in deportation hearings may be deported on the basis of information obtained in violation of the Constitution;[51] and defendants are not entitled to compel witnesses on their own behalf[52] or, apparently, to receive Miranda warnings when they are apprehended by the immigration service.[53]

Undocumented aliens are entitled to habeas corpus relief, however, if they can persuade a reviewing court either that established principles of justice were not observed during their deportation hearing[54] or that their expulsion was ordered on the basis of insufficient evidence.[55] Moreover, in most jurisdictions they are regarded as "legal persons," entitled at least to those civil rights unrelated to their violation of the Immigration and Nationality Act. Undocumented aliens can consequently sue, for example, for workmen's compensation,[56] breach of contract,[57] and personal injury.[58]

Most courts in the United States will assuredly maintain their hands-off position whenever the federal government is challenged on its substantive policy toward undocumented aliens. Soon, however, the courts may determine for the first time the extent to which civil disabilities may be imposed by individual states. Responding to popular pressure, during the 1970s state legislatures have enacted a surge of provisions designed to penalize undocumented aliens. Most notable among these provisions is section 21 of the Texas Education Code, which was amended in 1975 to permit individual school districts either to bar undocumented children altogether from their public schools or to accomplish the same end by charging them tuition.[59] Other states have prohibited undocumented aliens from engaging in certain occupations and, following the lead of the federal government, from receiving many specified social service benefits.[60]

If the courts outlaw at least some of these disabilities, they may do so on the ground that such they deprive affected aliens of their equal protection rights under the Fourteenth Amendment. According to the first clause of this amendment, "[no state] shall deny to any person within its jurisdiction the equal protection of the laws."[61] Whether, or to what extent, undocumented aliens are covered by this statute is to date unclear.

In 1896, the Supreme Court indicated that undocumented aliens were covered: "[The provisions of the Fourteenth Amendment's equal protection clause] are universal in their application within the territorial jurisdiction, without regard to the differences of race, color, or nationality."[62] In 1971, however, when the Supreme Court held that resident aliens merited "particular judicial solicitude," it carefully limited its ruling to noncitizens legally present in the United States,[63] and more recently the Court declared that the rights and benefits accorded by a state to legal residents do not necessarily extend to illegal aliens.[64]

In 1982, the high court is scheduled to render an opinion in *Doe v. Plyler,*[65] the case involving section 21 of the Texas Education Code. If the Court ultimately sustains the constitutionality of this provision, it may be on the basis of one or more arguments put forth by Texas in its defense.[66] According to the first of these arguments, by violating the terms of the Immigration and Nationality Act undocumented aliens have an "outlaw status" and are consequently precluded from asserting their rights in matters unrelated to immigration. According to the second argument, because undocumented aliens reside in this country illegally, they are not "within the jurisdiction" of the state in which they reside and are therefore beyond the purview of the equal protection clause. Finally, Texas defends its statute on policy as opposed to legal grounds—that is, by volunteering governmental bounty to any alien capable of eluding our immigration system, a state thereby provides an incentive for other aliens to enter this country surreptitiously.

If the Court finds the Texas provision unconstitutional, however, it may be on the basis of the logic employed by both the district and circuit courts in this case.[67] These tribunals found the Texas statute indefensible because it violated the equal protection clause, whose coverage extended to all human beings physically present within the United States. While both courts cited a number of reasons why such coverage is essential, they based their holdings on one paramount consideration, "the ultimate results that would obtain if illegal aliens were not afforded the equal protection of the laws."[68]

The circuit court noted in *Doe* that Texas was suffering the local effects of a national problem: "When national immigration laws are not or cannot be enforced, it is the States, most particularly the border States, that bear the heaviest burden."[69] Nevertheless, "the Court cannot suspend the operation of the Constitution to aid a state to solve its political and social problems."[70]

Courts must inevitably intervene on behalf of undocumented aliens, if not to grant their children educational benefits then to prevent even more egregious forms of discrimination. It is regrettable, however, that the courts must lead the attack on these "political and social" problems. Both Congress and the executive branch are better equipped and more appropriate bodies to address the inequities occasioned by illegal migration; moreover, state legislation such as that represented by section 21 can only be foreclosed indefinitely without broadly based federal action and international cooperation. Unfortunately, however, the majoritarian process is frequently unsolicitous of those who are powerless, and this lack of solicitude, evident in the Ninety-Seventh Congress, is apt to continue as long as undocumented aliens remain the focus of popular hostility. Thus, both by default and by necessity, the courts must intervene on behalf of undocumented aliens, the most defenseless of all minority groups.

The New Emphasis on Universal Human Rights

The extent to which a state bears responsibility for the treatment of aliens continues to inspire debate, notwithstanding frequent claims that the issue is no longer commanding—that is, that it has been preempted by human rights norms that for the purpose of international law have rendered irrelevant the traditional distinction between aliens and nationals.

A generation emerged from World War II appalled by the atrocities of which nations were capable and convinced that only fundamental revisions in classical international law could prevent such tragedies from recurring. Members of this generation accordingly set to work formulating doctrines that, if implemented, would protect the basic rights of all human beings, as against even sovereign authority, and guarantee protection of these rights on the international as well as the national level.

The Universal Declaration of Human Rights[71] and the International Covenant of Human Rights[72] were subsequently drafted, and both catalog and elaborate on the charter's general provisions. Regional agreements have also been enacted, first among the European nations and eventually among the American nations, which obligate participants to abide by a set of guarantees for the protection of human rights. Moreover, in excess of fifty related international instruments have been adopted on a global scale and more than twenty on a regional basis, and still a third series of agreements have been promulgated which are concerned with such specific subjects as racial discrimination and genocide. In light of these developments, many scholars are convinced that an effective system of international human rights law now exists.

Beyond their emphasis on human rights, a second unprecedented feature characterizes these post–World War II documents: They draw no significant distinctions between nationals and aliens. The language in most of these declarations is intentionally and almost invariably inclusive: "Everyone has the right to . . ." "No one shall be . . ."—indicating that the specific right at issue inheres in every human being, irrespective of nationality.

Article One of the European Convention, for instance, specifies that "the high contracting parties shall secure to everyone within their jurisdiction the rights and freedoms defended in Section One of this Convention."[73] The American Convention on Human Rights similarly proclaims in its preamble that fundamental human rights are not derived from an individual's being a national of a certain state but rather are based upon essential human attributes. In Section Two, after enumerating the rights to be protected, the convention states that "for the purpose of this convention, 'person' means every human being."[74]

When on infrequent occasions distinctions are drawn on the basis of alienage, they ordinarily concern activities such as voting or running for office that involve the "political community"—activities that states traditionally and at least defensibly have confined to their own nationals. When participation is then restricted, the pertinent language is unequivocal: for instance, Article One in the Universal Declaration of Human Rights states that "everyone has the right to take part in the government of his country, directly or through freely chosen representatives."[75]

None of the major human rights documents specifically cites alienage as an impermissible ground of discrimination, but given the inclusiveness of their guarantees, some legal scholars are convinced that hereafter states will be strictly curtailed in their efforts to differentiate on the basis of alienage.[76] Chen, McDougal, and Lasswell, in fact, envision a new world order characterized by an emerging set of standards that will apply to every sector of human interaction: "If we postulate that global connections will continue to gain in intensity, emerging networks of associations will cover more people, more localities, and more pluralization. To an increasing extent the protection of aliens will be taken for granted."[77]

The European Convention on Human Rights is a particularly notable postwar phenomenon. This singular institution, which enjoys substantial support from its contracting parties in Western Europe, has received and acted upon a multitude of petitions from nonnationals residing in the territory of member states. Since the convention confers its protection without regard to nationality, it represents a radical departure from traditional international law. Each contracting state pledges to secure enumerated rights and privileges to every individual within its jurisdiction, regardless of whether the individual is a national, an alien, or even a stateless person.

The postwar record of the European Convention, alongside other contemporaneous developments in the general area of human rights, has prompted some analysts to conclude that a system of individual human rights now exists and that this system effectively supersedes the basic statist principle that governments incur no international liability for the mistreatment of their own nationals.[78]

Many who welcome this new emphasis on human rights welcome as well the real or perceived waning of the doctrine of state responsibility toward aliens; according to their logic, the evisceration of this doctrine is necessary before there can emerge a system that is dedicated to the welfare of all human beings. Most ex-colonial and socialist states are also encouraged by any erosion in this doctrine, because they are either suspicious of or repudiate altogether the traditional principles of international law, many of which were systematized in the nineteenth century without their participation and have been applied thereafter at their purported expense.[79] Among the most challenged is the historic prescription itself that a state bears responsibility for the treatment of aliens in general, or for injuries to their persons and property in particular.[80]

Since World War II the collective political strength of these Third World and socialist states has been increasingly evident in the U.N. General Assembly; notably, the assembly recently drafted a

Charter of Economic Rights and Duties of States, which appears to
deny altogether the traditional law of state responsibility toward
aliens.

There remain some indications, however, that reports pro-
claiming the demise of the state responsibility doctrine may be exag-
gerated. Most significant, the International Law Commission, which is
entrusted by the U.N. charter with the primary responsibility for the
development and codification of international law, has shown renewed interest in formulating general principles of state responsibility toward aliens.

In 1972, the commission appointed Baroness Diana Louie Elles
to formulate a draft proposal that would enumerate the human rights
that states are obliged to accord their resident aliens. The baroness
formulated this Draft Declaration over a six-year period, and judging
from its growing acceptance her modus operandi has been effective.
She simply adopted many of the general human rights guarantees
that states have accepted over the years, and that have appeared in
numerous bilateral and multilateral treaties, and applied them exclusively to aliens.

The baroness's draft has received substantial support from an
unlikely source: developing countries. They were consulted throughout its preparation, which accounts in part for their enthusiasm, but
they are also becoming increasingly concerned about the treatment
their own nationals receive in other countries, and in particular with
the latter's continued right to repatriate their earnings. To date the
draft also has been approved by the U.N. Commission on Human
Rights.

While the draft represents a useful and necessary contribution to
the development of international law, for two reasons its significance
should not be overestimated. First, it applies only to permanent resident aliens, who comprise a very small percentage of the world's
migrant population. Second, despite indications of widespread endorsement, the draft has not yet been approved by the U.N. General
Assembly.

Notwithstanding some counterindications, therefore, it is uncertain whether or to what extent the doctrine of state responsibility
toward aliens has retained its erstwhile vigor. This is not necessarily
regrettable if its devitalization signifies the supplantation of an older,
assertedly imperialistic international law with a new system of human
rights norms applicable to all people. The fundamental question thus
becomes: Does an effective system for the protection of human rights
now exist, sufficient to guarantee at least fundamental justice to
aliens?

It is reassuring to contemplate a postwar era in which individual states have recognized certain basic human rights that apply to nationals and aliens alike; indeed, this era has witnessed a plethora of documents, declarations, treaties, commissions, conventions, and accords dedicated to the recognition and protection of human rights, and no amount of cynicism can minimize the significance of this phenomenon. Conversely, no amount of optimism can deny the reality of less heartening developments: Many countries, including the United States, are not yet parties to the bulk of these agreements, or have refused to be bound by any of their obligations that are "self-executing."[81] Conversely, the Soviet Union has ratified a number of international conventions and has also accepted the Helsinki Accords; the Organization of American States (OAS), as well, routinely passes, by unanimous vote, human rights provisions. Neither the Soviet Union nor a substantial proportion of the OAS signatories, however, are distinguished for their championship of human rights. The major rights' conventions are therefore either not among those treaties in force or contain provisions that at least on occasion are openly and notoriously flouted.

An effective system of human rights is impeded, as well, by the dominance of state sovereignty, which retains its formidable and largely unrivaled sway despite its anachronistic, perilous, and even defenseless character in today's interdependent world. Sovereignty remains so imperious a force that, regardless of the scope of the injustice, few states are willing either to tolerate international interference in their own operations or to implicate themselves in the "domestic jurisdiction" of another.[82]

As a consequence, James Watson is one of many who contend that little can be done to protect human rights in the current world legal order.[83] To buttress his thesis, Watson provides a surfeit of empirical evidence suggesting that human rights abuses, perpetuated by states indiscriminately on nationals and aliens alike, have receded neither in volume nor in brutality, despite a profusion of postwar commissions and conventions dedicated to the elimination of these abuses.

Many international scholars take issue with Watson's interpretation of the postwar environment and can cite a positive development to counter every dismal phenomenon that he details.[84] Regardless of whether the contemporary environment does or does not afford individuals more protection than they have received in the past, however, only those most committed to what Lowell F. Schechter calls "unsubstantiated optimism"[85] would conclude either that a "new world order" is imminent or that human rights norms have attained the scope and potency necessary to render superfluous the old doctrine of state responsibility for the protection of aliens.

What the Future Holds

The historic remedy for the protection of aliens is, then, neither superfluous nor outdated; rather, given the contemporary milieu, any move to dispense with this remedy is both foolhardy and dangerous. This remains true, despite two fundamental facts: (1) the doctrine is basically deficient, because under its authority the extent to which aliens receive adequate protection depends upon the will and the political clout of the affected sovereign; and (2) the doctrine will serve as a poor substitute for effective international mechanisms in the succeeding decades, when any one state or even grouping of states may lack the resources necessary to accommodate what demographers predict will be an unprecedented number of displaced people.

POPULATION PRESSURES

The world's alien population will swell in the decade ahead, perhaps in staggering proportions—a result, predictably, of overpopulation, poverty, and political upheaval. Demographers calculate that the world population in the 1980s will increase "inevitably" by 800 million, and possibly by 1 billion, of whom seven out of eight will be from the Third World and whose numbers will supplement the "estimated" 3 billion people who now live in poverty.[86]

The population boom means more young, who will migrate in search of the "opportunities" that purportedly abound in developed countries, and it means more people, young or old, who will migrate less for "opportunity" than from sheer necessity. Former President Houari Boumédienne of Algeria issued an ominous warning when he forecast that "no quantity of atomic bombs could stem the tide of millions . . . who will someday leave the poor southern parts of the world to erupt into the relatively accessible spaces of the rich northern hemisphere looking for survival."[87] This past decade, Vietnam, Cuba, and Uganda attest as well that population pressures can lead to mass expulsions.

Migration also will mount in response to the political unrest that will characterize the waning decades of the twentieth century. For instance, according to William Overholt, speaking before a recent

Task Force on Immigration and Refugee Policy, organized worker movements will escalate in Communist Eastern European countries,[88] and he prophesied that the movement toward Eastern European independence "would endanger the peace of all Western Europe and could produce a wave of refugees greater than the Eastern European wave of the 1950's."[89]

Comprising the bulk of the migrant population will be three classes of aliens that are particularly vulnerable and for whose protection international mechanisms are particularly inadequate. So-called "guestworkers" constitute the first class, those who find employment on a temporary basis in foreign lands as long as the latter remain in need of a cheap and plentiful supply of labor; according to recent studies, these workers seldom benefit from the economic and political safeguards that bi- and multilateral treaties have been designed to secure.[90] The second class is comprised of illegal/undocumented aliens, whose status subjects them to both legal and extralegal exploitation;[91] refugees compose the third class—those men, women, and children who now number in the millions and whose "well-founded fear of persecution" forces them to flee their native land amid circumstances that are always distressing and often tragic.[92]

Unfortunately, overpopulation and widespread displacement have not encouraged productive responses from either the developed or the developing nations. Rather, they have fostered a perverse form of nativism in the former and an authoritarianism in the latter which have rendered most countries more reluctant than ever to cooperate in large-scale international efforts or even to engage in the kind of preliminary debate that might encourage such cooperation.

Governments experiencing mounting populations show a tendency to repress internal critics, Richard Falk observed, concluding that "the global trend, manifest in the state level in all sectors of world society toward authoritative rule, is at once significant and discouraging."[93] This population pressure, coupled with the growing numbers of uprooted people, threatens to undermine national regimes and overtax international institutions, thereby jeopardizing the existence of and certainly the expansion of movements designed to protect human rights.

DEVELOPED VERSUS DEVELOPING NATIONS

These movements are further imperiled by the fundamental ideological differences that divide developed and developing nations. Denizens of poor lands often contend that there is a universal right to emigrate, or that developed nations have contributed to the welter of ills that afflict Third World countries and are consequently obliged not only to assist in the birth of a "new world order" but also, as Lowell Schechter phrased it, "[to take] people in as well as [give out aid]."[94]

Members of developed countries frequently resent these assumptions and maintain that the overpopulation and underdevelopment characteristic of Third World nations is largely attributable to their "irresponsible" failure to promote birth control, economic development, and democratic institutions. This resentment has contributed to a "neonativist" movement in many of these countries, manifest in such measures as those being undertaken in the United States to "crack down" on illegal aliens, restrict the annual number of refugee admissions, and reduce the country's foreign aid expenditures.

Developed countries are struggling with an array of economic and political problems that increasingly seem intractable, and their apparent "compassion fatigue"[95] may be understandable. While understandable, however, this "fatigue" represents a luxury no longer tolerable in a world where millions are uprooted, homeless, and desperate. What is more, developed nations no longer have the option of clutching old assumptions that may be neither realistic nor just in the second half of the twentieth century; instead, if not from altruism then from simple expediency they are obliged to identify those assumptions and then ask themselves the hard questions.

For those living in developed nations, the fundamental question is less whether they are their brothers' keepers than whether they owe their brothers anything at all.[96] If the answer is yes, the focus shifts to the nature and extent of this responsibility. Are they obligated to revitalize and abide by the traditional doctrine of state responsibility for injury to aliens, perhaps on the assumption that, for all its deficiencies, it still provides the most effective remedy available? Or, given the corresponding inadequacy of this remedy as the world's alien population continues to mount, are nations obliged to invest international mechanisms with the authority and resources sufficient to handle mass displacement?

Does the obligation persist if meaningful assistance on an international scale would necessitate a modest or even significant reduction in a country's standard of living? Or—of even more importance—if it requires a nation to sacrifice any of its hallowed sovereignty? This is a central question for people in the United States. This country guards its own "sovereign prerogatives" with jealous and unyielding fervor, and given its preeminent international status thereby encourages other countries to respond in kind.

THE UNITED STATES AND INTERNATIONAL HUMAN RIGHTS

Historically, however, the United States has pointed an accusing finger at countries that do respond in kind, earning a reputation for hypocrisy. While it has condemned other countries, such as Chile and the Soviet Union, for violating U.N. Charter obligations, its own courts have steadfastly maintained that the same obligations have no internal force in the absence of domestic legislation; while Congress requires the Department of State to report on the status of human rights in every other country in the world, it requires no such report on conditions at home. Louis Henkin concludes, "The United States has not been a pillar of human rights, only a flying buttress—supporting them from the outside."[97]

Most international human rights agreements are not among those treaties in force in the United States; neither are the bulk of the covenants and agreements concerning labor conditions sponsored by the International Labor Organization. Indeed, the U.S. Senate has yet to give its "advice and consent" to the Genocide Convention, drafted in the wake of Hitler's holocaust. The country has ratified only those human rights agreements that, like the U.N. Charter or the Universal Declaration, lack the status of law and hence impose no international obligations.[98] Finally, since the U.S. Constitution does not prohibit either the president or Congress from violating international law, courts in this country are rarely troubled when federal policy contravenes its prescriptions.

There is one commanding reason why the United States has failed to ratify most human rights treaties: it would thereby forfeit a modicum of its "plenary authority" over domestic relations. That other nations should participate even marginally in the country's internal affairs is as unacceptable to Congress as the specter of the nation being hauled against its will before an international tribunal. This attitude was particularly evident during the civil rights crises in the 1960s, when movements to eliminate racial discrimination through treaties provoked a backlash in Congress that manifested itself in renewed support for the Bricker Amendment.[99] According to the principal clause of this amendment, a treaty would become effective as domestic law only through legislation that would be valid in the absence of a treaty.

It is lamentable that the United States refuses to sacrifice any of

238

its sovereign authority by entering into binding human rights agreements. Beyond inspiring a similar reticence from other nations, the United States by its intransigence undermines the moral authority of multilateral agreements during a nuclear age when such agreements are crucial. Moreover, by its refusal to enter into such agreements, the nation passes up an opportunity to infuse its domestic law with new vitality. The standards embodied in such documents as the Universal Declaration of Human Rights reflect an international consensus, and by reference to these standards the courts could enrich the meaning of such familiar judicial concepts as "due process" and "equal protection," or provide a contemporary context within which to determine the meaning of the Eighth Amendment, for instance, which prohibits "cruel and unusual punishment," or the Ninth Amendment, which provides constitutional protection for fundamental "new" rights as they become evident through time and experience.

Finally, if the United States were to ratify human rights agreements, it would provide the courts in this country with an effective means by which to assist noncitizens. Since by virtue of the "supremacy clause"[100] treaties preempt contrary state legislation, they could be used by the judiciary in some circumstances where it otherwise would be reluctant to interfere, in particular where issues are involved that traditionally have been regarded as within a state's sole preserve—issues affecting education or the property rights of noncitizens, for instance, or labor relations that affect migrant workers. The judiciary should, of course, display the same restraint it does in most other contexts; it should not upset normal federal-state relations for "light and transient" reasons. By the prudent use of treaties, however, the Court could disallow the occasional state practice that departs flagrantly from accepted international norms.

To avoid worldwide havoc, the answer to a final question cannot be indefinitely postponed, and that is whether it is ethically justifiable for any country to close its borders for reasons that are less than compelling. To suggest otherwise is to challenge an attribute supposedly central to sovereignty, this being a state's absolute right to exclude from its territory any and all whom it chooses, and indeed for any reason it chooses. To suggest otherwise is to challenge as well a philosophic tenet that has prevailed scarcely without question throughout modern Western history: the thesis put forth by John Stuart Mill among others—that it is defensible for any state whose population is adjudged to be at or near its optimal level to prohibit the entry of any others whose presence sooner or later will upset the ideal.[101]

Eventually all these questions point beyond themselves, because in answering these questions both individuals and nations reveal those values that ultimately distinguish the just from the unjust.

Notes

1. Emerich de Vattel, quoted in Ram Prakash Anand, *New States and International Law* (New York: International Book Distributors, 1972), p. 39.

2. Judge Philip C. Jessup, quoted in Myres S. McDougal, Harold Lasswell, and Lung-chu Chen, "The Protection of Aliens from Discrimination and World Public Order: Responsibility of States Conjoined with Human Rights," *American Journal of International Law* 70 (1976): 443. (Hereafter the *American Journal of International Law* is cited as *AJIL.*)

3. Mixed Claims Commission: Parker, Umpire, American Commissioner; Kiesselbach, German Commissioner, 1924, United Nations Reports of International Arbitral Awards.

4. Elihu Root, "The Basis of Protection of Citizens Abroad," *AJIL* 4 (1910): 521–22.

5. The Calvo Doctrine was formulated by Carlos Calvo (1824–1906), an Argentine diplomat and legal scholar. An extension of his doctrine is the Drago Doctrine, developed in 1902 by Argentine foreign minister Luis Drago (1859–1921); according to the latter, a state is not permitted to react by force to secure public debts owed its aliens by a defaulting sovereign.

In 1957, Padilla Nervo participated in a debate in the International Law Conference, during which he explained why Latin Americans in general regard the "international minimum standard" with antipathy. As he said, "the history of the institution of state responsibility was the history of obstacles placed in the way of the new Latin American countries—obstacles to the defence of their [at that time] recent independence, to the ownership and development of their resources, and to their social integration" (*Yearbook of the International Law Commission, 1957*, 1: 155 ff, quoted from D. J. Harris, *Cases and Materials on International Law*, 2d ed. [London: Sweet & Maxwell, 1979], p. 425).

Most Third World nations have and continue to regard the doctrine of state responsibility for injury to aliens, and in particular the "international minimum standard" offshoot, as tools designed and enforced by and for the benefit of imperialistic nations. S. N. Guha-Roy is perhaps the most eloquent spokesman for these Third World nations:

> Imperialism . . . found in [the doctrine] a ready-made device to push itself forward under a sort of legal banner and at the same time helped the law to develop along certain lines. Once "the old Vattelian fiction" (that whoever ill-treats a citizen indirectly injures the state) underlying the state's right of diplomatic protection of its nationals is abandoned . . . , the sole theoretical basis of the right claimed as part of universal international law disappears and the only crutch left for this right to

lean on is custom. But custom is limited in its operation to states which either were its birthplace or adopted it.["Is the Law Responsibility of States for Injuries to Aliens a Part of Universal Law?" *AJIL* (1961): 880–881.]

Philip C. Jessup concurs in Guha-Roy's assessment: "The history of the development of international law on the responsibility of states for injuries to aliens is . . . an aspect of the history of 'imperialism' or 'dollar diplomacy.' The fact that several strong states found themselves simultaneously interested in the welfare of their nationals in states which were 'exploited' . . . assisted the legal development" (*A Modern Law of Nations* [New York: Macmillan Co., 1948], p. 96).

6. *United States* v. *Mexico*, 4 R.I.A.A. 60 at 64 (1926).

7. Ibid.

8. Harris, *Cases and Materials*, p. 421; see also Oliver J. Lissitzyn, *AJIL* 30 (1936): 632.

9. See Louis B. Sohn and R. R. Baxter, "Responsibility of States for Injuries to the Economic Interests of Aliens," *AJIL* 55 (1961): 545. The authors quote and analyze the Harvard Draft Convention, many articles of which relate to the judicial process and/or to procedural fairness antedating this process: art. 4 (sufficiency of justification); art. 5 (arrest and detention); art. 6 (access to a tribunal); art. 7 (fair hearing).

10. Restatement, Second, Foreign Relations Law of the United States Secs. 165–166, Comments and Reporters' Notes (1965), quoted in Burns H. Weston et al., *International Law and World Order* (St. Paul: West Publishing Co., 1980), p. 687.

11. 120 U.S. 479, 484 (1887).

12. Cited in McDougal, Lasswell, and Chen, "Protection of Aliens," p. 450.

13. Restatement, Second, Foreign Relations Law of the United States secs. 165–166 (2) (1965). For a thorough discussion of the current status of the state responsibility doctrine, see Richard B. Lillich, "The Current Status of the Law of State Responsibility for Injuries to Aliens," in Proceedings of the 73rd Annual Meeting of the American Society of International Law, Washington, D.C., April 26–28, 1979, p. 244.

14. According to Richard Lillich and Burns Weston, this phrase is generally thought to originate with Secretary of State Hull, who in 1938 attempted to formulate a doctrine of just compensation during correspondence between the United States and Mexico (*International Claims: Their Settlement by Lump Sum Agreements* [Charlottesville: University Press of Virginia, 1975], pp. 208–242). In practice, the authors note that "partial compensation" has become the general norm; since states cannot agree upon "valuation standards," they add that "what claimant States regard as 'partial,' respondent States may view as 'adequate,' 'just,' or even 'full'" (cited in Lillich and Weston, *International Claims*, p. 208).

15. To acquire permanent-resident status, an alien must obtain an immigrant visa by which he is "lawfully accorded the privilege of residing perma-

nently in the United States as an immigrant in accordance with the immigration laws" (8 U.S.C., sec. 1101 [a] [20]). Upon entry, a resident alien may live anywhere in the United States and engage in any activity permitted by law (8 U.S.C., sec. 1101 [a] [15]). After five years of residence in this country, most permanent aliens become eligible for citizenship (8 U.S.C., sec. 1427 [a]). Only three years' residency is required for the naturalization of an alien whose spouse is a United States citizen (8 U.S.C., sec. 1430). There are approximately 5 million resident aliens living in the United States on a permanent basis—about 2 percent of the total population (U.S. Bureau of the Census, *Statistical Abstract of the United States* (1978), Table 2).

16. The Immigration and Nationality Act (8 U.S.C.) imposes upon resident aliens certain obligations to which citizens are not subject. For example, the alien is required to register and report his or her address each year and within ten days to report any change of address. See also Appendix, *Hampton v. Mow Sun Wong*, 426 U.S. 88 (1976); in an appendix to its brief in *Hampton*, the government listed 243 statutory provisions that draw distinctions between citizens and aliens. As Gerald Rosberg pointed out, this list did not include Title 8, "Aliens and Nationality," in which almost every provision is premised on such a distinction (Gerald Rosenberg, "The Protection of Aliens from Discriminatory Treatment by the National Government," in *The Supreme Court Review*, ed. Philip B. Kurland and Gerhard Casper [Chicago: University of Chicago Press, 1978], pp. 275 and 276, n. 6).

17. 8 U.S.C., sec. 1184(a) (1976).

18. 8 C.F.R., sec. 214.5 (1979).

19. *Narenji* v. *Civiletti*, 617 F. 2d 745, 747 (D.C. Cir. 1979), *cert. denied*, 446 U.S. 957 (1980).

20. For discussion, see pp. 226–229.

21. A. Peter Mutharika provides a thorough discussion of the rights and restrictions imposed on aliens legally residing in the United States and details existing limitations on their right to own property, use natural resources, and engage in occupations (*The Alien Under American Law* [Dobbs Ferry, N.Y.: Oceana Publications, 1981]).

Weston et al. (*International Law and World Order*, p. 689) point out that the sole criterion regarding the reasonableness of conditions imposed upon resident aliens is the "international standard of justice." However, if a foreign national has entered the territory lawfully, and for a purpose lawful at the time of his entry, or lawfully acquired an interest in the state's property, new restrictions are ordinarily deemed unreasonable if they impose an undue hardship on the affected alien. For a discussion of the treatment to which resident aliens historically have been subject in the United States, see Elizabeth Hull, "Resident Aliens and the Equal Protection Clause: The Burger Court's Retreat from *Graham* v. *Richardson*," *Brooklyn Law Review* 47 (Fall 1980): 4–11.

22. Judge Benjamin Cardozo's opinion in *People* v. *Crane*, 214 N.Y. 154, 108 N.E. 427, affirmed 239 U.S. 195 (1915), upholding a statute limiting employment in public works projects to citizens, reflected the rationale

underlying the public interest doctrine. Finding that a state "may legitimately consult the welfare of its own citizens rather than that of aliens" in the allocation of the state's resources and "whatever is a privilege, rather than a right, may be made dependent on citizenship" (214 N.Y. at 164, 108 N.E. at 430), Judge Cardozo concluded that "it is not a denial of the equal protection of the laws when the government, in its capacity as proprietor, . . . bars the alien from the right to share in the property which [the state] holds for its own citizens" (214 N.Y. at 169, 108 N.E. at 432).

23. *Gizzarelli* v. *Presbrey,* 44 R.I. 333, 335, 117 A. 359, 360 (1922). Limitations upon aliens became almost ludicrous in their scope and variety, expressing the states' unwillingness to trust aliens "with animals, a corpse, or even a person's hair or beard." Simona F. Rosales, "Resident Aliens and the Right to Work: The Quest for Equal Protection," *Hastings Constitutional Law Quarterly* 2 (1977): 1037. See also *Miller* v. *City of Niagara Falls,* 207 App. Div. 798, 202 N.Y.S. 549 (4th Dept. 1924) (ordinance prohibiting aliens from selling soft drinks held constitutional because it served the welfare of the community); *Commonwealth* v. *Hana,* 195 Mass. 262, 81 N.E. 149 (1907) (peddler's licenses denied to aliens because of the opportunities to swindle purchasers).

24. 403 U.S. 365 (1971).

25. 403 U.S. at 376. According to a recently completed study of the schooling and earnings of immigrant families by T. Paul Schultz of Yale University and Julian L. Simon of the University of Illinois, "after about two to six years' residence in this country . . . immigrant families 'come to pay as much in taxes' as native families, and 'after that they pay substantially more'" (*New York Times,* September 22, 1980, p. A1, quoting Simon). The study, requested by the Select Commission on Immigration and Refugee Policy, also revealed that "immigrants contribute more to the public coffers than they take from them" (ibid., p. A15). Aliens admitted for permanent residence in the United States, it should be noted, are not exempt from induction into the armed forces (50 U.S.C. app. sec. 456 [a] [1976]).

26. *Sugarman* v. *Dougall,* 413 U.S. 634 (1973).

27. *In re Griffiths,* 413 U.S. 717 (1973).

28. *Examining Board of Engineers, Architects, and Surveyors* v. *Flores de Otero,* 426 U.S. 572 (1976).

29. *Nyquist* v. *Mauclet,* 432 U.S. 1 (1977).

30. 413 U.S. at 647. For discussion see McDougal, Lasswell, and Chen, "Protection of Aliens," p. 453. For a discussion of the "political community" doctrine, as applied by courts in this country, see Hull, "Resident Aliens," pp. 17–38.

31. *Skafte* v. *Rorex,* 191 Colo. 399, 553 P. 2d 830 (1976) (exclusion of aliens from voting in local school board elections upheld), *appeal dismissed,* 430 U.S. 961 (1977).

32. *Sugarman* v. *Dougall,* 453 U.S. at 647 (1973); *Boyd* v. *Thayer,* 143 U.S. 135, 161 (1892).

33. *Foley* v. *Connelie,* 435 U.S. 291, 297 (1978).

34. *Ambach* v. *Norwick,* 441 U.S. 68 (1979).

35. 435 U.S. at 304 (dissenting opinion).

36. *Mathews* v. *Diaz*, 426 U.S. 67 (1976).

37. U.S. Constitution, Art. 1, sec. 8, cl. 4.

38. The Supreme Court traditionally has subjected federal legislation affecting aliens to only the most perfunctory review. In *Mathews* v. *Diaz* the Court explained its reason for so doing:

> Since decisions in these matters may implicate our relations with foreign powers, and since a wide variety of classifications must be defined in the light of changing political and economic circumstances, such decisions are frequently of a character more appropriate to either the Legislature or the Executive than to the Judiciary. . . . The reasons that preclude judicial review of political questions also dictate a narrow standard of review of decisions made by the Congress or the President in the area of immigration and naturalization. [426 U.S. at 81–82.]

39. In *Yama Taya* v. *Fisher*, 189 U.S. 86 (1903), the Supreme Court upheld the exclusion of a Japanese alien on the ground that congressional power to exclude aliens, even on the basis of their race or national origin, is plenary. The Court again sustained Congress' action when it refused to allow people of Chinese ancestry to immigrate to the United States. See, e.g., *Fong Yue Ting* v. *United States*, 149 U.S. 698 (1893); *The Chinese Exclusion Case (Chae Chan Ping* v. *United States)*, 130 U.S. 581 (1889).

40. See *Kleindienst* v. *Mandel*, 408 U.S. 753 (1972).

41. *Fiallo* v. *Bell*, 430 U.S. 787 (1977). The Court upheld an immigration scheme that granted immigration preferences to "children" and "parents" of citizens; excluded from the preferential categories, however, were two classes of prospective entrants: (1) an illegitimate child of a citizen who is its natural father and (2) the natural father of a citizen who is his illegitimate child.

42. *Shaughnessy* v. *United States ex rel. Mezei*, 345 U.S. 206 (1953).

43. *United States ex rel. Knauff* v. *Shaughnessy*, 338 U.S. 537, 542 (1950).

44. *Fong Yue Ting* v. *United States*, 149 U.S. 698, 707 (1893).

45. For discussion, see Stanley Mailman, Statement on behalf of the Association of Immigration and Nationality Lawyers, Joint Hearing of the Subcommittee on Immigration and Refugee Policy of the Senate Committee on the Judiciary and the Subcommittee on Immigration, Refugees, and International Law of the House Committee on the Judiciary on the Final Report of the Select Commission on Immigration and Refugee Policy, May 6, 1981, pp. 12–16. In *Attorney General for Canada* v. *Cain*, The Judicial Committee of the Privy Council stated what continues to be a fundamental tenet of international law:

> One of the rights possessed by the supreme power in every State is the right to refuse to permit an alien to enter that State, to annex what conditions it pleases to the permission to enter it, and to expel or deport from the State, at pleasure, even a friendly alien, especially if it considers his presence in the State opposed to its peace, order, and good government, or to its social or material interests. [1906, A.C. 542 at 546.]

46. *Harisiades* v. *Shaughnessy*, 342 U.S. 580, 587–588 (1952).

47. Michael S. Teitelbaum, "Right Versus Right: Immigration and Refugee Policy in the United States," *Foreign Affairs* 59 (Fall 1980): 23.

John M. Crewdson notes that during the 1970s the United States absorbed 4 million immigrants and refugees, and in 1980 alone, with the inclusion of 160,000 Cuban and Haitian "boat people," there were more than 800,000 new arrivals. ("New Administration and Congress Face Major Immigration Decisions," *New York Times*, December 28, 1980, pp. 1, 120).

48. *Mathews* v. *Diaz*, 426 U.S. 67, 77 (1976).

49. C.F. 8 U.S.C., sec. 1252(b) (1970).

50. *Harisiades* v. *Shaughnessy*, 342 U.S. 580 (1952).

51. *Abel* v. *United States*, 362 U.S. 217 (1960). Immigration officials may undertake a search and seizure pursuant to an administrative arrest without violating the Fourth or Fifth Amendment, and any information uncovered during the search may be used to facilitate the petitioner's conviction.

52. *Low Wah Suey* v. *Backus*, 225 U.S. 460 (1912).

53. *Jolley* v. *Immigration and Naturalization Service*, 441 F. 2d 1245 (1971).

54. *United States ex rel. Vajtauer* v. *Commission on Immigration*, 273 U.S. 103, 106 (1927).

55. Ibid.

56. *Commercial Standard Fire & Marine Co.* v. *Galindo*, 484 S.W. 2d 635 (Tex. Civ. App.-El Paso 1972, writ ref'd n.r.e.).

57. *Gates* v. *Rivers Construction Co.*, 515 P. 2d 1020 (Alaska 1973).

58. *Martinez* v. *Fox Valley Bus Lines*, 17 F. Supp. 576 (N.D. Ill. 1936).

59. Sec. 21.031 of the Texas Education Code (Vernon Supp. 1976).

60. See, e.g., CALIFORNIA LABOR CODE sec. 2805 (a) (West Supp. 1978) (unlawful to knowingly employ workers lacking proper documentation); *Houston, Texas, Code of Ordinances* 745-63-8 (1978) (aliens seeking a driver's license to operate a taxi must produce proof that they are legally residing in the United States); 45 C.F.R., sec. 233.50 (1978) (Medicare eligibility restricted to citizens and lawful residents).

61. U.S. Constitution, Amendment 14, sec. 1.

62. *Wong Wing* v. *United States*, 163 U.S. 228, 238 (1976), quoting *Yick Wo* v. *Hopkins*, 118 U.S. 356, 369 (1886).

63. *Graham* v. *Richardson*, 403 U.S. at 365.

64. *Mathews* v. *Diaz*, 426 U.S. at 80.

65. No. 80-1538.

66. Brief for Appellant, James Plyler *et al.*

67. *Doe* v. *Plyler*, 458 F. Supp. 569 (1978); *Doe* v. *Plyler*, 628 F. 2d 448 (1980).

68. 628 F. 2d at 455.

69. 628 F. 2d at 461.

70. Ibid.

71. United Nations, *Human Rights: A Compilation of International Instruments of the United Nations*, U.N. Document ST/HR/1 (1973), p. 1.

72. Ibid., p. 1; see, e.g., art. 2: "Furthermore, no distinction shall be made on the basis of the political, jurisdictional, or international status of the country or territory to which a person belongs, whether it be independent, trust, non-self-governing or under any other limitation of sovereignty."

73. *European Convention on Human Rights: Collected Texts*, 9th ed. (1974), p. 2.

74. Preamble, American Convention on Human Rights, in *Basic Documents on International Protection of Human Rights*, ed. L. Sohn and T. Buergenthal (Indianapolis: Bobbs-Merrill Co., 1973), p. 125.

75. For Example, art. 3: "Everyone has the right to life, liberty and the security of person" (United Nations, *Human Rights*, p. 1).

76. McDougal, Lasswell, and Chen, "Protection of Aliens," pp. 457–458.

77. Ibid., p. 468.

78. See, e.g., Jeffrey M. Blum and Ralph G. Teinhardt, "Federal Jurisdiction over International Human Rights Claims: The Alien Tort Claim Act After *Filartiga* v. *Pena-Irala*," *International Law Journal* 22 (Winter 1981):53, 67.

79. For discussion, see Guha-Roy, "Law Responsibility of States," pp. 537–538.

80. Edwin M. Borchard summarizes some of the deficiencies that critics believe inhere in the doctrine of state responsibility for aliens:

> The clan conception is obsolete, and that protection abroad involves the people of two countries in a dispute essentially private; that its tendency is to place a premium on superior military strength in its contacts with weaker countries; that it substitutes the methods of politics for those of law; that it constitutes an invasion of the sovereignty and jurisdiction of weaker countries; that it makes the intervening state plaintiff, judge and sheriff in its own cause, without adequate opportunity for an impartial investigation of the facts; that it promotes injustice rather than justice; that in its support for economic nationalism it makes for imperialism and war. [Quoted in Weston et al., *International Law and World Order*, p. 696.]

81. A non-self-executing treaty requires implementing legislation, in contrast to a self-executing treaty, which confers rights directly enforceable in courts without congressional action.

82. After essaying the contemporary international environment, Eric Lane concluded that "today, state tremors over atrocities have stabilized and sovereign self-concern has reasserted itself as the dominant force of the world legal order. . . . As is evidenced by the experience in Uganda and Cambodia, the legal protection of human rights continues to remain solely a state matter" ("Mass Killing by Governments: Lawful in the World Legal Order?" *New York University Journal of International Law and Politics*, Fall 1979: 279–280).

83. "Legal Theory, Efficacy, and Validity in the Development of Human Rights Norms in International Law," *University of Illinois Law Forum*, 1979, no. 2: 609–613.

Watson notes that Article 2 (7) of the U.N. Charter, relating to nonintervention in matters of domestic jurisdiction, must be invalid if it does not allow a state to violate human rights. He contends that little can be done to protect human rights in the current world legal order and that any change may well be one for the worse.

84. See, e.g., Lowell F. Schechter, "The Views of 'Charterists' and 'Skep-

tics' on Human Rights in the World Legal Order: Two Wrongs Don't Make a Right," *Hofstra Law Review* 9 (Winter 1981): 357. Schechter cites a number of progressive moves in the area of human rights which have characterized the postwar environment. He notes at one point that "it is much more difficult . . . to produce the evidence for the other side—that is, violations that have not occurred or have taken a milder form because of the existence of international standards and enforcement machinery" (p. 363).

85. Ibid., p. 357. The author uses the phrase to summarize a tendency perceived by James Watson, who noted:

> With depressing regularity the reader of human rights literature in the international law field will find in the concluding paragraphs of the typical article an exhortation to optimism or hope, almost invariably expressed in the passive voice in order to increase its apparent authority. What such remarks indicate is of course that the true basis for the writer's argument is not to be found within the confines of international law, but rather in his or her perception of human nature. [Ibid., quoting Watson, "Legal Theory, Efficacy, and Validity," p. 627.]

86. Council on Environmental Quality and the Department of State, *The Global 2000 Report to the Press*, Vol. 1 (Washington, D.C.: Government Printing Office, 1980), p. 41.

According to Georges Tapinos, "the demographic situation in 1990 as we have described it will be the result of an ineluctable evolutionary pattern that no demographic policy, however coercive, can alter in such a brief period of time" ("The World in the 1980s: Demographic Perspectives," in Council on Foreign Relations, *Six Billion People: Demographic Dilemmas and World Politics* [New York: McGraw-Hill, 1978], pp. 74–75).

Phyllis Piotrow notes that the bulk of migration will be from the developing nations to the developed nations. She predicts that legal migration from Africa, Asia, and Latin America to Australia, Canada, and the United States, which doubled during the 1960s, will probably double again by the 1980s ("Population Policies for the 1980s: Meeting the Crest of the Demographic Wave," in ibid., p. 147, "Views of 'Charterists' and 'Skeptics,'" p. 387). Piotrow concludes that "by the 1980s, international migration will be a major issue. It will seem to some nations as important politically as their own national boundaries and as important economically as the price of their major commodity exports" (ibid.).

87. Otis L. Graham, Jr., "Illegal Immigration and the New Reform Movement," *FAIR Immigration Papers II*, February 1980: 11.

88. "A Global Survey of Political-Economic Tensions Which Could Stimulate Refugee or Rapid Migrations, 1980–2000" (Paper prepared for the Select Commission on Immigration and Refugee Policy, September 17, 1979).

89. Ibid.

90. See, e.g., Philip L. Martin and Mark J. Miller, "Guestworkers: Lessons from Western Europe," *Industrial and Labor Relations Review* 33 (April 1980): 315.

91. for discussion, see above, pp. 226–229.

92. The United Nations has defined a "refugee" in the following terms:

"[A person who], owing to well-founded fear of being persecuted for reasons of race, religion, nationality, membership of a particular social group or political opinion, is outside the country of his nationality and is unable or, owing to such fear, is unwilling to avail himself of the protection of that country. . . ." (Convention Relating to the Status of Refugees, July 28, 1951, 189 U.N.T.S. 150, as amended per Protocol Relating to the Status of Refugees, January 31, 1967, 19 U.S.T. 6223, T.1.A.S. No. 6577, 606 U.N.T.S. 267 [Basic Document 3.5]).

93. Richard A. Falk, *A World Order Perspective on Authoritarian Tendencies* (New York: Institute for World Order, 1980), pp. 3–4; quoted in Schechter, "Views of 'Charterists' and 'Skeptics,'" p. 395.

Ullman notes that "as governments feel increasingly hard pressed in their efforts to cope with burgeoning populations, they are more likely to direct repressive power against those who disagree with their goals or their means of achieving them" ("Introduction: Human Rights—Towards International Action," in *Enhancing Global Human Rights*, ed. Jorge I. Dominguez et al. [New York: McGraw-Hill, 1979], quoted in Schechter "Views of 'Charterists' and 'Skeptics,'" p. 385).

94. Schechter notes that a number of scholars detect a "neo-nativism" in the United States "that perceives present-day immigrants as contaminating society" ("Views of 'Charterists' and 'Skeptics,'" p. 388). That attitude is fueled by present fears over inflation, diminishing resources, and a generalized fear that the country is increasingly less able to care for its own (ibid.). While scholars disagree whether the net effect of immigration is good or bad for either sending or receiving countries, Schechter recognizes that it has already developed a strain between both sets of countries that can only grow worse during the 1980s, and in conclusion he forecasts dismal consequences:

> Migration problems will complicate and possibly subvert attempts to achieve further international cooperation in meeting basic needs and protecting political and civil rights. If, for example, at the onset of a recession, developed nations immediately begin laying off and expelling Third World migrant workers, they may cause economic chaos in the Third World countries and jeopardize human-needs programs. Additionally, when developed nations do not treat illegal aliens with a minimal degree of dignity, it undermines their argument to the developing states that human rights must be protected. [Ibid., pp. 389–390.]

Cornelius F. Murphy, Jr., discusses a number of issues upon which disagreement between First and Third World nations is profound ("Objections to Western Conceptions of Human Rights," *Hofstra Law Review* 9 [Winter 1981]: 433). He cites, e.g., the substantial division between these respective nations over the meaning of the right to own property, or the differences between them surrounding the interpretation of self-determinism, or over the meaning of "free expression" (ibid., pp.434–435), and he concludes that with regard to each of these issues "the general ideas about the nature of social life, the purpose of political authority, and the destiny of nations, as well as of individuals, are influential" (ibid.).

Keith Griffin, an Oxford economist, argues that developed countries

indeed bear responsibility, to varying degrees, for the problems characteriz-
ing most Third World nations:

> It is our belief that underdeveloped countries as we observe them today are a
> product of historical forces, especially of those forces released by European ex-
> pansion and world ascendancy. Thus they are a relatively recent phenomenon.
> Europe did not "discover" the underdeveloped countries; on the contrary, she
> created them. In many cases, in fact, the societies with which Europe came into
> contact were sophisticated, cultured, and wealthy. *Underdevelopment in Spanish
> America* (London: Allen and Unwin, 1969), p. 38, quoted in Schechter, "Views of
> 'Charterists' and 'Skeptics,'" p. 378.

For further discussion, see Carlos Diaz-Alejandro, "Delinking North and
South: Unshackled or Unhinged," in Albert Fishtow et al., *Rich and Poor
Nations in the World Economy* (New York: McGraw-Hill, 1978).

95. Quoted in Leon F. Bouvier, Testimony Before Joint Hearing of the
Senate and House Subcommittees on Immigration and Refugee Policy, May
7, 1981, p. 13.

96. According to Schechter, if developed countries were to accept at least
some degree of responsibility for nonnationals, the result would be "revolutionary":

> The crucial question is whether the governments of [developed countries] will
> accept a share of the responsibility for the well-being of the millions who live in
> absolute poverty—people who are not their own nationals, who come from differ-
> ent racial, cultural, and social backgrounds, and who live in countries thousands of
> miles away. Surely, such acceptance would involve a drastic change in the world
> legal order. We would be moving from the current situation where there is still
> vociferous debate over the extent of each state's international responsibility for its
> treatment of its own nationals to a system where each state would agree to be held
> at least somewhat responsible for the well-being of foreign nationals. ["Views of
> 'Charterists' and 'Skeptics,'" p. 378.]

97. Human Rights, Henkin continues, have been a "white man's burden," "for export only" ("Rights: American and Human," *Columbia Law Review* 79 [1979]: 421), and "Congress ordinarily invokes such human rights
standards only as a ground for sanctions against other countries." According
to Henkin, the United States has not accepted international human rights for
itself, and has supported the Universal Declaration of Human Rights only
because it would not possess the status of law or international obligation.
Henkin points out, in conclusion, that the United States has adhered to almost no international human rights agreements (ibid.).

98. Dean Rusk observes that while the United States has entered into
many bilateral treaty agreements that have an impact upon human rights,
major international covenants on human rights are absent from treaties in
force ("A Personal Reflection on International Covenants on Human Rights,"
Hofstra Law Review 9 [Winter 1981]: 516). Rusk notes, e.g., that on February
28, 1978, President Carter submitted to the Senate for its advice and consent
four major covenants: An International Covenant on the Elimination of All

Forms of Racial Discrimination (G.A. Res. 2106A, 20 U.N. GAOR, Supp. [no. 14] 47, U.N. Doc. A/6014 [1965]); an International Covenant on Civil and Political Rights (G.A. Res. 2200A, 21 U.N. GAOR, Supp. [no. 16] 52, U.N. Doc. A, sec. 6316 [1966]); an International Covenant on Economic, Social and Cultural Rights (G.A. Res. 2200A, 21 U.N. GAOR, Supp. [no. 16] 49, U.N. Doc. A, sec. 6316 [1966]); and the American Convention of Human Rights (see, e.g., American Convention on Human Rights, *signed* November 22, 1969, Organization of American States Official Records OEA/ser. K/XVI/1.1, doc. 65, rev. 1, con. 1 [January 7, 1970]). (Rusk, "Personal Reflection.") While Rusk notes that in each instance the United States played an active role in negotiating and drafting these covenants, none have yet been approved by the Senate. Neither has this body approved the Genocide Convention (Convention on the Prevention and Punishment of the Crime of Genocide, G.A. Res. 260A, U.N. Doc. A/810 [1948]).

99. See S.J. Res. 1, 83d Cong., 1st sess., 99 Cong. Rec. 6777 (1953). According to the principal clause of this Amendment, "a treaty shall become effective as internal law in the United States only through legislation which would be valid in the absence of a treaty."

100. U.S. Constitution, Art. 14.

101. For discussion, see Edwin Cannan, *Wealth: A Brief Explanation of the Causes of Economic Welfare* (1928; reprint ed., Westport, Conn.: Hyperion Press, 1980), p. 274; and Institute for Economic Affairs, *Economic Issues in Immigration: An Exploration of the Liberal Approach to Public Policy on Immigration,* Ser. i, No. 5 (London: Transatlantic, 1970), esp. William H. Hutt, "Immigration Under 'Economic Freedom,'" pp. 23–26.

CHAPTER 9

The International Setting
of American Refugee Policy

Leon Gordenker

Refugees move across national boundaries and involve governments, whatever their wishes, in international relationships and mutual sensitivities. Governmental reaction to these sensitivities led to the creation of international mechanisms and standards for the treatment of refugees. The result is a fragmentary and in some respects primitive international regime to guide and restrain actions of national authorities. As the leading land of permanent resettlement and increasingly the magnet for refugees arriving directly on its shores on their own initiative, the United States necessarily feels some of the impact of these international arrangements.

A Historical Overview

Neither the international structure for dealing with refugee problems nor American involvement in it has a lengthy history. It became a serious item on the agenda of continuing international cooperation only after the Russian Revolution of 1917 and the creation of the League of Nations. Earlier the relatively open American immigration policy accommodated European groups and solitary political fugitives from polities of European character with little strain, so long as they could find their way to the American shore. As Japan insisted at the Versailles peace conference, and as is repeatedly pointed out in the present volume, American treatment was anything but evenhanded among immigrants—and refugees—of other than the white race.[1] Yet no government rushed forward with proposals to reform such discrimination. In fact, immigration between the two world wars was a matter that international attention hardly touched, and then only by

251

sufferance of the governments involved. Fugitive individuals and groups could expect little response to claims of asylum or protection by right. They had to rely primarily on the tolerance or acquiescence of governments or on private initiative. This generalization applied to such varied groups as the victims of the Balkan wars of 1912–1914, the Greeks and Armenians driven from Turkey, and the fugitives from European fascist repression in Italy and Germany, and other less notorious cases.

The Russian revolution nevertheless impelled the first successful efforts to create standing machinery for dealing with some refugees. This effort began with initiatives by Fridtjof Nansen to provide documentation and some legal protection for fugitives from the Bolsheviks. It gradually became institutionalized in the structure of the League of Nations and ended with the adoption, if not the wide ratification, of a series of international conventions to provide rights to narrowly-defined groups of refugees, usually based on their national origins.[2] Thus, the organized international treatment of refugees implicitly emphasized impermanence, narrow definition, and origin of refugees. This was no general program but, seen from the vantage point of national capitals, a minimum gesture, carefully reserved and practical rather than reforming.

Official responses by the United States to such efforts could be characterized as irrelevant or proceeding from completely different assumptions. Reflecting as much as anything else exclusionary sentiments within an American society that paradoxically was permeated with recent immigrants, the authorities in Washington chose the moment of massive postwar movements of people to narrow the gates for immigrants. The restrictive law of 1924[3] conclusively dismissed the Japanese notion that migration was a proper subject for international concern and dealt equally cavalierly with the tentative gropings for protection for refugees undertaken in the League of Nations framework. American distance from the latter was consistent with Washington's failure to adhere to the Covenant of the League of Nations and with its fervent adoption of isolation as morality.

The refugees from fascism, however, created later reactions in the United States that could not altogether be overlooked by the government. The Roosevelt administration's antagonism to developments in Italy and Germany contradicted the exclusionary tone of the immigration laws. Because these would endure for the succeeding decades as a foundation of the American approach to refugees, the Roosevelt administration showed little ability or even inclination to deal with refugees on an international basis.[4] There was an unmistakable tension between national immigration policy and the implications of American treatment of fascism in Europe. One attempt to gain release from this produced the Évian Conference of 1938, where the United States, taking little account of existing international facilities, sought the creation of a new mechanism.[5] It received the title "Intergovernmental Committee on Refugees" (IGCR), and its primary task was to deal with the flow of fugitives from Nazi Germany. The moment of its creation could hardly have been more forbidding; the onset of the war loomed on the horizon, the damage to the German Jewish community had gone far, and the American polity was locked in a debate over its isolationism. That debate did little to alter a policy toward refugees based on barriers to immigration.

Not until the war was well advanced did the question of refugees get much serious American attention, and then only through the military back door. The Allied military expected to encounter displaced persons as it won territory back from the Germans. Many of these people served in the German slave labor battalions, while others were civilians flooded out of their homes by the tide of war. They needed care as humans, of course, and getting them out of the way of the military forces would help maintain fighting efficiency. As is often the case, by combining such mixed motives as humanitarian assistance and military efficiency, governments were able to act. Reacting favorably to a British suggestion, the United States led the way to the creation of the U.N. Relief and Rehabilitation Administration (UNRRA) in 1943. It became one of the largest multilateral administrative efforts ever mounted and by 1945 had several million displaced persons in its care. Most of the displaced persons were prepared to return to their homes, and it was UNRRA's mandate to help them. Some 7 million people received such assistance for repatriation.[6]

UNRRA had no formal mandate to deal with refugees, but some of the displaced persons refused to go home for political reasons. Others flowed from Eastern Europe primarily into camps in Western Europe and a few turned up in the Far East, seeking aid. UNRRA officials declined to force such people back to their homelands (although some violations of the policy occurred). At the same time, they could not simply continue to care for them and certainly had no means to resettle them. The IGCR had little capacity to offer, the evil auspices of its birth still darkening its ineffectual life, although it made some efforts.

Again the United States took the lead, as perhaps befitted the political and military leader of the world. As usual, the lead also

reflected internal politics. The United States proposed dismantling
UNRRA, partly because it wanted to end the association with the
Soviet Union with policymaking and benefits in that organization,
partly because doing so was a means of avoiding Soviet demands for
forced repatriation of anti-Communist refugees, and partly in order
to prune back a large-scale financial contribution. American efforts
were directed to the creation of the International Refugee Organization (IRO) by the United Nations.[7]

The IRO was approved by the U.N. General Assembly in an
unenthusiastic vote at the end of 1946, took form in an interim organization, came into official but designedly temporary existence in
1948, and ended its career in 1951.[8] Its task was to clear the growing
population of refugee camps by repatriation (a limited possibility), by
settlement in the country of first asylum (also limited in war-ravaged
Europe), and by resettlement elsewhere. Its mandate, which excluded
displaced persons, took in some 1.5 million persons, the majority of
whom were in Germany, Austria, and Italy, while others were scattered as far afield as Kenya, India, and Shanghai. They had claims to
some thirty different nationalities.

The United States took seriously the temporary character of IRO
and unwaveringly supported its termination. Its approach was made
easier by the fact that IRO's efforts to clear the camps proceeded
rapidly and efficiently. By 1950, the camp population had declined
sharply and the promise of further reductions seemed good. The way
appeared open to handling a small residual group and then returning
to the familiar road, opened by the League of Nations, of legal protection for refugees by a very small international establishment.

In that atmosphere, the United States and the Western European
and Commonwealth governments worked together to create the
office of the U.N. High Commissioner for Refugees (UNHCR), which
began to operate in 1951.[9] It was based on three main assumptions:
refugee problems were temporary; most of them could be dealt with
primarily by creating a legal regime which would provide a clear
status to a relatively few new refugees who would appear as a result of
unusual political circumstances; and migration could be separated
from refugee issues. At the same time, it was recognized that the IRO
wards who still had not left for new homes, as well as additional
people who would want to settle overseas, would need some continued assistance. To accomplish the remaining resettlements, the
principal countries of immigration joined with the Western European
governments to create the Intergovernmental Committee on European Migration (ICEM),[10] outside the U.N. structure.

The UNHCR was to perform its tasks of legal protection on the basis of a new codification of international practice and law regarding refugees. This was embodied in the U.N. Convention Relating to the Status of Refugees in 1951.[11] As a treaty, it required ratification by member governments before having a significant effect on domestic practices. UNHCR was given the duty of promoting accessions. This convention stood as the permanent protection for refugees wherever it came into force, and by 1981 ninety states had acceded to it.

UNHCR, however, was created as a subsidiary of the General Assembly and at first given only a three-year mandate. Like its predecessors, it too was to be temporary. Although the High Commissioner had some legal capacity to take initiatives, his role was carefully hedged with checks by the General Assembly and the Economic and Social Council. His capacity to raise funds was narrowly restricted. The General Assembly specifically denied the UNHCR an operational function: It could not undertake programs of assistance and resettlement which it planned, mounted, staffed, and directed. It was anything but a new version of UNRRA or IRO.

Meanwhile, the United Nations employed a different approach in the refugee situation which grew out of the 1947–1949 bloodshed attending the end of the League of Nations mandate in Palestine and the creation of the state of Israel. More than 700,000 Arabs precipitously fled or were driven from the territory that became Israel. They arrived in the surrounding countries in miserable conditions and were the immediate object of a large-scale relief effort. They hoped for nothing more than a return to their lands, but the bitter hostility between Israel and its Arab neighbors dictated that they would at least have a lengthy wait. Israel refused all but a handful of Arabs the right of repatriation. In these circumstances, the U.N. General Assembly, again with strong backing and leadership from Washington, established the U.N. Relief and Works Agency for Palestine Refugees (UNRWA).[12] The intention was to give the refugees shelter and employment until their return. The obvious implication was that their future depended on a political settlement in the Eastern Mediterranean area. The refugees thus had the status of interested parties and also of a fundamental element in the controversy between Israel and the Arab governments. Their return would require Israel to evacuate lands and properties. Their presence in the Arab countries produced international pressure on Israel. The Arab governments had little political incentive to offer permanent status, even if the refugees had clearly wanted it. Nor were proferred economic incentives sufficient to overcome political factors. Thus, the implicit goal of the entire

enterprise sought repatriation or nothing at all. Repatriation nevertheless depended on a broader political settlement. Needless to say,
the camps and the refugees, some of them of the third generation,
still are in place, and UNRWA still operates its program from
financial crisis to financial crisis.

Because the United States had taken the leading role in breaking
up UNRRA and in creating IRO and UNHCR, it had at least a moral
obligation to become an important country of resettlement. Its creation of an international framework for dealing with the European
refugees thus impinged on its immigration policy. Furthermore, the
atmosphere in postwar America, where broader publics had come to
understand what the Nazi government had done to Jews and other
subject peoples, and where anti-Communist sentiment encouraged a
welcome for fugitives from Soviet-occupied territories, promoted a
lowering of barriers. The United States did in fact adopt a series of
measures to make easier the entry and resettlement of certain categories of refugees from World War II and from a series of refugee-
producing incidents in the cold war framework.

Delay in U.S. Acceptance of New Norms

The American approach, however, long remained detached from the
international mechanisms it had helped create.[13] Until 1968, when
the United States at last adhered to the 1967 Protocol and thus accepted the provisions of the 1951 U.N. refugee convention, all U.S.
actions on behalf of refugees were taken within the framework of
American immigration law. Reacting to the immediate postwar situation, the United States sought to ease immigration by administrative
adjustments. It opened the way to the resettlement of displaced persons, including refugees, by borrowing from future places on existing
national-origin immigration quotas. This meant that sponsorship and
private support, often furnished by voluntary agencies, were required. When doors were opened wider to refugees fleeing from
Communist-controlled Eastern European countries in 1953, their
numbers were set as a specific exception to the usual immigration
controls. Hungarian refugees from the revolt and subsequent Soviet
repression in 1956 were brought in under this act and by means of
technical provisions for parole under the earlier laws. Similar patterns
were employed in 1956 to create some 18,000 nonquota places, and in
1958 an opening was made for Dutch nationals leaving Indonesia
under pressure. The first explicit connection with the international

mechanism came in 1960, when the United States joined in yet another effort to empty the European camps still supervised by the UNHCR. Congress expressly provided that the United States would accept not more than a quarter of those remaining; again the device employed depended on exceptions to the general immigration laws. Only in 1965 did the United States adopt legislation providing standing arrangements for admission of refugees under provisions akin to the 1951 Convention but maintaining geographical and political preferences. The admission of more than 500,000 Cubans and more than 300,000 Indo-Chinese up to mid-1980 took place under parole provisions, not under legislation squarely joining American practices to international norms. Only in 1980 did the United States embody the definition of refugees of the 1951 Convention and the 1967 Protocol, to which it was a party, in its domestic legislation. From 1946 to 1978, the United States admitted more than 1.3 million refugees as permanent residents; others were in the country without settled status; and yet others who would have qualified as refugees were able to arrange entry under the ordinary immigration laws.

Issues Arising from U.S. Refugee Policy

The factors conditioning the American response to refugees as a global problem create foreign policy issues with complex and shifting, but not unique, qualities. Considerations of national security affected the international commitments the United States agreed to undertake. In addition, a series of domestically rooted issues became interlocked with security considerations. These issues concerned the degree to which international norms would replace those controlled entirely by the domestic polity. They also had to do with the costs of refugee programs and, further in the background, the effects of refugees on American society. The latter issue stirred old nativist sentiments and touched on the common belief that new immigrants take jobs away from settled groups, and on the local impact of refugees.

National security during much of the last thirty-five years has been read in the United States in terms of competition with the Soviet Union and other Communist governments. The ease with which anti-Communism could be invoked to support military and related security policy spilled into the policy regarding refugees. This was apparent in the manner in which the United States welcomed those fleeing from Communist countries, including the Baltic lands, Hungary and other Eastern European countries, and the Soviet Union itself. Their appearance set off an almost immediate effort to offer them places for resettlement in the United States, whatever the attitude toward refugees from other countries.

Such actions were consistent with the international norms that the United States had promoted, including those listed in the U.N. Universal Declaration of Human Rights and the Convention on Refugees, but in a more profound sense their fit was inexact. While none of the legal protections of refugees or other humans implied a right of asylum or of immigration, they certainly did not point toward a policy of refugee resettlement on a particular political or ideological basis. Rather, the notion was that anyone could leave his country, implying that he could seek somewhere to go and that those who feared persecution if they returned should have at least temporary shelter. To have stated a doctrinal test for emigration or refugee status in an international norm-setting document would have been regarded by most governments as intolerably discriminatory.

The official American reaction both to the U.N. human rights movement and to the legal protection of refugees on the basis of an international treaty demonstrated an ancient fear of diluting the freedom of the United States to make its own choices. The legal documents that emerged from the U.N. General Assembly on both those issues obviously were intended to secure the voluntary limitation of national freedom of action. In accordance with venerable diplomatic practice, such limitations are subjected to painstaking negotiation prior to acceptance. Once ratified, they represent an obligation on the adhering governments. The interests of all, it is supposed, are promoted.

The United States gave enthusiastic support at first to the effort to create an international human rights regime, but it abruptly abandoned the effort when the Eisenhower administration decided not to challenge the criticism of Senator John Bricker and his associates of the effect of treaties on American law.[14] Both the U.N. Covenants on Human Rights, which would emerge from the drafting process only in 1966, and the Convention on Refugees held little attraction for those who set the whole treaty process, as a means of regulating international behavior, subordinate to unrestrained freedom to define the national interest. Their opposition implied a political price for a president who wanted to secure the advice and consent of the Senate. To this day, the Covenants on Human Rights, stamped heavily with American notions about civil and political rights and even about welfare of individual citizens, lie in senatorial limbo. The Convention on Refugees was ratified only in 1968, via the 1967 Protocol, after a delay long enough to demonstrate that *non-refoulement*[15] could hardly destroy the foundations of the republic; indeed, the Convention hardly created much stir, for almost no refugees had turned up on American shores directly from their points of departure. Furthermore, the process of transforming refugees into immigrants served anti-Communism and therefore national security interests, at least in one popular mode of reasoning.

In another important respect, the tensions between domestic and international demands bore on American policy. The United States had given the lion's share of financial support to UNRRA and IRO. It was also the principal, or at least the largest, financial backer of the entire network of international institutions which grew up mainly in the U.N. system. (This included UNRWA.) In dollar amounts the figures seemed large, even if in the aggregate they fell far below even one-tenth of one percent of the gross domestic product. Nevertheless, an eternal and irrepressible stream of public opinion firmly believed the United States had committed itself to an international "giveaway" campaign that includes bilateral aid and development programs as well as those with a multilateral base. Partly to meet criticism from this segment of opinion—it could rarely be separated from the sovereignty-protectors exemplified by Senator Bricker—the American government took care to limit its financial commitments. This tendency fit well with the notion that IRO would liquidate the camps once and for all, that legal protection would suffice for the few new refugees, and that the ICEM could systematically find places of resettlement in a skill-starved world. In addition, the existence of multilateral instruments for dealing with refugee problems would promote wide sharing of the burden. This reasoning allowed the United States to give impetus to the creation and work of UNHCR, the scope of which did not include expensive operations. Where there were operations, as in ICEM, American influence would in any case be greater than in the more diffuse U.N. structures.

American legal and financial commitments to the international handling of refugees have increased to impressive proportions. Whatever its expectations and its internal politics, the United States has become the principal land of resettlement and has remained the financial foundation of multilateral efforts. But the mixture of motives involved could be read clearly from the long delay in incorporating international norms explicitly into domestic law and in the continued special interest in refugees from Communist countries. As the latter usually comprised the main refugee groups, publics in the United States that had mainly humanitarian interests could merge with those that had political and ethnic goals in offering joint support to an unparalleled program of resettlement.

Tension in U.S. Refugee Policy

New strains in this consensus appeared recently. Acceptance of the Mariel fugitives from Cuba in 1980, and the trickle of Haitians arriving in Florida by boat, as refugees under the 1980 legislation and by implication under the U.N. Convention on Refugees caused serious domestic repercussions. Some of these repercussions would be expressed in local costs, such as schools, housing, and other social facilities in the areas where they landed and usually settled. Furthermore, such heavy waves would swamp the American legislation, which was intended to limit the target number of refugees accepted as immigrants to 50,000 per year. This number can be increased by the president after consultation with Congress. Thus, to accept the Cubans meant that the number of Indo-Chinese resettlers, defined as refugees from Communism and connected with the failure of the American policy in Vietnam, might have to be reduced. This would seriously affect the relationship of the United States with Thailand and other Southeast Asian states, where asylum for refugees was contingent upon their resettlement elsewhere.

In fact, the latest wave of Cubans overwhelmed the new American legislation and sorely tested its untried executive arrangements. By administrative sleight of hand, the Cubans were exempted from the operation of the 1980 act. The Haitians, who had been associated at least in time and in site and mode of arrival with the Cubans, received different handling. They were treated primarily as "economic refugees" and therefore illegal immigrants undeserving of protection afforded "political refugees." During late 1981, the Reagan administration reinforced the barriers by ordering U.S. Coast Guard vessels to stop on the high seas the perilous boats carrying Haitians so as to prevent their landing on American shores.[16] Thus, they could never claim refugee status.

The control of the flow of Haitians by the Coast Guard followed closely on a spate of news reports about a hardening attitude of the Reagan government toward immigration generally. Refugee policy had to be affected. The report of the Select Commission on Immigration and Refugee Policy, issued after a year's study, had concentrated on the domestic aspects of refugee policy.[17] It therefore emphasized such matters as the difficulties of resettlement, a point which merges with immigration issues. The report pointed toward tighter criteria for refugees and stricter control of immigration, with defined totals for all categories. Simultaneously, the perennial question of illegal immigrants from Mexico was raised and the discussion in the Congress and the press increasingly linked all these subjects together. A great deal of comment involved the alleged differences between "economic refugees" and the by now more familiar political variety. The Reagan administration announced that it would tighten up control over the American borders and in October 1981 submitted a comprehensive package of reform legislation.[18]

The details of the new proposals and the discussion that lay in the background have less importance perhaps than the tone, which demonstrated that the strong current of American opinion that had earlier backed restrictive immigration practices had never disappeared and could easily return to a leading if not dominant role in policymaking. Moreover, attempts to distinguish between economic refugees and political refugees appeared to contradict the spirit of decisions which welcomed those who fled from Communist governments even though there was little direct evidence of immediate persecution. Although the economic and social programs of the Soviet Union or Vietnam certainly damaged the interests and well-being of groups of their nationals, on this ground the departees from those lands could hardly be distinguished from some who left Chile or Argentina or South Africa but were not considered refugees anywhere. At the same time, it was difficult to understand the difference in principle between driving people out of a country by immediate terror and threatening them with imminent starvation and social exclusion through state practices. In both situations, those affected have real reason to fear for their lives. Thus, the notion of "economic refugees" tended to obscure a more general objection to the size of immigration flows.

In another respect, too, the emphasis on control began to raise the old notions of regulation by national origin. Usually when persons leaving Communist countries were involved, the question of national origin was given little emphasis by the U.S. government. Yet in districts where Indo-Chinese were concentrated, complaints were voiced about the lack of fit between their cultures and the American practices. This was also true of Cubans and Haitians and even of Russian immigrants. The treatment of the Haitians, however, was quickly distinguished from that of the Cubans. Against them were heard all the time-honored complaints: They worked for low wages, they did not speak English, they clustered in closed settlements, they had "strange

habits," and they had no fear of political persecution in their homeland. They were also the only group of blacks who had been able to
land in fairly large numbers directly on American beaches.

Usually in the muted phrases of diplomacy, representatives of
African governments also called attention to the difference between
American refugee policy for Indo-Chinese and Russians and that for
Africans.[19] Although no one explicity demanded large numbers of
resettlement opportunities for Africans, the numbers permitted to
enter the United States were so small as to suggest to the mildly
suspicious that the color of the candidates could have been involved.
It would not, however, be accurate to state that all Africans were
excluded, for some applied for resettlement and were admitted. Yet
appearances probably have more to do with shaping reactions than do
such explanations as the urgency of refugee situation, the ability to
create resettlement and opportunities, and the ease with which new
immigrants could be adjusted on the basis of their education and skills
to the United States.

Deepening U.S. Involvement
on the International Front

International arrangements for dealing with refugees take on colora-
tions that depend on the government viewing them. Table 9.1 shows
the global distribution of refugees in 1981. A government that has
just had to take notice of a massive flow of refugees from its neighbors
must interpret the rights of the newcomers without the luxury of
much time. It usually will first seek assistance to ward off a human
disaster, brought on by hunger, disease, or weather, on its soil. The
people have already arrived, more may be on the way, and not much
can be done to make them vanish instantly. If the government is
bound by the Convention on Refugees, respects the injunctions of the
U.N. General Assembly on human rights, or has a tradition of hospitality, it cannot even consider *refoulement*. Its situation has the character of an emergency. Only later will there be time to deal with
individual cases and to look for a method to bring the newcomers to
productive lives, whether at home or in new surroundings. This has
been the conventional and practical reactions of governments such as
Somalia, Sudan, and Pakistan and, earlier, those of Western Europe.

In a few instances, notably those recently in Southeast Asia, governments have deliberately threatened *refoulement* of refugees. Some
refugees who arrived from Vietnam by boat were simply pushed back

Table 9.1   *Distribution of Refugee Populations by Area, 1981[a]*

Area	Number of Refugees	Number of Displaced Persons[b]	Total
Africa	3,589,340	2,735,000	6,324,340
Asia	1,994,500	170,000	2,164,500
Europe	354,600	—	354,600
Latin America	189,600	50,000	239,600
Middle East	1,962,200	1,600,000	3,562,200
Total			12,645,240

Source: 1981 World Refugee Survey, ed. Michael J. de Sherbinin (New York: U.S. Committee for Refugees, 1981).

[a] This survey excludes people who have not yet acquired a new nationality but are formally resettled.

[b] Displaced persons have not left their own countries but may be fleeing military action, civil disorder, persecution, and so on. Legally speaking, they are not refugees, but they are sometimes assisted as if they were.

to sea, and others were flatly denied any organized material assistance, such as food, water, and shelter, after landing. The resultant outcry, along with demands from the affected governments, made certain that a large-scale emergency effort would be launched by transnational agencies. The willingness of the United States, above all, and some other countries to accept Indo-Chinese refugees won them the privilege of staying temporarily in the Southeast Asian countries while awaiting resettlement.

Both these patterns differ greatly from the prevalent understanding of refugee matters in the United States. Although the American government has supported efforts to assist refugees, it usually did so at a distance. This has also been the case in Western Europe most of the time since the dissolution of IRO and the creation of UNHCR. While the United States offered permanent resettlement to many refugees, and, as Table 9.2 indicates, ranks first among nations in resettlement, its approach had strong elements of selectivity. Before an individual refugee or a family could make their way to the United States, they had to be "processed," to use the ugly term of the bureaucratic art. They had to pass tests regarding health and often had to undergo inquiry regarding financial support and a political investigation. The latter aimed at exclusion of revolutionaries and other categories of activists whose proclivities seemed objectionable to the U.S. government. In brief, the international protection of refugees and assistance to them made it possible for the United States, and many other countries of permanent resettlement, to break the masses

264   LEON GORDENKER

Table 9.2   *Resettlement of Refugees, 1975–1980*

Country	Number	Country	Number
U.S.	677,000	Austria	4,300
China	265,000	New Zealand	4,100
Israel	105,700	Belgium	3,900
Malaysia	102,100	Argentina	2,800
Canada	84,100	Norway	2,700
France	72,000	Denmark	2,300
Australia	51,200	Romania	1,200
Germany (FRG)	32,100	Spain	1,100
U.K.	27,600	Italy	900
Tanzania	26,000	Chile	800
Hong Kong	9,400	Japan	800
Switzerland	7,500	Cuba	700
Sweden	7,300	Mexico	700
Netherlands	4,700		

Source: 1981 World Refugee Survey, ed. Michael J. de Sherbinin (New York: U.S. Committee for Refugees, 1981).

into individuals and to select from among them. It was an orderly procedure, a distinct contrast to the hungry, frightened arrival of the refugees in a temporary shelter.

American participation in the creation and expansion of the network of transnational agencies to deal with refugees had the effect of supporting orderly procedures to transform exiles into acceptable immigrants. Such orderly processes, on the one hand, provided a rationale for American participation at a relatively high level in international refugee programs and, on the other, fitted with the wing of U.S. immigration policy that emphasized the tradition of a land of refuge. As the number of immigrants from the ranks of refugees outstripped that of all other countries, the United States did indeed remain a land of refuge. In that function, U.S. policies toward refugees could be viewed as accepting the implications of the international arrangements. The United States participated not merely to keep refugees from its shores and from making claims on the government for something more than financial support.

Yet the arrival of the Cubans, the first refugees with histories like the waves of humanity in flight that have suddenly appeared elsewhere, caused reactions that suggest that the United States may change the quality of its international involvement with this issue. To begin with, the United States saw positive advantages in seeking international consultation about its handling of the stream of refugees. It asked other governments to provide asylum for Cubans.[20] Even if the refugees and those waiting to leave did not rush to take up such offers, which remained relatively few, U.S. officials and politicians had a first direct taste of a refugee crisis. Furthermore, the United States showed a closer integration with the international arrangements when it accepted some assistance from UNHCR in screening refugees on its own soil for conversion into normal immigrants.[21] Earlier UNHCR involvement had stopped, as it still does in Thailand and elsewhere in Southeast Asia, when the refugees enter the aircraft bound for the United States. In addition, ICM[22] had a brief role during the crisis caused by the occupation of the Peruvian embassy in Havana at the beginning of the 1980 outflow.

In another respect, American officials gave evidence of a new readiness to broaden the international structures for refugees. The proposal of a Fund for Durable Solutions under the wing of UNHCR signaled an attempt by the Carter administration to take advantage of cooperation for economic development to settle refugees.[23] The fund, to which contributions were to be voluntary, was to identify worthwhile development projects in which refugees could be involved, both for their self-support and for the benefit of the host economy. Such a proposal reflects the realization on the part of U.S. officials that conventional approaches to settlement of refugees had severe shortcomings, especially in the very poor areas, where most of them now appeared. The fund hardly performed, however, for Congress did not see enough merit in the notion to appropriate a contribution. Thus, an American idea for international cooperation had to get on without its principal potential backer.

The United States also strongly supported a program of orderly departures of refugees from Vietnam.[24] This required arms-length dealing between the Vietnamese government and the United States in matching lists of people applying for family reunification with the names of families that already were American residents. Again the United States was closely involved with international machinery in a novel enterprise quite unforeseen by those who created UNHCR with narrow duties.

Finally, the United States has been deeply engaged in a series of international conferences sponsored by the United Nations on specific refugee situations. The first of these dealt with the refugees from Vietnam. It was followed by another on Cambodian refugees and then by a major, if controversial, meeting organized by UNHCR to deal with African refugees.[25] Thus, what was once U.S. participation in programs that cared for refugees in distant places and delivered them in an orderly manner to the United States has been transformed. The United States now has a much deeper involvement in international efforts than ever before. It seeks a broadening of participation in dealing with refugee issues that it had never encountered earlier.

Issues, Opportunities, and the U.S. Role

The international setting in which the United States government approaches refugee issues owes much to policies designed in Washington. The United States has been a main source of both ideas and support for organized transnational efforts. It has never dropped its association with the institutions and programs that result in part from its involvement. At the same time, the international setting includes trends that have unexpectedly exceeded the limits that U.S. policymakers thought they were imposing on the participation of their government.

This review of U.S. involvement with refugees on a global basis leads easily to the conclusion that implicitly, if not explicitly, the United States has accepted that the issue is well-nigh permanent. It has enacted the international definition of refugees into its laws. It has stimulated new approaches to the issues and has itself borrowed help from the international agencies it helped to construct for purposes that impinged originally on the United States only when refugee-immigrants were landed. Compared to other governments, it has given massive financial support. Despite confusing internal pressures, it has continued to open its doors to a relatively large number of refugee-immigrants.

At the same time, policymakers in Washington have not often faced the full implications of the presence of large numbers of refugees in the world. The continuing growth of the world population, for instance, implies that the number of people who could be sent into flight increases constantly. Furthermore, much of the world exists in miserable conditions or is governed by such oppressive authorities that doubts can be raised about the alleged difference between "political" and "economic" refugees. This implies a deficiency in the concept of the "refugee" in the contemporary world. Nevertheless, the views of the United States in international deliberative bodies do not encourage opening up such conceptual issues. Rather, primary attention seems to go to short-term difficulties with organization and management and middle-term issues involving the design and scope of programs.

In addition to the pressure created by population growth, the relative ease with which news of opportunities for economic advancement travels and the relatively low cost of transportation suggests that large-scale migration may be an important long-term issue for many governments. Such migration tends to increase pressure on immigration practices. The United States has already encountered this pressure with regard to Mexican migrants who avoid immigration controls. Although in the short term little effective planning for such migrations could be created, a longer-term effort to explore the issue internationally may pay off handsomely for its participants. Such planning has an obvious bearing on the handling of refugees. Even if it would involve sensitive feelings, such a discussion might well be led by the United States as a primary target of migrants seeking better lives.

As the largest populations of refugees now can be found in some of the least developed countries in the world, an unavoidable issue involves the relationship between asylum-seekers and local development. This too is an issue that has had less consideration than the gravity of specific situations, such as that of Sudan or Pakistan, would appear to demand. The reluctance of the United States to take on more commitments for development obviously affects its position on this issue. Yet it is an issue that may offer real opportunities for leadership and benefits for all concerned.

Finally, the United States has vast experience with the resettlement of refugees and with the care of people in emergencies. More of this experience, especially when it has generated new techniques, might well be employed in the international programs to which the United States contributes. Making its technical capacity part of the common fund of knowledge available for refugees would be an important contribution. Since some of this experience rests in the skills and devotions of Americans who have worked with refugees, the United States could make a special effort to channel such people into international programs.

Notes

1. Japan unsuccessfully sought the inclusion of a treaty clause that guaranteed equal treatment of all races everywhere. The United States and the United Kingdom clearly understood the effect of such a clause on immigration. See the brief account of the negotiation in Paul Birdsall, *Versailles Twenty Years After* (New York: Reynal & Hitchcock, 1941), pp. 91–101.

2. Jacques Vernant, *The Refugee in the Post-War World: Preliminary Report of a Survey* (Geneva: 1951), p. 11.

3. Immigration laws excluding Chinese dated back to the 1880s. Quotas

based on nationality were adopted temporarily in 1921 and were made a permanent part of American law in 1924, forming the basis for additional legislation that stayed in place until 1965. A brief review of U.S. legislation may be found in Senate Committee on the Judiciary, *Review of U.S. Refugee Resettlement Programs and Policies,* 96th Cong., 2d sess., 1980. Hereafter cited as *Review.*

4. Robert A. Devine, *American Immigration Policy, 1924–1952* (New Haven: Yale University Press, 1957), pp. 92–104. How much presidential capital Franklin Roosevelt was willing to invest in this matter remains a very controversial issue. See Herbert Druks, *The Failure to Rescue* (New York: Robert Speller & Sons, 1977), chap. 1; and Arthur D. Morse, *While Six Million Died: A Chronicle of American Apathy* (New York: Random House, 1967). Morse says of Roosevelt: "Since he was afraid that the Jewish issue was a political liability, he helped to doom European Jewry by inaction even as he proclaimed America as the asylum for the oppressed" (ibid., p. 41). Morse admits that Roosevelt was personally sympathetic to the European refugees.

5. Devine, *American Immigration Policy,* pp. 95–97. See also John George Stoessinger, *The Refugee and the World Community* (Minneapolis: University of Minnesota Press, 1956), pp. 39–41.

6. UNRRA's course, fading from memories or altogether ignored, is chronicled in George Woodbridge, *The History of UNRRA,* 3 vols. (New York: Columbia University Press, 1950). It richly deserves a new study in the light of papers unavailable to Woodbridge.

7. The standard account is Louise W. Holborn, *The International Refugee Organization, Its History and Work, 1946–1952* (Oxford: Oxford University Press, 1956).

8. The IRO General Council began to anticipate the end of the organization and reported on its plans to the General Assembly in 1949 (U.N. Doc. A/C.3/528). It anticipated operating until October 1, 1951, and in the end kept going until the end of January 1952. By this time the General Assembly had established UNHCR. These proceedings disclosed a large body of abstainers and steady opposition from the Soviet Union and its allies.

9. The office of UNHCR was established by U.N. General Assembly Resolution 428 (V), adopted on December 14, 1950, by 35 votes in favor, 5 against, and 11 abstentions. See Holborn, *The International Refugee Organization,* 1: 57–86, for details of the political process from which the statute of the office and the associated Convention Relating to the Status of Refugees emerged. The office was originally established for a three-year term, was extended, and later was based on a five-year term. From a political point of view, therefore, the establishment of the office may be challenged every five years as the time for renewal approaches. The General Assembly has also adopted a substantial body of additional instructions to UNHCR.

10. See ibid., 1: 117–119. ICEM has had little scholarly attention.

11. U.N. Treaty Series no. 2545, vol. 189, p. 137. Adopted by a conference in 1951, it came into force in 1954.

12. The standard study is Edward H. Buehrig, *The U.N. and the Palestin-*

ian Refugees: A Study in Nonterritorial Administration (Bloomington: Indiana University Press, 1971). See also David P. Forsythe, "UNRWA, the Palestine Refugees, and World Politics," *International Organization* 25 (Winter 1971): 26–45.

13. *Review*, p. 3.

14. Vernon Van Dyke, *Human Rights, the United States, and the World Community* (New York: Oxford University Press, 1970), pp. 129–141.

15. This term derives from Article 33 of the U.N. Convention on the Status of Refugees, which prohibits the expulsion or return of a fugitive to territories where his life would be threatened for, in effect, political or social reasons.

16. In November 1981, President Reagan ordered U.S. Coast Guard vessels to intercept in international waters boats suspected of leaving Haiti with persons aboard who would seek refugee status in the United States. By December, the attorney general reported the policy was a success: the numbers arriving in the United States were down sharply (*New York Times*, December 16, 1981, p. A23).

17. Select Commission on Immigration and Refugee Policy, *U.S. Immigration Policy and the National Interest*, Final Report, March 1, 1981 (Washington, D.C.: Government Printing Office, 1981). See above, Chapter 2, for a fuller discussion of the work of the Select Commission.

18. The Reagan government reacted to the Select Commission report by establishing a Task Force on Immigration and Refugee Policy to report to the president. It urged the interception of boats carrying Haitians, legislation to speed up deportation and exclusion proceedings, detention of those Cubans and Haitians who arrived without visas, and legislation to adjust the status of Caribbean boat people (*New York Times*, April 28, 1981, p. A1). The reduced budgets for assistance to the poor, proposed by the Reagan administration, also affect the fate of refugees within the United States.

19. See, e.g., U.N. Doc. A/AC.96/588, October 20, 1980, p. 20: "Many speakers voiced once again their opinion that Africa, the continent with the largest number of persons of concern to the High Commissioner and with some of the gravest humanitarian situations in the world, should receive a commensurate proportion of the total available resources. A higher level of assistance in Africa . . . would ensure equality of treatment for the persons of concern to the High Commissioner through the world."

20. As did Peru. On May 8, 1980, delegates of eighteen governments and representatives of international agencies met in Costa Rica (*New York Times*, April 10, 1980, p. 3, and May 10, 1980, p. 11).

21. U.N. Doc. A/AC.96/577, p. 140. The United States sought help in screening refugees, especially in dealing with convicted criminals. Two UNHCR officials joined in the task (*New York Times*, May 22, 1980, p. 30, and May 29, 1980, p. 13).

22. As a result of its broadening operations, ICEM dropped the "European" from its title in 1980 and has since used the acronym, ICM. Its role extended to intra-American flights after the Cuban government interrupted

a brief airlift to Costa Rica during May 1980. See ICEM, "Monthly Dispatch for the Press," June 6, 1980.

23. The proposal for such a fund was made by UNHCR in 1979 (U.N. Doc. A/AC.96/569). This proposal had strong U.S. backing; interviews point to the conclusion that it originated with the United States. A year later the fund, now formally established, had a contribution of $25,000 and limited authority to tap other UNHCR funds.

24. This agreement was actually negotiated mainly by a U.S. national serving as Deputy High Commissioner. It was announced by Vietnam on May 30, 1979, and since then the process of matching lists of prospective emigrants from Vietnam to lists of family members who would receive them in, primarily, the United States has gone at a modest pace after a halting start; more than 1,000 people left Vietnam between May and December 1979 on UNHCR charter flights and 800 more by commercial means (U.N., General Assembly, Official Records, 35th Session, *Report of the U.N. High Commissioner for Refugees,*p. 49). Whether these emigrants are refugees in any but a remote legal sense is an open question.

25. UNHCR acted on behalf of the United Nations in organizing the conference, which resulted from a resolution by the U.N. General Assembly (Resolution 35/42) that had the strong support of the African governments but not unanimous backing among the senior UNHCR officials. Governments were asked to submit specific projects related to refugees. Their proposals required a total of more than $1.2 billion in financing (U.N. Doc. A/Conf. 106/1 and Add. 1). The conference, held on April 9 and 10, 1981, resulted in pledges of just under $600 million, not all of which was a net addition to earlier pledges.

CHAPTER 10

Immigration Reform:
The United States and
Western Europe Compared

Mark J. Miller and *Demetrios G. Papademetriou*

United States immigration issues often are seen as unique. The fact that the United States shares an almost 2,000-mile-long border with Mexico, for example, is frequently cited as a reason to set off or demarcate U.S. issues from discussion of immigration issues faced by advanced industrial democracies in general.[1] The assumption of fundamental dissimilarity or uniqueness contributes to the data problem that has stymied U.S. immigration reform since accumulated knowledge concerning immigration-related phenomena in other advanced industrial democracies is not viewed as pertinent to the debate over U.S. immigration policy. To many, comparing U.S. immigration issues to Western European immigration issues is like comparing proverbial apples and oranges.

Yet, while everyone would agree that the national histories and sociopolitical contexts of each advanced industrial democracy are original, there would seem to be ample ground on which to question the assumption of U.S. uniqueness in migration matters vis-à-vis Western Europe. The matter of the shared border with Mexico actually underscores a problem common to all advanced industrial democracies (with the possible exception of Japan): their inability to regulate and monitor all comings and goings by aliens. Advanced industrial democracies are vulnerable to determined clandestine migrants. The long border with Mexico makes the problem of undocu-

The first author would like to thank the German Marshall Fund of the United States for research support on European and American immigration policy.

271

mented aliens in the United States quantitatively more serious, but not qualitatively different in any fundamental sense. The 2,000-mile-long border with Mexico presents the United States with a problem of border control of such magnitude that some observers feel that any effort by the United States to bolster border control in the Southwest would represent so much money and effort wasted. But the point is that other advanced industrial democracies have porous boundaries as well.

Take the case of France. Granted, and to their credit, the French do make a more significant effort, relatively, to police their frontiers than the United States. And France is not contiguous with Algeria, Morocco, or any other Third World country such as Mexico. But France still is vulnerable to clandestine entry and sojourn. French officials, like Americans, assume that their boundaries are porous. Instead of Mexican *campensinos* wading across the Rio Grande, the French must contend with Moroccans and other North and Black Africans who journey to Spain and then surreptitiously enter France across the Pyrenees. Or they must contend with Africans and Asians who are smuggled in by trucks from Belgium, Switzerland, or Italy. According to French Ministry of Interior estimates, 500,000 aliens enter or transit through France each day.[2] The sheer magnitude of this inflow makes French immigration law vulnerable to massive violation. Whether illegal aliens from Third World countries wade across rivers to advanced industrial society or overstay their tourist visas seems less important than the fact that both the United States and the nations of Western Europe have large illegal alien populations that are the object of malaise and concern.

Comparison of Western Europe and the United States in the realm of immigration, as in other issue areas, is justified by the underlying similitude of these societies: democratic, liberal, capitalistic, highly industrialized, and all products of the Judeo-Christian tradition. Of course, there are important differences from one advanced industrial democracy to the next, but nothing like the differences separating Ghana, for example, from France, or Bulgaria from the United States. Unless duped by the idiographic fallacy, or the mistaken idea that all societies are unique, comparison between the United States and other advanced industrial democracies makes sense because a host of societal variables pertinent to the comparison can be controlled for or assumed to hold constant from one advanced industrial democracy to the next. As Adam Przeworski and Henry Teune have argued, a "most similar systems" approach to comparison, such as that being advocated here, logically has less theoretical or explanatory potential than a "most dissimilar systems" approach to comparison, because of the large number of variables held constant in the former as opposed to the latter.[3] But for purposes of comparative public policy analysis, only a comparison between most similar political systems, in this case advanced industrial democracies, seems to make sense. And significant dissimilarities affecting policies in Western Europe and the United States need to be elucidated even if we assume that it makes sense to compare the United States and Western Europe in this issue area. Suzanne Berger and Michael J. Piore have shown the pitfalls of assuming that industrial democracies are everywhere evolving into or moving toward one "postindustrial" society.[4] Instead, significant discontinuities between advanced industrial societies persist.

Contextual Differences Between the U.S. and Western Europe

Unlike most Western European countries, the United States traditionally has welcomed permanent immigration. It is an immigration land, and this quality is usually seen as sharply differentiating the United States from Western European political systems. Yet this historical distinction, while significant, may not be as sharp as commonly thought. European countries differ in their historical experiences with immigration as in other issue areas. Of all European states, France seems to come closest to sharing an immigration-land tradition with the United States. France has welcomed and assimilated successive waves of immigrants since the late nineteenth century. Following World War II, France openly proclaimed itself an immigrant-welcoming country. It is only since the economic downturn of the 1970s that a French minister could declare that "what was formerly an immigration country will become an emigration country."[5] Other European nations with significant immigrant-welcoming traditions include Great Britain, Belgium, and more recently Sweden. However, in none of these cases has immigration played as central a historical role as in the United States.

More typical of Europe as a whole are the cases of the Federal Republic of Germany and Switzerland, which pointedly maintain that they are not immigration lands even in the face of massive de facto immigration by guestworkers and their dependents. West German officials from all political persuasions have been particularly persistent in their rejection of the immigration-land label. In doing so, the history of immigration to Germany has tended to be overlooked. As the German novelist and political activist Günter Grass has recently noted, the official conception that Germany is not an immigrant land is somewhat at variance with German history.[6] Large numbers of

Huguenots fleeing persecution in seventeenth-century France successfully integrated into German society despite oftimes maintaining
their native language and religion to this day. After the modern German state was born in 1870, hundreds of thousands of Poles came to
work in German agriculture and in the mines and industries of the
Ruhr area. After World War II, millions of ethnic Germans from
throughout Eastern Europe were by and large successfully assimilated despite cultural differences and other barriers.

Switzerland, too, officially rejects the immigration-land label, but
it also has experienced considerable immigration in modern times.
Indeed, *überfremdung,* the term used in Switzerland to connote fear of
loss of national identity due to an excessive presence of aliens, dates
from the World War I period. Ironically, this now notorious term
originally referred to excessive numbers of German migrants in Switzerland.[7]

The U.S. immigration tradition versus European insularity distinction, then, should not be overdrawn. And it is obvious that the
transatlantic difference has been diminished by the "settling" of
guestworkers and their dependents in recent years. Nonetheless, the
nature and extent of immigration constitutes a key dissimilarity
limiting comparison between Western Europe and the United States.
This dissimilarity, however, does not preclude public-policy-relevant
transatlantic comparison. Indeed, it is precisely the fundamental difference between European society and the United States in migration
matters which has generated so much contemporary interest in European migrations on the part of Americans.

As was noted in Chapters 1, 2, and 4, the United States traditionally has welcomed permanent immigration and, officially at least,
regarded temporary foreign worker authorization as an exception.
U.S. reluctance to authorize nonimmigrant labor policy stands in
sharp contrast to post–World War II European decisions to authorize
massive foreign worker employment. Between 1960 and 1973, some
30 million migrant workers and their dependents entered Western
Europe before guestworker recruitment was stopped in 1973–1974 as
a result of the worsening economy and mounting integration problems between natives and aliens.[8] The post–World War II European
experience with guestworker policy takes on significance in the debate
over the future of U.S. immigration policy because of persistent advocacy of an expanded U.S. nonimmigrant worker policy. In other
words, a policy reform has been proposed which, if implemented,
would attenuate differences in migration policies between Western
Europe and the United States. Hence, European foreign labor

policies can serve as a pertinent point of reference with which to examine the pros and cons of nonimmigrant labor policy in advanced industrial democracies. An effort to draw out the implications of European guestworker policies for the debate over the future course of U.S. immigration policy is further justified by the relative paucity of the U.S. experience with nonimmigrant labor policy. Vernon Briggs' assessment of those limited if persistent U.S. experiences with nonimmigrant labor policy (see Chapter 4) already would indicate that the United States should proceed with the utmost caution, if at all, with expanded temporary foreign worker policy.

At this point, several further comparative caveats are in order. First, European guestworker policies developed during a period of extremely low unemployment in Western Europe. It would be unthinkable for European officials to consider authorizing new foreign worker employment at a time of high domestic unemployment, such as experienced by the United States in recent years. When unemployment loomed as a potential problem, the Europeans quickly stopped recruitment of foreign labor. Second, European societies are much better prepared to regulate foreign worker employment and residency than the United States. Many European countries have networks of employment agencies which enable them to determine when and where labor shortages exist. The United States lacks this capability, thereby condemning decisions to authorize foreign worker employment to controversy. This difference in U.S. and European policy contexts has become more significant as Reagan administration budget cutbacks have further reduced the ability of state and federal officials to pinpoint labor shortages. Also, most European governments require some form of identity card for citizens and resident aliens (British citizens are a major exception to this rule). Consequently, in many respects European societies were better prepared institutionally to administer guestworker-type policy than the United States.

It is evident that what transpired with Western Europe's foreign labor policies need not be replicated in the U.S. context if a decision is taken to expand categories of temporary workers to be admitted or to inaugurate guestworker policy. A host of variables, such as length of stay permitted, number of workers admitted, and legal rights granted to them, would determine the outcome of a U.S. temporary foreign worker policy initiative. Further, a multitude of transatlantic variables, only some of which have been elucidated above, suggest that similar decisions taken in the two contexts could have markedly different consequences. But temporary foreign worker policy in any

advanced industrial setting is shaped by answering several key questions. How many workers should be admitted? How is need for alien
labor determined? What rights shall alien workers have? How long
can they stay? Can they bring in dependents? Is repatriation
obligatory? It is instructive to consider European responses to these
questions, because the United States will have to respond to these
same questions if it is to expand foreign worker policy.

Growing Misgivings over Guestworkers

With some limited exceptions, European governments did not intend
decisions to admit foreign labor to eventuate in alien workers becoming permanent residents. Rather, foreign labor was conceived of as a
complementary labor supply that would offset temporary labor shortages. It was widely anticipated that foreign workers would return
home of their own volition or when they lost their jobs in economic
downturns. Limited exceptions to the temporariness assumption behind postwar European foreign labor policies occurred in France
(which encouraged the permanent immigration of Italians and
Spaniards, while considering North Africans temporary sojourners),
Belgium, Great Britain, and Sweden.

Under the Treaty of Rome, which created the European Economic Community (EEC), workers from member states would eventually gain virtually unrestricted access to labor markets within the
EEC. Italians were able to look for work in Germany and, if they
found it, to receive an automatically renewable five-year work permit.
Hence, community workers had privileged status, since they could
stay on permanently; but it was expected that most of them would one
day return home. EEC workers, however, comprised fewer than half
the foreign workers within the EEC by 1959, and by 1978 they represented fewer than one-quarter of all foreign workers within the enlarged EEC.[9] The overwhelming majority of foreign workers
admitted to Western Europe since 1945 first came with one-year work
and residency permits with no guarantee of renewal. Because Switzerland is not a member of the EEC, virtually all its foreign workers came
in with one-year, temporary permits.

The number of foreign workers admitted was a function of labor
market demand. Europe experienced unprecedented, sustained
growth that created severe manpower shortages, especially in blue-
collar, manual-labor jobs. There was little or no competition between
foreigners and natives for work, since aliens were funneled into jobs

and areas with discernible labor shortages. Broad consensus existed on the need for recourse to foreign labor, and unions consented to alien recruitment as long as alien workers were assured rights and salaries so that working conditions were not undercut. In the three principal countries recruiting foreign labor—France, West Germany, and Switzerland—permit systems restricted the type of work that aliens took and where they took it for up to ten years. Alien workers, however, were free to change employers after the first year of work.

European foreign worker policies developed on an ad hoc basis and in a flush of confidence that temporary foreign worker policy benefited all parties involved. When West Germany admitted its one-millionth guestworker in 1964, he was presented with a motor scooter by thankful German officials.[10] European economies were growing rapidly, and the assumption that guestworkers would voluntarily return home went unchallenged. When interviewed, most alien workers planned to stay for only a few years—enough time to save up a nest egg. Guestworker permits were routinely renewed. Then a brief recession struck in 1967. In Germany, hundreds of thousands of foreign workers lost their jobs and went home. Most returned home of their own volition. Only a minority seemed to have been forced to leave through nonrenewal of permits. In short, assumptions surrounding guestworker policy seemed borne out by the facts— guestworkers were temporary and disposable.

Foreign-worker recruitment, however, soon surged again as the economic downturn bottomed out. Foreign workers and, increasingly, their dependents, who were allowed to come after a wait of one year to fifteen months by the late 1960s, flooded into France and Germany. But in Switzerland, growing public controversy over foreign labor policy had prompted restrictive measures by 1964. At this time, aliens comprised 30 percent of the total work force, and integration problems were mounting. The government pledged to stabilize and then reduce the foreign population, but at the same time to ameliorate the rights and living conditions of the foreign population. There was growing concern over the growing average length of stay of alien workers, as more and more stayed on despite expectations of return. The Swiss could not, or more appropriately would not, force out aliens with steady work. They could only reduce the number of seasonal workers who had permits valid for less than a year and stop authorizing new recruitment of workers with year-long contracts beyond a set ceiling. The number of seasonal workers plummeted from a high of 206,000 in 1964 to 61,000 by 1976.[11]

The size of the foreign work force and population relative to the

Swiss population probably accounts for the early politicization of foreign labor policy in Switzerland. However, foreign worker policies very quickly would become controversial throughout Europe. As foreign populations grew, the restricted legal status and under-privileged socioeconomic status of aliens became issues. In France, foreign workers and their families frequently lived in shantytowns. Pressure mounted for European governments to ameliorate the lot of foreign workers at the same time that integration problems, some-times exacerbated by racism, mounted. When the Arab-Israeli war of 1973 prompted an oil embargo, European governments would justify stopping foreign worker recruitment on economic grounds: forecasts of economic stagnation with attendant downturns in employment. Unofficially, European officials were equally concerned with the pro-pensity of alien workers to stay on longer than expected and to bring in their families. A new awareness of the potentially serious sociopolit-ical consequences of foreign labor policy arose in 1973 following mas-sive street protests by foreign workers in France and a wave of foreign worker strikes in Germany.

As a result of international agreements which stipulated that most economic and social restrictions placed on foreign labor should end after five years of continuous employment, European govern-ments did not even have the legal option to withdraw residency and work permits from many foreign workers when economic and social conditions soured. By and large, all they could do was stop new re-cruitment and encourage voluntary foreign worker repatriation. From the ending of recruitment to 1980, roughly 2 million foreign workers lost their jobs, and many of these workers returned home.[12] In Germany, foreign worker employment declined to 1.8 million in 1978 after reaching a high of 2.6 million in 1973.[13] However, most foreign workers stayed on, and return flows of workers were more than offset by an inflow of dependents. Increasingly, dependents qualified for work permits despite numerous restrictions placed upon their labor market entry. Consequently, in recent years, foreign worker employment has increased again, despite the continuing re-cruitment halts (which do not apply to EEC workers and seasonal workers) and skyrocketing unemployment among native and foreign workers. Only unemployed foreign workers stand to lose their resi-dency permits.

European misgivings about the long-run consequences of deci-sions to admit "temporary" foreign workers stem mainly from the unanticipated volume of foreign worker recruitment, the result of unprecedented economic growth and the unanticipated propensity of

foreign workers to stay. Actual return rates fluctuate from one nationality group to the next, with Italians in Germany apparently returning at a much higher rate than Turks (90 percent versus 30
percent), but the key consideration is the size of apparently permanent alien populations representing between 6 and 8 percent of the
total populations of France and Germany and about one-quarter of
the total population of Switzerland.[14]

Due to high birthrates and continuing family reunification, alien
shares of the total population will probably increase in the foreseeable
future. Germany experienced a net increase of 300,000 aliens, or 7.6
percent of the total alien population, in 1980 alone.[15] European efforts to encourage repatriation have met with very limited success.
Between 1976 and 1981, the French offered cash payments to foreign
workers and their dependents who renounced their residency rights
and rights to French social security. Despite vigorous protests that
such a policy was unfair, the government hoped to reduce sharply the
foreign population, especially the North African population. Less
than 75,000 workers and dependents took up the offer, and only 3
percent of those who did were Algerians.[16] One of the first things the
new socialist president of France did in office was suspend the cash
bonus return offer. Not only did the socialists regard the offer as
morally repugnant, they also realized it was very costly and simply did
not work.

Out of the welter of alien worker permit groups in Western
Europe, only seasonal workers in France and Switzerland, numbering
about 225,000 together, have exhibited apparently high repatriation
rates in the range of 95 to 100 percent. Seasonal workers are required
to return home after fulfilling a less than one-year-long contract and
are limited to jobs of a temporary nature. Seasonal workers in Switzerland and non-Spanish seasonal workers in France are not permitted to bring in their dependents, although visits by dependents are
allowed. Seasonal worker programs also have not been problem-free.

In Switzerland, the clandestine entry or overstaying of seasonal
worker dependents has long been a major component of the Swiss
illegal alien population.[17] In France, areas where large numbers of
seasonal workers are employed also seem to have disproportionately
large numbers of illegal aliens.[18] Unauthorized employment of Spanish seasonal worker dependents is widespread and unofficially tolerated by authorities. Both countries have had problems with so-called
faux saisonniers, false seasonal workers, whose seasonal employment in
fact is permanent in nature. Both countries have had to adjust the
status of *faux saisonniers* who can prove that their employment entitled

them to permanent residency rights. During the French legalization program of 1981–1982, seasonal workers participated in strikes and demonstrations to obtain permanent status.

Seasonal labor programs, like European foreign worker policies in general, have become very controversial. Alleged Swiss mistreatment of Italian seasonal workers was a major factor in strained Italo-Swiss diplomatic relations in the early 1960s.[19] The plight of seasonal workers, who truly live at the margins of Swiss and French society, has sparked calls for elimination of this status. A recent referendum seeking to abolish the seasonal worker program in Switzerland was voted down by a large majority in 1981.[20] One reason the referendum was voted down was a trade-union-backed plan to overhaul the seasonal worker program. While not eliminating seasonal worker employment, this plan would end numerous abuses and enhance seasonal worker rights.

The French and Swiss seasonal worker programs closely resemble the American temporary foreign workers admitted under the H-2 program. It is ironic that when expanded temporary worker policy was being advocated in the United States it was also being advocated in Germany, where despite high unemployment employers also complain that they cannot find workers to take secondary labor market-type jobs. Leading state government officials in Bavaria and Baden-Württemberg, the two most conservative German states, argued that seasonal worker policy would bring only benefits and no costs, because aliens would be forced to return home after a stay of less than a year. The proposal was rejected out of hand by the German trade union movement and the federal government as unthinkable at a time when German and foreign worker unemployment was so high. Key German officials also felt that such a program would exacerbate an apparently growing problem of illegal alien employment. Further, they thought they had learned a lesson from their prior experience with foreign labor policy: A policy of mandatory rotation is incompatible with democratic society.[21]

Foreign worker policy in the United States presumably would never match the dimensions or scale of French, Swiss, or German foreign labor policy. The highest number of permits advocated is in the range of 750,000 to 850,000 yearly. Nonetheless, the European experience with foreign labor policy warns against placing excessive confidence in the temporariness of temporary foreign worker policy and in its presumed benefits. It may be possible to rotate migrants in and out of truly temporary jobs, but it would be difficult to shuttle foreign workers in and out of permanent jobs. The European experience suggests that long-term sociopolitical costs associated with guest-worker policy outweigh benefits to individual employers and the foreign workers themselves. Guestworker policy has very uneven distributional costs and benefits to various segments of society—a small group of employers are the major beneficiaries, while blue-collar workers are the major losers. It also seems obvious on the basis of recent European history that foreign worker integration into advanced industrial democracies is possible only when foreign workers are allowed to stay for periods of time after which it seems inhumane to force them to leave. An acceptable degree of foreign worker intergration is incompatible with short-term rotation policy such as that practiced in the case of French and Swiss seasonal workers. At the same time, however, integration measures mitigate against voluntary return.

Postwar foreign labor policies have given rise to one of the principal dilemmas facing contemporary Europe. When considered along with largely unhappy U.S. experiences with temporary labor policy in the past, it should give pause to advocates of expanded U.S. temporary foreign worker policy. Reflection upon the problems encountered by the Europeans (or encountered during the *bracero* or U.S. Virgin Islands program, for that matter) is neither absurd nor thoughtless, as sometimes charged, unless history has no meaning.[22] In fact, European foreign labor policies have been cited both in support of and in opposition to expanded U.S. temporary foreign worker policy. The European comparison already has become part of the debate over the future of U.S. immigration reform. Only a modern-day Dr. Pangloss, however, could find support for the idea of an expanded U.S. temporary worker policy in the history of European nonimmigrant labor policy. In the end, the Europeans would have been better off with American-style immigration policy, because whether they like it or not, they too have become immigration lands.

The realization that European countries have become at least de facto immigration lands should encourage further efforts at transatlantic comparison. European experiences with employer sanctions and legalization programs for illegal aliens also seem germane to the debate over the future course of U.S. immigration reform, since employer sanctions and legalization figure prominently in proposals to reform U.S. policy. Again, the Europeans have had concrete experience with policy instruments that are being proposed in the United States.

Employer Sanctions in Europe

Employer sanctions are the key component in Western European efforts to curb illegal alien employment and residency. With a few notable exceptions, all Western European governments now have laws that punish employers of illegal aliens with fines and/or prison terms. Once detected and convicted, employers also may be obliged to pay back wages and social security taxes that ordinarily would have been paid if an alien worker had been legally employed. Further, European employers often are obliged to pay the repatriation costs for illegal aliens in their employ. Recurrent violation of laws governing the employment of aliens may result in employers' losing the right to hire aliens all together.

Although the specific nature of employer sanctions and the administrative processes behind their enforcement vary considerably among Western European countries, the fact that Western European democracies have emphasized this particular policy option in their broader efforts to stem flows of illegal immigrants into their countries is of considerable interest to the United States. Reference to Western European practices and experience in light of the present debate in the United States over the advisability of imposing employer sanctions helps put the issues being debated here in perspective.

The Western European experience with guestworkers is pertinent to the issue of proposed employer sanctions in the United States because, despite the fact that large-scale legal opportunities were made available to aliens, illegal immigration and illegal alien employment proved to be persistent problems in Europe. In the early 1970s, it was estimated that a number of aliens, equivalent to 10 percent of legally admitted alien populations, resided illegally in most Western European countries.[23] As in the United States, in Europe there are few statistics on illegal aliens, and estimates concerning their total numbers vary considerably. Nonetheless, it is certain that the illegal alien population of Western Europe is much smaller than the illegal alien population in the United States. Whether this apparent difference is due more to European policies legally admitting alien workers on a temporary basis or to sanctions taken against illegal employment in Europe is not clear.

Since the 1973–1975 recruitment bans, which are unlikely to be lifted in the foreseeable future, European governments have strengthened employer sanctions, but illegal alien populations seem to have remained stable or to have grown. Some observers impute the presumed increases in illegal immigration and illegal alien employment to the ending of recruitment, but any causal relationship is difficult to establish because significant illegal alien populations and patterns of illegal alien employment had developed alongside and perhaps because of postwar guestworker populations.

In the case of France, many of the post–World War II foreign workers came illegally but quickly had their residency and employment status legalized through a "regularization" program. In 1968, over 80 percent of incoming migrant workers had their technically illegal status "regularized," which indicates that illegal immigration was largely condoned by the government during periods of labor shortages. Mounting political opposition to foreign workers in general, but particularly against illegal aliens (*immigration sauvage*), led to a progressive reversal of policy. By 1974, the French government had made it clear that it would no longer tolerate illegal immigration and that adjustment of status for illegal aliens would end. From 1975 to 1980, the French government only occasionally permitted adjustment of status for illegal aliens, estimated to number between 250,000 and 400,000 throughout France.[24] Since the 1981 elections and change of government, however, a new, one-time only legalization program has been inaugurated, and French officials expected up to 300,000 illegal aliens to adjust their status by January 1982.[25] However, to the disappointment of some observers, only 83,000 clandestine workers ended up receiving papers. It was widely felt that employer resistance to the legalization program and a requirement for proof of stable employment had resulted in many clandestine workers not coming forward or not qualifying for papers. Despite the generosity and goodwill behind the program, a significant illegal alien problem remained.[26]

Unlike the French, the Germans and Swiss have rejected adjustment of status policy. While some aliens were permitted to legalize their status in Germany until 1972, both the Swiss and the Germans reject the French approach, in part because large-scale illegal alien inflows were never tolerated and consequently illegal alien populations apparently have not been as large. It is estimated that there are between 300,000 and 500,000 illegal aliens in Germany, while the number of illegal aliens in Switzerland is thought to be small, with no official estimate available.

Use of the term "illegal alien" in the context of Western Europe actually refers to four distinctive violations, as it does in the American context. Hence, illegal aliens can be (1) individuals who enter the country without undergoing any sort of control, (2) individuals who are entitled to stay but who illegally extend their period of stay, (3) individuals who are entitled to stay but work without authorization,

and (4) individuals who had been authorized to work but work beyond the authorization period or take jobs for which they lack authorization.[27] Compared to the French and the Germans, the Swiss
seem to have experienced very little of the first kind of immigration-
law violation; what problems they have seem to involve primarily the
second and third types of violations.

The policy context of employer sanctions in Western Europe,
then, differs considerably from country to country in Europe and
between Western Europe and the United States. Countries like Belgium, the Netherlands, Great Britain, and France have permitted
adjustment of status or have decreed amnesties for illegal aliens as
part of broader policies aimed at reducing illegal alien populations,
while other countries, such as Germany and Switzerland, have not. As
noted earlier, most continental European countries have some form
of national identity card for citizens, while legally admitted foreign
workers and their dependents are required to carry residency authorization at all times. Among major Western European states, Great
Britain is exceptional in that it resembles the U.S. situation of not
requiring citizens to obtain some sort of national identification card.
Like Americans, the British see identity papers as a potential threat to
civil liberties.

Several other factors serve to facilitate efforts to thwart illegal
immigration and illegal alien employment in the European context as
opposed to the United States. In several Western European countries,
police forces and other authorized officials are freer to conduct identity checks aimed at discovering illegal aliens than in the United
States. Until the recent change of government in France, for example,
the police regularly checked identity papers in the Paris metro and,
less frequently, cordoned off entire neighborhoods thought to contain large numbers of illegal aliens while systematically demanding
identity papers from individuals suspected of being illegal aliens. In
1980, a law was passed in France that would have enabled the government to computerize records pertaining to national identity cards and
alien work and residency permits. However, the new French government intends to abolish the law which would have permitted the stor-
age of such information in a nationwide computer system. In many
European countries, such as in Germany, Switzerland, and France,
official monitoring of aliens is facilitated by regulations that require
aliens to report to the local police when they take up residency in a
town or city, and then to report any change of address. In Belgium
and Switzerland, special police forces have been created to regulate
the inflow and outflow of aliens.

More generally, Western European countries are more ethnically homogeneous than the United States, especially if one can disregard for the purposes of this discussion so-called national or regional minorities such as the Scots in Great Britain or the Bretons and Corsicans in France. The relative ethnic homogeneity of European countries facilitates administrative control of aliens in general and detection of illegal aliens in particular as compared to the United States. European countries with significant minority populations that could suffer prejudice as a result of random identity checks or an obligation to prove citizenship before taking a job include France, which has a large population of citizens of North African, sub-Saharan African, and West Indian descent; Great Britain, with its large immigrant citizen populations from India, Pakistan, and the West Indies; and the Netherlands, with its citizens from former colonies in the Caribbean region and from Indonesia. Simmering resentment over frequent identity checks actually seems to have been a factor in the 1981 British "youth" disturbances, and French identity controls also have resulted in incidents between the police and citizens of North African background who feel they are being harassed.[28] In countries like Norway or Germany, by contrast, there are relatively few citizens who physically and linguistically resemble major resident populations of legally admitted aliens and illegal aliens.

In addition to border control and alien transit problems similar to those in France, countries such as the Federal Republic of Germany have special problems in regulating alien entry. Because of the special status of West Berlin, for example, it is quite easy for aliens to fly to East Berlin and then enter West Berlin on the subway that links the divided halves of that city, since there are no identity controls. Large numbers of aliens from the Near East, India, and Pakistan have been able to take up illegal residency and employment in West Berlin, and from there throughout West Germany, because of the peculiar status of Berlin. The permeability of Western European frontiers to potential illegal aliens, the impossibility of stopping all would-be illegal aliens at national borders because of international and bilateral travel conventions, tourist industries, foreign student admissions, and visiting rights accorded families of legally admitted aliens, together with the reluctance of democratic societies to inhibit the free circulation of individuals, have been decisive factors in European decisions to adopt employer sanctions as a primary means of preventing illegal alien residency and employment. Hence, one should not exaggerate the putative uniqueness of the U.S. immigration situation arising from the long border with Mexico. European countries also have enormous problems regulating alien inflows.

Penalties against the employers of illegal aliens in Western

Europe became important features of governmental policies toward migrants only in the 1970s. Two major factors seem to account for the European-wide emphasis upon employer sanctions by the mid-1970s: (1) the adoption in 1975 by the International Labor Organization (ILO) of Convention 143, pertaining to migration in abusive conditions and to equality of opportunity and treatment for migrants, and (2) the general economic recession brought on by the oil crisis. A third factor would appear to be the politicization of postwar foreign labor policies and resultant pressure to stop or more closely restrict additional foreign worker employment.

Part I of Convention 143 requires each ratifying government to seek to determine whether there are illegally employed aliens in its territory. Governments are required to take all necessary measures to suppress clandestine movement of aliens and their employment, including measures against employers of illegal aliens. ILO conventions, if ratified, have the force of international treaties. Although no Western European states have as yet ratified Convention 143, its adoption by the ILO meant that member states would be asked to report on what measures, if any, they had taken to comply with the provisions of Convention 143. Generally, Western European states are responsive toward ILO instruments, especially if key domestic interest groups embrace them. Organized labor, among other interest groups in Western Europe, generally supported the idea of employer sanctions enunciated in Convention 143, as well as approving penalties against traffickers of aliens. In addition to employer sanctions, legislation stipulating harsh penalties for people involved in smuggling aliens or otherwise abetting clandestine entry and residency by aliens has become a key element of European policies aimed at stemming illegal immigration.

In 1978, the EEC commission announced its intention to seek a joint European policy against illegal immigration.[29] The EEC, now more appropriately referred to as the European Community, is composed of ten Western European states, including France and the Federal Republic of Germany but not Switzerland. The EEC commission wished to see employer sanctions resembling those of Germany adopted by the entire community. At present, employers of illegal aliens in Germany are subject to fines of up to 100,000 deutsche marks (roughly $42,000) and/or prison terms of up to five years. The EEC commission's statement concerning employer sanctions, however, was an advisory opinion only. Nonetheless, it added momentum to the now nearly uniform movement by Western European states toward adoption of employer sanctions.

Table 10.1 *Types of Employer Sanctions in Western Europe*

Country	Fines	Imprisonment	Requirement to Pay Back Wages, Social Security, and/or the Cost of Repatriation of Illegal Alien	Lose Rights to Hire Aliens after Repeated Violations
Austria	Yes	No	Yes	Yes
Belgium	Yes	—	Yes	—
France	Yes	Yes	Yes	Yes
Germany	Yes	Yes	Yes[a]	Yes
Luxembourg	Yes	Yes	Yes[a]	—
Netherlands	Yes	—	Yes	—
Norway	Yes	Yes	—	—
Sweden	Yes	Yes	Yes	Yes
Switzerland	Yes	Yes	Yes	Yes
United Kingdom	No	No	No	No

Primary source: International Labour Conference, *Migrant Workers*, Report 111 (Part 2) (Geneva: ILO, 1980).
[a] Excluding repatriation.

Table 10.1, listing the types of employer sanctions adopted or not adopted by ten Western European states, indicates that most European countries have adopted some form of employer sanctions. Fines and jail terms for convicted employers of illegal aliens generally are stiff, although Austrian law does not permit imprisonment of employers of illegal aliens. In Great Britain, where there are no employer sanctions per se, employers can be punished if it is determined that they are abetting illegal alien residency. In Switzerland, provisions of the legislation governing alien employment and residency do not explicitly include penalties for illegal alien employment, but de facto employer sanctions (fines and prison terms) exist.

EMPLOYER SANCTIONS IN FRANCE

Perhaps because of past tolerance of large-scale illegal alien immigration and employment up to 1973–74, the French government moved decisively in 1976 to curb illegal immigration and employment. A law providing for fines of up to 3,000 francs (roughly $600) and jail terms of up to one month was enacted. The penalties could be doubled for repeat offenders. Simultaneously, an interagency (or interministry) authority was established to coordinate governmental efforts to curb illegal immigration and illegal alien employment. No less than five distinct enforcement agencies may impose employer sanctions in France.

French law requires employers to maintain a special register indicating the names of alien workers, the date of their hiring, their nationality, and the nature of the document authorizing aliens to work. All people not in possession of French national identity cards or passports must have valid work and residency permits to seek employment. In the cases of most aliens from former French colonies, their residency permits must be stamped "salaried worker" before employers can legally hire them. Employers are obliged to notify authorities when they hire alien workers. These notifications must include the name and nationality of the alien hired and the date of his hiring.

The various agencies involved with enforcement of laws against illegal alien employment are free to inspect factories and other known places of employment. However, they generally need court authorization to inspect private residences. A corps of inspectors is specifically assigned to suppression of illegal alien employment. In 1979, these inspectors who specialized in migrant workers are recorded to have made 5,044 field inspections involving firms employing 139,234 people, of whom 48,151 were aliens.[30]

France has a total population of around 53 million and a labor force of about 22 million, including almost 2 million legally employed aliens and over 4 million legally resident aliens. Hence, the work force inspected in the field by agents specializing in suppressing illegal alien employment amounts to only a small percentage of the total work force. The decline in investigations subsequent to field inspections of agents cannot be imputed to variations in rates of inspection, which have remained roughly constant over the years. Rather, according to French governmental sources, the decline in investigations indicates a decline in relatively easy-to-detect illegal employment in urban areas.[31] Employer sanctions and their enforcement have had an obvious deterrent effect upon many employers, but French authorities are careful to note that sanctions have driven some employers and the illegal aliens they hire further underground. Employers of illegal aliens in urban areas have become more sophisticated, as evidenced by the scandal discovered in the Parisian garment industry in 1980. Employers were able to hire large numbers of illegal aliens and escape detection because they used apparently legitimate "front" corporations to cover illegal business transactions. Industries that seem particularly prone to illegal alien employment include agriculture, hotels, and restaurants, which employ large numbers of seasonal workers.

Table 10.2 reveals the number and nature of court actions taken against employers of illegal aliens in recent years. The high number of dismissals stems from a certain inadaptation of the legal system to the problem of illegal alien employment and certain evidentiary problems. A recent report made to the Ministry of Labor recommended stiffer penalties for employers of illegal aliens and regulatory reforms that facilitate convicting such employers.[32]

Convicted employers of illegal aliens are also subject to an administrative fine levied by the National Immigration Office. The fine is five hundred times the minimum guaranteed wage per hour. In 1980, this fine amounted to 4,275 francs (roughly $1,000). Not all convicted employers have been assessed the fine, however, because of administrative foul-ups.

Although employer sanctions in France have a discernible deterrent effect, they have not resulted in a detectable decline in illegal alien residency and employment after four years. One can safely assume that the French illegal alien population would be much larger in the absence of employer sanctions. The new French government will

Table 10.2   *Sanctions Levied Against Employers of Illegal Aliens in France, 1976–1979*

Sanction	Year			
	1976	1977	1978	1979
First offense, case				
dropped	57	231	209	128
Case dismissed	105	321	324	243
Nolle prosequi	12	36	48	51
Penalty forgiven	—	1	3	12
Fines (in francs)				
Less than 600	285	1,069	1,504	1,310
600–2,000	46	297	444	353
2,000+	12	47	70	32
Suspended fine	8	28	62	30
Imprisonment				
Less than 2 mos.	—	25	11	16
2–6 mos.	1	43	36	23
6 mos.+	—	30	15	10
Suspended sentence	3	65	64	84
Total cases	529	2,193	2,790	2,293

Source: Mission de liaison interministerielle pour la lutte contre les trafics de main d'oeuvre, *Bilan* (Paris: Ministry of Labor, 1980), pp. 12–13.

probably step up enforcement of laws against illegal alien employment. Employers convicted of hiring illegal aliens were pointedly not extended amnesty or parole, as were so many other offenders when President Mitterand took office.

IMPLICATIONS OF EUROPEAN EMPLOYER
SANCTIONS FOR THE U.S. DEBATE

Even though most Western European states have employer sanctions that have had some positive impact upon efforts to suppress illegal alien immigration and employment, similar employer sanctions in the U.S. context would clearly not necessarily produce the same beneficial results. The significant historic, ethnic, and other contextual differences both among Western European states and between Western Europe and the United States must be constantly borne in mind. Nonetheless, reflection upon the Western European experience with employer sanctions is instructive in several ways.

First, the fact that most Western European states have adopted employer sanctions reinforces international expectations that the United States also adopt employer sanctions. While the United States' sovereign prerogative to decide who to admit is universally recognized, there exist international norms pertaining to immigration policy which cannot be ignored. In this age of interdependency, successful immigration policy requires international cooperation with reference to international norms and guidelines such as those contained in ILO Convention 143.

Second, the experience of France, which has a considerable citizen population of the same ethnic background as legally and illegally present alien populations, would tentatively indicate that employer sanctions will not necessarily result in additional discrimination against minority groups and legally resident aliens who employers might suspect to be illegal aliens. Despite serious problems of racism and discrimination in France against persons of North African and sub-Saharan African descent, both citizens and noncitizens, it does not appear that employers have discriminated against legal job-seekers of North African and black African background because of a fear that they will be running a risk of unintentionally hiring illegal aliens, being discovered, and then punished. France has had an anti-discrimination law since 1972, and there seem to be few, if any complaints of discrimination against people of North African descent, because of the adoption of employer sanctions. There are tremendous problems of discrimination and racism in France, but employer sanctions are seen as lessening discrimination by punishing employers who exploit aliens rather than as exacerbating problems of discrimination. Since a major fear in the United States is that employer sanctions will result in additional discrimination against U.S. citizens and legally resident aliens of Hispanic background, the apparent absence of such an effect in France is worth noting.

On the other hand, in terms of the U.S. debate over employer sanctions, the fact that employer sanctions in France have had the effect of driving employers of illegal aliens further underground lends credence to the fear often expressed in the United States that employer sanctions would worsen the employment conditions of illegal aliens, not end them. The illegal-alien problem in France is apparently as serious now as it was in 1973. Employers of illegal aliens have proven to be ingeniously adaptive, but perhaps the arrival in power of a government even more committed to stopping illegal alien immigration and employment than the previous government will remedy this disquieting problem. If it should, the French "model" would certainly be studied closely, not only by the United States, but also by other advanced industrial democracies.

Employer sanctions have been the keystone of European policies aimed at halting illegal immigration for some time now. Europeans see employer sanctions as the most effective means of preventing the discrimination and other untoward socioeconomic consequences flowing from clandestine migration. But employer sanctions have had a less-than-hoped for deterrent effect. Consequently, the governments of France and West Germany have increased penalties for employers. The German government, however, did not authorize the hiring of three hundred additional labor inspectors, which the Ministry of Labor felt were required to enforce the new law adequately.[33]

Employer sanctions in any advanced industrial democracy are more difficult to enforce than to legislate. As the Western European experience indicates, they are not a cure-all to illegal immigration. There are no simple solutions to the undocumented-alien problem and only employer sanctions with teeth—criminal penalties, heavy fines, and possible jail terms—combined with rigorous enforcement, would seem to hold out the possibility for meaningful reform of U.S. immigration policy.

A Final Comparative Note: Hispanophobia

At the bottom of the debate on numbers, limits, and the "desirable" ethnic composition of migrant flows to any advanced industrial democracy is a basic concern with the future ethnic, cultural, and linguistic profile of the society in question. Although American concern over this is often couched in perfectly neutral terms, the fear is of an unduly Hispanic United States fifty or one hundred years from now. The Germans, by way of contrast, are more blunt in expressing their fears of the Turks.[34]

One could take issue with the methodology of these projections and the assumptions that underpin them both in the United States and in Germany. We will not do so here. Instead, we will limit ourselves to what we perceive as a usually latent but increasingly open sentiment of Hispanophobia. We will begin by pointing out a well-established fact of American history: Established immigrant groups have almost invariably opposed new immigration. The tension between myth and reality in American immigration history has always defined the U.S. policy debate. The myth has been indelibly etched on our consciousness by the immortal words of the poetess Emma Lazarus. The reality, however, is one of intolerance and suspicion of foreigners. Lazarus' moving words inscribed on the Statue of Liberty ignore the long history of American anti-immigrant sentiment. Thomas Jefferson heads a list of an endless roll call of distinguished Americans who have repeatedly admonished the nation about the potentially deleterious impact of new immigrants on the American polity. Writing in 1782, he asked:

> But are there no inconveniences to be thrown into the scale against the advantage expected from a multiplication of numbers by the importa- tion of foreigners? . . . They will bring with them the principles of the governments they leave, inbibed in their early youth; or, if able to throw them off, it will be in exchange for an unbounded licentiousness, pass- ing, as is usual, from one extreme to another. . . . In proportion to their numbers, they will share with us the legislation. They will infuse into it their spirit, warp and bias its directions, and render it a heterogeneous, incoherent, distracted mass.[35]

Senator Alan K. Simpson of Wyoming, the influential chairman of the Senate Subcommittee on Immigration and Refugee Policy, most recently echoed this sentiment when he contrasted the "humanitarian" and "compassion" standard (liberal immigration pol- icy) with the dictates of the "national interest" (restrictive immigration policy). He came squarely in favor of the latter, which he defined partly as the

> maintenance of . . . freedom, safety, an adequate standard of living, and political independence and stability. It also includes the preservation of cultural qualities and national institutions . . . [and] an even more funda- mental interest: the maintenance of the attributes of America which make it familiar to them and, uniquely, their homeland.[36]

One can appreciate the Senator's concerns, but not share his fears. The "humanitarian" standard is not necessarily antithetical to the "national interest," any more than immigration is inimical to national interest. A broad and constantly changing concept such as the "na- tional interest" cannot be projected with confidence into the future in the United States or anywhere else. The Senator's remarks, however, reflect the point of view and the concerns of a majority of the popula- tion. Hispanophobia ranges from its extreme form of conjuring up images of culturally/linguistically spearheaded separatist movements in the Southwest, to the more neutral observations that decisions about whom we admit today will shape the contours of the future of the United States (especially in such matters as language and foreign policy). One need not deny that the dominance of Hispanics in both legal and clandestine immigration flows will influence the future direction of United States foreign policy and its cultural/linguistic profile to reject the value judgment inherent in such formulations, that is, that America as a whole will be a worse nation for it. After all, this has been the judgment passed by settled groups on each substantial successive wave of immigrants—not only in the United States, but in Europe and elsewhere as well.

Underlying the anti-immigrant animus in the United States are fears that Hispanics are not assimilating at the rates and completeness with which other groups have. In spite of the ahistoricism of this image (one has only to look at cultural/linguistic retention patterns of the German immigrants to the United States throughout the nineteenth century), the proponents of that view at times go as far as to imply that, sometime in the future and because of the concentration of Hispanics in the Southwest, we may be faced with our own "Quebec," that is with a separatist movement. Lawrence Fuchs, former executive director of the Select Commission on Immigration and Refugee Policy, addressed himself to the differences between the two cases.[37] First, he pointed out that arguments in favor of language preservation by Mexican-American leaders are not made to the exclusion of the acquisition of English—in sharp contrast to the French of Quebec; second, the role of the church is different. The American Catholic church is national and assimilationist. The church in Quebec has been active in promoting monoculturism and, less directly, separatism; third, unlike the French Canadians, most Mexican Americans have not shown any particular proclivity for unique behavior in such matters as geographic mobility or attachment to the dominant mythology and symbols of the United States.

The points that Fuchs raised are important and go to the heart of comparisons among cases across distinctive social, historical, and political settings. For instance, it is well known that ethnic and/or linguistic and/or religious and/or racial conflict is responsible for severe problems in such diverse societies as Canada, Belgium, Lebanon, Northern Ireland, and South Africa. Yet, although the historical setting is different in each case, each is rooted in a violent recent past, in a tradition of ethnic, religious, linguistic, and racial conflict. What distinguishes these situations from that of the United States is that the dominant tradition goes back for a relatively long time and is a tradition of accommodation rather than conflict. This tradition of accommodation, and the indigenous institutions which it has spawned, have now become integral parts of the myths and symbols of the United

States. That, however, is not to deny the possibility of conflict along ethnic and linguistic lines.

The extensive literature on "cleavages" (societal divisions and conflict) indicates that ethnically diverse societies are under serious danger of disintegration only when a system of "cumulative inequalities" entrenches itself. Such a system reinforces the natural centifugal forces or discontinuities of a society and leads to severe instability. To make all this relevant to the U.S. debate, what restrictionists seem to be saying is that "we" can keep "them" (the Hispanics) under control if "their" numbers do not grow beyond a certain threshold. Since we cannot divine what this numerical threshold is, anyone can choose a percentage or a number beyond which Hispanic demands are deemed to take an irresistible force of their own.

Of course, such estimates (and the fears they generate) are always based on untestable assumptions and immense inferential leaps. For instance, Hispanophobes assume that new Hispanic immigrants will share a common set of symbols and attachments, a common culture, a common vision, and a common system of values with older, established, and presumably better adapted Hispanic Americans; they further assume that Hispanics from different countries of origin will unite into an all-engulfing pan-Hispanic movement.

Let us play the devil's advocate. Even if pan-Hispanism was possible, and even if it could lead to a genuine separatist movement, is immigration control the proper remedy for this projected "problem"? We would say not, for this "solution" would address the symptoms rather than the root causes of the problem. Based on the literature on inequalities and cleavages, the means by which this feared separatist movement will not materialize are to be found in the aggressive incorporation of Hispanics on an equal footing into the social, economic, and political mainstream of the American society, for it is in officially sanctioned or tolerated discrimination that societies' fissiparous forces thrive. That is why guestworker policy is so noxious and German fears over their Turkish population more warranted than U.S. fears over Hispanics.

To echo the 150-year-old predictions of Alexis de Tocqueville and to paraphrase Gunnar Myrdal at the same time, the greatest threat to national unity—the continuing "American Dilemma"—is the pervasive and historical racism of American society. The myth of cultural pluralism usually works well only when *race* does not intrude as a variable. Race, and latent racism, then, is the variable we must confront and successfully wage war against if we are not to make the predictions of an incipient "Quebec" in the Southwest become a self-fulfilling prophecy.

Notes

1. See, e.g., Franklin W. White, "Who Needs A Guestworker Program?" *Caribbean Review* 11 (Winter 1982): 46.

2. *Le monde,* May 31, 1979, p. 13.

3. Adam Przeworski and Henry Teune, *The Logic of Comparative Social Inquiry* (New York: John Wiley & Sons, 1970).

4. Suzanne Berger and Michael J. Piore, *Dualism and Discontinuity in Industrial Societies* (New York: Cambridge University Press, 1980).

5. Lionel Stoleru, quoted in *Le nouveau journal,* October 6, 1978.

6. Remarks made at the Social Democratic Party Wählerinitiativ-Deutschland ist ein Einwanderungsland, November 15, 1981, in West Berlin.

7. See Hermann Hagman, *Étrangers: Chance ou tourment pour la Suisse* (Geneva: Payot, 1970).

8. Figures based on a calculation made by Philip C. Martin using Système d'Observation Permanente des Migrations (Organization for Economic Cooperation and Development) statistics.

9. Ray C. Rist, "The European Economic Community and Manpower Migrations: Policies and Prospects," *Journal of International Affairs* 33 (Fall/ Winter 1979): 201.

10. *Der spiegel,* No. 50, December 7, 1981, p. 27.

11. Mark J. Miller, "Seasonal Workers in France and Switzerland: Western Europe's *Braceros*" (Paper delivered at the Europeanist Conference, Washington, D.C., October 25, 1980).

12. W. R. Böhning, "International Migration in Western Europe: Reflections on the Past Five Years," *International Labour Review* 118 (July–August 1979): 401.

13. Federal Ministry of Labor Statistics.

14. Return rates calculated by W. R. Böhning. See W. R. Böhning, "Guestworker Employment, with Special Reference to the Federal Republic of Germany, France, and Switzerland: Lessons for the United States," Paper prepared for the Center for Philosophy and Public Policy, University of Maryland, 1980.

15. *Week in Review* (German Information Center publication), March 27, 1981, p. 2.

16. *Presse et immigrés en France,* no. 88, November 1981, p. 3.

17. See Jonathan Power, *Migrant Workers in Western Europe and the United States* (London: Pergamon, 1980), p. 34.

18. Mission de liaison interministerielle pour la lutte contre les trafics de la main d'oeuvre, *Bilan* (Paris: Ministry of Labor, 1981).

19. Ann Sue Matasar, "Labor Transfers in Europe" (Ph.D. diss., Columbia University, 1968).

20. See "La Suisse face à l'immigration," *Problèmes et évenements,* no. 22, April 1982, pp. 2–6.

21. Based on a series of interviews, November 1–15, 1981

22. See note 1 for an example of rejection of transatlantic learning on the immigration issue.

23. Jacques Houdaille and Alfred Sauvy, "L'immigration clandestine dans le monde," *Population* 29 (July–October 1974): 725–742.

24. Jacqueline Costa-Lascoux and Catherine de Wenden-Didier, "Immigrés: le travail clandestin," *Encyclopedie Universalis*, 1982, p. 287.

25. *Le monde,* April 8, 1982, p. 26.

26. Jean-Paul Garson and Yann Moulier, "Les clandestins et la regularisation de 1981–1982 en France," Restricted working paper, Service de la Migration Internationale pour l'Emploi, International Labor Organization, Geneva, 1982.

27. Costa-Lascoux and de Wenden-Didier, "Immigrés: le travail clandestin," p. 284.

28. See, for illustrations, *Jeune Afrique*, no. 948 (March 7, 1979), p. 45, and *Droit et liberté*, no. 379 (April 1979), p. 7.

29. Jonathan Power, "The Great Debate on Illegal Immigration," *Journal of International Affairs* 33 (Fall/Winter 1979): 245.

30. Mission de liaison interministerielle pour la lutte contre les trafics de la main d'oeuvre, *Bilan* (Paris: Ministry of Labor, 1980), p. 26.

31. Ibid., p. 6.

32. Mission de liaison interministerielle pour la lutte contre les trafics de la main d'oeuvre, *Le travail illegal* (Paris: Ministry of Labor, 1980), p. 23.

33. Based on interviews at the Ministry of Labor, November 1981.

34. John Vinocur, "Foreign Workers in West Germany Live Under the Shadow of Prejudice," *New York Times*, February 22, 1982, p. A3.

35. Quoted in Stephen Steinberg, *The Ethnic Myth: Race, Ethnicity and Class in America* (New York: Atheneum, 1981), p. 12.

36. Select Commission on Immigration and Refugee Policy, *U.S. Immigration Policy and the National Interest*, Final Report, March 1, 1981 (Washington, D.C.: Government Printing Office, 1981), pp. 407–408.

37. Lawrence Fuchs, "Immigration, Pluralism and Public Policy: The Challenge of the *Pluribus* to the *Unum*" (Paper presented to the Rockefeller, Ford and Johnson Foundations' Workshop on Immigration Issues, August 1981).

Index